RENAISSANCE C
Reappraisals and Reflections

Civic humanism has been one of the most influential of all concepts in the history of ideas. In this volume, an eminent team of political theorists and historians have been brought together to reassess the impact on the subject of the pioneering work of Hans Baron (1955) and J. G. A. Pocock (1975), creating a fresh intellectual landscape in which Renaissance civic humanism can be discussed.

Drawing from medieval to early modern traditions of political thought, this book evaluates civic humanism in the light of the emergence of oligarchy, imperialism, patronage politics, and the Medici ascendancy in Florence in the fourteenth to sixteenth centuries. It proposes new understandings of the evolution of important republican concepts such as liberty, the rule of law, virtue, and the common good. This thought-provoking collection represents a significant contribution to the study of republican political ideology in the Renaissance and modern periods.

JAMES HANKINS is Professor of History at Harvard University. His publications include *Plato in the Italian Renaissance*, 2 vols. (Brill, 1990), and numerous studies on Renaissance humanism and Platonism. He is the General Editor of the I Tatti Renaissance Library.

IDEAS IN CONTEXT

Edited by QUENTIN SKINNER (*General Editor*),
LORRAINE DASTON, DOROTHY ROSS and JAMES TULLY

The books in this series will discuss the emergence of intellectual traditions and of related new disciplines. The procedures, aims and vocabularies that were generated will be set in the context of the alternatives available within the contemporary frameworks of ideas and institutions. Through detailed studies of the evolution of such traditions, and their modification by different audiences, it is hoped that a new picture will form of the development of ideas in their concrete contexts. By this means, artificial distinctions between the history of philosophy, of the various sciences, of society and politics, and of literature may be seen to dissolve.

The series is published with the support of the Exxon Foundation.

A list of books in the series will be found at the end of the volume.

RENAISSANCE CIVIC HUMANISM

Reappraisals and Reflections

EDITED BY
JAMES HANKINS

PUBLISHED BY THE PRESS SYNDICATE OF THE UNIVERSITY OF CAMBRIDGE
The Pitt Building, Trumpington Street, Cambridge, United Kingdom

CAMBRIDGE UNIVERSITY PRESS
The Edinburgh Building, Cambridge CB2 2RU, UK
40 West 20th Street, New York NY 10011–4211, USA
477 Williamstown Road, Port Melbourne, VIC 3207, Australia
Ruiz de Alarcón 13, 28014 Madrid, Spain
Dock House, The Waterfront, Cape Town 8001, South Africa

http://www.cambridge.org

© Cambridge University Press 2000

This book is in copyright. Subject to statutory exception
and to the provisions of relevant collective licensing agreements,
no reproduction of any part may take place without
the written permission of Cambridge University Press.

First published 2000
First paperback edition 2003

Typeset in Baskerville 11/12.5 pt [VN]

A catalogue record for this book is available from the British Library

Library of Congress Cataloguing in Publication data
Renaissance Civic Humanism: Reappraisals and Reflections / edited by James Hankins.
p. cm. – (Ideas in Context; 57)
Includes bibliographical references.
ISBN 0 521 78090 X hardback
1. Italy – Politics and government – 1268–1559. 2. Humanism – Italy. 3. Renaissance – Italy.
4. Republicanism – Italy – History. I. Hankins, James. II. Series.
DG533.R44 2000
320′0945′09024–dc21   99-057079

ISBN 0 521 78090 X hardback
ISBN 0 521 54807 1 paperback

Contents

List of contributors		*page* ix
	Introduction *James Hankins*	1
1	The republican idea *William J. Connell*	14
2	"Civic humanism" and medieval political thought *James M. Blythe*	30
3	Civic humanism and Florentine politics *John M. Najemy*	75
4	The two myths of civic humanism *Mikael Hörnqvist*	105
5	Rhetoric, history, and ideology: the civic panegyrics of Leonardo Bruni *James Hankins*	143
6	De-masking Renaissance republicanism *Alison Brown*	179
7	Civic humanism, realist constitutionalism, and Francesco Guicciardini's *Discorso di Logrogno* *Athanasios Moulakis*	200
8	Bruni and Machiavelli on civic humanism *Harvey C. Mansfield*	223
9	Rhetoric, reason, and republic: republicanisms – ancient, medieval, and modern *Cary J. Nederman*	247

10	Situating Machiavelli *Paul A. Rahe*	270

Index of manuscripts and archival documents   309
General index   310

Contributors

JAMES M. BLYTHE, Professor of History at the University of Memphis, is the author of *Ideal Government and the Mixed Constitution in the Middle Ages* (1992), and has recently translated Ptolemy of Lucca's *On the Government of Rulers* (1997).

ALISON BROWN, Professor of Italian Renaissance History in the University of London, is the author of *Bartolomeo Scala, 1430–1497, Chancellor of Florence: The Humanist as Bureaucrat* (1979) and *The Medici in Florence: The Exercise of Language and Power* (1992). She has recently edited Guicciardini's *Dialogue on the Government of Florence* for the series Cambridge Texts in the History of Political Thought (1994).

WILLIAM J. CONNELL, the Joseph M. and Geraldine C. La Motta Chair in Italian Studies in the History Department at Seton Hall University, is author of *La città dei crucci* (2000) and editor (with Andrea Zorzi) of *Florentine Tuscany: Structures and Practices of Power* (2000). He has written numerous articles on the history of the Renaissance, and he is Secretary to the Board of Directors of the *Journal of the History of Ideas*.

JAMES HANKINS, Professor of History at Harvard University, is the author of *Plato in the Italian Renaissance*, 2 vols. (1990), and numerous studies on Renaissance humanism and Platonism. He is the General Editor of the I Tatti Renaissance Library.

MIKAEL HÖRNQVIST, Researcher in the Department of the History of Science and Ideas at Uppsala University, is the author of *Machiavelli and the Romans* (1996) and a number of essays on Renaissance political thought.

HARVEY C. MANSFIELD, William R. Kenan Professor of Government at Harvard University, is the author of numerous books and articles on modern political thought, including *Machiavelli's New Modes and Orders: A*

Study of the Discourses (1979) and *Machiavelli's Virtue* (1996). He has translated Machiavelli's *Prince* (1985) and *Discourses* (with Nathan Tarcov, 1996) for the University of Chicago Press and the *Histories* (with Laura F. Banfield, 1988) for Princeton University Press.

ATHANASIOS MOULAKIS, Herbst Professor of Humanities at the University of Colorado, is the author of *Homonoia: Eintracht und die Entwicklung eines politischen Bewusstseins* (1973); *Beyond Utility: Liberal Education for a Technological Age* (1994); *Simone Weil and the Politics of Self-Denial* (1998); *Republican Realism in Renaissance Florence: Francesco Guicciardini's Discorso di Logrogno* (1998) and numerous essays on the history of political thought.

JOHN M. NAJEMY, Professor of History at Cornell University, is the author of *Corporatism and Consensus in Florentine Electoral Politics, 1280–1400* (1982) and *Between Friends: Discourses of Power and Desire in the Machiavelli–Vettori Letters of 1513–1515* (1993), and numerous essays on Florentine history and on Machiavelli.

CARY J. NEDERMAN teaches political science at the University of Arizona. The author or editor of nine books, most recently, *Worlds of Difference: European Discourses of Toleration, 1100–1550* (2000), he has also published more than sixty journal articles and book chapters, including contributions to *American Political Science Review*, *Journal of the History of Ideas*, and *Political Theory*.

PAUL A. RAHE, Jay P. Walker Professor of History at the University of Tulsa, is the author of *Republics Ancient and Modern: Classical Republicanism and the American Revolution* (1992), and numerous articles on ancient, European, and American political thought.

Introduction

James Hankins

When in 1925 the young German historian Hans Baron, in a short review in Meinecke's *Historische Zeitschrift*, coined the term "civic humanism" (*Bürgerhumanismus*), he could not possibly have imagined the extraordinary celebrity and influence this expression, and the political ideal it expressed, would come to enjoy by the end of the twentieth century.[1] The term became well known to historians in English-speaking countries only after 1955, when Baron (now fifty-five years old and an American citizen) published his classic work, *The Crisis of the Early Italian Renaissance: Civic Humanism and Republican Liberty in an Age of Classicism and Tyranny*.[2] In this study, possibly the most important monograph in Renaissance history written since the Second World War, Baron depicted a Florentine Renaissance that had been inspired to achieve cultural greatness through its devotion to ideals of patriotism, popular government, and public service. These ideals, inherited from ancient Greece and the Roman republic, had been rediscovered and popularized by a politically committed movement of intellectuals and educators whom Baron labeled "civic humanists." Twenty years later, J. G. A. Pocock, in his equally famous work, *The Machiavellian Moment: Florentine Political Thought and the Atlantic Republican Tradition*,[3] reinterpreted civic humanism (or "classical republicanism") as a distinct tradition in early modern political thought. According to Pocock, civic humanism con-

---

I should like to thank my colleagues Bernard Bailyn, Mark Kishlansky, and Harvey Mansfield for their help with this introduction.

[1] For Baron's review (of F. Engel-Jànosi's *Soziale Probleme der Renaissance*) see R. Fubini, "Renaissance Historian: The Career of Hans Baron," *Journal of Modern History* 64 (1992): 541–74 at 560, which contains a learned analysis of the term's genesis in Weimar culture and politics. For the later development of Baron's thought, see now K. Schiller, "Hans Baron's Humanism," *Storia della storiografia* 34 (1998): 51–99.

[2] The work was first published in 2 vols. by Princeton University Press, 1955; revised edition in one volume, 1966.

[3] Also published by Princeton University Press (1975).

stituted a distinct political discourse which (via a "Machiavellian moment") had passed from Renaissance Florence to Oliver Cromwell's England, and thence to colonial America, where it formed the ideological matrix of the American Revolution. Pocock's study helped liberate a generation of American historians and political theorists from the unquestioned and unquestionable assumption that American public philosophy descended directly from the liberal tradition of John Locke and seventeenth-century contractarian and rights theorists. In England, recovering the history of republicanism became a central activity of the "Cambridge school," associated above all with the names of Pocock and Quentin Skinner. Pocock, Skinner, and their followers and colleagues used the study of republicanism to illustrate the merits of their new approach to the history of ideas, which emphasized reconstructing the history of political languages and discourses. In the 1980s, civic humanism passed from the realm of scholarship to that of public policy, where, under the guise of "communitarianism," it became a rallying-point for political theorists dissatisfied with Marxism, socialism, and liberalism.[4] In the 1990s communitarianism was hailed, no doubt with considerable exaggeration, as the governing philosophy of both the Clinton administration in America and the Blair administration in the United Kingdom, while in France and Italy Jacques Delors and Romano Prodi were said to be sympathetic to certain themes of the movement.[5]

By any standard, the idea of "civic humanism" has been enormously successful. Yet while politicians and political theorists have been eager to jump on the republican bandwagon, professional historians (to borrow an image from J. H. Hexter) have been busy loading republicanism onto

[4] The movement has been associated with prominent names in philosophy and political theory such as Alisdair MacIntyre, Charles Taylor, Michael Sandel, Richard Walzer, and Richard Bernstein (not all of whom would accept the label "communitarian"). See Michael Sandel, ed., *Liberalism and Its Critics* (Oxford: Blackwell, 1984). On the relationship of Pocock's work to communitarianism, see J. C. Isaac, "Republicanism vs. Liberalism? A Reconsideration," *History of Political Thought* 9.2 (1988): 349–77. See also Benjamin Barber, "Unscrambling the Founding Fathers," *New York Times Book Review* (13 January 1985). Barber is closely linked to the Democratic Leadership Council, the "New Democrat" think-tank formerly chaired by Bill Clinton. The term "republicanism," though commonly used in England, is (like the term "civic humanism") for obvious reasons more problematic in an American political context.

[5] See "Rebuilding Civil Society," a symposium in *The New Democrat* (March/April, 1995), a journal associated with the Democratic Leadership Council and the Progressive Policy Institute; "Freedom and Community," *The Economist* (24 December 1994): 65–8; Chris Wilkens, "Blair's Tory Agenda," in the *Guardian* (24 March 1995): 27; Jacques Delors (chairman), *Learning, the Treasure Within: Report to UNESCO of the International Commission on Education for the Twenty-First Century* (Paris: UNESCO, 1996); Pierpaolo Donati, "Può essere la vera alternativa al tramonto del Welfare State," *Liberal* (January 1996): 105–7. William A. Galston, a major theorist of communitarianism, was a policy adviser in the first Clinton administration.

Introduction 3

the tumbrils.⁶ In the two decades since Pocock's *Machiavellian Moment* they have grown increasingly doubtful about the value of such terms as "civic humanism" and "classical republicanism" for describing or explaining the ideological landscape of early modern Europe and colonial America. Such doubts are of more than antiquarian interest. Modern civic republicanism has always claimed to be a uniquely historical movement – to be continuing or reviving a tradition of political reflection based on the actual practice of ancient and early modern polities – and therefore to be free of the tendencies to abstraction, scientism, and utopianism that have helped discredit its chief rivals, liberalism and Marxism. American communitarians have often made strong claims for the rootedness of their political ideas in the ideology of the American Revolution. Doubts about the correctness of these claims, naturally enough, have often come from historians of a liberal or Marxist persuasion.⁷

Historians who criticize the republican thesis have followed several strategies. Some deny that republicanism ever existed as a coherent ideology in the early modern Atlantic world. Recent critics of J. G. A. Pocock, for example, have argued that the language of virtue and corruption, active participation in political life and devotion to the common good coexist in solution, as it were, in premodern political discourse with proto-liberal and proto-capitalistic language; that republicanism, in other words, cannot be said to constitute a distinct tradition or language of political discourse.⁸ In the political literature of

---

⁶ A funeral oration was pronounced over "the republican hypothesis" in early American history by Daniel T. Rodgers, "Republicanism: The Career of a Concept," *Journal of American History* 79 (June, 1992): 11–28. See also Thomas L. Pangle, *The Spirit of Modern Republicanism: The Moral Vision of the American Founders and the Philosophy of Locke* (Chicago: University of Chicago Press, 1988), esp. 28–39, and Paul A. Rahe, *Republics Ancient and Modern: Classical Republicanism and the American Revolution* (Chapel Hill, N.C.: University of North Carolina Press, 1992).

⁷ For a critique of the inner coherence of the republican tradition from the liberal side, see Isaac, "Republicanism vs. Liberalism?"; and Alan Patten, "The Republican Critique of Liberalism," *British Journal of Political Science* 26 (1994): 25–44. Peter Berkowitz, *Virtue and the Making of Modern Liberalism* (Princeton: Princeton University Press, 1999), argues that communitarianism caricatures the history of liberalism and that its "discourse of virtue" can be situated within the tradition of liberal theory. A Marxist critique of the republican idea in the thought of Hans Baron, William J. Bouwsma, and J. G. A. Pocock is found in R. Pecchioli, *Dal "mito" di Venezia all' "ideologia americana": Itinerari e modelli della storiografia sul repubblicanesimo dell' età moderna* (Venice: Marsilio, 1983); see Pocock's reply in "Between Gog and Magog: The Republican Thesis and the *Ideologia Americana*," *Journal of the History of Ideas* 48.2 (1987): 325–46.

⁸ A summary statement of Pocock's view can be found in his essay, "Virtues, Rights, and Manners: A Model for Historians of Political Thought," in *Virtue, Commerce, and History: Essays on Political Thought and History, Chiefly in the Eighteenth Century* (Cambridge: Cambridge University Press, 1985), 37–50. For an overview of his work see Iain Hampsher-Monk, "Political Languages in Time: The Work of J. G. A. Pocock," *British Journal of Political Science* 14 (1984): 89–116, with a bibliography of Pocock's writings.

the time, they claim, there was no strict and necessary opposition between private self-interest, understood as the acquisition of property, and commitment to the common good; men devoted to republican principles could without embarrassment also come to the defense of commercial society.[9] Other critics point out that early modern "republicans" cannot even be identified with an anti-monarchical position, since some of them, at least, were prepared on Aristotelian grounds to admit a role for the royal principle in a mixed polity.[10] Still others have contested Pocock's attempt to obscure the role of Locke in the formation of American political ideology. Thanks to recent research on Locke, it is fair to say that his eclipse as a source for American Revolutionary thought has proven to be temporary.[11] The ideology of the American Revolution in the latest historical literature is seen to be pluralistic in its sources, making use of a variety of political languages and traditions.[12]

A second line of attack on the republican thesis has sought to bury civic humanism in an unusable historical past. The putatively conservative, hierarchical, elitist, and even racist character of much English and American republican thought has been stressed by some liberal historians of political thought, while others have pointed out the inconvenient implications of traditional republicanism for its modern epigoni.[13] The

[9] Christopher Nadon, "Aristotle and the Republican Paradigm: A Reconsideration of Pocock's *Machiavellian Moment*," *Review of Politics* 58.4 (Fall 1996): 677–99, argues that both liberalism and republicanism can be construed from the Aristotelian tradition, and that Pocock's strict opposition between republican and liberal paradigms is a distortion of the Western political tradition. Isaac ("Republicanism vs. Liberalism?") also argues against Pocock's view that liberalism and republicanism constitute two distinct traditions in the history of political thought. For the view that republican language was being integrated with a new ideology of commercial society in late seventeenth-century England, see Steve Pincus, "Neither Machiavellian Moment nor Possessive Individualism: Commercial Society and the Defenders of the English Commonwealth," *American Historical Review* 103 (1998): 705–36. On the lack of an "interesting disagreement between liberals and republicans" on the question of liberty, see Patten, "The Republican Critique," with Quentin Skinner's response in his recent *Liberty before Liberalism* (Cambridge: Cambridge University Press, 1998), 84. In his review of the latter book (*London Review of Books* [5 February 1998]: 15), Blair Worden similarly maintains that "in those [Whig] commonplaces [of the 18th century] . . . [Skinner's] neo-roman and negative conceptions of liberty, far from contending with each other, mingled freely."

[10] See Blair Worden, "English Republicanism," in *The Cambridge History of Political Thought*, ed. J. H. Burns (Cambridge: Cambridge University Press, 1991), 446–7. On this see also chapter 5, note 22.

[11] See Michael P. Zuckert, *Natural Rights and the New Republicanism* (Princeton: Princeton University Press, 1995).

[12] See Rodgers, "Republicanism: The Career of a Concept."

[13] See Don Herzog, "Some Questions for Republicans," *Political Theory* 14.3 (August, 1986): 473–93, especially his disturbing explication (or rather exposé) of the republicanism of Benjamin Rush. Isaac Kramnick in "Republican Revisionism Revisited," *American Historical Review* 87 (1982): 629–64, comments (653) that Aristotle, unlike modern republicans, was a "theorist of hierarchy and privilege."

partisan commitments of most modern communitarians sits ill, for example, with the enthusiasm of traditional republicans for an armed and militant citizenry.[14]

A third strategy, particularly favored by Straussian critics, has been to slice up Pocock's long republican tradition into unrelated sections, usually by means of a frontal assault on his interpretation of individual texts. Hence some historians have sought to drive wedges between Aristotle and Machiavelli, or Machiavelli and Harrington, or Harrington and the so-called "neo-Harringtonians."[15] They argue, in effect, that the republicanisms espoused by these writers differ from each other to such an extent that it is sheer equivocation to place them in the same "tradition" of thought. Straussians in particular argue that to create a diachronic unity out of a common political language is purely factitious when it is not expressive of a deeper conceptual unity. Some critics such as Paul Rahe and Pierre Manent have gone further and have argued that both modern republicans and modern liberals share deeply in modernity through their common rejection of Aristotle's idea of nature; for them, the two centuries between Machiavelli and Rousseau constitute a fundamental break in the history of Western political thought.[16]

This is not to say that all criticism of the republican idea in early modern thought has come from scholars hostile to civic republicanism. Some of the most trenchant revisionism derives from what might be called the "internal" critique of Quentin Skinner, the most important modern student of classical republicanism. Less dogmatic than Hans Baron, more empirical than J. G. A. Pocock, Skinner has shown a remarkable willingness to rethink fundamental descriptions and categories in his work on the republican tradition. Already in his first major work, *The Foundations of Modern Political Thought*, he subjected Hans Baron's *Crisis* to a searching critique, concluding that many of the ideas Baron credited to his "civic humanists" had a long prehistory in medieval scholastic and rhetorical traditions. Since the early 1980s, he has

---

[14] See David C. Williams, "Civic Republicanism and the Citizen Militia: The Terrifying Second Amendment," *Yale Law Journal* 101 (1991): 551–615, with references to earlier literature.

[15] Vickie B. Sullivan, "The Civic Humanist Portrait of Machiavelli's English Successors," *History of Political Thought* 15.1 (1994): 73–96; Nadon, "Aristotle and the Republican Paradigm"; Vickie B. Sullivan, "Machiavelli's Momentary 'Machiavellian Moment': A Reconsideration of Pocock's Treatment of the *Discourses*," *Political Theory* 20.2 (May 1992): 309–18; Jonathan Scott, "The Rapture of Motion: James Harrington's Republicanism," in *Political Discourse in Early Modern Britain*, ed. N. Phillipson and Q. Skinner (Cambridge: Cambridge University Press, 1993); Gary Remer, "James Harrington's New Deliberative Rhetoric: Reflections of an Anticlassical Republican," *History of Political Thought* 4 (1995): 532–57. See also Isaac, "Republicanism vs. Liberalism?" and the contributions of Athanasios Moulakis, Harvey C. Mansfield and Paul A. Rahe in this volume.

[16] Pierre Manent, *La cité de l'homme* (Paris: Fauard, 1994).

moved gradually away from the description of civic humanism formulated by Pocock. Skinner now recognizes – in contrast with Pocock – that Renaissance republican theorists did not promote "positive liberty," participation in politics as a mode of self-realization, or (to be more Aristotelian) as a way of perfecting one's nature through the exercise of reason and virtue. Instead, he believes that Renaissance theorists (primarily Machiavelli) advocated active citizenship, not as a "primary good" (in Rawls's sense), but because it contributes to the maintenance of "negative liberty," i.e., freedom from arbitrary power and corruption.[17] This recognition implies a further distancing from Pocock, who characteristically sees Machiavelli, and civic humanists in general, as constituting a revival and continuation of the Aristotelian tradition, a tradition distinct both from the theologically based politics of the scholastics and modern liberalism and socialism. Skinner, too, sees Renaissance republicanism as a middle way, but now prefers to find its roots in Roman writers like Cicero, Sallust, and Seneca rather than in Aristotle.[18] His emphasis on the Roman sources of civic humanism, and his recognition that not all civic humanists were anti-monarchical, seem to have led Skinner in his most recent book to a significant change in terminology, for he now appears to prefer the label "neo-Roman" to "classical republican."[19]

Among scholars of the Italian Renaissance, however, Skinner's openness to revision is the exception rather than the rule. While seminars devoted to early modern republicanism have been ringing with lively debate, the papers of most Renaissance scholars on the same subject are received with a silent chorus of nodding heads. Especially in

[17] This view was first adumbrated in Skinner's article, "Machiavelli on the Maintenance of Liberty," *Politics* 18 (1983): 3–15; see also "The Idea of Negative Liberty: Philosophical and Historical Perspectives," in *Philosophy in History*, ed. R. Rorty, J. B. Schneewind, and Q. Skinner (Cambridge: Cambridge University Press, 1984), 193–221. The fullest expression of this conception is in his "The Republican Idea of Liberty," in *Machiavelli and Republicanism*, ed. G. Bock, Q. Skinner, and M. Viroli (Cambridge: Cambridge University Press, 1990), 293–309. For a criticism of this view as a reading of Machiavelli, see John Charvet, "Quentin Skinner on the Idea of Freedom," *Studies in Political Thought* 2 (1993): 5–16. In *Liberty before Liberalism*, Skinner moves away from this "instrumental republicanism" to embrace a concept of negative liberty as "non-domination," a view indebted to the work of the modern republican theorist Philip Pettit; see the latter's *Republicanism: A Theory of Freedom and Government* (Oxford: Oxford University Press, 1997).

[18] Skinner, "Ambrogio Lorenzetti: The Artist as Political Philosopher," *Proceedings of the British Academy* 72 (1986): 56: "It was from these humble origins, far more than from the impact of Aristotelianism, that the classical republicanism of Machiavelli, Guicciardini and their contemporaries originally stemmed. The political theory of the Renaissance, at all phases of its history, owes a far deeper debt to Rome than to Greece."

[19] See his *Liberty before Liberalism*, esp. 11, 54–5; for Blair Worden's criticism of Skinner's new terminology see his review in *London Review of Books*, 5 February 1998.

Quattrocento studies, the Baronian model of Renaissance republicanism remains virtually unchallenged. The irony, as William J. Connell points out in the first essay of the present volume, is that republicanism as a subject of historical study was practically the invention of Renaissance scholars. So perhaps we are simply witnessing the phenomenon, observed by historians of technology, whereby the cultures that are the first to innovate are the last to update. In any case, historians of Renaissance political thought have made few serious attempts to revise the orthodox view of civic humanism as established by Baron and Pocock. Certain generalizations as well as facts and interpretations relating to particular texts have been challenged, it is true,[20] but attempts to move beyond technical criticisms to a broader reinterpretation of humanist political thought and its role in the development of Western political theory have not made much headway.[21] The relative absence of serious revisionism within Renaissance studies is attested by the numerous examples of more or less unreconstructed Baronianism one can find in the recent historical literature, even in the work of well-informed scholars.[22]

This book aims to challenge that complacency. It hopes to stir up new debate on civic humanism among scholars of the Italian Renaissance, to take stock of where recent research has brought us, and to press further along the various paths of exploration and reappraisal that have opened

---

[20] See my article, "The Baron Thesis After Forty Years," *Journal of the History of Ideas* 56 (1995): 309–38, for a conspectus of the criticisms made of Baron's *Crisis* since 1955.

[21] The present writer has attempted a fresh valuation in "Humanism and the Origins of Modern Political Thought," in *The Cambridge Companion to Renaissance Humanism*, ed. Jill Kraye (Cambridge: Cambridge University Press, 1996), 118–41. For a reinterpretation of the period of Baron's "crisis," see John Najemy, "The Dialogue of Power in Florentine Politics," in *City States in Classical Antiquity and Medieval Italy*, ed. A. Molho, K. Raaflaub, and J. Emlen (Ann Arbor: University of Michigan Press, 1991), 269–88. Many scholars have noted the tendency of Baron's critics to become bogged down in technical issues, but this was a tendency inherited from Baron himself: see Najemy again in "Baron's Machiavelli and Renaissance Republicanism," *American Historical Review* 101.1 (February, 1996): 128, where he speaks of Baron's "tendency to displace problems of interpretation onto puzzles of chronology."

[22] Unreconstructed Baronianism is more common in Italy than in England or America: see, for example, Cesare Vasoli, "Leonardo Bruni alla luce delle più recenti ricerche," *Atti e memorie della Accademia Petrarca di lettere, arti e scienze di Arezzo* 50 (1988): 3–26; Eugenio Garin, "Leonardo Bruni: politica e cultura," in *Leonardo Bruni cancelliere della repubblica di Firenze*, ed. P. Viti (Florence: Olschki, 1990), 3–14; Antonio Lanza, *Firenze contro Milano: Gli intellettuali fiorentini nelle guerre con i Visconti* (Rome: De Rubeis, 1991); Paolo Viti, *Leonardo Bruni e Firenze: Studi sulle lettere pubbliche e private* (Florence: Bulzoni, 1992), esp. chapter 1. Despite many reservations and modifications, a fundamentally Baronian perspective is maintained by Albert Rabil, Jr., "The Significance of 'Civic Humanism' in the Interpretation of the Italian Renaissance," in *Renaissance Humanism: Foundations, Forms, and Legacy*, 3 vols. (Philadelphia: University of Pennsylvania Press, 1988), I: 141–74; and by Ronald G. Witt, "The *Crisis* after Forty Years," *American Historical Review* 101 (February, 1996): 110–18.

up in the last two decades. The essayists in this book have no new grand thesis to replace the "Baron thesis." Unlike Pocock, they propose no sweeping new visions of the history of republicanism. In their own politics they represent a broad ideological spectrum and are united only by a common discomfort with current orthodoxies. Attentive readers will notice that the authors in this volume often disagree with each other, sometimes sharply. Yet despite the diversity of backgrounds, methods, and conclusions represented here, certain consistent themes have emerged from our research and reflection.

The first theme concerns the relationship of Renaissance civic humanists to the medieval tradition. It is now well established that many of the republican ideas Baron claimed had emerged around 1400 in the writings of Italian humanists had, in fact, a long prehistory in the medieval scholastic and rhetorical traditions. In his essay for this volume James Blythe takes this revisionist line much further, showing that the relationship of humanists to scholastics was not that of republicans to monarchists, but of popularizers to theorists. The late medieval scholastic tradition boasted a very rich republican (or commonwealth) tradition, including both monarchical and anti-monarchical republicans, who took their analysis from Aristotle's *Politics* but applied that analysis to contemporary society. Ptolemy of Lucca, the most extreme republican of the later Middle Ages, was, in Blythe's analysis, a much more populist figure than any civic humanist of the Quattrocento. Long before Leonardo Bruni, late medieval scholastics had produced a "desacralized" account of Roman history, and had criticized the Roman empire of the Caesars as tyrannical and corrupt. They had defended the value of the active life against the monastic and neo-Platonic traditions and insisted on the value of participation in political life. Where Pocock saw a strict separation between the scholastic juridical tradition (the source, in his view, of the liberal stress on rights and negative liberty) and the civic humanist tradition's discourse of virtue and participation, Blythe demonstrates that on a doctrinal if not a discursive level this supposed dichotomy is difficult to defend.[23]

The lack of any clear break in doctrinal terms between late medieval scholastics and civic humanists raises in acute form the issue of Machiavelli's relationship to the humanists of the Quattrocento. As William J. Connell suggests in his essay, the efforts of Baron, Pocock, and Skinner to assimilate Machiavelli to the civic humanist tradition have grown

---

[23] On this point see also Blythe's *Ideal Government and the Mixed Constitution in the Middle Ages* (Princeton: Princeton University Press, 1992).

increasingly problematic in recent years.[24] The thesis of an unbroken "republican tradition" stretching from Aristotle to Jefferson, as was said above, has sustained numerous attacks from historians of political theory, who emphasize the differences between major figures in the supposed tradition on key points of doctrine, such as participation and the analysis of human nature. Cary J. Nederman tries to resolve this problem by pointing to the pluralistic character of the republican tradition, especially the tension between "discursive" and "rational" republicanism found in the writings of the greatest Roman republican, Cicero. The unity of the republican tradition can be saved, he suggests, if it is recognized that that unity embraces considerable diversity.

Harvey Mansfield and Paul A. Rahe take a different approach to "situating Machiavelli." Building on recent literature, both represent Machiavelli as a radically modern figure. Mansfield's point of comparison is the *Laudatio Florentinae urbis* of Leonardo Bruni. Bruni, for him, is still a traditional figure, firmly within the Aristotelian cosmos. He uses a traditional rhetoric of idealization, whereas Machiavelli uses a rhetoric of rationalization: deeds justify words, not vice versa. Bruni wants to imitate the ancients in a gestural, external way, by recovering their thought and language; Machiavelli rejects their ideology but wants to find out the secrets of their power. Bruni is a republican; Machiavelli is not, at least in any unequivocal sense. Neither is a civic humanist, less because they fail to fit Baron's description than because, on a deeper level, the civic is irreconcilable with the humanist. Rahe agrees that Machiavelli is to be classed with the moderns, but takes Aristotle as his primary point of comparison. Aristotle is ancient because of the political anthropology he shares with other ancient writers, both Greek and Roman. The purpose of a polity is to perfect human nature by maximizing the scope for virtue and rationality. Since individuals and populations differ in virtue and rationality, politics is a matter of prudence: choosing the regime that allows the best people to be fully human in a given set of circumstances. Machiavelli is modern because his reason is purely instrumental; like Hobbes and Hume, he thought reason should be the slave of the passions. The republican constitution is preferable, not because it provides a focus for "common meanings and purposes," but because it has a greater chance of satisfying both the desire of the nobles to rule and that of the populace to live in security. Machiavelli's republic therefore embodies both positive and negative liberty. But

[24] For a fascinating account of how Baron came to see Machiavelli as a civic humanist, see Najemy, "Baron's Machiavelli and Renaissance Republicanism," 119–29.

liberty does not exist to enable the exercise of the Good Life, but subserves an illimitable desire for survival, profit, and acquisition.

If Machiavelli is radically modern and represents in many respects a rejection rather than a continuation of the civic humanist tradition, it is natural to ask if his generation's new understanding of human nature and the instrumental role of reason have their roots in some other Florentine tradition of political reflection. Athanasios Moulakis and Alison Brown address this question in their contributions to this volume. Both authors see the thought of Machiavelli and Guicciardini as emerging from what Moulakis calls "realist constitutionalism," a tradition of thought associated with the political practice of Florentine statesmen, rather than with the normative, exhortatory writings of the humanists. Realist constitutionalism was nourished by the political culture of fifteenth-century Florence, which was marked by a "quasi-permanent abrogation" of her constitutional order. Oligarchic and later Medicean statesmen sought to solve the problem of how a state whose *ordinamenta* were descended from the corporatist guild republicanism of the late Middle Ages could refashion itself in such a way as to be both legitimate and effective. As Alison Brown suggests, part of the answer lay in the appropriation and manipulation of images, which went together with a growing consciousness of the conventional character of terms such as "liberty." The burgeoning consciousness of liberty, not only as a political ideal, but also as a "system of representation," led, in Guicciardini's *Dialogue on the Government of Florence*, to "one of the earliest and most incisive attacks" on the republican idealism of the civic humanists. The new realism implies, according to Moulakis, a new political anthropology wherein politics is seen as artificial and unnatural. Men are forced into politics by necessity, not by a desire to realize their nature; political activity is motivated by ambition and shaped by rational calculation. Virtue is a power of canalizing necessity, not a *physis* in the Aristotelian sense, a principle of self-realization.

If Machiavelli and Guicciardini cannot be readily situated within the tradition of classical and late medieval republicanism, and if Quattrocento republicanism is indistinguishable on a doctrinal level from the republicanism of the late medieval scholastics, it remains to establish whether or to what extent the civic humanists of the fifteenth century may be said to represent a new departure. It remains, in other words, to determine how they are related to modernity. It has been suggested that the innovations of the civic humanists were chiefly a matter of audience and language, of selecting and reshaping materials already present in the scholastic and rhetorical traditions. If this is the case, then it is natural to ask to what end the humanists of the early fifteenth century constructed their civic homilies. John Najemy suggests that, in Florence, their project was essentially a conservative one that served the interests of the post-Ciompi oligarchy. The audience for civic humanism was in part the Florentine oligarchy itself, but more importantly those "politically infantilized nonelite office-holders" that were the key to the stability of the regime. Humanists like Salutati and Bruni created a new civic myth which, by reshaping the old language of guild republicanism, effectively delegitimized and supplanted it. The new political language of virtue replaced the language of class and collective interests which the middling ranks of society had often embraced in the past. Virtue now meant serving the common good, but the common good as defined by patrician statesmen. Participation was about office-holding rather than decision-making: patronage, not self-rule. Civic humanism was thus a form of socialization, effectively supporting a "culture of conformity and surveillance," even if some contemporaries regarded it as a way to transcend class tensions and achieve social consensus.

If in domestic affairs the ideology of civic humanism reinforced the hegemony of the post-Ciompi oligarchy, in foreign affairs, as Mikael Hörnqvist shows, civic humanists actively promoted Florentine imperialism in Tuscany and Italy. While Hans Baron had presented civic humanism as "an ideology of self-defense and peaceful co-existence" between states, Hörnqvist discloses the role Leonardo Bruni and his followers played in justifying, and indeed glorifying, "expansionism and the pursuit of empire." The humanists exploited their studies of classical antiquity to construct an imperial myth for Florence, modeled on that of republican Rome, whose aim was to reinforce the legitimacy of Florentine rule and attract the loyalty of new Florentine subjects. His reading of imperialistic writings by civic humanists leads Hörnqvist to rethink the meaning of Florentine liberty. Florentine political thinkers promoted a conception of negative liberty (due process and equality under the law), Hörnqvist suggests, because a positive, "exercise concept" of liberty as self-rule would have been incompatible with the realities of Florentine imperial rule. Florentine subjects in the *contado*, like the lower classes within Florence, could not be offered a real share in political power; their sovereignty had to be limited in key ways by the imperial center. The concept of liberty used by the Florentine *reggimento* and the humanist intellectuals who supported it could not help but reflect and respond to that situation.

The present writer, through a detailed analysis of Leonardo Bruni's civic panegyrics, lends further support to the positions of Najemy and Hörnqvist. Leonardo Bruni was not the fiery republican ideologue and populist of Hans Baron's imagination. Close attention to the rhetorical form and context of Bruni's famous orations shows them to be consciously artificial productions, not intended to reflect either historical reality or Bruni's own political convictions. Their primary purpose was to serve as propaganda vehicles, and their primary audience was foreign elites. Bruni's biography and his other writings show him to be a faithful servant of the post-Ciompi oligarchy and, later, of the Medici party. His fundamental political convictions were compatible with a range of regimes, though, like Aristotle, he preferred monarchy or aristocracy. Civic humanism for him was primarily about the need for virtuous rulers, whether princes or leading citizens of a republic. It was more about governors than about governments.

The essays in this volume, in short, see the civic humanism of the early and high Renaissance within an optic quite different from that of Hans Baron. Baron presented Florence and Venice as embattled outposts of freedom and democracy in an age moving inexorably towards absolutism. By courage and sacrifice these cities had preserved through dark times the highest civic ideals of Athens and republican Rome, to be inherited in modern times by the Western democracies. Pocock explained how this *translatio reipublicae* had been effected, while quietly purging his republican tradition of its nonegalitarian biases and attributing to it a universalist conception of liberty, which was, in reality, quite foreign to it. A less ingenuous view – some would say a more cynical one – might rather see Renaissance republicanism, at least in Italy, as transitional. It represents a step away from the populist guild republicanism of the thirteenth and fourteenth centuries and a step towards the aristocratic and monarchical regimes of the early modern period. Civic humanism was in origin a discourse that changed the self-understanding of Florentine elites by helping them see their polity, not as a congeries of self-ruling corporations set within the larger medieval juridical order, but as a sovereign secular state led by an aristocracy of virtue. This was its contribution to modernity. But Machiavelli, reacting in part against the normative pieties of civic humanism, invented a political anthropology and a political science that were modern in a far more radical sense.

It may be asked what relevance, if any, historical revisionism of the kind attempted in this volume has to modern debates about communitarianism and republicanism. An obvious answer would address

Introduction

the issue of ideological pedigrees. Contemporary republicans should, I think, accept that key assumptions of their movement, especially its egalitarianism and universalism, are fundamentally modern, and derive from the same ideological factory that produced liberalism and socialism: namely, the Enlightenment. It is also true, of course, that many elements in modern republicanism derive from older traditions going back to classical antiquity. But the historical study of these older republicanisms must raise serious questions for those who wish to revive the republican outlook in modern times. Even those (like the present writer) with some sympathy for communitarianism may find disquieting the uses to which its ancestors have been put in the past. Does the emphasis on virtue, it may be asked, provide "ideological cover" for elitism? Is the opposite of virtue corruption, or is it criticism of authority? Are the civic humanist attacks on *tyrannia quoad exercitium* intended to distract attention from *tyrannia absque titulo*? Is the common good the good of all, or the good of those who control political discourse? Is the nondomination model of liberty compatible with imperialism and graduated citizenship? Should we not rather demand of a political philosophy that it exclude these possibilities? Is the negative liberty of Renaissance republics, even the reconstructed, "instrumental" version of it described by Quentin Skinner, sufficient to secure equal liberties and universal civic participation?[25] Are the civic humanists correct to suppose (as Harvey Mansfield asks) that the common good never derogates from one's individual good? History cannot, perhaps, give compelling answers to such questions, but it can give us cause to question the answers we sometimes receive.

[25] See Patten, "The Republican Critique," 29, who criticizes from a theoretical point of view the idea that we can derive an (individual) duty to participate from a (collective) need for some virtuous persons to participate.

CHAPTER I

The republican idea

William J. Connell

In recent years, while the history of republicanism has become one of the most hotly contested subjects in the fields of American and English history, historians of the Italian Renaissance have been paying less and less attention to what was long a staple of our trade. The fortune of the *vita civile*, as it developed in the cities of medieval Italy and as it variously survived or perished during the Renaissance, was a central theme of most Italian histories written since the time of Sismondi. Of late, however, a number of scholars have denied the importance of the *vita civile*, and there has now developed a large body of historical writing on the Renaissance that pays little attention to it.[1] Certainly, the patient philological work of Nicolai Rubinstein has continued to expand our knowledge of the changing political vocabulary of Florentine thinkers and statesmen.[2] And Machiavelli remains as interesting as ever: although much of the best recent work on Machiavelli has focused on his rhetorical strategies rather than looking to his role in a longer republican tradition, or, in more precise ways, at the immediate historical context of *The Prince* and the *Discourses*. As an overall effort, however, few would disagree that the study of republican thought in Renaissance Italy

---

A first version of this essay was delivered at a round-table discussion at the Harvard Center for Italian Renaissance Studies, Villa I Tatti, in 1992. A shortened and somewhat different version appeared in the volume, *Girolamo Savonarola: Piety, Prophecy, and Politics*, ed. Donald Weinstein and Valerie R. Hotchkiss (Dallas: Bridwell Library, 1994), 95–105. Paul Kristeller, James Livingston, Thomas Mayer, Karl Morrison, and John Najemy offered helpful comments on this material.

[1] See, for instance, the remarks of Edward Muir, "The Italian Renaissance in America," *American Historical Review* 100 (1995); 1095–118; and also his "Una replica," *Quaderni storici*, no. 88 (1995): 247–51. For a similar though less radical trend in Reformation historiography, see R. Po-Chia Hsia, "The Myth of the Commune: Recent Historiography on City and Reformation in Germany," *Central European History*, 20 (1987): 203–15. The noted polemic of Philip Jones, "Economia e società nell'Italia medievale: il mito della borghesia," in his *Economia e società nell'Italia medievale* (Turin: Einaudi, 1980), 3–189, is much moderated in his *The Italian City-State: From Commune to Signoria* (Oxford: Clarendon Press, 1997), 332–650.

[2] Rubinstein's bibliography appears in *Florence and Italy: Renaissance Studies in Honour of Nicolai Rubinstein*, ed. Peter Denley and Caroline Elam (London: Westfield College, 1988), 515–23.

has gone little beyond the point to which it was brought in the 1970s by an extraordinary group of mostly German and American scholars.³

It was Hans Baron who with great energy opened the way for the study of republican political thought in relation to its cultural and political context in the Renaissance. Baron's death in 1988 became the occasion for a number of thoughtful essays on his contribution to Renaissance studies, although, to my mind, these have not adequately treated the impact of Baron's writings on the study of republicanism.⁴ As the author of one of these essays noted, the discussion concerning Baron's great "thesis" – according to which the cultivation of ancient republican ideas by Florentine humanists in the early fifteenth century was the result of a lengthy military and diplomatic struggle between Florence and Milan – has tended to obscure rather than illuminate the general significance of Baron's idea.⁵ For Baron's thesis was never strictly a claim concerning events which took place at Florence in the period

---

³ Hans Baron, *The Crisis of the Early Italian Renaissance: Civic Humanism and Republican Liberty in an Age of Classicism and Tyranny*, 2 vols. (Princeton: Princeton University Press, 1955); rev. edn in one volume (Princeton: Princeton University Press, 1966); Rudolf von Albertini, *Das florentinische Staatsbewusstsein im Übergang von der Republik zum Prinzipat* (Berne: Francke, 1955); Felix Gilbert, *Machiavelli and Guicciardini: Politics and History in Sixteenth Century Florence* (Princeton: Princeton University Press, 1965), with revised bibliographical essays in the 1984 Norton paperback edition; William J. Bouwsma, *Venice and the Defense of Republican Liberty* (Berkeley: University of California Press, 1968); Nicolai Rubinstein, *The Government of Florence under the Medici (1434 to 1494)* (Oxford: Clarendon Press, 1968; revised edn, 1997); Donald Weinstein, *Savonarola and Florence* (Princeton: Princeton University Press, 1970); J. G. A. Pocock, *The Machiavellian Moment: Florentine Political Thought and the Atlantic Republican Tradition* (Princeton: Princeton University Press, 1975); Gene A. Brucker, *The Civic World of Early Renaissance Florence* (Princeton: Princeton University Press, 1977). For suggestive discussions of this postwar scholarship, see Anthony Molho, "American Historians and the Italian Renaissance: An Overview," *Bulletin of the Society for Renaissance Studies*, 9 (1991): 10–23; and his "The Italian Renaissance, Made in the USA," in *Imagined Histories: American Historians Interpret the Past*, ed. Anthony Molho and Gordon S. Wood (Princeton: Princeton University Press, 1998), 263–94. Interestingly, the most original recent contributions to the history of the *vita civile* have not been made by historians of Florence or Venice. See, for example, Quentin Skinner's attempt to demonstrate the non-Aristotelian origins of the Italian civic tradition in his "Ambrogio Lorenzetti: The Artist as Political Philosopher," *Proceedings of the British Academy*, 72 (1986): 1–56; and Antony Black's critical reexamination of the European legal tradition concerning guilds and corporatism in his *Guilds and Civil Society in European Political Thought from the Twelfth Century to the Present* (Ithaca: Cornell University Press, 1984).

⁴ Alison Brown, "Hans Baron's Renaissance," *The Historical Journal*, 29 (1990): 991–1003; John M. Najemy, review of Hans Baron, *In Search of Florentine Civic Humanism*, *Renaissance Quarterly*, 45 (1992): 340–50; Riccardo Fubini, "Renaissance Historian: The Career of Hans Baron," *Journal of Modern History*, 64 (1992): 541–74; James Hankins, "The 'Baron Thesis' After Forty Years and Some Recent Studies of Leonardo Bruni," *Journal of the History of Ideas*, 56 (1995): 309–38. See also the essays by Ronald Witt, John M. Najemy, Craig Kallendorf, and Werner Gundersheimer in the *American Historical Review*, 101 (1996): 107–44. Among earlier tributes, the essay of Eugenio Garin, "Le prime ricerche di Hans Baron sul Quattrocento e la loro influenza fra le due guerre," in *Renaissance Studies in Honor of Hans Baron*, ed. Anthony Molho and John Tedeschi (Florence: Sansoni, 1971), lxi–lxx, is especially informative.

⁵ Fubini, "Renaissance Historian," 542.

around 1400; it was instead a thesis about the relationship of those events to what he considered to be "modern" culture, broadly understood. This is indicated in the subtitle to the 1988 collection of Baron's writings: *Essays on the Transition from Medieval to Modern Thought*.[6] In contrast with Jacob Burckhardt, whose perspective on modernity (and also the Renaissance) was far less sunny than is often acknowledged, Baron's writings offered a thoroughly positive evaluation of what he considered the essential aspects of modern society: participatory politics, constitutional government, and security for private property.[7] In Baron's view, the most important political writers of antiquity, particularly Aristotle and Cicero, had endorsed a regime founded on similar values. Baron's great historical project became the charting of the European world's recovery of the ideals of ancient republicanism during the Renaissance.

It was only natural that the early fifteenth-century writings of the Florentine chancellor Leonardo Bruni should have drawn Baron's attention, since Bruni was the most important of the early humanists engaged in the diffusion of the political and moral thought of the ancient world during the century that revived classical learning.[8] It was natural, too, that Baron should have been drawn to Niccolò Machiavelli, whose importance in the formation of modern political thought remains undisputed (even though there is little agreement on the character of his contribution), and who – at the very least because of where and when he lived – might plausibly be claimed to have inherited the fifteenth-century republican tradition that was begun by Bruni and his contemporaries. If Bruni's interest in ancient republicanism could be explained, and if the influence of the early humanists on Machiavelli could be established, Baron would be in a good position to describe the role played by the Florentine Renaissance in making ancient republican thought once again influential in modern Europe.

In order to draw the necessary connections between these republican thinkers, it was especially important for the success of Baron's project that the corpus of Machiavelli be somehow cleansed, so that works indicating disagreement with the civic values of the ancients and of humanists of the early fifteenth century should not be seen as detracting

[6] Hans Baron, *In Search of Florentine Civic Humanism: Essays on the Transition from Medieval to Modern Thought*, 2 vols. (Princeton: Princeton University Press, 1988).

[7] On Burckhardt's less than sanguine view of modernity, see Riccardo Fubini, "Rinascimento riscoperto? Studi recenti su Jacob Burckhardt," *Società e storia*, 16 (1993): 583–607. Baron continually measured his writings against those of Burckhardt: see his *In Search*, II: 155–81, 190, 198, 208.

[8] See, for example, the collection *The Humanism of Leonardo Bruni*, ed. Gordon Griffiths, James Hankins, and David Thompson (Binghamton: Medieval and Renaissance Texts and Studies, 1987).

from the republicanism at the core of his thought. It was above all Machiavelli's authorship of *The Prince* that prompted persistent doubts concerning the claim that the Florentine secretary was heir to the republicanism of the civic humanists. But in an article entitled "Machiavelli, the Republican Citizen and the Author of *The Prince*," published in the *English Historical Review* in 1961, Baron claimed to have surmounted this difficulty, for the essay turned Machiavelli's *Prince* into an isolated composition, composed well before the Florentine secretary began to write the work that represented his true republican thinking, the *Discourses on Livy*.[9] With Machiavelli now a true republican, it became possible to undertake the project, one in which many scholars would participate, of constructing the stages, or "crises," or "Machiavellian moments," in which the classical republican ideas revived by the Florentine humanists were transmitted to the modern world.[10]

Important to a general acceptance of Baron's more republican Machiavelli was a little-noticed "conversion" of Felix Gilbert to a somewhat similar view of the relation between Machiavelli and the humanists. In a 1939 essay on *The Prince* Gilbert had offered a perceptive account of Machiavelli's "refutation" of the ideas of earlier humanists, but in the postwar years he can be shown to have changed course. Already by the time of his essay on the dating of the *Discourses*, published in 1953, it is clear that Gilbert, like Baron, was reading *The Prince* as an exceptional work in Machiavelli's *oeuvre*, while he saw the *Discourses* as a more important work that emerged from a republican humanist tradition.[11]

---

[9] Hans Baron, "Machiavelli the Republican Citizen and Author of *The Prince*," in his *In Search*, II: 101 51; and his earlier "The *Principe* and the Puzzle of the Date of the *Discorsi*," *Bibliothèque d'Humanisme et Renaissance*, 18 (1956): 405 28.

[10] Compare Randolph Starn, "Historians and 'Crisis,'" *Past and Present*, 52 (1971): 3 22.

[11] To trace Felix Gilbert's changing views on Machiavelli's relationship to Renaissance humanism, begin with his 1939 essay, "The Humanist Concept of the Prince and *The Prince* of Machiavelli," reprinted in his *History: Choice and Commitment* (Cambridge, Mass.: Harvard University Press, 1979), 110 12, which discusses Machiavelli's "refutation" of the humanists. Note that the article suggests (e.g. at 92 and 472 n. 3) no fundamental difference between the viewpoint of *The Prince* and the *Discourses*. Then compare Gilbert's 1953 essay, "The Composition and Structure of Machiavelli's *Discorsi*," also in his *History*, 115 33, esp. 133, in which he reads the *Discourses* "as a first sign of Machiavelli's inclination to accept orthodox humanism," and therefore quite different from *The Prince*. Later, in 1977, Gilbert wrote that he had now become convinced that Machiavelli's interest in humanistic literature went back "to his early years," long before the composition of the *Discourses* when it became more pronounced (see in his *History*, 115 [at bottom]). But as doubts concerning the "classical" quality of the republicanism in the *Discourses* began to emerge in the Machiavelli literature, Gilbert stepped back somewhat from his earlier positions. In 1984 he wrote that "[c]ertainly Pocock's emphasis on Machiavelli's humanist legacy goes too far"; Gilbert, *Machiavelli and Guicciardini*, Norton paperback edn, 321. Perhaps Fubini ("Renaissance Historian," 543) alludes to these changes of direction when he refers to Gilbert's "very pragmatic attitude" in interpreting Machiavelli.

With the passing of the years, it has become easier to see how the great disagreement between Baron and Gilbert over the dating of *The Prince* and the *Discourses* obscured a more consequential point on which both were agreed: in urging the primacy of the *Discourses*, and by reading that work as typical of Florentine humanism, Baron and Gilbert were turning Machiavelli into a classical republican.[12] Thanks to their influential writing, by the late 1960s the rehabilitation of Machiavelli was probably as complete as it could ever be, with the former counselor of evil now seen as an apostle of republican virtue.

Baron, who was working at the Newberry Library in Chicago in the 1950s and 1960s, became increasingly absorbed by the intricate polemics surrounding the chronologies he had constructed for the development of the thought of Bruni and Petrarch. It was at this time that Gilbert became especially influential in encouraging the historiography of republicanism. It was not just that Gilbert, first at Bryn Mawr and then at the Institute for Advanced Study (from 1962), stood at the center of a great network of professional friends and acquaintances at American universities.[13] Nor was it sufficient that Gilbert had a well-acknowledged gift for making good suggestions to other scholars, such as his recommendation to William Bouwsma that he undertake the study of Paolo Sarpi that became *Venice and the Defense of Republican Liberty*.[14] What made Gilbert so important was that he significantly transformed the terms of the republican discussion. Where Baron had formulated the civic humanist thesis in a rather uncomplicated way, one that now seems reminiscent of Toynbee's "challenge and response," Gilbert's goal was to study the fortunes of classical republicanism against

---

[12] Gennaro Sasso, *Niccolò Machiavelli*, 2 vols. (Bologna: Il Mulino, 1980–93), I: 314–20, is most perceptive on the Baron–Gilbert controversy.

[13] *Felix Gilbert as Scholar and Teacher*, ed. H. Lehman, German Historical Institute, Occasional Paper no. 6 (Washington, D.C., 1992). Among the Bryn Mawr colleagues with whom Gilbert worked closely was Caroline Robbins, whose work on the "commonwealthmen" would figure prominently in English and American versions of the republican thesis. See Caroline A. Robbins, *The Eighteenth-Century Commonwealthman: Studies in the Transmission, Development and Circumstances of English Liberal Thought from the Restoration of Charles II until the War with the Thirteen Colonies* (Cambridge, Mass.: Harvard University Press, 1959).

[14] Personal communication. But note that Bouwsma, *Venice and the Defense of Republican Liberty*, xiii, states that the first suggestion was Baron's — perhaps an indication of the extent to which both scholars influenced new scholarship. Sometimes seen as a Venetian version of Baron's *Crisis* (see, e.g., Renzo Pecchioli, *Dal "mito" di Venezia all' "ideologia americana"* [Venice: Marsilio, 1983]), Bouwsma's volume should perhaps be understood instead as a test study of Trevor-Roper's thesis, advanced in a famous essay *contra* Weber and Tawney, that suggested a linkage between Erasmian religious sentiment and merchant capitalism in Europe's free republics. Compare H. R. Trevor-Roper, "Religion, the Reformation and Social Change," in *Religion, the Reformation and Social Change, and Other Essays*, third rev. edn (London: Weidenfeld and Nicolson, 1984), 1–45.

the background of what he called "traditional political assumptions." Methodologically, this involved a significant raising of the stakes.

The more sophisticated approach was already evident in Gilbert's 1949 article on "Bernardo Rucellai and the Orti Oricellari." The ideas of individual thinkers such as Machiavelli and Guicciardini, "were not isolated phenomena," Gilbert wrote, "for they proceeded from political and historical concepts which were the common property of a whole group of Florentine writers." Since Gilbert further postulated that the political thought of the Renaissance was "structured in terms of schools," one of the chief tasks of the historian was to develop an adequate taxonomy. "Ideologies" replaced "ideas" as the historian's currency: the classical republicanism of Bernardo Rucellai and his friends was a "political ideology" they adopted as a means to power.[15]

There was a bravura to Gilbert's work that it is not always easy now to recognize. In the essay on Rucellai, as in his subsequent treatments of "Florentine Political Assumptions in the Period of Savonarola and Soderini" (1957) and *Machiavelli and Guicciardini* (1965), Gilbert developed a sustained and elegant case for studying political thought through the reading of a wide range of texts by a wide range of authors. *Machiavelli and Guicciardini*, arguably Gilbert's best-known work, is often considered a disappointing exercise by readers looking for a guide to the two Florentine writers; but a close reading of major texts was not at all what Gilbert had in mind. Indeed, the book's introduction notes with some pride how few times Machiavelli and Guicciardini are mentioned in later pages![16]

Gilbert flirted quite openly with a structuralist approach.[17] His stated ambition – "to place the ideas of Machiavelli and Guicciardini in [the] context" of "the prevailing trends and tendencies in politics and history" – was quite clearly pointing toward the then-developing method of Quentin Skinner and the Cambridge school of historians of political thought.[18] By determining the "political ideology," "system of values and concepts," "political assumptions," "conceptual framework," or "prevailing mode of thinking" (all phrases used by Gilbert), evidenced

[15] Gilbert, "Bernardo Rucellai," in his *History*, 217, 245.
[16] Gilbert, *Machiavelli and Guicciardini* (1965; 1984), 3.
[17] See, for example, ibid., 28–9. He need not have been influenced directly by Thomas Kuhn, as Pocock would later be. Compare Quentin Skinner's 1969 essay, "Meaning and Understanding in the History of Ideas," in *Meaning and Context: Quentin Skinner and His Critics*, ed. James Tully (Princeton: Princeton University Press, 1988), 292–93, nn. 17–18.
[18] Gilbert, *Machiavelli and Guicciardini* (1965; 1984), 3; Skinner, "Meaning and Understanding," esp. 56–67. See also John H. Geerken, "Structuralist Explanation in History," *Journal of the History of Philosophy*, 17 (1979), 309–18.

across a broad spectrum of texts, the historian was afforded a way of integrating the study of the theoretical, political, and social systems of past societies.[19] An old disciplinary barrier that stood between intellectual history and the world of socio-political power was in the process of being pulled down.

At the same time, Gilbert managed to inject a significant dose of class analysis into his interpretation of the Florentine ideological struggles of the fifteenth and sixteenth centuries. Here, his difference with Baron is quite revealing. Baron, in accordance with an older liberal historiography, had made quite clear his belief that early modern capitalism and republicanism were closely connected and mutually supportive historical phenomena. In several essays devoted to the theme of "civic wealth," Baron claimed that humanist arguments to the effect that private wealth contributed to public prosperity and that some forms of "avarice" could be defended (if not entirely endorsed), were an important concomitant to the development of an ethic favorable to the *vita activa* and to participatory government.[20] Although Baron made clear his debts to Werner Sombart and Amintore Fanfani, he was the first writer to connect a specifically republican ideology with the rise of a new positive attitude toward wealth.[21]

Gilbert, however, saw the relationship between wealth and republican ideals somewhat differently. It is clear from his writings that he was especially drawn to the calls to sacrifice, so common in republican literature, that appeared during times of necessity or crisis.[22] Gilbert's republicanism was an ideology that sought to redistribute existing resources for the common good, while Baron's republicanism was postulated upon exuberant economic growth. Interestingly, as Gilbert interpreted it, a republican ideology could easily become an instrument

---

[19] Compare Clifford Geertz's 1964 essay, "Ideology as a Cultural System," in his *The Interpretation of Cultures: Selected Essays* (New York: Basic Books, 1973), 193–233.

[20] See especially Baron, *In Search*, I: 158–288 (chaps. 7–10).

[21] Werner Sombart, *Der Bourgeois. Zur Geistesgeschichte des modernen Wirtschaftsmenschen* (Munich: Duncker and Humblot, 1913); Amintore Fanfani, *Le origini dello spirito capitalistico in Italia* (Milan: Vita e pensiero, 1933); and cf. Baron, *In Search*, I, 261. It is possible that Baron's argument concerning wealth and the *vita civile* may have influenced Trevor-Roper's attack on Weber, discussed at note 14 above. It is curious that in the essays published in *In Search*, Baron makes no mention of Lester K. Little's *Religious Poverty and the Profit Economy in Medieval Europe* (Ithaca: Cornell University Press, 1978), nor of Little's preliminary essays.

[22] This was the larger significance of Gilbert's detailed 1973 essay, "Venice in the Crisis of the League of Cambrai," republished in his *History*, 269–91. Baron, too, was attracted to the "concepts of 'devotion and sacrifice'" he found in Machiavelli's thought (see John Najemy, "Baron's Machiavelli and Renaissance Republicanism," *American Historical Review*, 101 [1996]: 127), but where Baron was clear on the importance of private wealth for communal well-being, Gilbert was silent.

adopted and manipulated by both parties in a particular episode of class struggle – by the Florentine *popolo*, to be sure, but also by an upper class of *grandi* or *ottimati*. In cities of longstanding civic traditions, such as Florence and Venice, republican exhortations were powerful political weapons that could be used not just to democratize a republican regime but also to undermine it.

The fact that Gilbert's version of republicanism, unlike Baron's, was indifferent to private property would become an important factor in the development by American historians of a "republican paradigm," as we shall see. To understand the American historical profession's attraction to the republican tradition in the 1960s, it will be useful to consider the extent to which the republican idea that emerged from Renaissance historiography offered an exciting alternative to what was more or less a situation of gridlock in the field of American intellectual history. At that time, largely as a result of the work of Charles Beard and Louis Hartz, historians of both the left-leaning and the liberal schools were largely in agreement in interpreting the English and American regimes as embodiments of Lockean self-interest.[23] Historians on the left thought that John Locke's political ideas should be seen as the offspring of nascent bourgeois capitalism; historians on the right thought Locke's ideas instead represented a reasonable response to a plurisecular history of institutional conflict. From both perspectives, it seemed, future historians would be condemned to a dismally unvarying diet of Locke.[24]

For two Americanists, Bernard Bailyn and his student Gordon Wood, developments that were then taking place in Renaissance history arrived as emancipatory tidings. Encouraged in part by Gilbert's example, these Americanists discovered in the history of ideology a way to address simultaneously the concerns of intellectual and social historians.[25] Both Bailyn and Wood noted the predominance of classical republicanism in the pamphlet literature and political treatises of the revolutionary and postrevolutionary periods. Bailyn, in his study of

---

[23] Charles A. Beard, *An Economic Interpretation of the Constitution of the United States* (New York: Macmillan, 1913); Louis Hartz, *The Liberal Tradition in America: An Interpretation of American Political Thought since the Revolution* (New York: Harcourt Brace, 1955).

[24] John P. Diggins, *The Lost Soul of American Politics: Virtue, Self-Interest, and the Foundations of Liberalism* (New York: Basic Books, 1984), 18–47, is especially insightful.

[25] Gilbert's Bancroft Prize-winning *To the Farewell Address: Ideas of Early American Foreign Policy* (Princeton: Princeton University Press, 1961) guaranteed him, as a Europeanist, an unusual degree of attention from American historians.

the pamphlet literature surrounding the Stamp Tax Act, published as the *Ideological Origins of the American Revolution* in 1967, encountered a powerful rhetoric of communal liberty and the right of resistance rather than expressions of Lockean individualism.[26] Although he thought classical republicanism was ultimately unimportant in the Revolution,[27] and he rejected the term "civic humanist,"[28] Bailyn's discovery of a communitarian ideology in the American colonies provided Gordon Wood with the conceptual starting-point for a thorough-going reinterpretation of the Revolution as a phenomenon that had little to do with Lockean self-interest. In Wood's *Creation of the American Republic*, published in 1969, the Revolution was not about the protection of colonial tax exemptions but rather about brotherhood, self-sacrifice, and the defense of the community. Only with the drafting of the constitution, that elaborate mechanism for balancing and defusing the conflict of particular interests, did the forces of Lockean reaction take over.[29] What was so particularly suggestive in Wood's model was that the communitarian and republican ideals of the revolutionary period might be said to offer an alternative and prior standard for the measurement and correction of the republic's institutional arrangements – or even for disobeying them.[30] Published at a time when American society was becoming increasingly disenchanted with its institutions, Wood's book immediately found a receptive audience. The impact of Wood's conceptual model was such that by the early 1970s it was possible for Robert Shalhope to conclude that there was an emerging "republican synthesis" in American historiography.[31]

Charting the lineage of this American republicanism – legitimating it by situating it within an ancient European and Western tradition – was the ambitious task that was taken up by J. G. A. Pocock. Pocock's *The Machiavellian Moment: Florentine Political Thought and the Atlantic Republican Tradition* drew connections with a whole series of republicanisms,

---

[26] Bernard Bailyn, *Ideological Origins of the American Revolution* (Cambridge, Mass.: Harvard University Press, 1967; enlarged edn, 1992).
[27] Bernard Bailyn, *Faces of Revolution: Personalities and Themes in the Struggle for American Independence* (New York: Knopf, 1990), 225–78.
[28] See his preface to the 1992 enlarged edition of *Ideological Origins*.
[29] Gordon S. Wood, *The Creation of the American Republic, 1776–1787* (Chapel Hill: University of North Carolina Press, 1969).
[30] See also Gordon S. Wood, *The Radicalism of the American Revolution* (New York: Knopf, 1992).
[31] Robert E. Shalhope, "Toward a Republican Synthesis: The Emergence of an Understanding of Republicanism in American Historiography," *William and Mary Quarterly*, 29 (1972): 49–80. See also his "Republicanism and Early American Historiography," *William and Mary Quarterly*, 39 (1982): 334–56.

stretching from the *politeia* of Aristotle, to the Florence of Bruni and Machiavelli, to Venice, England, and the American Republic.³² In elaborating the stages of a great republican *translatio virtutis*, Pocock did not seek to determine specific connections by looking for evidence that certain books were read or cited by certain people in certain times and places;³³ he tried instead to survey an array of important texts, most of them by well-known writers, in order to demonstrate that there were structural continuities in republican language that could be found to have endured through the centuries. One of the casualties along the way was the previously omnipresent Locke, whose incipient liberalism Pocock and others were busily writing out of the eighteenth century.³⁴ By the time of the American Revolution, the language of classical republicanism, anchored in Aristotle and Machiavelli, was so dominant that, according to Pocock, it excluded other possibilities. "Not all Americans were schooled in this tradition, but there was (it would appear) no alternative tradition in which to be schooled."³⁵ Where Gordon Wood had seen republicanism's influence coming to an end with the framing of the constitution, Pocock saw it as an enduring presence in the American psyche. It explained typical American attitudes toward the frontier, toward corruption, and toward time itself – since a notable quality of republican ideology, according to Pocock, was a tendency toward millenarianism.

One of the most interesting and indicative of the many transformations Pocock effected in Baron's original concept appears in his discussions of wealth and the market. Here Pocock followed Gilbert, by asserting that "virtue" and property stood in fundamental opposition to one another. Where Baron thought that republicanism was properly protective and nurturing of property, Pocock asserted that the republic should be ever on guard to combat the corrupting effects of private

---

[32] On Pocock's volume, see J. H. Hexter, "Republic, Virtue, Liberty, and the Political Universe of J. G. A. Pocock," in his *On Historians* (Cambridge, Mass.: Harvard University Press, 1979), 255–303; and Cesare Vasoli, "*The Machiavellian Moment*: A Grand Ideological Synthesis," *Journal of Modern History*, 49 (1977): 661–70. Note Pocock's two vigorous defenses of his work: "*The Machiavellian Moment* Revisited," *Journal of Modern History*, 53 (1981): 49–72; and "Between Gog and Magog: The Republican Thesis and the *Ideologia Americana*," *Journal of the History of Ideas*, 48 (1987): 325–46.

[33] As Vasoli ("*The Machiavellian Moment*," 662) suggests he should have done.

[34] John Dunn, "The Politics of Locke in England and America in the Eighteenth Century," in *John Locke: Problems and Perspectives*, ed. John W. Yolton (Cambridge: Cambridge University Press, 1969), 45–80; J. G. A. Pocock, "The Myth of John Locke and the Obsession with Liberalism," in *John Locke: Papers Read at a Clark Library Seminar, 10 December 1977*, ed. J. G. A. Pocock and Richard Ashcraft (Los Angeles, 1980), 3–24.

[35] Pocock, *The Machiavellian Moment*, 507.

wealth. Pocock so emphasized the subordination of private wealth to the good of the commonwealth that for many American historians today the rhetoric of "civic humanism" has come to stand for a kind of communitarianism, if not socialism, offering a response even to that hoary question, "Why is there no socialism in the United States?" For if – so the argument goes – for various historical and structural reasons (such as the absence of feudalism) America remains impervious to European socialism, its republicanism is a historically grounded political tradition which, like socialism, also prizes the sacrifice of private interests for the good of the community.

Certainly this communitarian reading of republicanism was one of the most important reasons for the diffusion of the Pocock model among American historians, who have used it to produce influential interpretations of the Jacksonian period and of early labor movements. Lately the republican model has been extended even to treatments of Wilsonian diplomacy, Jane Addams at Hull House, and the CP-USA during the Popular Front period. We should perhaps leave it to our Americanist colleagues to decide whether it makes sense for their graduate students – who have certainly never heard of Hans Baron – to spend time tracing throwaway references to the Pisistratidae or the Gracchi in the soap-box oratory of the nineteenth century.[36] But the fact that they are doing so stands as almost eerie testimony to the impact a group of Florentine historians has had on contemporary historical research.[37]

Meanwhile, back in Florence, historians for the most part have been content to address their own moment in the republican tradition in its more narrow aspects, steering clear of many of its more important historical and methodological ramifications. In particular, the controversy over the "validity" of Baron's thesis that classical republican values were rediscovered during the war with Milan has resulted in what Riccardo Fubini has called the "misdirection" of historical research.[38]

To begin with, the critics of Baron among the Florentinists have not done nearly so much damage to the Baron thesis as has often been

---

[36] Compare the skepticism toward classical allusions evident in the portrayal of the labor organizer Slackbridge in Charles Dickens, *Hard Times*, ed. Kate Flint (Harmondsworth: Penguin, 1995), 141 ff.

[37] Daniel T. Rodgers, "Republicanism: The Career of a Concept," *Journal of American History*, 79 (1992): 11–38, offers a highly critical discussion of the republican thesis as a Kuhnian-style paradigm. As an essay about fashions in scholarship this is terrific; but the historical problems associated with the republican idea – the reasons for its survival, transmission, and transformation – cannot be dismissed so easily. Baron, Gilbert, Pocock, and the other historians of republicanism, were engaged in something more serious than propagating paradigms.

[38] Fubini, "Renaissance Historian," 542.

claimed.³⁹ Virtually all scholars now object to Baron's use of such terms as "democracy" and "democratic values" to describe the Florentine regime of the late fourteenth and early fifteenth centuries. As we know from a good many studies, the government for which Leonardo Bruni worked was oligarchical.⁴⁰ But it bears keeping in mind that oligarchies are still republics, and there is still something distinctly different about the rule of a self-governing, self-legitimating oligarchy as compared with the rule of a monarch or a tyrant.

Criticisms to the effect that the Florentine republic was imperialist in its foreign policy, rather than defensive as Baron claimed, have been made since the 1960s. Baron was wrong here, too; but history has known other republics that were aggressor states.

A great deal of attention has been paid the Florentine chancellors, whose rhetoric of republicanism, it is alleged, was insincere, a concomitant of their professional lives.⁴¹ But even if it was true that some of the most important early Florentine humanists were not sincere republicans, there remains a problem of audience, since the Florentine oligarchs who *hired* the chancellors had quite clearly developed a taste for the humanist rhetoric of classical republicanism in roughly the years Baron designated.⁴²

In the 1960s and 1970s it was established by Charles Davis, Nicolai Rubinstein, and Quentin Skinner, among others, that major aspects of the kind of republican civic consciousness that Baron thought originated in the Florentine crisis of 1400–1402 were already present in Italy during the communal period.⁴³ But even such a drastic revision of republican-

---

[39] For a good survey of the *fortuna critica* of the Baron thesis, see Albert Rabil, Jr., "The Significance of 'Civic Humanism' in the Interpretation of the Italian Renaissance," in *Renaissance Humanism: Foundations, Forms and Legacy*, 3 vols. (Philadelphia: University of Pennsylvania Press, 1988), I: 141–74.

[40] Peter Herde, "Politische Verhaltensweisen der Florentiner Oligarchie, 1382–1402," in *Geschichte und Verfassungsgefüge. Frankfurter Festgabe für Walter Schlesinger*, ed. Klaus Zernack (Wiesbaden: Steiner, 1973), 161–249.

[41] Jerrold Seigel, "'Civic Humanism' or Ciceronian Rhetoric? The Culture of Petrarch and Bruni," *Past and Present*, 34 (1966), 3–48; Peter Herde, "Politik und Rhetorik in Florenz am Vorabend der Renaissance," *Archiv für Kulturgeschichte*, 50 (1965): 141–220. See also Robert Black, "The Political Thought of the Florentine Chancellors," *Historical Journal*, 29 (1986): 991–1003.

[42] This is the argument of Ronald G. Witt, *Coluccio Salutati and his Public Letters* (Geneva: Droz, 1976), 73–88. See also Gene Brucker, *Civic World*, 300–2. For an excellent discussion of one of the ways in which professional rhetoricians responded to new social and institutional developments, see Witt, "Civic Humanism and the Rebirth of the Ciceronian Oration," *Modern Language Quarterly*, 51 (1990): 167–84.

[43] Charles T. Davis, *Dante's Italy and Other Essays* (Philadelphia: University of Pennsylvania Press, 1984); Nicolai Rubinstein, "Florentina Libertas," *Rinascimento*, n.s., 26 (1976): 3–26; Quentin Skinner, *The Foundations of Modern Political Thought*, 2 vols. (Cambridge: Cambridge University Press) I: 3–65. For a recent appraisal see J. H. Mundy, "In Praise of Italy: The Italian City-Republics," *Speculum*, 64 (1989): 815–34.

ism's early chronology did not touch the larger project – we might call it a "republicanist" project – concerning the continuity of republican political language through Machiavelli and beyond. This, indeed, was the goal of Skinner's two-volume study on *The Foundations of Modern Political Thought*.

Florentine historians, after years of the sometimes quite bitter polemics precipitated by Baron's writings, have taught us a great deal more about Renaissance Florence; but with respect to the larger republican thesis they have done little more than change the chronology. Indeed, the more imposing challenges to the republican thesis have come in other fields, namely American history, the study of classical antiquity, and in the studies on Machiavelli of a number of political theorists and literary scholars.

In the field of American history, John Locke has quite correctly returned to center stage, as such scholars as Joyce Appleby, John Diggins, and Paul Rahe reconstruct the intellectual and cultural world of the Founding Fathers.[44] What becomes clear from this recent work is the extent to which the generation of Madison, Hamilton, and Jefferson embraced liberal ideals that can only be called "Lockean," while furthermore adopting an often critical approach to the republicanism of the ancient world. Although there were differences between them, the Founders of the United States made clear again and again that they hoped to replace classical factions with modern interests, classical virtue with modern industry, classical direct democracy with diluted modern representation. As a result of these studies we can now see the extent to which the most important English and American republican theorists of the early modern period believed that a great historical divide separated them from the republics of classical antiquity.

And, indeed, there may really have been such a divide. As the work of ancient historians increasingly reminds us, the world of ancient politics was radically different from our own. Fierce civic religions, chattel slavery, the exclusion of foreigners, the domestic enslavement of women, and the subordination of private wealth to the *res publica*, institutions that the modern republic deems inimical or can tolerate only with difficulty, were necessary to the perpetuation of the primacy of politics in classical republican regimes.[45] The idea that the coming of

[44] See Joyce O. Appleby, *Capitalism and a New Social Order: The Republican Vision of the 1790s* (New York: New York University Press, 1984); Diggins, *Lost Soul*; Paul A. Rahe, *Republics Ancient and Modern: Classical Republicanism and the American Tradition* (Chapel Hill: University of North Carolina Press, 1992).

[45] Paul A. Rahe, "The Primacy of Politics in Classical Greece," *American Historical Review*, 89 (1984): 265 93; Christian Meier, *The Greek Discovery of Politics*, trans. David McLintock (Cambridge,

modernity has drastically changed the kinds of moral philosophy now possible has been emphasized by a number of writers, most notably Alasdair MacIntyre, who offers a model that is explicitly historical and which therefore deserves to be tested by intellectual and social historians who have been slow to take up his challenge.[46]

If the relationship of the Founding Fathers to antiquity was more problematic than we have thought, so too was their relationship to the Italian medieval republics, which they studied with a view to modern concerns – interests, industry, and representation – rather than for shining instances of civic virtue. If any of the early American statesmen took the time to read Leonardo Bruni, it is extremely unlikely they arrived at assessments similar to Hans Baron's.[47] The Americans were impressed by Machiavelli, but not because they thought he was a classical republican, or because they wished to imitate the faulty Florentine institutions they read about in his *Florentine Histories* – a work that John Adams characterized as a "humorous entertainment," while transporting great sections of it into his *Defence of the Constitutions*.[48] Instead, Adams, Madison, and Jefferson were attracted to the Machiavelli whom they thought had opened a way for creating a new kind of republic that would be more successful than any of the regimes of classical antiquity.

And it is precisely in the area of Machiavelli studies that challenges to

Mass.: Harvard University Press, 1990); Pierre Vidal-Naquet and Nicole Loraux, "La formation de l'Athènes bourgeoise," in Vidal-Naquet, *La Démocratie grecque vue d'ailleurs. Essais d'historiographie ancienne et moderne* (Paris: Flammarion, 1990), 161–209. See also the valuable collection of essays, *City-States in Classical Antiquity and Medieval Italy*, ed. Anthony Molho, Kurt Raaflaub, and Julia Emlen (Stuttgart: Franz Steiner Verlag, 1991). The point was not fully grasped by M. I. Finley, *Politics in the Ancient World* (Cambridge: Cambridge University Press, 1983), notwithstanding the contribution in this direction of many of his earlier writings.

[46] Alasdair MacIntyre, *After Virtue*, second edn (Notre Dame, Ind.: University of Notre Dame Press, 1984). For some recent attempts in this direction, see F. Edward Cranz, "A Common Pattern in Petrarch, Nicholas of Cusa, and Martin Luther," in *Humanity and Divinity in Renaissance and Reformation*, ed. John W. O'Malley, Thomas M. Izbicki, and Gerald Christianson (Leiden: Brill, 1993), 53–70; and Louis Dupré, *Passage to Modernity: An Essay in the Hermeneutics of Nature and Culture* (New Haven: Yale University Press, 1993). See also James Hankins, "Humanism and the Origins of Modern Political Thought," in *The Cambridge Companion to Renaissance Humanism*, ed. Jill Kraye (Cambridge: Cambridge University Press, 1996), 137.

[47] John Adams owned a copy, now in the Boston Public Library, of the 1610 Strasbourg edition of Bruni's *Historiae Florentinorum*, but he did not rely on it for his major work of political theory and history, *A Defence of the Constitutions*; Alfred Iacuzzi, *John Adams Scholar* (New York: Scolar Press, 1952), 95–6, 279 n. 5.

[48] John Adams, *A Defence of the Constitutions of the Government of the United States of America*, 2 vols. (1787–88; rpt. New York: Da Capo, 1971), II: 114. In fact, Machiavelli's *Prince* and Guicciardini's *History of Italy* arrived with the Pilgrims at Plymouth Plantation, where William Bradford kept them in his library. See Thomas Goddard Wright, *Literary Culture in Early New England, 1620–1730* (1920), 27; and Giorgio Spini, *Autobiografia della giovane America. La storiografia americana dai Padri Pellegrini all'Indipendenza* (Turin: Einaudi, 1968), 17.

the thesis of a continuous republican tradition or "language" are now taking hold. Although Pocock, Skinner, and other English-language scholars accept Baron's late dating of the *Discourses*, thirty-three years after the publication of Baron's revisionist article European authorities hold fast to the view that *The Prince* was composed during an interruption in Machiavelli's work on the *Discourses*.[49] Indeed, it has become more common now for writers to seek similarities of outlook in *The Prince* and the *Discourses*, or to read the *Discourses* in the light of *The Prince*, as in the work of Mark Hulliung, Hanna Pitkin, and Victoria Kahn.[50] Albert Hirschmann's *Passions and the Interests*, written at the same time as Pocock's *Machiavellian Moment*, reveals a somewhat different Machiavelli, one who anticipates the ideas of early capitalist theorists, rather than a Machiavelli who recapitulates the classical doctrine of the suppression of the appetites.[51] In these studies we find a serious effort to restore to our reading of Machiavelli his forceful *critique* of classical political thought, as evidenced in his espousal of very different ideas concerning imperialism, faction, class, and the moral appetites. Thus the important ways in which Machiavelli's republicanism differed from that of Aristotle or Cicero are becoming once again visible.[52] One can hardly

[49] For endorsements of Baron's chronology, see Pocock, *The Machiavellian Moment*, 185–86; Quentin Skinner, *Machiavelli* (New York: Hill and Wang, 1981), 50; John M. Najemy, *Between Friends: Discourses of Power in the Machiavelli–Vettori Letters of 1513–1515* (Princeton: Princeton University Press, 1993), 335–6; and David Wootton's introduction to his translation of Machiavelli's *Prince* (Indianapolis: Hackett, 1994). For the more widely accepted view that the *Discourses* existed in some preliminary form before the writing of *The Prince*, see John H. Geerken, "Machiavelli Studies Since 1969," *Journal of the History of Ideas*, 37 (1976): 357; Bernard Guillemain, *Machiavel. L'anthropologie politique* (Geneva: Droz, 1977), 151–7; Sasso, *Niccolò Machiavelli*, I: 314–20; Paul Larivaille, *La pensée politique de Machiavel. Les Discours sur la première Décade di Tite-Live* (Nancy: Presses universitaires de Nancy, 1982); and Francesco Bausi, *I "Discorsi" di Niccolò Machiavelli: genesi e struttura* (Florence: Sansoni, 1985).

[50] Mark Hulliung, *Citizen Machiavelli* (Princeton: Princeton University Press, 1983); Hanna Fenichel Pitkin, *Fortune is a Woman: Gender and Politics in the Thought of Niccolò Machiavelli* (Berkeley and Los Angeles: University of California Press, 1984); and Victoria Kahn, "*Virtù* and the Example of Agathocles in Machiavelli's *Prince*," *Representations*, 13 (1986): 63–83; Kahn, "Reduction and the Praise of Disunion in Machiavelli's *Discourses*," *Journal of Medieval and Renaissance Studies*, 18 (1988): 1–19. See now Kahn's *Machiavellian Rhetoric: From the Counter-Reformation to Milton* (Princeton: Princeton University Press, 1994).

[51] Albert O. Hirschmann, *The Passions and the Interests: Political Arguments for Capitalism before its Triumph* (Princeton: Princeton University Press, 1977), 13, 33, but see also 41.

[52] In an attempt to rescue most of the thesis of republican continuity—all save Aristotle and Greece, which he is willing to let go—Quentin Skinner has recently posited a third, intermediary strain of republicanism, lying between the ancient republicanism of Aristotle, on the one hand, and the liberal, modern republicanism of Locke, on the other. But whether this republicanism based in law is of a kind substantially different from modern republicanism is open to question. See Quentin Skinner, "The Republican Ideal of Political Liberty," in *Machiavelli and Republicanism*, ed. Gisela Bock, Quentin Skinner, and Maurizio Viroli (Cambridge: Cambridge University Press, 1990), 293–309 and the essay by Paul Rahe in this volume.

approach the writings of Machiavelli now without wondering whether the continuities in republican vocabulary registered by Pocock might not have obscured radical differences of meaning.[53]

What we are witnessing in a sometimes tentative and disharmonious manner in the various fields of scholarship I have discussed is a more careful historicization of the republican tradition than we have had so far. To understand better the changes that took place, one of the places to which we shall have to return is Florence – but with a new set of questions that regard not so much the imitation and rebirth of the culture of the ancient world, as the relationship of medieval and early modern culture to the culture of modernity. This is not a new agenda – in fact it was Burckhardt's – but perhaps at the end of the twentieth century we are in a better historical position to assess the advantages and disadvantages of modern culture. If republicanism is still one of the important cords that links us to the ancient world, it is clear that the composition of its threads has changed dramatically over time. Rather than distancing ourselves from the history of republicanism and the *vita civile*, what is needed instead is to focus critical attention on the demonstrable changes that took place in the republican idea – and to undertake the substantial and important task of constructing historical explanations for those changes.

[53] Machiavelli's meaning certainly was not intentionally concealed, as Leo Strauss (*Thoughts on Machiavelli* [Glencoe, Ill.: Free Press, 1958]) and some of his followers would have it. What is needed is much patient philological and historical work to reveal Machiavelli's new meanings, which appear, of course, alongside older ones. Such an effort is evident, above all, in the lifework of Gennaro Sasso (see especially his *Machiavelli e gli antichi e altri saggi*, 4 vols. [Naples and Milan: Ricciardi, 1987–97]); while Najemy's recent *Between Friends* offers another excellent model for combining the historical and the philological in studying Machiavelli.

CHAPTER 2

"Civic humanism" and medieval political thought

James M. Blythe

Hans Baron's fame rests largely upon his characterization of what he called "civic humanism." Central to this is what he saw as the emergence in early fifteenth-century Florence of a new emphasis on the participation of the citizen in the government and civic life of a city-republic, and on the necessity of such participation for the nurturing of individual virtue and the prosperity and liberty of the city. Although his idea stirred controversy from the start, the term itself has become part of the common historical vocabulary, in spite of the shortcomings of Baron's formulation. That formulation has come under attack from both medievalists and Renaissance historians who disagree about the evolution and content of the phenomenon, its connection with republicanism, its chronology, and its geographical origin and extent. In particular, there has been much debate over Baron's claim that civic humanism arose during the intense struggle between Milan and Florence, in which Florence was saved only when Giangaleazzo Visconti of Milan died suddenly of plague in September 1402.

A review article by James Hankins shows that the controversy continues. After reprising the many assaults on Baron, Hankins concedes that the term "civic humanist" may have some validity, but only if we reconstrue it:

> If we continue to use the term "civic humanist," it should be clearly recognized that the attempt to reform and revalorize the life of the city-state in accordance with ancient models . . . was never confined to Renaissance republics . . . It is a style of thought inherited from ancient Rome . . . [which] aims at the reform of political communities generally by improving the moral behavior of their ruling elites . . . If Baron was wrong to read his humanists as fervent partisans of republicanism, he was correct in seeing that humanism, as a cultural program, sought more than the cultivation of the individual. It aimed also to bring

scholarship and learning to bear on the task of building the virtues necessary to the preservation of civil society.¹

Above all Baron identified civic humanism with a fundamental change in values: from the medieval preference for the contemplative life to the Renaissance exaltation of the active and civil life, which was "increasingly respected as a precondition for the full realization of human nature; action and political engagement, therefore, seemed to represent the only truly humane way of life." In contrast, medieval thought had "no access to the later argument – so central to Quattrocento humanists – that virtue must be constantly tested and practiced and that contemplative withdrawal causes human nature to fragment."²

For Baron, these new values were intimately connected with a "new type of historical thinking," which freed the concept of Rome from theological and apocalyptic associations and allowed for a new appreciation of the Roman republic at the expense of the Roman Empire. This desacralization of Rome allowed for it to be seen as an exemplar for the growth and decay of other states. Part of the reason for the emergence of these ideas around 1400 was that the northern Italian cities, threatened by native Italian monarchies, were dominated by purely secular concerns. Once the supernatural justification for hierarchical government was jettisoned, there were grounds for the appreciation of various kinds of states – particularly the city-state – in which all citizens could take an active role.³

Baron believed that the struggle of Florence against Milan around 1400 was the stimulus for the emergence of full-fledged civic humanism, but conceded that the latter built upon Petrarch's rediscovery of Republican Rome in the 1340s and Salutati's recovery of Cicero as a patriot and statesman in the late fourteenth century, and drew as well, of course, on the whole late medieval Italian rhetorical tradition. Despite these influences, Baron basically insisted upon a break with medieval thought, tradition, and world outlook. He insisted that this occurred later than many other Renaissance historians postulated and had been

---

[1] James Hankins, "The 'Baron Thesis' after Forty Years and some Recent Studies of Leonardo Bruni," *Journal of the History of Ideas* 56 (1995): 329–30. The year after this article appeared, there was a forum on Baron's legacy in the *American Historical Review* 101 (1996): 107–144.
[2] Hans Baron, "A Defense of the View of the Quattrocento First Offered in *The Crisis of the Early Italian Renaissance*," in his *In Search of Florentine Civic Humanism*, 2 vols. (Princeton: Princeton University Press, 1988), II: 195–6.
[3] Ibid., 195–7.

brought about by the alleged "big and decisive changes" around 1400 in art and philosophy as well as politics.⁴

J. G. A. Pocock finds a similar disjunction between medieval and Renaissance thought with regard to the concept of the citizen. "It can be argued," he writes, "that the ideal of the citizen implied a totally different conceptualization of the modes of political knowledge and action from that implicit in the scholastic-customary framework."⁵ And later: "To affirm the republic, then, was to break up the timeless hierarchic universe into particular moments."⁶

In contrast, much recent work by both medievalists and Renaissance historians has stressed the continuity of political thought from the twelfth to the sixteenth century. Although a recent controversy has opened the question of whether or not these historians have anachronistically identified the thought of disparate periods, it nevertheless seems clear that a great deal of continuity exists. But this is by no means the same as saying there was an identity of outlook.⁷ Again and again political theorists of various periods have put emphasis on some aspect of earlier theory, or twisted its meaning, or reinterpreted it in new historical circumstances, and have thereby created a new paradigm partially or largely out of old elements. While it is true that the civic consciousness of fifteenth-century Florence, or at least northern Italy from the late fourteenth century on, represents something considerably different from what had existed before, none of Baron's indicia for civic humanism were lacking in the thought of some late thirteenth- and fourteenth-century scholastic writers. In the thought of one of these writers, Ptolemy of Lucca, we can find almost all of them.

Since this article is written from a medievalist's perspective, it will not consider the degree to which the purported content of these ideas accords with the political and social reality of Renaissance Italy, with the centrality of republicanism to civic humanism, or with the sincerity of the republican commitment of those of its proponents who stress repub-

---

⁴ Hans Baron, *The Crisis of the Early Italian Renaissance* (Princeton: Princeton University Press, 1966), 3.

⁵ J. G. A. Pocock, *The Machiavellian Moment: Florentine Political Thought and the Atlantic Republican Tradition* (Princeton: Princeton University Press, 1975), 49.   ⁶ Ibid., 54.

⁷ For a survey and bibliography of this controversy, see Francis Oakley, "Nederman, Conciliar Theory and Constitutionalism: Sed Contra," *History of Political Thought* 16 (1995): 1–19 and Cary Nederman's reply, "Constitutionalism—Medieval and Modern: Against Neo-Figgisite Orthodoxy (Again)," *History of Political Thought* 17 (1996): 179–94. Nederman has written widely about this and other issues relevant to this volume. Many of his articles have now been collected in Cary Nederman, *Medieval Aristotelianism and its Limits: Classical Traditions in Moral and Political Philosophy, 12–15th Centuries* (Brookfield, Vt.: Variorum, 1997).

licanism. To do so would be to make even more apparent the continuity of medieval and Renaissance thought, for Renaissance humanists are considerably more elitist than these concepts suggest, much more open to a variety of political forms, more devoted to the common good as the *raison d'être* of government, and more inclined to stress the harmonious workings of all the various human parts of a polity.

This essay will concentrate on several aspects of Baron's argument: appreciation of the Roman Republic and criticism of the Empire, rejection of the medieval theology of the Roman Empire, exaltation of republican government, and appreciation of nonmonarchical government in general. It will only touch upon the idea of civic life as necessary to human fulfillment and virtue, the necessity of testing virtue, the model of Cicero as a statesman, and rhetoric as the highest calling for a statesman, all of which were also developed before 1400.[8] Nor, for the most part, will it discuss the medieval rhetorical tradition, which many scholars have analyzed to defend a wide range of positions, from claiming that it and civic humanism are quite different, to virtually identifying them and thereby questioning the very existence of civic humanism as a new phenomenon.[9]

Many previous authors have criticized Baron on various points of his theory, and I am indebted to their work. But one prejudice that still remains, even among Baron's critics, is the tendency sharply to distinguish scholastic writers as either Italian republicans or northern monarchists. In the High and Later Middle Ages there was a marked contrast between the governmental experimentation of northern Italy, from

---

[8] A few portions of this essay have been adapted from my book, *Ideal Government and the Mixed Constitution in the Middle Ages* (Princeton: Princeton University Press, 1992). There is also some overlap with my introduction (written at about the same time as this essay) to Ptolemy of Lucca, *On the Government of Rulers (De Regimine Principum), with portions attributed to Thomas Aquinas*, trans. James M. Blythe (Philadelphia: University of Pennsylvania Press, 1997). All translations and paragraph numbers here of either author's part of *De Regimine Principum* are derived from this edition. For the sake of consistency in this volume, I render the word "regimen" here as "regime," instead of the "government" I used there (although, of necessity, I have kept the English title of the book as *On the Government of Rulers*). I have also made some other minor changes to fit the context here better, and I have corrected a few small errors. All other translations are also my own unless otherwise noted.

[9] Paul O. Kristeller, "Humanism and Scholasticism in the Italian Renaissance" and "The Humanist Movement," reprinted in *Renaissance Thought and Its Sources*, ed. M. Mooney (New York: Columbia University Press, 1979), 85–105 and 21–32, respectively; Ronald Witt, "Medieval '*Ars Dictaminis*' and the Beginnings of Humanism: A New Construction of the Problem," *Renaissance Quarterly* 35 (1982): 1–35; Quentin Skinner, "Machiavelli's *Discorsi* and the Pre-Humanist Origins of Republican Ideas," in *Machiavelli and Republicanism*, ed. Gisela Bock, Quentin Skinner, and Maurizio Viroli (Cambridge: Cambridge University Press, 1990); Jerrold Seigel, "'Civic Humanism' or Ciceronian Rhetoric? The Culture of Petrarch and Bruni," *Past and Present* 34 (1966): 3–48 and *Rhetoric and Philosophy in Renaissance Humanism* (Princeton: Princeton University Press, 1968).

fairly broadly based republics to tyrannies, and the monarchies that dominated in northern Europe. Popular works, chronicles, speeches, public correspondence, and the like show that there was also a much greater interest in republican ideas in Italian cities than elsewhere. Yet scholars throughout Europe traveled widely to study and teach at universities and to carry out the business of the Church and their clerical orders and drew on a common education and common readings in Aristotelian and other republican political works. So we should not be surprised that in many cases they came to conclusions that are not predictable from their place of birth. Even northern proponents of monarchy were aware of the political situation in Italian cities, understood their affinity with the ancient Greek city-states, and often used Italian republican examples in attempting to understand or apply Aristotelian principles. They were also quite capable of defending republicanism or of incorporating republican principles into their theories of monarchy.

This blending of monarchist and republican ideology suggests that the words "monarchist," and "republican," do not in themselves sufficiently characterize a writer's attitude toward participation in government. Therefore, the common practice of treating Engelbert of Admont, Nicole Oresme, and John of Paris, to name only a few, simply as northern monarchists and of contrasting them with purported Italian republicans such as Ptolemy of Lucca and Marsilius of Padua, as Quentin Skinner tends to do, does not make sense. It makes even less sense (considering the writings of John of Paris, Engelbert of Admont, and Peter of Auvergne, among others) to say, as he does, that "in the half-century after Moerbeke's translation began to be widely used, almost all the original and influential adaptations of Aristotle's ideas came from Italian writers."[10] Most confusing of all is his treatment of Thomas Aquinas, whom he classifies as an Italian, and therefore presumably more receptive to the republican perspective, yet it is not clear why this should be so, since Aquinas was raised in southern Italy in one of the most centralized monarchies in Europe. Each writer developed ideas somewhat differently because of specific political experiences and contingencies, and this certainly is important, but it is not the entire story. Many civic humanist ideas were anticipated both in the north and south, as the writings of northerners like Nicole Oresme, especially, demonstrate; his writings will be discussed more fully below.

[10] Quentin Skinner, "Political Philosophy," in *The Cambridge History of Renaissance Philosophy*, ed. Quentin Skinner et al. (Cambridge: Cambridge University Press, 1988), 395.

While my own work has been mostly concerned with the Aristotelian elements in medieval political thought, I sympathize with the tendency of scholarship in the past few decades to downplay the revolutionary nature of the introduction of Aristotle's *Politics* in the mid-thirteenth century and to emphasize how medieval writers used the new vocabulary and theoretical framework to bolster their own political outlook. There has been increasing interest in other "voices" in medieval political thought. For example, Antony Black lists five "languages" spoken by educated medieval people, each with its own political vocabulary: theological, native, juridical, Ciceronian, and Aristotelian. All but the native "language" were written in the same Latin.[11] To understand the change in thinking between the medieval and Renaissance periods, it is necessary to understand how all of these languages interacted and how they changed over time. Of particular concern here is the Ciceronian voice in the Middle Ages, since the recovery of Cicero as a statesman and orator is central to Baron's concept of civic humanism.

On the other hand, the introduction of Aristotle did have an important effect in giving political thinkers a way to explain the political situation, focus the political activity of citizens, defend existing political traditions, or advocate reforms. Nicolai Rubinstein argues that, in the case of Italy, 150 years of independent city-republics with widespread citizen participation had made little impact on formal political theory, and even on native Italian theory, which remained rudimentary and pragmatic, but that all this changed within fifty years under the impact of the *Politics*.[12] While this underplays the influence of Cicero, it is true that these years saw an explosion of political thought based on Aristotle, and, once assimilated, Aristotelian language spurred the evolution of new ways of thinking and new attitudes toward government.

THE ROMAN REPUBLIC AND EMPIRE

Let us now turn to the question of Rome. To evaluate Baron's position, we need to look at the images of both the Republic and Empire in the Middle Ages and to determine whether these were connected to a theological-hierarchic view of politics. One of the key events for Baron is Leonardo Bruni's assertion in his *Panegyric of the City of Florence* that

---

[11] Antony Black, *Political Thought in Europe, 1250–1450* (Cambridge: Cambridge University Press, 1992), 7–10.

[12] Nicolai Rubinstein, "Political Theories in the Renaissance," in *The Renaissance. Essays in Interpretation*, ed. André Chastel (London: Methuen, 1982), 153–5. Quentin Skinner questions this assessment of Italian political thought in "Machiavelli's *Discorsi*."

Florence was founded under the Roman Republic, and not, as had been previously asserted, under the Empire. For Baron, this symbolizes the new attitude toward ancient Rome. But, as Rubinstein notes, Giovanni Villani (*c.* 1280–1348) had already tied contemporary Florence to the ancient Republic, not through its original foundation, but through its alleged refounding in the time of Charlemagne, who decreed that Florence "should rule and govern itself as Rome had done, that is by means of two consuls and by a council of one hundred senators."[13]

Many other historians have shown that there was extensive appreciation of the Roman Republic before Bruni, and even before Petrarch. Beryl Smalley criticized Baron specifically on this point, demonstrating the pervasive influence of Sallust on medieval education and, through education, on medieval views of ancient Rome. She shows that medieval writers appreciated that Rome had grown great under the Republic, cited republican heroes as models, and, even more importantly, considering the Baron thesis, grounded republican success on the virtue of these republican heroes. Smalley writes: "Petrarch could reinterpret, but not rediscover what Sallust had made part of the heritage of learning."[14] Charles Till Davis points out that in addition to Sallust, "Florus, Lucan, Virgil, Servius, Cicero, Juvenal, and Valerius Maximus were popular, and whether or not the medieval writers attacked the Empire, they all praised pristine virtue and republican heroes." He also mentions numerous examples of early medieval writers who esteemed the Republic, including Paul the Deacon, John of Salisbury, and Arnold of Brescia.[15] He goes on to show in detail how Ptolemy of Lucca, Remigio de' Girolami, and even the imperialist Dante Alighieri all praised the virtue of the ancient Romans during the Republic and, together with other Tuscan writers of the late thirteenth and early

---

[13] Giovanni Villani, *Chronicle*, 3.3. "si reggesse e governasse al modo di Roma, cioè per due consoli e per lo consiglio di cento sanatori." Cited in Rubinstein, "Political Theories in the Renaissance," 164.

[14] Beryl Smalley, "Sallust in the Middle Ages," in *Classical Influences on European Culture 500–1500*, ed. R. R. Bolgar (Cambridge: Cambridge University Press, 1971), 167–8. Nicolai Rubinstein, "Some Ideas on Municipal Progress and Decline in the Italy of the Communes," in *Fritz Saxl, 1890–1948: A Volume of Memorial Essays*, ed. D. J. Gordon (London: Nelson, 1957), 165–83, also discusses the role of Sallust in northern Italy. More recently, Patricia J. Osmond (de Martino) has written several articles showing the pervasive influence of Sallust from the thirteenth through the sixteenth centuries, most relevantly, "*Princeps Historiae Romanae*: Sallust in Renaissance Political Thought," *Memoirs of the American Academy in Rome* 40 (1995): 101–43.

[15] Charles Till Davis, "Ptolemy of Lucca and the Roman Republic," *Proceedings of the American Philosophical Society* 118 (1974): 30.

fourteenth century, showered praise upon Cicero as statesman.[16] Although few rejected the Empire, Davis suggests that at this period in Tuscany: "streams of classical influence flowed together, and all dealt with subjects that concerned the Roman Republic. Perhaps it is at this point that we find the 'rediscovery of pre-imperial Rome' which Baron defers until Petrarch, and in regard to Cicero, until Coluccio Salutati."[17]

Baron himself admits that there were a few isolated instances of advocacy of the Republic before Bruni: he cites Petrarch's *Africa* and Ptolemy of Lucca who, he wrote, "showed an astonishing openness of mind toward the role played by free city-republics in the ancient world; [he] had formed the clear-cut judgment that the power of Rome had been built up under the consuls and free councils of the Republic." In spite of this, and his attribution of the "rediscovery of pre-imperial Rome" to Petrarch, Baron feels that neither Petrarch nor Ptolemy had ventured any kind of coherent historical critique of the Empire (by this he means in terms of the decline of virtue); the former expressed merely a form of racial nationalism, the latter simply reflected the republican ideals of the existing northern Italian communes.[18]

In response, let me outline the attitudes of several scholastic writers toward the Roman Empire and Republic. In *On the Government of Rulers*, an unfinished advice manual directed to the king of Cyprus, later completed by Ptolemy of Lucca, the author, traditionally considered to be Thomas Aquinas (*c.* 1225–74), sowed the seed for the later scholastic critique of the Roman Empire and for appreciation of the Republic.[19] Thomas remarks that although kingship is the best form of government, tyranny is the worst. Rome expelled the kings, created an aristocratic republic, and "instituted for themselves consuls and other magistrates. These began to govern and direct them, and, as Sallust reports: 'It is incredible to relate how the Roman city grew in a short time once liberty had been obtained.'" Since the citizens perceived that the common good was in their own hands, they worked for it with enthusiasm, even

---

[16] Ibid., 32–50. See also Davis, "Roman Patriotism and Republican Propaganda: Ptolemy of Lucca and Pope Nicholas III," *Speculum* 50 (1975): 411–33.   [17] Davis, "Ptolemy of Lucca," 41.
[18] Baron, *Crisis of the Renaissance*, 55–7. I must admit that I do not understand why Baron considers the latter a limitation.
[19] I have used different editions for the two parts: Ptolemy of Lucca, *De Regimine Principum*, in Thomas Aquinas, *Opuscula Omnia necnon Opera Minora: Opuscula Philosophica*, ed. R. P. Joannes Perrier (Paris: P. Lethielleux, 1949), I: 267–426 and Thomas Aquinas, *De Regimine Principum*, in Thomas Aquinas, *Opera Omnia*, ed. Roberto Busa (Stuttgart-Bad Cannstatt: Frommann Verlag and Günther Holzboog, 1980), 595–601.

giving their private wealth for the good of the Republic.[20] But afterwards:

when they were worn out by the continual dissensions which escalated into civil wars – during which liberty, for which they were very zealous, was ripped from their hands – they came under the power of the emperors. From the beginning the emperors were unwilling to be called kings, because this title was odious to the Romans. Some of them procured the common good faithfully, as is the true royal custom, and through their zeal the Roman Republic was increased and preserved. But most of them were tyrants to their subjects yet idle and feeble toward their enemies, and these led the Roman Republic to naught. There was a similar process among the Hebrew people. First, while the judges governed them, their enemies ravaged them on all sides. For they did "what was good in their own eyes." But when kings had been divinely given to them at their own insistence, they fell away from the cult of the one God because of the kings' evil and were finally led into captivity.[21]

This is not an unqualified attack on the empire or defense of the Republic; the author's concern is for the common good, which could be served by either. When emperors governed well, they advanced the commonwealth as much as or more than when aristocrats dominated. Since kingship, when it is exercised correctly, is the best regime of all, the great growth of the Roman Republic presumably stems from its emancipation from tyranny rather than from the specific form of good government that replaced the evil kings. There is no inkling that participation is beneficial in itself or necessary for the individual –

---

[20] Thomas Aquinas, *De Regimine Principum*, 1.5.2: "Horum quidem exemplum evidenter apparet in Romana republica. Regibus enim a populo Romano expulsis, dum regium vel potius tyrannicum fastum ferre non possent, instituerant sibi consules et alios magistratus per quos regi coeperunt et dirigi, regnum in aristocratiam commutare volentes et, sicut refert Salustius: 'incredibile est memoratu, quantum, adepta libertate, in brevi Romana civitas creverit'." Sallust, *The War with Catiline*, 7.3. See also Augustine, *The City of God*, 5.12. In recent years the attribution of book 1 and book 2 up to the middle of 2.4.7 of *De Regimine Principum* to Thomas has been questioned. The strongest case, which I discuss in the introduction to my translation, is made by Walter Mohr, "Bemerkungen zur Verfasserschaft von dem *De Regimine Principum*," in *Virtus Politica*, ed. Joseph Möller and Helmut Kohlemberger (Stuttgart and Bad Cannstatt: Friedrich Frommann Verlag and Günter Holzboog, 1974), 127 45. The question is still open in my mind, and for convenience I will continue to refer to Thomas as the author.

[21] Thomas Aquinas, *De Regimine Principum*, 1.5.5 6, citing 1 Kings 3.18 and 12.13 15: "Sed cum dissensionibus fatigarentur continuis, usque ad bella civilia excreverunt, quibus bellis civilibus eis libertas, ad quam multum studuerant, de manibus erepta est, sub potestate imperatorum esse coeperunt, qui se reges a principio appellari noluerunt, quia Romanis fuerat nomen regium odiosum. Horum autem quidam more regio bonum commune fideliter procuraverunt, per quorum studium Romana respublica et aucta et conservata est. Plurimi vero eorum in subditos quidem tyranni, ad hostes vero effecti desides et imbecilles, Romanam rempublicam ad nihilum redegerunt. Similis etiam processus fuit in populo Hebraeorum. Primo quidem dum sub iudicibus regebantur, undique diripiebantur ab hostibus, nam unusquisque quod bonum erat in oculis suis, hoc faciebat. Regibus vero eis divinitus datis ad eorum instantiam, propter regum malitiam, a cultu unius Dei recesserunt et finaliter ducti sunt in captivitatem." The first quotation actually refers to the Judge Samuel's comment about God: "Let him do what is right in his own eyes."

indeed, in all of Thomas's writings popular participation is included only to pacify the people by making them feel that they have a stake in the government – and here there is not even this element of democracy, since Thomas sees the republic as an aristocracy. The weakness of each of the good, simple forms of government – monarchy, aristocracy, democracy, and empire (as a kind of monarchy) – is the same: as a pure form it is not easily prevented from degenerating into oppressive perversions of itself.

Nevertheless, it is clear that even in this earliest of the scholastic appreciations of the Republic and critiques of the Empire we find some of the very elements that Baron says are missing before civic humanism. The Republic represented the active involvement of an aristocratic class of citizens, and its success was largely due to the virtue of these citizens working ardently for it and liberty; conversely, it was only after virtue failed and dissension ensued that this liberty could be taken away. The comparison with the Hebrews suggests that Thomas identified this fall from virtue with concern for self-interest rather than for the common good. The "similar process" to which Thomas refers is the transformation to tyrannical kingship from purely aristocratic government under the Judges, who, since they were not checked by other elements, were able to ignore the common good, in preference to their own. This contrasts both with the initial uncorrupted period of the Judges' rule and with the earlier Hebrew government, which Thomas praises in the *Summa Theologiae* as one in which both democratic and aristocratic elements had had a role under a monarchical Moses.[22] In either case, turning away from civic virtue led to loss of freedom and oppression under tyrannical kings or emperors.

Although it is possible to extract a pro-republican position from Thomas's words, one can do so only by failing to appreciate the context of his argument, which is how to avoid the pitfalls of the best form of government – monarchy. Thomas does not generally support a republic over a monarchy or oppose the Empire *per se*.[23] Such a critique of empire

---

[22] Thomas Aquinas, *Summa Theologiae*, 1 2.105.
[23] Ronald Witt, "The Rebirth of the Concept of Republican Liberty in Italy," in *Renaissance Studies in Honor of Hans Baron*, ed. A. Molho and J. Tedeschi (Dekalb, Ill.: Northern Illinois University Press, 1971), 193 4, comments that Thomas's statement is "unmistakably republican in its criticism of the Emperors as a group and . . . provides a rationale for the putative superiority of republicanism over monarchy," but realizes that Thomas "used this historical discussion precisely to show that a government of many fell under the power of a tyrant more easily than did a government ruled by one. The republican interpretation of Roman history, therefore, was buried in a series of arguments designed to prove the superiority of monarchy." On Thomas's putative republicanism, see below. See also Ronald Witt, "The *De Tyranno* and Coluccio Salutati's View of Politics and Roman History," *Nuova rivista storica* 53 (1969): 440 5, 449 50.

does figure in the portion of *On the Government of Rulers* that Ptolemy of Lucca (*c.* 1236–1327) wrote. This differs in many important ways from Thomas's portion, not least in that it shows a decided hostility to kingship in general, accepting it only if the population is unworthy of a better form.

In the process of developing his anti-monarchical ideas Ptolemy rehabilitates the Roman Republic at the expense of the Empire. He frequently cites approvingly the praise of the Roman Republic found in 1 Maccabees:

no one wore a diadem or assumed the purple so as to be glorified by those things, and they held court to consult daily with the 320, always taking counsel about matters concerning the multitude so that they might do those things that were worthy. They committed their magistracy to one person to exercise lordship over all the lands for a single year, and all obeyed that one, and there was neither ill-will nor jealousy among them.[24]

This may describe the greatest period in Roman history, but for Ptolemy the Roman Republic was at all times "political." This word is used with various meanings by scholastic writers, but for Ptolemy it normally includes the participation of many, rule by law, alternation of rulers, election of rulers, mild rule, and salaries for rulers.[25] He delineates an evolution of republican institutions, as segments of the community were gradually elevated to an active role in government:

First the two consuls were created; then, as the histories tell us, the Dictator and the Master of Equites, to whom belonged the whole civil government, and so Rome was governed by an aristocratic rule. Later, tribunes were set up to favor the plebeians and the people, so that the consuls and the others I mentioned could not exercise government without them, and in this way democratic rule was appended. In the course of time the senators took over the power of governing.[26]

---

[24] 1 Maccabees 8.14–16; see Ptolemy of Lucca, *De Regimine Principum*, 2.8.1, 2.8.4, 3.6.3, 3.12.5, 3.20.3, 3.20.6, 4.1.4, 4.2.1, 4.7.4, 4.19.4, 4.25.2. "Nemo portabat diadema nec induebatur purpura ut magnificaretur in ea, et quia curiam fecerunt in qua consulebant quotidie trecentos viginti, consilium habentes semper de multitudine ut quae digna sunt gerant, et quia committunt uni homini magistratum suum per singulos annos dominari universae terrae, et omnes obediunt uni, et non est invidia nec zelus inter eos." The quotation given is from 3.6.3 and differs in a few insignificant words from 1 Maccabees.

[25] Ibid., 4.1 and passim.

[26] Ibid., 4.19.5. "Primo enim creati fuerunt consules qui erant duo, postea dictator et magister equitum, ut historiae narrant, ad quos pertinebat totum civile regimen; et sic principatu aristocratico regebatur. Ulterius inventi sunt tribuni in favorem plebis et populi sine quibus consules et alii praedicti regimen exercere non poterant; et sic adjunctus est democraticus principatus. Processu vero temporis senatores assumpserunt regendi potestatem, licet senatores primo a Romulo sint inventi."

The key word here is "appended": old institutions and rulers were not replaced; rather, the system became more representative of all social groups. The emperors ended this, doing away with political rule and personally assuming all power. For scholastic writers who distinguished political, regal, and despotic as separate categories of rule, each valid in its proper place, this would not have necessarily been bad, since they considered only tyrannical rule, the perversion of monarchical rule (and not the same as despotic rule), to be always harmful. But Ptolemy conflates all nonpolitical rule and sees regal rule as inevitably despotic and tyrannical. He is careful to argue that the rule of the dictator and consuls was aristocratic, not monarchical, since plurality of rule exists as long as there is alternation of rule, participation in rule (as with the senate and tribunes), and election. The case of Julius Caesar is different; Ptolemy considers his coup to be usurpation, the destruction of polity, and his rule to be despotic or tyrannical. This is why he concludes that Caesar was slain for abuse of power.[27]

Ptolemy sees the first signs of decay in the Roman Republic during the period of the civil wars when a few men converted the republic into an oligarchy.[28] Before this, the virtue of the Roman people as a whole made republican government possible, and the Republic was greatest when the greatest number of citizens participated. One sign of this greatness was the world-wide expansion of Roman power. This empire of Rome (as opposed to the Roman Empire) flourished under the Republic. As virtue declined, authority became concentrated in fewer and fewer hands until Caesar's tyranny ended the Republic. In his view of the end of the Republic, if not of its evolution, Ptolemy follows Aquinas in emphasizing the conversion of the common good to the good of the few.

Ronald Witt reminds us that we should be wary of equating anti-Caesarist comments with anti-imperialism, since the former were usually personal and not attacks on the Empire itself or on the line of emperors beginning with Augustus.[29] To some extent we can see this in Ptolemy, although I disagree with Witt's comment that Ptolemy's remarks are "too vague to be significant." As will be seen below, Ptolemy identifies Caesar's "usurpation of empire" with the end of Rome's role as a world monarchy, and in this sense Augustus can be no other than Caesar's successor, whose rule represents the destruction of the true

[27] Ibid., 4.1.4, 2.9.6, 3.8.5, 3.12.5.   [28] Ibid., 4.19.5.
[29] Ronald Witt, "The Rebirth of the Concept of Republican Liberty in Italy," 193 4; "The De Tyranno," 443 50.

polity of the Roman Republic. Ptolemy was not a consistent thinker. He was equally capable of condemning the empire or supporting it as the political arm of the papacy. What is significant is that he is at times capable of providing a coherent critique of the Empire in terms of the decline of virtue and the incompatibility of any monarchy with the needs of any "virile and virtuous people." He himself would perhaps see no inconsistency, since he could have argued that with the loss of virtue among the ancient Romans came the inability to govern themselves and the necessity of an oppressive monarchy.

As one example of Witt's point, Marsilius of Padua (c. 1275–after 1342), a supporter of the Empire, condemns Julius Caesar for violating and usurping the Republic, and, unlike Augustus, taking power without a grant from the Roman people.[30] Interestingly, he too thinks that it was the exceptional virtue of the Roman people under the Republic that made the Romans worthy of an empire,[31] which grew into a tree in whose shade "all the kings, princes, and tyrants of the age with all their peoples relax and enjoy the blessings of peace."[32] Here Marsilius specifically refers to the republican period, but he says that these virtues extended into the empire under Augustus and his successors. Besides military prowess, these virtues included "peaceful liberty, the cultivation of justice, reverence for laws, friendships with neighboring nations, mature counsel, and dignified speech and action."[33] Like Ptolemy, Marsilius thinks that these virtues induced foreigners to submit themselves voluntarily to Roman rule.[34]

Marsilius's combination of an attack on Caesar with a pro-imperial position illuminates the view of Engelbert of Admont (c. 1250–1331). While he did not reject the Empire out of hand – indeed, he was a qualified imperialist – he insisted that no rule could be valid without the participation of the many and provided arguments that could be used in a general critique of the Empire. Because Caesar (like Tarquin) refused participation, he became a tyrant who substituted his personal good for

---

[30] Marsilius of Padua, *De Translatione Imperium*, in *Marsile de Padoue: Œuvres Mineures*, ed. Colette Jeudy and Jeannine Quillet (Paris: Editions du Centre de la Recherche Scientifique, 1979), chap. 2. For a translation, see *Marsiglio of Padua, "Defensor minor" and "De Translatione Imperium,"* ed. Cary Nederman (Cambridge: Cambridge University Press, 1993).

[31] Marsilius of Padua, *Defensor minor*, in *Marsile de Padoue: Œuvres Mineures*, chap. 12.

[32] Marsilius of Padua, *De Translatione Imperium*, chap. 1 (Nederman's translation): "omnes reges saeculi principes et tyranni cum populis omnibus, in pacis pulchritudine quiescebant."

[33] Ibid: "Romani . . . libertate quieta, iustitiae cultu, legum reverentia, finitimarum gentium amicitiis, maturitate conciliorum, gravitate verborum et operum obtinuerunt, ut orbem subjicerent suae dicioni."

[34] See also Marsilius of Padua, *Defensor minor*, chap. 12.

the common good.³⁵ In this regard, Engelbert cites favorably Cicero's story of a senator's remark: "If you will not have me as Senator, I will not have you as emperor."³⁶ Engelbert is also concerned with a ruler's need to honor existing constitutions, a great concern of medieval lawyers. In the Cicero anecdote he specifically cites the obligation to honor contracts and agreements.

Nicole Oresme (c. 1320–82) is a monarchist, but like Engelbert he emphasizes participation. He therefore condemns the Roman empire decisively, since the Roman people turned over all their power to the emperor and ended what Oresme believed was a perfect republican monarchy. The result was the corruption of the polity and the decline of Roman power.³⁷ In contrast, the Republic flourished while the multitude acted rationally and established limited institutions: a monarchical consulate checked by an aristocratic senate and a democratic tribunate. Oresme made analogies between the Roman Republic and Sparta and Carthage (Aristotle's examples of mixed constitutions), the government of the ancient Jews, and the France of his own day under Charles V.³⁸ These ideas are further blows to Baron's thesis that no reasoned opposition to the Empire and support for the Republic based on an analysis of the decline of virtue existed in this period or country, and shows how medieval authors can easily combine republicanism with monarchy. Oresme's analysis is precisely in the terms Baron demands: the Republic flourished because of the virtue and participation of a rational multitude and was transformed into the despotic Empire only when the multitude lost its reason.

THEOLOGY OF THE ROMAN EMPIRE

Having sketched some medieval views of the Roman Republic and Empire, we must now address Baron's contention that medieval

---

³⁵ Engelbert of Admont, *De Regimine Principum* (Regensburg, 1724), 7.35, 253: "Seditiones faciunt ... quando Princeps seu Dominus nullum dignum honore vel lucro permittet eis participare, sed vult omnia solus esse. Haec enim fuit causa seditionis Senatus contra Julium Caesarem, quod, ut dicit Lucanus de ipso, 'Omnia Caesar erat.'"

³⁶ Ibid., 3.21, 74: "Et secundum Articulum adhuc addit Tullius in Primo Officiorum, videlicet quod distincta iura et honores contractionibus et collocutionibus singulis a singulis exhibeantur et serventur pro debito et decenti. Sicut legitur quidam Senator Romae dixisse ad Imperatorem: 'Si tu non habebis me in Senatorem, neque ego te habebo ut Imperatorem.'"

³⁷ Nicole Oresme, *Le Livre de Politiques d'Aristote*, ed. Albert Douglas Menut, *Transactions of the American Philosophical Society*, n.s., 60 (6) (1970): 6.25, 242–43: "Mes depuis que le peuple transporta ou bailla toute posté au prince et que il mist le prince sus la lay, assés tost apparut que leur policie ala en empirance et leur prosperité en deffaillant et leur domination en declinant."

³⁸ Ibid., 2.21, 108; 6.12, 274.

thought about the Empire always included a theological or apocalyptic element. Earlier citations have already begun to discredit this idea, since those who regard the Empire as tyrannical or avoidable would not also claim that it was God's chosen regime. While this latter outlook was common, it was fairly rare among scholastic writers. Even those who support the empire usually do so for purely earthly political reasons.

This also suggests that Baron was mistaken when he said that medieval thinkers lacked a concern with or understanding of secular historical development, and that it was only the civic humanists who developed a new type of nontheological historical thinking that allowed for a new appreciation of the Roman Republic and its consequent use as an exemplar for the growth and decay of other states. Whatever the merit of their conclusions, medieval thinkers had already begun to seek for purely historical explanations, and these explanations were often headed in the same direction that the later humanists would take. Nicolai Rubinstein has pointed out that various translations of Roman historical works into the vernacular, as well as contemporary histories, show that fourteenth-century Italians were both increasingly interested in and knowledgeable about ancient Roman history, and, more significantly, that contemporary "political thinkers considered . . . history . . . relevant to the political problems of their time and coloured it with their own political preoccupations and ideals." As a result, Rome came to be seen as a model for political organization and an object lesson in the rise and decline of political fortunes. This can be found not only in the works of scholars like Ptolemy and Thomas but also in poems, chronicles, sermons, speeches, and the products of civic chanceries. By the mid-thirteenth century, as Rubinstein notes, there are many examples of using an analysis of the connection between Roman internal discord and its decline to warn against the civic factionalism in Italy.[39]

One must also consider how theology is commonly used in scholastic political thought. Citations of the Bible are frequent, but are usually given merely for support or illustration of ideas or conclusions reached by reason, or to provide a basis for discussion through reason. A perfect example of this can be seen in Ptolemy's musings on seemingly contradictory models of kingship in the Bible.[40] The texts provide the basis for a purely secular discussion of the nature of monarchy, the conclusions of which illuminate the texts. But biblical texts are rarely used to make an assertion about the nature of government that is unsupported by secular political ideas.

---

[39] Rubinstein, "Political Theories," 161-2. [40] Ptolemy of Lucca, *De Regimine Principum*, 3.11.

This was not true for all medieval writers. There were two common suprahistorical conceptions of the Roman empire. The first, derived from a common interpretation of the book of Daniel, conceives of Rome as the last of four world empires which collectively are divinely ordained to remain until the Last Days. Jerome and Augustine mention this theory, but, although Augustine at times accepts Rome's part in God's plan, he does not deduce from this any special virtue for it or place any special hope in it.[41] The second conception is that the Roman Empire represents the City of God on earth. Augustine popularized this expression, but adamantly denied that Rome, or any secular government, or even the Church, could be identified with it. Although "City of God" was not applied to Rome before Augustine, the conception goes back a century to the euphoria over the conversion of Constantine, as reflected in the work of Eusebius of Caesarea.[42] Both ideas became common in the early Middle Ages and were eventually combined with the idea of the transfer of the empire in the time of Charlemagne and on several later occasions. Increasingly, they were also combined with hierocratic political thought, in which the pope was given authority over the Empire and in the selection of the emperor. These concepts were developed in the papal curia of the eighth and ninth centuries, in the course of the great struggles of Church and State in the eleventh and twelfth centuries, and by canon lawyers from the twelfth century on.

One influential twelfth-century writer who propagated such ideas was Otto of Freising, uncle of the emperor Frederick Barbarossa. He writes that after the conversion of Constantine there is really only one City, since with few exceptions the emperors were good Christians.[43] Rome will endure until the Last Days, but then will come to represent the forces of evil and be overthrown. At first, he thought the Investiture Controversy initiated an irrevocable schism heralding the end of the world, but a renewed Church–State harmony and the resurgence of Roman power under Frederick Barbarossa made him abandon his pessimism for a vision of a new golden age of the City of God, a revival of the Roman Christian Empire as it was under Constantine, Theodosius, Charlemagne, and Henry III.[44]

Scholastic writers of the late thirteenth century, even imperialist ones, markedly reduce or secularize the part played by such conceptions –

---

[41] Augustine, *The City of God*, 18.22.
[42] Eusebius of Caesarea, *Ecclesiastical History*, especially book 10.
[43] Otto of Freising, *The Two Cities*, trans. Charles Christopher Mierow (New York: Columbia University Press, 1928), prologue to book 5 and passim.
[44] Ibid., prologue to book 1; *The Deeds of Frederick Barbarossa*, trans. Charles Christopher Mierow (New York: Columbia University Press, 1953), prologue to book 1.

though they do not vanish. Engelbert of Admont, for example, mentions the four empires, but in an entirely naturalistic setting, saying that each of these empires attained its power through just wars, not a divine plan.[45] He places the Roman Empire and all polities firmly within a framework of historical change. He scoffs at the theory of transfer of empire and the idea that Rome will last until the End, insisting that all temporal things come into existence, evolve, degenerate, and eventually fail, and that all kingdoms are unstable over time since human ideas of peace, justice, and power change and human minds have a tendency to discord, injury, and violence.[46]

Oddly, Ptolemy of Lucca, the most republican of these writers, and the only one who hates monarchy, also preserves the teleological approach to Rome more than any other. We have seen that he condemns the Empire as a tyranny and defends the independent republics of Italy. But as an even stronger supporter of the Roman Church he is unwilling totally to abandon the Empire as Christendom's universal secular arm. So after giving reasons to banish teleology from politics, he proceeds to revive it, accepting the four biblical world empires, allegorically described in Nebuchadnezzar's vision of a statue:

> the prophet Daniel . . . relates this vision to the four monarchies: that of the Assyrians because of the gold head, that of the Medes and the Persians because of the silver arms and breast, that of the Greeks because of the brass belly and thighs, and, finally, that of the Romans because of the iron legs and the feet partially iron and partially clay. "But after these," says the prophet, "the God of heaven will raise up a kingdom that will not be dissipated throughout eternity, and his kingdom will not be handed over to another people, and it will crush all kingdoms and will itself stand for eternity." We say that all of this refers to Christ, and to the Roman Church in his place, if it directs itself to feeding the flock.[47]

By "monarchy" Ptolemy does not here mean the usual one-person rule, but the rule of one nation or Church over all peoples. That the

---

[45] Engelbert of Admont, *Tractatus de ortu, et progressu statu et fine Romani Imperii*, in *Politica imperialia*, ed. Melchior Goldast (Frankfurt: J. Bringer, 1614), 10, 759.

[46] Ibid., 20–21, 770.

[47] Ptolemy of Lucca, *De Regimine Principum*, 3.10.9, with reference to Daniel 2.44: "visionem Daniel propheta . . . ad quatuor monarchias adaptat, Assyriorum videlicet pro aureo capite, Medorum et Persarum pro argento in brachiis et pectore, Graecorum vero monarchiam pro aereo ventre et femore, sed Romanorum ultimo pro tibiis ferreis et pedibus partim fereis partim vero fictilibus. 'Sed post haec suscitabit,' ait Propheta, 'Deus coeli regnum quod est in aeternum non dissipabitur, et regnum eius populo alteri non tradetur, comminuetque universa regna et ipsum stabit in aeternum,' quod totum ad Christum referimus, sed vice eius ad Romanam Ecclesiam si ad pascendum gregem intendat." Daniel (2.37–45) interprets the dream somewhat in this manner, but does not specify which empires in particular are signified.

internal government need not be monarchical is shown by his treatment of Rome. When he speaks of the Fourth Monarchy, he does not mean the period of formal Empire, but rather the preceding Republic. Repeatedly, he identifies the Fourth Monarchy with the Rome of 1 Maccabees,[48] which, as we have seen, was the period of widest participation. It is true, he says, that the Romans commit their magistracy to one person for a year, and at one point he refers to this consulate as a "monarchy,"[49] but he distinguishes this from the governmental form of monarchy: consuls were elected, their power depended on the many, and there was alternation of office and continuous consultation with the senate.[50] This changed with Julius Caesar and then Augustus, when the Fifth Monarchy, that of the Church, came to power.

Charles Till Davis argued that, for Ptolemy, Augustus served as a vicar for Christ.[51] This may be true, but only because declining Roman virtue had previously undermined the Republic. Ptolemy says that Rome's monarchy (that is, the Fourth Monarchy) lasted until Caesar's "usurpation of empire,"[52] making Augustus simply a place-holder for Jesus, and not a legitimate ruler in his own right. In Ptolemy there is no trace of the common theory, found, for example, in Dante, that the birth of Christ under the Roman Empire indicates God's acknowledgment of the legitimacy of that rule; on the contrary, it indicates a transfer of universal power from Rome to the Church. It may be, as Davis claims, that this viewpoint elevates the Republic as a precursor to Christ, but the reverse is more in accord with Ptolemy's way of thinking – Rome deserved this position because of its great virtue and perfect republican government. The rise of the Fifth Monarchy removes any theological justification for secular government. If God expresses his will through the Universal Church, no universal secular monarchy is necessary, and each state must govern itself for the common good of its people, independent of any religious concerns other than subordinating itself to the Roman Church.

As so often, however, Ptolemy has trouble accommodating all his contradictory views, and he sometimes defends the Empire as an adjunct to the papal monarchy. He shows that most Christian emperors obeyed the pope in both secular and theological matters,[53] and accepts the view that the pope transferred the Empire when this was necessary to defend the Church: from the Greeks to the Franks, from the Franks to

---

[48] Ibid., 3.6.3, 3.12.5. [49] Ibid., 3.12.5. [50] Ibid., 3.20.1 3, 2.8, 4.1.
[51] Davis, "Ptolemy of Lucca," 42 3. [52] Ptolemy of Lucca, *De Regimine Principum*, 3.12, 4.1.
[53] Ibid., 3.17 18.

the Saxons, and finally from the Saxons to the Germans.[54] But he also knows that the emperor need not subordinate himself to the Church, and indeed has not always done so. This suggests that Ptolemy supports the Empire for practical, not teleological, reasons, and this is confirmed by the fact that he does not use teleological language in writing about it. It is simply that his overwhelming emphasis on the Church leads him sometimes to overlook his anti-monarchical sentiments. Perhaps this is one reason why he classifies imperial rule as a form midway between regal and political rule: political in that it is elective and not generally hereditary and because not all emperors were noble. But this still gives the emperors the powers that Ptolemy believes make regal government inherently tyrannical: government by the will instead of law, and lack of plurality (in the sense that there is neither citizen participation nor regular alternation of rulers).[55]

Although Ptolemy never states this explicitly, there is a way around this dilemma for him. The pope's monarchy is exempt from the problems of secular monarchy, since it is divinely established and led by the pope as vicar of God. Insofar as the emperors are agents of the pope, they should also have monarchical powers, according to Ptolemy's principle of subordinate power.[56] This could still allow for independent republics for virtuous peoples, under the overall direction of Church and empire and could justify a universal role for the Roman Empire in ending factionalism and inter-city strife, thereby creating the peace necessary for republics to flourish.

What is most notable about Ptolemy is that he stands alone among scholastic writers in giving even an ambivalent teleological role to the Roman Empire. Much more decisive in its critique of the Empire is a gloss in Nicole Oresme's commentary on the *Politics* on "a question which I have not seen disputed elsewhere... whether a kingdom can be too big and if there should be several kingdoms in the world not subject to one."[57] Earlier he had declared that such a temporal world monarchy was neither reasonable nor possible,[58] and now he seeks to prove it, by giving and refuting sixteen arguments in favor of universal empire and adding thirteen against.

Most of these arguments address purely secular issues, but Oresme does discuss the traditional series of empires, only to discount the entire idea:

[54] Ibid., 3.19.1–2.   [55] Ibid., 3.20.   [56] Ibid., 3.22.6–8.
[57] Nicole Oresme, *Le Livre de Politiques*, 7.10, 289–90.
[58] Ibid., 3.10, 128.

I say, first, that such great kingdoms were not true kingdoms, but violent and tyrannical usurpations . . . I say that none of these rulers I have named had sovereignty over all the world. This is because, according to the prophecy of Daniel, the kingdom or empire of Rome was the greatest of all, and nevertheless, it did not have sovereignty over all peoples, as Saint Augustine showed . . . But it is true that when one ruler has many countries under him, one is accustomed to say that all the world obeys him, and it is a common manner of speaking . . . And such a manner of speaking is often found in Holy Scripture.[59]

The very idea that a universal monarchy could exist and lead to peace is like a "poetic fiction or mathematical fantasy," or the false prophecy of those who promise the millennium.[60] According to Oresme, we must take the world as it is, and in this real world, it is not possible for such a sovereign monarchy to come into existence, and if it could, it could not last long. Even if somehow it could be done there would be insurmountable difficulties: rebellions, dissension, and more evils than before, since there would be many imperial contenders.[61]

Throughout Oresme's writing there is a similar insistence on considering real historical conditions and discounting metahistorical justifications for government in general or particular governments. As far as universal empire is concerned the only admissible questions are whether such a government is possible or desirable, and, as we have seen, he argues that it is not.

Other writers also evaluate the Roman Empire solely on the basis of how it fulfills the functions of good government. These include Marsilius of Padua and William of Ockham, two early fourteenth-century writers who spent much of their time defending Emperor Ludwig of Bavaria and attacking the papacy's pretensions to political authority.

Marsilius ascribes the authority of any government to a grant by the legislator, which he defines in the *Defensor minor* as the community of human beings subject to law in each region, or its weightier part, which, according to the *Defensor pacis*, includes all but the very few "deformed"

---

[59] Ibid., 7.10, 293: "je di, premierement, que telz grans royalmes ne furent pas vrais royalmes, mes estoient usurpations violentes et tyranniques . . . Apres je di que nul des princeys desus nommés ne autre ne eut onques seigneurie sus tout le munde. Car selon la prophecie Daniel, le royalme ou empire de Rome fu le plus grant de tous, et toutesvoies, il ne eut onques seigneurie sus tous gens, si comme monstre Saint Augustin . . . Mes verité est quant un prince a pluseurs païz sous lui l'en seult dire que tout le munde lui obeïst, et est commune maniere de parler . . . Et ceste maniere de parler est mout de foiz en la Sainte Escripture."
[60] Ibid., 7.10, 294: "comme une fiction poëtique ou comme une ymagination mathemetique."
[61] Ibid.

persons.⁶² The Roman Empire is exceptional only in its universality, in that each of the world's peoples approved such a grant, but without surrendering the right to revoke it at will. The emperor's power is a temporary grant from the Roman people, who in turn have authority beyond the city of Rome only so long as non-Romans authorize it. The same is true of the transfer of the empire, which Marsilius accepts, but restricts the pope's role to publicizing it with permission of the human legislator, or at most to carrying it out under a temporary authority granted by the human legislator.⁶³

Unlike Marsilius, William of Ockham (c. 1285–1347) alludes to the Assyrians and Medes as great monarchies to be compared to the Roman empire, but only to deny them any special significance – they are from God only in the sense that any government is, and they all originate from the people.⁶⁴ William explains how this view can be reconciled with the seemingly contradictory one that the empire is from God alone by distinguishing different senses of jurisdiction from God. It can be without human agency, as with Moses or Peter; it can be directly from God but requiring human agency, as with baptism; or it can come from God, but only after someone else has conferred it:

> The empire is from God alone in the third way – because, namely, although it would have been from God with the concurrence of some human ordinance, so that men with power to confer temporal jurisdiction on someone truly conferred jurisdiction on the emperor (just as they truly conferred on him, and transferred from themselves to him, power to make laws), nevertheless, once that conferring of jurisdiction by God and men had been done, it depended regularly on no one but God alone, although on occasion it might depend also on men (since on occasion the people had power to correct the emperor).⁶⁵

---

⁶² Marsilius of Padua, *Defensor pacis*, ed. Richard Scholz (Hanover: Hanische Buchhandlung, 1933), 1.12; *Defensor minor*, chap. 12. In *Defensor pacis*, Marsilius gave a similar definition, but said that the legislator was the efficient cause of the law. For a discussion of Marsilius's position on the empire, see Cary Nederman, "From *Defensor pacis* to *Defensor minor*: The Problem of Empire in Marsiglio of Padua," *History of Political Thought* 16 (1995): 313–29.

⁶³ Marsilius of Padua, *Defensor pacis*, 2.30.8; *De Translatione Imperium*, chap. 8. In chapter 9, Marsilius refers the reader to *Defensor pacis*, 2.30.

⁶⁴ William of Ockham, *Breviloquium de Principatu Tyrannico*, in Richard Scholz, *Wilhelm von Ockham als politischer Denker und sein Breviloquium de Principatu Tyrannico* (Leipzig: K.W. Hiersemann, 1942). Translation is from William of Ockham, *A Short Discourse on Tyrannical Government*, trans. John Kilcullen (Cambridge: Cambridge University Press, 1992), 4.3.

⁶⁵ William of Ockham, *Short Discourse*, 4.5–6: "imperium est a solo Deo tertio modo, quia, scilicet fuerit sic a Deo, quod humana ordinatio concurrebat ita, ut homines habentes potestatem conferendi alicui iurisdictionem temporalem, vere conferebant imperatori iurisdictionem, quemadmodum vere conferebant sibi et transtulerunt a se in eum potestatem condendi leges; tamen, postquam ista collatio iurisdictionis a Deo et hominibus facta fuit, a nullo regulariter dependebat, nisi a solo Deo, quamvis casualiter dependeret etiam ab hominibus, eo quod in casu populus habebat potestatem corrigendi imperatorem."

"Civic humanism" and medieval political thought

This obviously gives more power to the emperor than Marsilius did, since the grant of power is not as easily revocable, and the emperor has no temporal superior corresponding to the Marsilian legislator, but it does as clearly secularize the Empire. It, like all other governments not specified in Scripture as divine grants, comes originally from the people and is only then approved by God. As such, the pope has no more authority over the emperor than over any other ruler, such as the king of France.[66] In the case of a crime, whether secular or ecclesiastical, the right to judge and depose belongs:

> to the Romans, calling "Romans" those to whom it belongs to manage and regulate the Roman Empire, such as the princes who elect the emperor – if such a power has been transmitted to them, who seem to have succeeded to the place of the senate. If they were reprehensibly negligent in correcting an emperor or in deposing him if he deserved to be deposed, all these functions would devolve upon the Roman people: the empire arose from the people, they transferred to the emperor the power of making laws and doing other things pertaining to the administration of the Empire, they gave (or someone by their authority and in their name gave) to the electors power to elect, correct, and depose the emperor.[67]

The pope may have a special function in investigating an ecclesiastical crime, but in judging he is simply one of the Roman people.

The grant of the Roman people sufficiently explains the legitimacy of the Roman government at home, but not the empire. William knows that it is legitimate, because Jesus acknowledged it as such, but he denies that this happened by divine mandate, since this is not mentioned by Scripture.[68] Thus, its legitimacy, like that of any other government, requires an explanation in purely secular terms. Unlike most of the authors we have been discussing, William does not rely on the idea of Roman virtue; in fact, he conditionally accepts Augustine's attribution to them of a corrupt lust to dominate others.[69] He suggests as a possibility that the Empire may take its legitimacy from a combination

---

[66] Ibid., 6.2, 4.14.
[67] Ibid., 6.2: "In primo casu ventilatio et examinatio totius cause et sententie executio spectat ad Romanos, vocando Romanos, qui de Romano habent imperio disponere et ordinare, cuiusmodi sunt principes electores imperatoris, si in eos huiusmodi est derivata potestas, qui loco senatus successisse videntur. Si autem isti in corrigendo imperatorem vel in deponendo, si esset dignus deponi, essent dampnabiliter negligentes, predicta omnia devolverentur ad populum Romanum, a quo ortum est imperium, et qui in imperatorem transtulit potestatem condendi leges et alia faciendi, que ad administrationem spectant imperii, et qui, vel aliquis auctoritate et nomine eius, dedit electoribus potestatem eligendi et corrigendi et deponendi imperatorem."
[68] Ibid., 4.10.   [69] Ibid., 4.11.

of just wars and the voluntary submission of other nations who realized the utility of world government.[70]

Thus, despite a number of different approaches, the writers considered here from the late thirteenth century on, and many others who have not been considered, generally share a secular approach to the Roman Empire, whether or not they can be classified as anti-imperialist, qualifiedly imperialist, or imperialist. One important factor in the development of this approach was the renewed interest, from the early twelfth century on, in Roman law, which treated Rome in a purely secular context and placed original political power with the Roman people, who then transferred it to the emperor. The only question was whether this grant was revocable. As one among many examples, the fourteenth-century writer Lupold of Bebenberg cites Roman law texts to argue that the Roman people, like any other, has the right by international law to choose its own ruler, and does so today through their representatives, the prince electors. In the past the army represented them for imperial election and the senate for legislation. Further, since collectively the Roman people are greater than the emperor, they retain the power to legislate, to depose an emperor, or to transfer the Empire to another nation.[71]

Three other important factors shaping a secular approach to the Roman Empire are the growth of secular monarchies and other governments unwilling to recognize even the theoretical hegemony of the Empire; the influence of ancient political thought; and the general shift in secular ideology from the time of the Investiture Controversy on, when apologists for governments began to realize that the Church always had the upper hand in theological arguments. To defend government as independently legitimate they needed to ground it in nontheological principles such as the common good or the right of any people to choose a government. The Roman Empire would continue to have a special aura for many, as it still would for humanist imperialists such as Aeneas Sylvius Piccolomini, but it would be defended by rational arguments such as its utility or Roman virtue, and God would be brought in only to give his *a posteriori* blessing to a purely human community. Just as there can be a prehumanist attack on empire, Piccolomini demonstrates that there can be a humanist defense of empire, and both can equally be couched in terms of virtue, which Baron sees only in defense of republi-

[70] Ibid., 4.10 11.
[71] Lupold of Bebenberg, *De Iure Regni et Imperii*, in *De iurisdictione, autoritate, et praeeminentia imperiali ac potestate ecclesiastica deque iuribus regni et imperii*, ed. Simon Schard (Basel, 1566), 5, 352; 17, 406.

canism.⁷² As a number of authors have argued, the ideals of civic humanism seem quite flexible, applicable even to Renaissance despotisms, and, as Hankins indicates in the quotation that opens this essay, it seems likely that we can preserve the term only by reconceptualizing it. The Renaissance may bring a greater appreciation of the Republic at the expense of the Empire, but it does not seem to have brought either a greater appreciation of the Republic *per se*, or a greater desacralization of the Empire. Both were well established in the Middle Ages, the first by the twelfth century and the second from the late thirteenth century.

NONMONARCHICAL GOVERNMENT: REPUBLICANISM

Now let us turn to the question of appreciation of nonmonarchical government, which is much less rare in the Middle Ages than Baron believes. Quentin Skinner has built upon the work of Smalley and perhaps Davis to show that many aspects of the humanist republican ideology can be found from the twelfth century on in the tradition of the *Ars dictaminis* and in treatises on city government written to give advice to city officials.⁷³ He stresses the influence of ancient writers other than Aristotle, specifically Sallust and Cicero. In this, he is trying to refute not only Baron but even those, like Rubinstein, who take the more moderate position that no civic ideology developed corresponding to northern Italian civic practice until the political and ethical works of Aristotle became known in the thirteenth century.⁷⁴ In any case, both the rhetorical and scholastic traditions provided a basis for a reasoned defense of republicanism and liberty long before 1400.⁷⁵

There are two paths to the scholastic appreciation of nonmonarchical government. The first, followed by Ptolemy of Lucca, and arguably by Marsilius of Padua, identifies some other form as best or, at least, prefers nonmonarchical government in general. The second path begins from the assumption that the best form of government varies, depending upon local conditions. In one sense there is only one category, since none of the authors treated here believe that nonmonarchical govern-

---

⁷² Cary Nederman discusses Aeneas Sylvius Piccolomini's imperialism and humanism in two recent articles: "Humanism and Empire: Aeneas Sylvius Piccolomini, Cicero, and the Imperial Ideal," *Historical Journal* 36 (1993): 499–515 and "National Sovereignty and Ciceronian Political Thought: Aeneas Sylvius Piccolomini and the Ideal of Universal Empire in Fifteenth-Century Europe," *History of European Ideas* 16 (1993): 537–43.
⁷³ Skinner, "Machiavelli's *Discorsi*," 121–41.   ⁷⁴ Ibid., 121.
⁷⁵ See also Quentin Skinner, *The Foundations of Modern Political Thought*, 2 vols. (Cambridge: Cambridge University Press, 1978), I: 27–65.

ment is appropriate in all circumstances. The distinction, rather, is between those who praise nonmonarchical government *per se* and those who think that the choice between monarchical and nonmonarchical governments is best made by considering the particular circumstances. This distinction allows overlap, and I will mention several of the authors under both categories.

In another sense, as mentioned before, there is an inherent problem in discussing medieval attitudes toward nonmonarchical government, and I present the issue in this way only to respond to Baron. Understanding the medieval contribution to civic humanist ideas is complicated by Baron's and others' tendency to equate nonmonarchical and republican government and to distinguish sharply between monarchical and republican government. Except for Ptolemy of Lucca this is problematic with respect to medieval political thought; perhaps it is Baron's artificial demands that blind him to medieval thought that could be considered republican. Almost all scholastic writers favor some participation in government, though many view participation as possible within a monarchy or monarchical mixed constitution and greatly restrict those who may participate. At the same time many of them defend some version of popular sovereignty or at least consent, again often within the context of a monarchy.[76] Here, I will concentrate on what can be considered more or less pure republican sentiment. It is difficult even to define precisely what this is, since popular or aristocratic participation may strictly circumscribe a king or even transform the monarch into a figurehead or a temporary ruler. Conversely, officials ordinarily considered republican in character, such as the Roman consuls or the Italian *podestà*, can be interpreted as monarchs. Nicole Oresme, who favored participatory monarchy, takes this approach, as do the thirteenth- and fourteenth-century proponents of the "myth of Venice," the Thomist Henry of Rimini and Benzo d'Alessandria.[77] Another complication is that it is possible to see the people as the sovereign force in a government, and even as the best day-to-day rulers in most circumstances, and still allow them to institute for a time a monarchical or other government under their ultimate authority.

This is what Marsilius of Padua argues, although he usually praises participation of all the citizens, and it is also the position of a number of civil lawyers and corporate theorists, beginning at least with the Glossator Azo (*c.* 1150–1230). As Quentin Skinner notes, Azo:

---

[76] This is one of the pervasive themes of Blythe, *Ideal Government*.
[77] See ibid.

argued that the consent of the whole people considered as a *universitas* is always needed if the highest powers of *iurisdictio* are to be lawfully instituted. He derived this conclusion from his interpretation of the *Lex Regia*, the law whereby the people of Rome were alleged to have made the original grant of *iurisdictio* to the emperor ... Azo parts company with his teachers, however, when he goes on to argue that, even after the establishment of a prince with full *iurisdictio*, "the power to make laws, if it was a power the people possessed before that time, is one they will continue to possess afterward."[78]

Even allowing for the final qualification, which, like most Roman law, limits claims of popular sovereignty to those peoples who had demonstrable authority to create the government, Azo makes a powerful corporate defense of the inalienability of sovereignty. Marsilius will later defend inalienability functionally, by arguing that the people as a whole are most qualified to decide upon proposals formulated by the wise.

There are three attitudes toward popular participation that are significant here. First, Aristotle taught that humans were political animals who needed to participate in government in order to complete their natures.[79] This perhaps begs the question of whether popular participation benefits government, but it gives the multitude a claim to a part of rule by distributive justice and by the principle that nature does nothing in vain. This principle also suggests that their participation will be positive. Second, Thomas Aquinas discounted the capacity of the multitude, but believed that it should have a role in order to make each person feel a part of the polity and thus minimize dissent.[80] Finally, Peter of Auvergne, in his continuation of Thomas's *Commentary on the "Politics"* and elsewhere, developed the idea of bestial and nonbestial multitudes. The former is perverse and incapable of contributing to good government; it, therefore, can have no right to rule. But since a nonbestial multitude can contribute, it does have this right.[81] Peter's distinction provides a justification for participation at the cost of any absolute right to participation. This suggests a connection between sin and the form of a regime. Once stated, this principle seemed obvious,

---

[78] Skinner, "Political Philosophy," 392–3. For a discussion of the ruler's obligation to maintain contractual agreements see Peter Riesenberg, *Inalienability of Sovereignty in Medieval Political Thought* (New York: Columbia University Press, 1956), 129–44.
[79] Aristotle, *Politics*, 1.2.1253a1–2.   [80] Thomas Aquinas, *Summa Theologiae*, 1–2.105.2.
[81] See Thomas Aquinas, *In Libros Politicorum Aristotelis expositio*, ed. R. M. Spiazzi (Turin: Marietti, 1966), book III, 9, 435, 438. Books III, 7 through VIII, attributed by Spiazzi to Thomas, are actually by Peter of Auvergne. See also Peter's "Questiones super Politicum", Paris, Bibliothèque Nationale MS lat. 16,089, ff.295rb (book III, qu. 15) and 295vb (book III, qu. 16). Aristotle, *Politics*, III.11.1282a, casually introduced the terminology of the bestial multitude, but did not develop its implications.

for to allow the perverse to govern seems almost to guarantee an undesirable result. These ideas inform almost all later medieval discussions, whether or not Peter's terminology, which becomes commonplace, is used. It is even possible to reconcile this view with the purely Aristotelian one by saying, as Marsilius implies, that the perverse are perverse in that their nature has been deformed. It is likely that this idea influenced Peter's choice of words: if the multitude is bestial its members lack the human quality of being political animals.

None of the medieval scholastics argue for universal and equal participation. Unless they advocate a minor role for all the people simply to keep them happy, all restrict self-government to those sufficiently wise and virtuous, and this even applies to Marsilius, although he expects this group to be the overwhelming majority of the free, male, adult population. The same thing is true of the civic humanists, none of whom advocated universal participation, and many of whom advocated narrow restriction of the ruling class, in most cases much more narrowly than the medieval scholastics did.

Brunetto Latini, who composed his *The Book of the Treasure* in the 1260s under the influence of Aristotle's *Ethics*, but with no apparent knowledge of the *Politics*, is perhaps the first to use the Aristotelian classification of polities to argue for a republic, by flatly reversing Aristotle's conclusion in the *Ethics* that monarchy is best. He writes of the three good forms of lordship – that of kings, of a group of good men, and of the "communes" – that the last is the best.[82] However, he does not go on to critique the other constitutional types or even indicate the extent of participation in a commune, since his emphasis is on the *podestà*'s duties. Only Ptolemy of Lucca is hostile to the very idea of monarchy. This is understandable for one brought up in republican Italy and writing at a time when many city-states were falling into the hands of despots, and at times he appears to interchange kingship and despotism. For example, Ptolemy writes that Aristotle distinguished two kinds of rule, political and *despotic*, but then goes on: "Rule is political when a [polity] is ruled ... according to its statutes ... in *regal* dominion ... [the king] is not obligated by law ..."[83] He repeatedly

---

[82] Brunetto Latini, *Li Livre dou Tresor*, ed. F. J. Carmody (Berkeley: University of California Press, 1948), 2.44. There is a recent translation, *The Book of the Treasure*, trans. Paul Barrette and Spurgeon Baldwin (New York: Garland Publishing, 1993).

[83] Ptolemy of Lucca, *De Regimine Principum*, 2.8. Italics mine: "Duplex enim principatus ab Aristotele ponitur in sua *Politica* ... politicus videlicet et despoticus ... Politicus quidem quando regio sive provincia sive civitas sive castrum per unum vel plures regitur secundum ipsorum statuta ... per regale dominium ... dum, non legibus obligatus, per eam censeat, quae est in pectore principis ..."

states that we can "reduce despotic rule to regal," or regal to despotic, and often uses these terms and "tyrannical" almost synonymously. Since Ptolemy equates political and republican rule, he sees all rule as either republican or despotic.

However, he also often says that monarchy is necessary for most peoples and occasionally gives *a priori* arguments for monarchy. Implicit in this is Peter of Auvergne's distinction between a bestial and nonbestial multitude. This means that Ptolemy is not a republican *per se*, although this is how he is often presented.

Nonetheless, it is clear that a republican form is the only one he considers to be good; his objection is simply that it is not always possible. It is also the only natural form. If humans are naturally political animals, government must have existed before the Fall, in a noncoercive sense:[84] "there was political, not regal lordship, there was no lordship then that involved servitude, but rather preeminence and subjection existed according to the merits of each for disposing and governing the multitude, so that whether in influencing or receiving influence each was disposed proportionately according to its own nature."[85] It could not be argued, as it could be in postlapsarian society, that a regal king, restricted only by reason, could best handle changing circumstances,[86] since everything in Paradise acts according to natural law, and therefore the law is sufficient for any contingency.

Ptolemy ties the optimal republican government to secular virtue, represented most clearly by the pagan Roman Republic: "Therefore, political government was better for wise and virtuous persons, such as the ancient Romans, since it imitated this state of nature."[87] Original sin has become a sin like any other that people of sufficiently good character can overcome. Ptolemy attempts to equate true virtue, which for Augustine can mean nothing less than harmony with God, with the political virtue of people living in the best community. He even feels that the internal harmony of such a republic can render it immune to the forces of decay and collapse,[88] thus suggesting an earthly analogue of

---

[84] Ibid., 3.9.6.
[85] Ibid., 2.9.4: "non fuisset regale regimen sed politicum, eo quod tunc non fuisset dominium quod servitutem haberet, sed praeeminentiam et subiectionem in disponendo et gubernando multitudinem secundum merita cujuscumque, ut sic vel in influendo vel in recipiendo influentiam quilibet esset dispositus secundum congruentiam suae naturae." See also *Determinatio Compendiosa de Juribus Imperii*, in *Fontes Iuris Germanici Antiqui*, ed. Marius Kramer (Hanover: Bibliopolius Hahnianus, 1909), 17.36.
[86] Ptolemy of Lucca, *De Regimine Principum*, 2.9.5.
[87] Ibid., 2.9.4: "Unde apud sapientes et homines virtuosos, ut fuerunt antiqui Romani, secundum imitationem talis naturae regimen politicum melius fuit." [88] Ibid., 4.23.4.

Augustine's City of God, and looking forward to Renaissance ideas of the possibility of permanence for time-bound republics.[89] Girolamo Savonarola would later use Ptolemy's ideas explicitly to combine the two in his theory of millenarian republicanism.[90]

Charles Till Davis has demonstrated how Ptolemy used "obsequious respect, together with a shameless flair for misquotation" to systematically pervert the message of Augustine in *The City of God* and turn condemnation for self-love and lust for power and glory into praise for the love of the Romans for their fatherland.[91] Ptolemy "finds" three Roman virtues in Augustine, each of which makes them worthy of dominion and republican rule: love of their fatherland, zeal for justice, and piety and civil benevolence.[92] The first he identifies with divine love, since it brings love to the community and springs from the love that prefers the common good to one's own. The second refers to Augustine's dictum that justice is what makes lordship legitimate, but conveniently ignores his further point that this cannot occur without true love of God, and so never in an earthly state. The third (Ptolemy uses "piety" in both the religious and secular Roman senses) explains why foreign nations came to love the Romans and how they were led voluntarily into subjection as friends and allies. Each of these virtues Ptolemy illustrates with many examples from Roman republican history.

Not only are such virtuous people capable of self-government, it is their nature to reject any other mode. In part this is a function of the geographical region in which they live and their astrological sign, which to a great degree determine national characteristics. Since Rome, Athens, and the contemporary Italian cities are governed by the constellation of Mars, they resist having any superior.[93] Others are geographically situated so as to be predisposed to servitude, and Ptolemy contrasts the servile nature of those who endure kingly rule with the virility of those who are predisposed to liberty.[94]

One consequence of the Romans' spirit is that since no one arrogated sole command there was "neither ill will nor jealousy among them." The consuls "exercised governance with a certain forgiving spirit" and

---

[89] See Pocock, *Machiavellian Moment*, 74–80 and passim, where it is suggested that this idea was original to the Renaissance.
[90] See Donald Weinstein, *Savonarola and Florence* (Princeton: Princeton University Press, 1970), 290, 293, 304, 309.
[91] Davis, "Ptolemy of Lucca and the Roman Republic," 33.
[92] Ptolemy of Lucca, *De Regimine Principum*, 3.4–3.6.   [93] Ibid., 2.8.4.
[94] Ibid., 2.9.6, 4.8.4.

earned the citizens' love and benevolence. This strengthened their rule more than any quantity of arms could have done.[95]

One theme of civic humanism generally lacking in the scholastic writers is the Sallustian idea that virtue develops through exercising it and being challenged by civic participation. The virtue of citizens to which they frequently refer is a rather static thing; virtue is needed for participation, but it does not necessarily wither without participation nor increase with it. But here Ptolemy suggests that there may be a progression in virtue, in that good government leads to an increase in the virtues of love and benevolence. Although geographical factors may make certain regions more suited to republican rule, participation in civic affairs has a beneficial effect on the citizen. Ptolemy argues that the subjects in a republic become more confident from taking turns exercising lordship, and this makes them even more bold in pursuing liberty and opposing kings.[96] Virtue also radiated outward and inspired others in less fortunate regions to join with the Romans and to acquire some of their virtue.[97] The implication is that, although they may not be naturally suited to republican rule, they may become at least partially worthy of it through association with the virtuous Romans. This may be one way that those whom original sin made unsuited for good government can find their way back to it. Thus, those who are virtuous, through a combination of natural conditions and acquired traits, have been restored to full human status as political animals and as such cannot be happy unless they are in charge of their own destinies and government.

Ptolemy's extensive treatment of the origins of human society clarifies and extends the connection between participation and virtue.[98] He wants to show the intimate connection between the human community and the virtue of both the sensitive and rational parts of the human spirit. Thomas Aquinas had reported, in a formulation that was not authentic, but which Ptolemy and most other scholastic writers followed, that Aristotle called humans "social and political animals" instead of simply "political animals."[99] Although this is consistent with Aristotle's meaning, it shifts the emphasis from a natural need to participate in government to a natural need to live together in communities. One aspect of this is the human appetite for sharing one's activities with the multitude. Ptolemy cites Cicero, Archytas of Taren-

---

[95] Ibid., 2.8.4.   [96] Ibid., 2.8.5.   [97] Ibid., 3.6.   [98] Ibid., 4.2 3.
[99] For example, Thomas Aquinas, *De Regimine Principum*, 1.1.3; Ptolemy of Lucca, *De Regimine Principum*, 3.5.3, 3.9.6.

tum, and Boethius to the effect that no one would do a virtuous act or enjoy even a vision of the universe in the absence of human society or companionship.[100]

It is interesting that Ptolemy chooses to cite Cicero in this context: "nature loves nothing that is solitary."[101] Although he does not elaborate, it seems clear that he is rejecting what Baron sees as the universal medieval preference for the contemplative versus the active life, for it is only in civil society that natural human needs and, as we shall see, virtues can exist and develop. It could be objected that "civil society" may include the Church as Fifth Monarchy, or even monasteries, but what is most significant is that certain necessary virtues can develop there only to the degree that these communities are similar to the city. This will be clearer as we look at Ptolemy's discussion of the virtues pertaining to the different parts of the human spirit.

With regard to the sensitive (bodily) virtues, Ptolemy reviews all the ways that human beings, unlike other animals, lack the specific resources to take care of themselves as individuals.[102] These needs establish an intimate connection between the sensitive virtues and the establishment of human community. But it is in regard to the rational spirit that human beings are unique, and so Ptolemy believes that the virtues connected with the rational spirit are even more dependent upon human society. He analyzes the parts of this spirit and shows that all of them also require society; the moral virtues, in particular, can only be defined with respect to more than one person.[103]

The same is true of the speculative virtues, which require teaching and hence many persons, and also of other intellective actions such as the creation of order. There are two educable senses, vision and hearing, and hearing presupposes a multitude. Speech and writing make even less sense without a multitude.[104]

Justice (doing double duty as both a practical and volitional virtue) and friendship are virtues of the will that follow a similar pattern, in that they are directed to others. Justice, whether legal, distributive, or commutative, can only exist in cities, which in turn need justice to survive. Neither can friendship, which no one chooses to live without, exist without a community. Besides the positive advantages of friendship there is the possibly more important negative advantage, especially for the young, of holding one back from sinning.[105]

---

[100] Ptolemy of Lucca, *De Regimine Principum*, 4.3.11.
[101] Ibid., 4.3.11, in reference to Cicero, *On Friendship*, 23. "Natura nihil solitarium amat."
[102] Ibid., 4.2.   [103] Ibid., 4.3.1 4.   [104] Ibid., 4.3.4 7.   [105] Ibid., 4.3.8 9.

Now what is implicit in this whole discussion is that not only do many virtues require community, but they can only develop and grow in the context of human society. In the abstract discussion of these virtues Ptolemy leaves unanswered the question whether the political participation of each individual is necessary for that individual's moral advancement, or whether simply living in a community provides sufficient opportunity. But his treatment of the close connection of republicanism and virtue shows that these virtues can only be fully achieved in a republic. And while this does not always demand the participation of every citizen, his praise for Rome shows that the republic is most effective and the virtue of the citizens most widespread when this is the case.

Ptolemy is the only author to reject monarchy for a virtuous people unconditionally. Other writers acknowledge the benefits of kingship, but some also praise republican government, quite apart from their common appreciation of the Roman Republic. Thomas Aquinas, for example, occasionally sounds like a republican. His comments come in a discussion of Rome, but they are general:

> It often happens that persons living under a king strive for the common good rather sluggishly, inasmuch as they reckon that what they devote to the common good does not benefit themselves but [the king], under whose power they see the common good to be. But when they see that the common good is not in the power of one, each attends to it as if it were their own, not as if it were something pertaining to someone else. For this reason experience seems to show that one city administered by rectors chosen for a year can sometimes do more than one king who has three or four cities, and small services that kings exact weigh more heavily than great burdens imposed by the community of citizens [on themselves].[106]

In context, this is by no means purely republican. In discussing why monarchy is the best government, Thomas pauses to discuss how its perversion, tyranny, is the worst and shows how the Romans were able to advance under a republic once they had expelled the tyrannical kings. But he is equally at pains to point out the dangers of a republican

[106] Thomas Aquinas, *De Regimine Principum*, 1.5.3: "Plerumque namque contingit, ut homines sub rege viventes, segnius ad bonum commune nitantur, utpote aestimantes id quod ad commune bonum impendunt non sibi ipsis conferre sed alteri, sub cuius potestate vident esse bona communia. Cum vero bonum commune non vident esse in potestate unius, non attendunt ad bonum commune quasi ad id quod est alterius, sed quilibet attendit ad illud quasi suum: unde experimento videtur quod una civitas per annuos rectores administrata, plus potest interdum quam rex aliquis, si haberet tres vel quatuor civitates; parvaque servitia exacta a regibus gravius ferunt quam magna onera, si a communitate civium imponatur." Cf. Ronald Witt, "Rebirth of Republican Liberty," 193.

government; in fact, he believes that the latter is more likely to lead to tyranny than is a monarchy. This is the point of his discussion of the collapse of the Roman Republic:

> The regime of all the many has usually ended in tyranny, as appears clearly in the case of the Roman Republic. After it had long been administered by many magistrates, rivalries, dissensions, and civil wars arose, and it fell under the cruelest tyrants. If you diligently consider past deeds and the contemporary situation everywhere, you will discover that more have exercised tyranny in lands governed by many, than in those guided by one.[107]

Although he has considerably altered his meaning, Thomas here relies on Aristotle's statement that most tyrants are demagogues who seized power by getting popular support against the nobles;[108] he then applies it to the "contemporary situation," no doubt with the northern Italian cities in mind, some of whose despots came from popular leaders or especially from "captains of the *popolo*," supposedly representing the "democratic" power of the guilds. In Thomas's time members of the Della Torre family in Milan and Mastino della Scala in Verona, for example, had used this office to achieve great personal power.

Thomas is arguing not for republicanism as such, but rather, to use his word, for a "tempered"[109] monarchy in which aristocrats and the people are given some share of government. He aims both to prevent the monarch from becoming a tyrant and to give the people the feeling that they have a stake in the polity. Even under a king, this would eliminate the perception that the common good was in the hands of one. Although Thomas does not believe that the multitude can contribute positively to government, their desire to have a part of political power must reflect their nature as political animals. By satisfying this natural desire, without surrendering a destructive amount of control to the masses,[110] the best government, a mixed constitution, is able to overcome all the problems of each government taken individually.

Northern Italy naturally provides the bulk of specific contemporary examples of republicanism, so it is interesting that a German, Engelbert of Admont (*c.* 1250–1331), makes extensive use of these by enumerating

---

[107] Ibid., 1.6.3: "Nam fere omnium multorum regimen est in tyrannidem terminatum, ut in Romana Republica manifeste apparet; quae cum diu per plures magistratus administrata fuisset, exortis simultatibus, dissensionibus et bellis civilibus, in crudelissimos tyrannos incidit, et universaliter si quis praeterita facta et quae nunc fiunt diligenter consideret, plures inveniet exercuisse tyrannidem in terris quae per multos reguntur, quam in illis quae gubernantur per unum."

[108] Aristotle, *Politics*, 5.10.1310b.14–16.   [109] Thomas Aquinas, *De Regimine Principum*, 1.7.2.

[110] Thomas defends this most clearly in *Summa Theologiae*, 1–2.105.1.

and exemplifying each of the acceptable simple forms of government and all of their possible combinations in mixed constitutions, something no other medieval or Renaissance author attempted. Altogether there is a total of fifteen, since he includes oligarchy as an acceptable, if basically undesirable, form. He is especially enthusiastic about what he says are the best-governed cities in Italy, which combine aristocracy and democracy in the offices of a *podestà* and a group of consuls, called Elders, chosen from the common people. He singles out for praise the method of election by secret ballots to allow all to express their opinion without fear and the fact that all are allowed to give counsel. He also mentions that since nobles generally seek their own power and benefit rather than the common good, well-governed cities usually try to avoid oligarchy by insisting on virtue as a qualification for office.[111]

Engelbert is implicitly defending the Italian popular republics threatened in his day by oligarchy. During the earlier period of the *popolo* the right to hold office and to participate in government was most widely extended during the Middle Ages, and many city-states passed "anti-magnate" legislation to bridle the hereditary nobility. These laws were never totally successful and, by 1300, the magnate class had turned the tables in some cities and installed despots (*signorie*). Most other cities were also threatened, and even the most republican eventually saw a drastic narrowing of the ruling class.[112] The only other form for which Engelbert shows much enthusiasm also includes the participation of the aristocracy and the people, but with the addition of a monarchical element. This form, he says, had existed in Hungary.[113]

One thing shown by Engelbert, and indeed by most medieval writers with the exception of Ptolemy of Lucca (and Thomas Aquinas to some extent) is that support or praise of republicanism depends upon the Aristotelian criterion of its ability best to provide for the common good, and not on its ability to fulfill basic human needs or allow for the growth of virtue. Even writers who insist on universal consent or the people's right to institute any government it so desires, regardless of the implications of its choice for the common good, do not base this requirement on the two latter factors. As Cary Nederman has shown, only a few medieval writers follow through on Aristotle's claim that humans are by

---

[111] Engelbert of Admont, *De Regimine Principum*, 1.7, 22. "Elders" refers to a common office in many cities (*anziani*), analogous to the priors in Florence.
[112] See J. K. Hyde, *Society and Politics in Medieval Italy* (New York: St. Martin's Press, 1973), 112–15, 146.
[113] Engelbert of Admont, *De Regimine Principum*, 1.8, 22–4.

nature political animals. The variation "social and political animals" allows the emphasis to be put upon humans coming together for material needs, and many authors, such as John of Paris and Marsilius of Padua, substitute Cicero's version of the origin of society, in which the primitive condition was nonsocial, and from which society emerged only through the guidance of a wise and eloquent statesman.[114]

Nor did civic humanists consistently and exclusively base their republicanism on these factors; they, too, placed much emphasis on the common good, or sometimes even on the good of the republic as an independent goal. But the total omission of these factors in Marsilius of Padua's thought makes his republicanism, though profound, considerably different from that of the civic humanists. To demonstrate this, consider how Marsilius defends his famous definition:

> Let us say, then, in accordance with the truth and the counsel of Aristotle in the *Politics*, Book III, c.6 that the legislator, or the first and proper efficient cause of the law is the people or the corporation of citizens or its weightier part, through its election or will in the general congregation of citizens ordering or determining through its express speech that something should be done or not done concerning human civil acts under temporal punishment or penalty. I say "weightier part" taking into consideration the quantity and quality of the persons in that community over which law is made, whether that corporation of citizens mentioned or its weightier part makes it immediately by itself, or whether it entrusts that which is to be done to one or more persons, who is not and cannot be the legislator simply, but only for some purpose and for a time, and according to the authority of the first legislator.[115]

It seems clear that Marsilius intends the "weightier part" to include all free adult males of all classes, with the exception of a very few "deformed" men, whose lack of reason would impede or prevent the implementation of the common good.[116] He provides several arguments to justify this: the best laws come from the citizens as a whole,

[114] Cary Nederman, "Nature, Sin, and the Origins of Society: The Ciceronian Tradition in Medieval Political Thought," *Journal of the History of Ideas* 49 (1988): 3–26.

[115] Marsilius of Padua, *Defensor pacis*, 1.12.3: "Nos autem dicamus secundum veritatem atque consilium Aristotelis 3° Politice, capitulo 6°, legislatorem seu causam legis effectivam primam et propriam esse populum seu civium universitatem aut eius valenciorem partem, per suam eleccionem seu voluntatem in generali civium congregacione per sermonem expressam precipientem seu determinantem aliquid fieri vel omitti circa civiles actus humanos sub pena vel supplicio temporali: valenciorem inquam partem, considerata quantitate personarum et qualitate in communitate illa super quam lex fertur, sive id fecerit universitas predicta civium aut eius pars valencior per seipsum immediate, sive id alicui vel aliquibus commiserit faciendum, qui legislator simpliciter non sunt nec esse possunt, sed solum ad aliquid et quandoque, ac secundum primi legislatoris auctoritatem."

[116] I have argued this elsewhere; see Blythe, *Ideal Government*, 196–7.

the law will be better observed if it is made by all, that which affects the well-being of all must be established by all, and the making of law by any proper subset of the whole would result in the misdirection of the common good to the particular good of that subset.[117] All of these arguments bear directly on the common good or on the right of the people to establish government, and all go to show that the best laws and the most stable polity result when the people as a whole (a category explicitly including farmers, artisans, and "mechanics") evaluates laws proposed by the wise and educated men who possess leisure. On the other hand, the legislator will usually delegate executive decisions and even legislative ones at times. This argues that a republican form of government is best, but that other forms are acceptable if the legislator institutes them. It also, however, bases the people's wisdom and virtue on their inherent understanding of their needs, rather than on an inherent need to be active politically or on a developmental process in which virtue and wisdom evolve through participation in the regime.

For these reasons, I disagree with Quentin Skinner when he argues that Marsilius represents a more developed version of Ptolemy's republicanism. Skinner cites Ptolemy's conclusion: "Certain others have a virile spirit, a bold heart, and a confidence in their intelligence, and these cannot be ruled other than by political rule . . . Such lordship is especially strong in Italy," and adds: "A similar commitment lies at the heart of Marsilius's *Defensor pacis.*" One difference, according to Skinner, is that, although Ptolemy had merely stated his preference for popular sovereignty, "Marsilius offers a careful argument in favour of equating the *legislator humanus* with the *universitas civium.*"[118] But the conceptions are entirely different. Ptolemy stated no such thing; he argued for popular sovereignty only in the case of a virtuous people, something he thinks is rare, and saw a republic as part of the process of building still greater virtue. Marsilius, by contrast, believed in popular sovereignty in every case as the best means to the common good and as necessary for achieving the people's absolute right to consent to government. It is Ptolemy's view which is closer to that of the civic humanists.

---

[117] Marsilius of Padua, *Defensor pacis*, 1.12.5 8.
[118] Skinner, "Political Philosophy," 400 1; Ptolemy of Lucca, *De Regimine Principum*, 4.8.4. Skinner uses a different translation.

NONMONARCHICAL GOVERNMENT: CIRCUMSTANTIALISM

Now let us turn to the other kind of appreciation of nonmonarchical government: that it is sometimes the best form. The idea that the best government can be determined only by considering particular circumstances became more common in fourteenth-century political thought, though Ewart Lewis claims that it always was a primary characteristic of medieval Aristotelian political thought. Lewis calls this approach "expediency," but, to avoid confusion with the later idea of "Reason of State," I have previously called it "relativism."[119] Since there are many other meanings of that word, I have now chosen to use "circumstantialism."[120] This should not suggest that the form of government is completely open, since these writers retain an absolute measure of success: the regime's fulfillment of the common good. A shift appears to begin with Engelbert of Admont (c. 1250–1331) that perhaps was later fueled by the rise of philosophical nominalism. The circumstantialist view is not precisely the same as Oresme's insistence on understanding the real world, since he concludes that limited, participatory monarchy under law is best in every case, whereas others such as William of Ockham feel that any form might be best in a particular instance. But both views lead to more careful observation of local conditions and a greater historical sense. It is significant that both William and Oresme (as well as Marsilius of Padua and others) treat the Church as a polity and apply Aristotelian arguments to discuss its regime and whether this should be changed.

To some extent circumstantialism, as Lewis argued, derived directly from the *Politics*, which argued that contingencies such as climate, temperament, local custom, the nature and quality of a given people, and even astrological influences might affect best or possible regimes. Most scholastic authors accept these factors to some extent, though many would still insist on one form or another as best in all or most situations. But a new direction appears around the turn of the fourteenth century. Instead of simply making a gesture of respect toward Aristotle's circumstantialistic statements, some authors now embraced them wholeheartedly and insisted on the contingency of political or-

---

[119] Ewart Lewis, "Natural Law and Expediency in Medieval Political Theory," *Ethics* 50 (1939–40): 144–63; Blythe, *Ideal Government*, 165–79.
[120] I take the term from Harold J. Johnson, "Ethical Relativism and Self-Determination: Political Theory in Aquinas and Some Others," in Christian Wenin, ed., *L'Homme et son univers au moyen age. Actes du septième congrès international de philosophie médiévale*, 3 vols. (Louvain-la-Neuve: Editions de l'Institut supérieur de Philosophie, 1986), II 835–44.

ganization. While this obviously does not lead to an unalloyed republicanism, it at least involves an appreciation of it in the proper circumstances.

In some ideal sense Engelbert of Admont feels that monarchy is best, but he rejects any absolutist position:

> we do not intend to say that this or that polity is the best or worst of all; because, just as Aristotle says in the third book of the *Ethics:* "Perhaps the best polity has not yet been discovered" . . . "not yet discovered" is to be understood according to use rather than according to understanding, because to find such a king who does nothing beyond reason, or a good and virtuous consul who in nothing exceeds the mean of virtue, or a rich and powerful individual who intends nothing according to reason and virtue but all according to his will – this happens rather according to imagination and intellect than according to the thing and act. We can more readily invent such persons mentally than discover them in reality.[121]

However useful, the whole Aristotelian classificatory schema is an abstraction that ignores particular circumstances. Any judgment on the value of such ideals must also be an abstraction about forms that never exist absolutely. In practice we must take the actual regime and contingencies into account. Engelbert repeats Aristotle's argument that hot climates make for easily subjected people, cold climates for anarchy, and temperate climates (Greece and Italy) for civil rule. In order to live well, he writes, different cities must establish different regimes according to such conditions.[122] This is similar to what Ptolemy has said as well, although he is more neutral than Ptolemy about those not suited for republican rule. Legislators must also consider the different languages, customs, and rites of different peoples.[123] In order to make useful laws, he writes, you need to know everything about a locality.[124]

---

[121] Engelbert of Admont, *De Regimine Principum*, 1.17, 38: "non intendimus dicere, quod ista vel illa politia sit optima omnium vel pessima: quia sicut dicit Philosophus Tertio Ethicorum, 'nondum forsitan inventa est optima politia' . . . 'nondum inventa est optima politia,' hoc intelligendum est secundum usum potius quam secundum intellectum: quia invenire talem Regem, qui in nullo faciat aliquid praeter rationem, vel Consulem bonum et virtuosum, qui in nullo excedat medium virtutis, vel talem divitem seu potentem, qui nihil intendit secundum rationem et virtutem, sed omnia secundum suam voluntatem, hoc contingit potius secundum imaginationem et intellectum, quam secundum rem et actum. Tales enim homines plus mentaliter fingere possumus, quam realiter invenire."

[122] Ibid., 3.19, 70; 2.2, 45. See also 6.8, 178 9.

[123] Engelbert of Admont, *De ortu*, 16, 765. See also 14, 763. Engelbert does say that there can be universal government and law with respect to those things held in common, i.e., natural law and the law of nations (ibid., 1.18, 768).

[124] Engelbert of Admont, *De Regimine Principum*, 3.9, 63.

Engelbert recognizes that historical development partially determines the appropriateness of particular regimes, and also that different-sized polities generally require different kinds of regime. In ancient times monarchy was common in cities, but now cities are best served by aristocratic, democratic, oligarchic, and mixed regimes, and monarchies are proper only for large areas.[125]

This distinction between what is good for small and large polities is one made by a number of medieval and early modern writers. Ptolemy of Lucca, Engelbert's contemporary, says that political rule is more common in cities and monarchy in kingdoms or provinces;[126] in fact, he says that "cities live politically in all regions, whether in Germany, Scythia, or Gaul, although they may be circumscribed by the might of the king or emperor to whom they are bound by established laws."[127] In the mid-fourteenth century, the jurist Bartolus of Sassoferrato (1313–57) developed a slightly more complicated schema. Towns must submit to larger polities; small cities, like his native Perugia, are suited to political rule; large cities, like Florence and Venice, are suited to aristocratic rule; and large polities comprising many cities and provinces, like the Roman empire, are suited to monarchy – an argument picked up much later by Rousseau.[128] Nevertheless, Bartolus is always willing to grant legitimacy to any form of regime established by custom. He is sometimes regarded as favoring republicanism absolutely, but he never goes beyond this circumstantial sense, and even here he does not exclude a superior lord. Though an expert in Roman law and a supporter of the overall hegemony of the Empire, he praised the Roman Republic. But he did this in circumstantialistic terms, not as a form inherently better than the imperial, but as suited to the size of Rome in its early days; it served first as an example of political rule and then, when it grew larger, of aristocratic government.[129]

These views reflect a common tendency of medieval political thought to combine a guiding overall monarchy with local self-government. This can be seen quite clearly in Dante's fervent imperialism and equally

---

[125] Ibid., 1.12, 31. See also 1.6, 19; 2.2 3, 44 6; and *De ortu*, 12, 761; 13, 761 2.
[126] Ptolemy of Lucca, *De Regimine Principum*, 4.2.1.
[127] Ibid., 4.1.5: "Considerandum etiam quod in omnibus regionibus, sive in Germania sive in Scythia sive in Gallia, civitates politice vivunt sed circumscripta potentia regis sive imperatoris, cui sub certis legibus sunt astricti."
[128] Bartolus of Sassoferrato, *Tractatus de Regimine Civitatis*, in *Consilia, Questiones et Tractatus Bartoli cum Additionibus Novis* (Venice, 1495), f. 128r; Jean-Jacques Rousseau, *The Social Contract*, chap. 3. This presentation of Bartolus differs from that of Skinner, *Foundations*, I: 62, who says that Bartolus favored the rule of the whole people in all but the biggest polities.
[129] Bartolus of Sassoferrato, *Tractatus*, f. 128ra b.

fervent republicanism or in Ptolemy's advocacy of papal monarchy combined with political rule in cities and republican rule among the virtuous. It can even help to explain some of the contradictions in Ptolemy's attitudes toward the Roman Empire. For Roman lawyers such a schema was the only way to preserve some vestige of the imperial ideal. In Italy the idea also seemed natural to some, considering the factionalism and violence that pervaded the northern city-states from the thirteenth century on, and it survived throughout the Renaissance. But we see that the same idea occurred also in northern European thought.

One of the most articulate defenders of circumstantialism was William of Ockham (c. 1285–1347), not coincidentally the chief representative of radical nominalism, which insisted on the contingency of the created universe. Although it is difficult to isolate Ockham's own political position, since he often gives several points of view without identifying his own, he most frequently and in most cases considers the best government only in relation to the particular time, place, and culture. Even though he has a tendency to favor monarchy abstractly, when it comes to particular cases he considers only pragmatic concerns – and for this the sole criterion is the common good, which may make any form most desirable at a given time.[130] If the common good requires, he writes, any government can be changed, even one that was originally ordained by God, such as the papal monarchy.[131]

I cannot leave the subject of circumstantialism without mentioning two other figures, who while preferring one form or another, acknowledge the legitimacy of a wide variety of forms. The monarchist and populist John of Paris wrote that the people has an absolute right to choose the form of rule to which it is to be subject, and this right can be exercised at any time – even when there is an existing regime: "it pertains to [the people] to subject itself to whom it desires without prejudice of another."[132] The people can change the government for good reason, or even if there is no good reason, if it is the people's will: "just as jurisdiction is given by the consent of humans, so it is taken away

---

[130] William of Ockham, *Dialogus*, in *Monarchia Sancti Romani Imperii*, ed. Melchior Goldast (Frankfurt, 1614; reprint Graz: Akademische Druck- und Verlagsanstalt, 1960), 3.1.2.9, 796; 3.1.2.15, 800; 3.1.2.20, 806; 3.1.2.21 4, 808 11; 3.1.2.17, 802; *Octo Questiones*, in *Guillelmi de Ockham Opera Politica*, ed. H. S. Offler, 3 vols. (Manchester: Manchester University Press, 1974), I: 3.9, 111; 5.3, 156.
[131] William of Ockham, *Dialogus*, 3.1.2.20, 808.
[132] John of Paris, *De Potestate Regia et Papali*, in *Johannes Quidort von Paris: Über königliche und päpstliche Gewalt*, ed. F. Bleienstein (Stuttgart: E. Klett, 1969), 15, 151: "cuius est se subicere cui vult, sine alterius praeiudicio."

by a contrary consent."[133] In a way this is opposite to the views of Ockham just mentioned, since for him the agency of establishing government is secondary to the criterion of the common good, while the reverse is true for John.

In some ways the views of Marsilius of Padua are similar to those of John of Paris. He recognizes the right of the citizen legislator to choose any government it wishes. Marsilius is most concerned with defending secular power against the papacy and therefore is not clear about his optimal political form. This has left him open to the charge that he really did not care about the type of government, and that he formulated the concept of legislator solely as an *ad hoc* theoretical obstacle to the secular claims of the pope, purposely made vague to apply to any reasonably well- or long-established government.[134] Although Marsilius supports a government with universal participation in general, he does leave the particular form of government open and subject to local conditions, customs, and needs, but behind the particular officials and constitutional organs he demands the consent of a much wider "legislator" if the regime is to be legitimate.

CICERO

Finally, let us consider briefly the medieval appreciation of Cicero, asking whether it changed radically around 1400 as Baron claims. It has always been known that Cicero remained an important classical source, particularly in education, for the entire Middle Ages, and Baron admits that beginning around 1300, in Italy at least, Cicero, "began to be recognized along with Aristotle as the most effective guide to civic obligations." He specifically mentions in this regard two Dominicans, Ptolemy of Lucca and Remigio de' Girolami, and comments that their writings, "allow us to trace in detail how devotion to the community was

---

[133] Ibid., 25, 209: "Et ideo sicut per consensum hominum iurisdictio datur, ita per contrarium consensum tollitur." The same holds true for the Church; the pope, if he be unwilling to resign, "can be deposed in such a case by the consent of the people, because the pope himself and any other prelate rules not for himself but for the people . . . the consent of the people in such a case to depose him (although he is unwilling) if he seems totally useless, and to choose another, is more efficacious than his will to renounce voluntarily . . . when the people are unwilling" (24, 201).

[134] Conal Condren, "Democracy and the *Defensor pacis*: On the English Language Tradition of Marsilian Interpretation," *Il pensiero politico* 13 (1980): 301–16. For a more recent treatment of Marsilius as not particularly concerned with the type of regime, see Cary Nederman, *Community and Consent: The Secular Political Theory of Marsiglio of Padua's "Defensor pacis"* (New York: Rowman and Littlefield, 1994). Nederman does put emphasis on consent and the functional participation of the entire community.

preached from the pulpits and how it influenced contemporary writings on politics and history."¹³⁵ However, he feels that Cicero's political career, about which little was known in 1300, but which Petrarch uncovered in 1345, was unacceptable to the medieval preference for the contemplative life and even to Petrarch's sometime ideal of intellectual leisure. It was only Salutati and Bruni, according to Baron, who rescued Cicero the politician and praised exactly those traits to which Petrarch objected. Baron attempts to demonstrate, "how the aspect of Cicero the Roman citizen and thinker was but timidly recognized throughout the medieval centuries, only to be seized upon in the Quattrocento by humanists as an essential aid in their efforts to break away from many of the assumptions held during the Middle Ages."¹³⁶

I have already touched upon the question of medieval devotion to the contemplative life, and concluded that, however much this may have been a feature of religious writing, it is simply missing from the political writings of the scholastic philosophers. Although they may not praise the participatory life to the degree that the civic humanists did, there is no criticism of participation as a second-rate activity, as we would find in the Fathers and in the early Middle Ages. Only Marsilius of Padua mentions a life of leisure at all, and he does this in a sense far different from the religious, contemplative life that Baron imputes to the Middle Ages or even to Petrarch's life of intellectual development in leisure. Marsilius argues that the citizens as a whole are best qualified to decide whether a particular proposal is good, but that in proposing law, "Such inquiry . . . can be carried on more appropriately and be completed better by those men who are able to have leisure, who are older and experienced in practical affairs, and who are called 'prudent men,' than by the mechanics who must bend all their efforts to acquiring the necessities of life."¹³⁷ In other words, Marsilius is referring to those citizens who have devoted their efforts to the polity and have not had to be distracted by extraneous responsibilities. That is, precisely, the Ciceronian citizen-statesmen.¹³⁸

---

¹³⁵ Hans Baron, "The Memory of Cicero's Roman Civic Spirit in the Medieval Centuries and in the Florentine Renaissance," in his *In Search of Florentine Civic Humanism*, 2 vols. (Princeton: Princeton University Press, 1988) I: 114.
¹³⁶ Ibid., 97.
¹³⁷ Marsilius of Padua, *Defensor pacis*, 1.12: "Inquisicio hec conveniencius fieri potest et compleri melius ex observacione potencium vacare, seniorum et expertorum in agilibus quos prudentes appellant quam ex mechanicorum consideracione, qui ad acquirenda vita necessaria suis operibus habent intendere."
¹³⁸ See Cary Nederman, "The Union of Wisdom and Eloquence before the Renaissance: The Ciceronian Orator in Medieval Thought," *Journal of Medieval History* 18 (1992): 90 3.

It is Petrarch whose thought is in opposition to the prevailing scholastic opinion on this point; the latter is much closer to the civic humanist perspective. Without making too much of the motives of the early humanists, one possible explanation is that some of the medieval thinkers that Baron considers representatives of a transitional viewpoint, lacking the earmarks of civic humanism – such as Petrarch – are ones who have been affected by the disasters of the fourteenth century. In this atmosphere one should not be surprised that some thinkers withdrew from the ideal of virtue in the active life which was common at the turn of the fourteenth century and which was compatible with the civic humanist ideal.

With regard to the medieval image of Cicero, Cary Nederman has disproved the assumption of Baron and other Renaissance scholars that "the Ciceronian idea of the orator as the man who employs reasoned eloquence in order to speak publicly about matters touching upon the common good was unappreciated in the Middle Ages but formed a central tenet of the Renaissance humanist outlook."[139] Nederman surveys a wide range of medieval writing, from Cicero commentaries by Thierry of Chartres and others to the mid-thirteenth century *Book of Treasure* of Brunetto Latini, to the political works of scholastic thinkers like John of Paris and Marsilius of Padua, and finds in all these sources an appreciation for the Ciceronian union of eloquence and civic involvement. His work supports Kristeller's thesis that "the eloquence of the humanists was the continuation of the medieval *ars aregendi* just as their epistolography continued the tradition of the *ars dictaminis*."[140] But he goes much further; while Kristeller refers only to oratory as a practical activity, Nederman wants to show a connection between humanism and medieval theoretical work, including scholasticism. He concludes:

Thus, both humanism's praise of wise eloquence, and its connection of oratory with a concern for and devotion to public affairs, may be taken as continuations of medieval theoretical frameworks as well as actual practices. Even scholasticism, which is so often denigrated as the implacable enemy of humanism, could grasp these "authentic" features of Cicero's thought . . . Nothing in Cicero's ideal of the wise and eloquent orator was precluded by or incompatible with the most cherished presumptions of medieval rhetorical and political authors.[141]

---

[139] Ibid., 77. Nederman has written a number of other articles on Cicero in the Middle Ages, most notably, "Nature, Sin, and the Origins of Society: The Ciceronian Tradition in Medieval Political thought," *Journal of the History of Ideas* 49 (1988): 3–26.

[140] Nederman, "The Union," 94, citing Paul Kristeller, *Renaissance Thought and Its Sources* (New York: Columbia University Press, 1979), 94.

[141] Ibid., 94–5.

Although he concurs that Roman writers such as Cicero and Sallust were widely used in the Middle Ages, Richard Tuck has argued that a significant change of attitude toward them did occur around 1400. From that time there was a tendency to subordinate Aristotle to the Roman writers, both through a greater emphasis on these writers and by reinterpreting Aristotle. One result was that, beginning with Pier Paolo Vergerio and Bruni, "Ciceronians were quite prepared to assert absolutely plainly, for the first time since antiquity, the straightforward superiority of *action* over contemplation, and in particular the superiority of a life of political activity devoted to the common good of a city."[142] While there may have been a change of attitude, the study of Aristotle actually increased in this period, and, in any case, medieval writers were no less capable than these "Ciceronians" of advocating an active political life directed to the common good. If anything, any subordination of Cicero to Aristotle would lead to a greater emphasis on aristocracy and thus work against the theory of popular participation. This reflects the actual trend in Renaissance cities; as Lauro Martines has demonstrated, the culture of humanism was elite to an extent unknown in the Middle Ages.[143]

CONCLUSION

Whether or not civic humanism is, as Baron argued, a phenomenon arising out of particular Florentine conditions or, as Hankins suggests, something that is ubiquitous in fifteenth-century humanist writings throughout Italy,[144] there is certainly a major difference between civic humanists and the medieval writers discussed here: only a few of the latter were direct participants in the government of a republic. Most were writing from an academic position; for them the political life, however admirable, was not something in which they felt it was necessary for them personally to take part. Those who were committed to political activity were, for the most part, writing as exiles or opponents of the regimes from which they were excluded. From the first group, we do not feel the passion that seems to inform writers such as Bruni and

[142] Richard Tuck, "Humanism and Political Thought," in *The Impact of Humanism on Western Europe*, ed. Anthony Goodman and Angus McKay (New York: Longman, 1990), 55.
[143] Lauro Martines, *Power and Imagination. City States in Renaissance Italy* (Baltimore: Johns Hopkins University Press, 1979), 191–217. On the continuing importance of Aristotle, see David Lines, "The Importance of Being Good: Moral Philosophy in Italian Universities, 1300–1600," *Rinascimento* n.s. 36 (1996): 139–88.
[144] Hankins, "'Baron Thesis,'" 328–30.

others, and the very real passion of the second group is directed differently from that of the civic humanists. For both groups we have to dig to find those ideas that seem so close to those of civic humanism; they are not omnipresent and insistent. In this regard the debate over whether Bruni and others were dedicated republicans or merely talented rhetoricians telling people what they wanted to hear seems not to be so important, since their positions must have found a response in the underlying attitudes or aspirations of the community. The events of 1402 that Baron feels are so important may well have contributed to the particular manifestation of civic ideas associated with Bruni and early Quattrocento Florence. But he goes too far when he claims that the intellectual elements of this attitude were something new, or that the basic civic attitude was something originally unique to Florence or necessarily bound to anti-monarchical political forms.

There is also a sense in which civic humanist ideas serve as a cover for the decline of actual participation. The most plausible explanation for the rise of civic humanism at this time is the one John Najemy develops in chapter 3 of this volume. Starting from the observation that civic humanism in no way reflected political reality in Florence during the fifteenth century, he concludes that it developed as a civic myth to silence thirteenth-century guild republicanism and justify the new oligarchic era of participation without power. He writes that civic humanism was "deeply conservative in its denial of the legitimacy of class interests and conflict and in its affirmation of a natural leadership of patrician fathers over their citizen/children. It may also have served as the intellectual foundation of a culture of conformity and surveillance."[145]

Najemy correctly points out that civic humanists promoted ideals that were quite different from those of the period of the *popolo*, but they did use and transform those ideals, as well as scholastic theories widely circulated in the thirteenth and fourteenth centuries. By so doing, Bruni and other late fourteenth- and fifteenth-century writers brought ideas developed in the universities into a form that resonated with the aspirations of the burgeoning Renaissance elites of the Italian cities.

[145] See p. 103, below.

CHAPTER 3

Civic humanism and Florentine politics

John M. Najemy

For forty-five years now historians have debated the arguments advanced by Hans Baron in *The Crisis of the Early Italian Renaissance*,[1] and elaborated in many separate studies and essays,[2] according to which a tenacious defense of republican liberty and an ethic of civic participation suddenly emerged among early fifteenth-century Florentine citizens and humanists as a consequence of Florence's struggle for survival against the expansionist ambitions of the Visconti dukes of Milan. Baron's thesis has enjoyed (and suffered) a degree of attention and controversy that has not abated even now, a decade after his death and in a completely transformed world of historiographical assumptions and practices.[3] One reason for this is certainly the dramatic quality of Baron's thesis – its claim that big and lasting changes in the intellectual history of the Renaissance occurred as a direct and immediate response to what Baron saw as the Florentines' life-and-death conflict with Milan. Other reasons for the continuing debates may be less clear, less related to the merits and weaknesses of Baron's historical arguments, and rooted, perhaps, in the political agendas and ideological stakes that still surround modern versions of civic

---

[1] Hans Baron, *The Crisis of the Early Italian Renaissance: Civic Humanism and Republican Liberty in an Age of Classicism and Tyranny*, 2 vols. (Princeton: Princeton University Press, 1955); and the revised one-volume edition with an epilogue (Princeton: Princeton University Press, 1966).
[2] Many of them collected in Hans Baron, *In Search of Florentine Civic Humanism: Essays on the Transition from Medieval to Modern Thought*, 2 vols. (Princeton: Princeton University Press, 1988).
[3] Some recent essays on Baron and his thesis: Albert Rabil, Jr., "The Significance of 'Civic Humanism' in the Interpretation of the Italian Renaissance," in *Renaissance Humanism: Foundations, Forms, and Legacy*, 3 vols. (Philadelphia: University of Pennsylvania Press, 1988), I: 141–74; Riccardo Fubini, "Renaissance Historian: The Career of Hans Baron," *Journal of Modern History* 64 (1992): 541–74; James Hankins, "The 'Baron Thesis' after Forty Years and some Recent Studies of Leonardo Bruni," *Journal of the History of Ideas* 56 (1995): 309–38; and the papers by Ronald Witt, Craig Kallendorf, and myself, with a comment by Werner Gundersheimer, in the *AHR Forum* on Baron and the *Crisis* in the *American Historical Review* 101 (1996): 107–44.

humanism.⁴ Whatever the reasons, the problem of when and why civic and republican attitudes emerged in Renaissance Florence still generates a good deal of debate.

The question of Florentine civic humanism, as understood *both* by Baron and most of his critics, has typically been framed around three points: the genesis, the originality, and the accuracy of the civic humanist representation of republican politics in fifteenth-century Florence. Baron's answers to these questions are well known. For the origin or cause of the civic humanist ideas of republican liberty and the active life, he focused on the long wars with Milan. As for their originality, he argued that they represented a radical break with the more militantly classical and essentially apolitical humanism of the fourteenth century, and a significant departure as well from the earlier civic ethos of the medieval city-states that was – in his view – largely untouched by the focus on Roman history and culture that later became the trademark of humanism. And on the question of the accuracy of the civic humanist view of Florentine politics, Baron believed that its defense of liberty, equality, and citizen participation in government reflected the lived experience of Florentine citizens and the animating spirit of the republic's institutions.

Baron's critics have disagreed with him on all these points. About the birth of civic humanism, some have contended that the appearance of the crucial texts cannot be correlated with any foreign policy crisis,⁵ while others have suggested that Baron focused on the wrong crisis.⁶ About the originality of fifteenth-century civic humanism, some critics have asserted that most or even all of its chief ideas about liberty, law, and the pursuit of the "common good" can be found in the theorists of communal government as far back as the thirteenth and early fourteenth

---

⁴ The papers read in the lecture series on "Humanism and Public Life" at the University of Washington in 1988-9, and published in *Modern Language Quarterly* 51 (June 1990): 101-271, make only occasional reference to Baron, but the imprint of his work is unmistakable in the common aim of these essays to explore the connections between politics and humanism in a variety of medieval, Renaissance, and early modern contexts. Two of the essays are particularly relevant to the Italian context: Lauro Martines, "The Protean Face of Renaissance Humanism," 105-21; and Ronald G. Witt, "Civic Humanism and the Rebirth of the Ciceronian Oration," 167-84.

⁵ Dismantling Baron's key date of 1402 was one of the aims of Jerrold Seigel in "'Civic Humanism' or Ciceronian Rhetoric? The Culture of Petrarch and Bruni," *Past and Present* 34 (1966): 3-48.

⁶ Gene Brucker has observed that "Not until a decade after [the Milanese duke] Giangaleazzo's death" – and in the aftermath of the war against Ladislaus of Naples – "do clear signs of what Baron calls 'the new politico-historical outlook' appear" in the records of the consultative assemblies convened by the Florentine government; *The Civic World of Early Renaissance Florence* (Princeton: Princeton University Press, 1977), 300.

centuries;[7] others claim that the fundamental assumptions of civic humanism were not peculiar to republican Florence, but rather the common property of humanist circles throughout northern Italy.[8] And about the accuracy, or lack of it, of the civic humanist view of things, many historians have rightly insisted that the polity of early fifteenth-century Florence was something less than a paradise of citizen equality and participatory liberty, that the city was in fact governed by a restricted oligarchy, and that this self-proclaimed defender of republican liberty could be quite ruthless in subjugating its neighbors in Tuscany.[9]

Questions about the precise "cause" of civic humanism, of whether it was an original or derivative political philosophy, and of the extent to which it accurately represented Florentine political life may now have exhausted their usefulness, at least in the terms in which they have usually been posed. Few historians now accept that the military crisis of 1402 could have been the single decisive factor in the emergence of civic humanism, and the question that needs to be asked about Baron's argument is what *kind of role*, if any, foreign policy played in the development of Florentine political attitudes, and in what relation to domestic politics. The issue of originality may never have had much usefulness. All political ideas build on preceding traditions of discourse, and in this sense there are probably no absolutely radical breaks in the history of political thought. On the other hand, claims that it had all been said before usually ignore the ways in which context and circumstance change the meaning and force of ideas. In any case, Baron's claim was not that civic ideals were unknown in Florence and the other city-states before the "crisis"; what was new, in his view, was the combination of these civic ideas with the humanist educational and moral program that began with Petrarch.

But it is the question of civic humanism's "truth" – its more or less faithful representation of the alleged realities of Florentine politics – that

---

[7] See especially Quentin Skinner, *The Foundations of Modern Political Thought*, 2 vols (Cambridge: Cambridge University Press, 1978), I: 69–84; also Skinner's essay on "Machiavelli's *Discorsi* and the Pre-Humanist Origins of Republican Ideas," in *Machiavelli and Republicanism*, ed. G. Bock, Q. Skinner, and M. Viroli (Cambridge: Cambridge University Press, 1990), 121–41.

[8] A suggestion made by James Hankins in "The 'Baron Thesis'," 327–30.

[9] The classic statement of this assessment of the medieval Italian republics, including Florence, is by P. J. Jones, "Communes and Despots: The City-State in Late-Medieval Italy," *Transactions of the Royal Historical Society*, 5th ser., 15 (1965): 71–96. Tending more cautiously in the same direction, and with a sharper focus on the Florentine situation, is Nicolai Rubinstein, "Florentine Constitutionalism and Medici Ascendancy in the Fifteenth Century," in *Florentine Studies*, ed. N. Rubinstein (Evanston: Northwestern University Press, 1968), 442–62. For a recent restatement of this approach, see Hankins, "The 'Baron Thesis'," 316–17 and 321–3.

may be the trickiest point of all. Baron's critics are quite right to point out the gap separating Leonardo Bruni's laudatory accounts of Florentine liberty, civic equality, and participatory government from what the political historians have established about the oligarchic character of the republic in the early fifteenth century.[10] It is undeniably the case that the writings of the civic humanists did not accurately or objectively represent the realities of Florentine politics. This has led some critics, from Jerrold Seigel thirty years ago to James Hankins very recently, to explain the gap by asserting that the "civic humanists" were professional rhetoricians and not political philosophers.[11] In his important essay on Baron and Bruni studies, Hankins asks: "Were men such as Salutati and Bruni really as rooted in the values and attitudes of the Florentine ruling classes as they had seemed to Baron?"[12] His answer of course is that they were not: "if we admit that Bruni's *impostazione* is primarily that of a rhetorician, the problem [of his inconsistencies] disappears." Thus Hankins concludes that we ought to "do away with the anachronism that men like Bruni and Salutati were ideologues (in the sense of having an exclusive commitment to one political ideology such as republicanism) . . . [and] admit that Florentine republicanism as presented by Salutati and Bruni was a rhetorical artifact not necessarily in keeping with either their private beliefs or the political realities of the time . . . [Their] attitude was that of permanent under-secretaries, loyal to Florence rather than to the regime and carrying out to the best of their abilities the changing policies of successive political masters. They were also, undeniably, professional rhetoricians in the most basic sense of being paid salaries to produce propaganda for the state. They were made by their political masters to write letters and speeches that were sometimes inconsistent with or hostile to their own private convictions, but no one thought the worse of them for that."[13]

There is potentially much to agree with here, but there are also

---

[10] See especially Dale Kent, *The Rise of the Medici: Faction in Florence, 1426–1434* (Oxford: Oxford University Press, 1978); and Brucker, *Civic World*. Nicolai Rubinstein's study of *The Government of Florence Under the Medici (1434 to 1494)* (Oxford: Clarendon Press, 1966) is often, and rightly, cited in support of this gap, but it should not be overlooked that among Rubinstein's main arguments is that the Medici regime, at least in its early decades, adhered far more than is commonly supposed to the constitutional norms and restraints of republicanism.

[11] Eugenio Garin has expressed some useful caution about the tendency to see "rhetoric" as the single key to understanding the political ideas of the humanists in his "Leonardo Bruni: politica e cultura," in *Leonardo Bruni cancelliere della repubblica di Firenze*, ed. Paolo Viti (Florence: Leo S. Olschki, 1990), 3–14. Nicolai Rubinstein explores Bruni's dependence on specific rhetorical models, as well as the political purposes to which he put his rhetoric, in "Il Bruni a Firenze: retorica e politica," in ibid., 15–28.

[12] Hankins, "The 'Baron Thesis'," 318.   [13] Ibid., 325–6.

difficulties that stem, I think, from the way in which key terms are used. About "rhetoric" and "professional rhetoricians," one can agree that Salutati, Bruni, and the other chancellors were indeed professional rhetoricians, and that they were paid to defend the policies of the governments they worked for. But Bruni was not yet chancellor when he wrote the *Laudatio* or when he drafted the most republican and anti-imperial portions of his *Histories of the Florentine People*.[14] And into what category should we place those writers, like Gregorio Dati and Matteo Palmieri, who were never chancellors and were never paid to write on behalf of the republic, but who nonetheless display many of the ideas and attitudes that one finds in Bruni? What about a much later figure like Alamanno Rinuccini, who was not only never chancellor but indeed recapitulated much of the civic humanist ethos in an angry denunciation of the Medici regime? Writers like Dati, Palmieri, and Rinuccini alert us to the fact that the civic and republican ideas that emerged from the rhetoric of the chancery were not limited to that context. One should not for a moment dismiss the importance of rhetoric in the formation and sense of intellectual vocation of the humanists, whether professional or citizen, civic or classical. But Renaissance rhetoric, with its commitment to education and moral philosophy, should itself not be reduced to the figure of the "professional rhetorician" who simply did the bidding of his employer. "Professional rhetoricians" certainly existed, but they do not account for the full range and popularity of civic humanist ideas.

It might also be possible to agree that "Florentine republicanism as presented by Salutati and Bruni was a rhetorical artifact not necessarily in keeping with either their private beliefs or the political realities of the time." But to argue that, if we "admit" this, "we can at least save them from some of the more serious charges against their moral character" implies that Bruni and Salutati ought otherwise to fall under some suspicion of moral failure because of the gap between the "rhetorical artifact" and the "private beliefs" and/or "political realities" to which their utterances should have been anchored, and that the "charges" against them can be reduced once we realize that the poor devils were beholden to "political masters" and merely trying to keep their jobs. The clear inference here is that we have morally acceptable thinkers when we can certify the authenticity or integrity of their utterances as

[14] A recent study that emphasizes the continuity of Bruni's thought from the early *Laudatio* through the chancery letters is by Paolo Viti, *Leonardo Bruni e Firenze: studi sulle lettere pubbliche e private* (Rome: Bulzoni, 1992), especially the first essay, "Il primato di Firenze," 3–91.

faithful reflections of either consistent "private beliefs" or objectively verifiable "political realities." The problem with the first of these tests is that "private belief" is often mutable and almost never of a piece; and the problem with the second is that no political thinker of any conceivable interest could pass it.

But there is at least a third possibility: namely, that political thinkers and writers move within, and help both to constitute and to modify, social, historical, and political traditions of discourse whose "authenticity" is reducible neither to private belief nor to objectively verifiable truth. Such traditions might usefully be called myths, which for these purposes I define not as lies or pure inventions, but as powerful stories that organize experiences, aspirations, fears, and memories into more or less coherent accounts of how the world is perceived to be and how it ought to be – but usually *not* how it actually is. In fact, one of the most important things that myths of this kind do is to help people *not* to see aspects of their world that are incompatible with prized beliefs or ideals. Such myths can also be called ideologies – not in the sense of consistently held private convictions (which I would prefer to call philosophies), but in the sense of collective belief systems that are often inconsistent with the "facts," but no less powerful or historically significant for those inconsistencies. When the founders of the American republic, in justifying their rebellion against the authority they had previously recognized, appealed to the "self-evident" and thus common belief that "all men are created equal," and proceeded to create a polity in which only propertied white men enjoyed political rights, they were reasoning from within the parameters of such a myth or ideology: a body of beliefs that helped them not to see how the facts on the ground flagrantly violated the principles at the core of those same beliefs.

I argue that civic humanism was such an ideology, and that in this sense the civic humanists can be considered ideologues – self-conscious promoters of a particular vision of Florentine politics and society that they did not invent (but to which they contributed significantly), and which had the political and intellectual support of powerful elements in that society. This vision of things could never be a matter of merely private conviction; its expression was a social and even ritual process, a way of belonging to the consensus that, as we shall see, was the core of the ideology. And it was not, even in the intention of its promoters, a dispassionate analysis of political realities; it was a normative discourse that couched itself in hortatory and educational rhetoric, even when it "described" the institutions of the republic. One of the most important senses in which civic humanism deserves to be called an ideology is precisely its role in persuading people of truths that would not easily have withstood being tested against the political realities on the ground.

Florentine civic humanism may sometimes appear on the surface to be a straightforward defense of republicanism against monarchy, and from this impression has flowed much of the attention to the foreign-policy dimension of its origins and polemical aims. But the Florentines did not need civic humanism in order to defend the autonomy of their republican state against threats from differently constituted polities. They had been doing that for a long time. It was rather the transformation of domestic politics from the 1380s into the opening decades of the fifteenth century — the half-century from the collapse of the last guild-based popular government in 1382 through the decades that preceded the victory of the Medici faction in 1434 — that generated the ideology of civic humanism. Two very different kinds of republicanism confronted each other in this period of transformation, and civic humanism was the intellectual expression and ideological product of the ascendancy and triumph of the newer form of Florentine republicanism. I contend that civic humanism's real antagonist — the enemy it sought to defeat — was less the duke of Milan than the popular, guild republicanism that had periodically surfaced to challenge the hegemony of the elite in the thirteenth and fourteenth centuries.

The confrontation of rival republicanisms in Florence developed from longstanding class antagonisms. From the early thirteenth century down to the 1370s and 1380s, the Florentine guild community regularly presented itself as an alternative to the oligarchical governments favored by the great families. The guild community's brand of republicanism made of the guilds the constituent parts of the republic and authorized their systematic representation in the offices and councils of the commune. The republicanism of the guilds envisioned a society of separate and not always compatible interests, in which difference and division were acknowledged as legitimate, and in which government emerged from the constitutionally ordained representation and confrontation of these differences. The guild republic was thus a federation of autonomously constituted parts, each with a voice of its own. The institution of the guild itself, as a legal corporation or *universitas*, served as the model for this popular republicanism. The members of a guild voluntarily constituted the authority to which they subjected themselves, and each guild developed structures of representation (often of its own internal subdivisions) and systems of delegation and accountability of power. With their regular emphasis on the participation of the members in various assemblies and councils, the guilds were in effect miniature republics from whose experience and example the communal popular governments of 1292–5, 1343–8, and 1378–82 drew direct inspiration.[15]

Guild republicanism was the creation of the broad middle ranks of communal society, the class that the Florentines called the *popolo*: the regional merchants, notaries, moneychangers, manufacturers of cloth for the local market, retail clothdealers, and other professional groups of the major guilds who did not belong to lineages of great wealth or social prestige; and the shopkeepers, providers of services, builders, and artisans of various sorts in the minor guilds. Popular governments were made possible by coalitions between these two groups – the nonelite major guildsmen and the minor guildsmen – against the elite families, who constituted a minority, albeit a politically and economically potent one, within the major guilds. Until the end of the fourteenth century, the nonelite members of the major guilds were the fulcrum of Florentine politics. When they allied themselves with their fellow major guildsmen from the elite families, they helped forge oligarchic governments that reduced the influence of the guilds in general and thereby diminished the role of the minor guildsmen in government. But when the nonelite major guildsmen became dissatisfied with the leadership of the great families (which could happen because of fiscal mismanagement, economic crisis, or foreign-policy disasters), they sometimes turned to the rest of the guild community and supported constitutional reforms according to which all the guilds shared, more or less equally, in the offices and committees of communal government. These regimes regularly insisted on the frequent consultation of the full guild community. As an advisory committee to the Signoria recommended during the popular movement of 1378, legislation can only be said to enjoy "the consent [or pleasure: *contentamento*] of the whole city" if and when all the guilds have been consulted and have had the chance to voice their opinions.[16]

Each popular government in Florence was more radical than its

---

[15] On the republicanism of the guilds and their contributions to the popular governments of the commune, see Brucker, *Civic World*, chap. 1, 14–59; my *Corporatism and Consensus in Florentine Electoral Politics, 1280–1400* (Chapel Hill: University of North Carolina Press, 1982), and my essays, "Guild Republicanism in Trecento Florence: The Successes and Ultimate Failure of Corporate Politics," *American Historical Review* 84 (1979): 53–71; "*Audiant Omnes Artes*: Corporate Origins of the Ciompi Revolution," in *Il Tumulto dei Ciompi: un momento di storia fiorentina ed europea* (Florence: Leo S. Olschki, 1981), 59–93; and "Stato, comune, e 'universitas,'" *Annali dell'Istituto Storico Italo-germanico in Trento* 20 (1994): 245–63.

[16] Florence, Archivio di Stato, Capitoli, Protocolli, 7, f. 190v; quoted in my "Guild Republicanism," 66.

predecessor, bringing larger numbers of "new men" from further down the social hierarchy to some voice in government, either directly through election to communal offices or indirectly through systems that allowed for the representation of a greater number of guilds. This progressive radicalization of popular politics culminated in the explosive summer of 1378 when thousands of workers in the textile industries, previously denied any right of corporate association, organized themselves into three new guilds, which collectively claimed no less than a third of the posts in the governing committee of the Signoria (with another third going to the minor guilds). Although the largest of these new guilds was disbanded within a matter of weeks, the other two continued to exist as members of an expanded community of minor guilds for three and a half more years within a regime that gave the minor guilds exactly one-half of the seats in the Signoria. And the vast majority of the major guildsmen who held the other half of the seats during these years came from the ranks of the nonelite members of their guilds. The popular government of 1378–82, more than its predecessors of 1343–8 and 1292–5, nearly completely excluded the elite families of Florence from the political offices that these families considered their birthright. But it was not only the elite families that were fearful of the policies of this most radical of Florentine popular regimes. The nonelite major guildsmen could now see that the constitutional reforms they had supported at the beginning of the popular challenge to the elite had gone far beyond their intentions. Perhaps more than anything else, it was the spectacle of workers and artisans in the textile industries enjoying an autonomous corporate existence, and thus the right to bargain collectively with the cloth manufacturers of the wool guild, that made even the nonelite members of the major guilds realize the profound threat to their own interests of popular regimes that were willing to open the doors to new members of the guild federation from the working classes.

The fear and loathing that the popular regime of 1378–82 engendered in the Florentine upper classes became the stuff of legend. Such sentiments are alluded to in the famous dictum of Gino Capponi, who, by way of saying how unthinkable submission to foreign lords (in this case Ladislaus of Naples) would be for the Florentines, claimed that it would be "better to live under the government of the Ciompi than under the tyranny of that king."[17] Only the popular movement of 1378, in other words, could rival the loss of liberty to foreign tyrants as a source of

---

[17] Brucker, *Civic World*, 388.

terror for the Florentine upper classes. And about the entire regime of 1378–82, there is the testimony (reported by the historian Giovanni Cavalcanti) of Rinaldo degli Albizzi's emotional diatribe in 1426 – nearly fifty years after the target of his denunciation – against "those forty damned months" when the guilds and their consuls "held this people in servitude."[18] Patrician contempt for the working classes was of course nothing new, but one has only to go to the chronicle of Marchionne di Coppo Stefani to see the angry reactions against the regime of 1378–82 from the very nonelite elements of the major guilds that had once strongly promoted guild republicanism. Stefani, who in other moments was capable of being sternly critical of the arrogance of the Parte Guelfa and the elite families, denounced the unskilled woolworkers as the latter-day equivalent of Christ-killers, incapable of any rational political action, and easily seduced by demagogues.[19] But his anger was not limited to the Ciompi alone. Commenting on the economic policies of the guild regime of 1378–82, he wrote: "So great was the power of the [nonelite] guildsmen that in every matter under deliberation they achieved their aims in the legislative councils . . . Thus whoever has more power gets what he wants, with little concern however for whether it is good or useful for the city; everyone seeks his own advantage as best he thinks he can: neither law nor statute counts for much in such matters."[20] Stefani's reaction to the independent guild of the dyers negotiating terms of labor and piece-rates with their former masters in the wool guild was an especially irate one. He again denounced the "soperchio homore che soprabbondava negli artefici" and the "insolence" and "arrogance" of the dyers who "had no concern for who they were" or for the fact that they "used to be governed by and subject to the cloth manufacturers from whom they had their laws and to whose statutes they were [previously] subject." Their requests were "so alien to the cloth manufacturers and so abominable to the citizens that it was beyond all measure."[21] It is worth underscoring that these denunciations of the guild regime came not from some reactionary *arciguelfo* in the elite of great families, but from a man of modest family

---

[18] Giovanni Cavalcanti, *Istorie fiorentine*, 2 vols., ed. F. Polidori (Florence, 1838), I: 82; Brucker, *Civic World*, 473.
[19] *Cronaca fiorentina di Marchionne di Coppo Stefani*, ed. N. Rodolico, in *Rerum italicarum scriptores*, vol. XXX, part I (Città di Castello, 1903–1955), 194, 199.
[20] Ibid., 382: "Ma tanto era la forza degli artefici, che in ogni cosa di diliberazione vinceano ne' consigli ciò che volieno . . . E così va a chi più può, non guardando però s'è bene o utile della città, e ciascuno tira acqua a suo mulino, come meglio vede potere; nè legge, nè statuto vale nelle cose."
[21] Ibid., 386; see also Brucker, *Civic World*, 52.

whose father, Coppo di Stefano, had been a rank-and-file member and occasional office-holder in the not very elite major guild of Por Santa Maria.

A half-century later, Leonardo Bruni's *Histories of the Florentine People* would make clear how crucial the memory of the Ciompi and fear of social revolution were to civic humanism's view of the Florentine past. His account of the events of 1378 contains a memorable passage that simultaneously evokes the still vivid fears of the workers in the minds of the Florentine upper classes and denies any legitimacy to their political aims: "Every day new movements were born, because some people were eager to plunder the possessions of the rich, others to gain revenge against their enemies, and still others to make themselves powerful. This may stand as a lesson for all time [*perpetuum documentum*] to the distinguished men of the city: never to let political initiative or arms into the hands of the multitude, for once they have had a bite, they cannot be restrained and they think they can do as they please because there are so many of them." Well-meaning but misguided attempts at reform had resulted in "making poor guildsmen and men of base condition the rulers of the city" and in putting noble and distinguished families at the mercy of the "stupidity of the aroused multitude. For there was no end or order to the unleashed appetites of the poor and the criminals, who, once armed, lusted after the possessions of rich and honorable men, and who thought of nothing except robbing, killing, and exiling citizens."[22] A similar attitude toward the poor is evident in Giovanni Morelli's advice about hiding grain harvested from one's farm: "If a poor man sees that you have grain to sell and that you are holding on to it to increase its price, he will damn and curse and rob you and burn your house, if he has the power to do so, and he will make you hated by the entire lower class, which is a most dangerous thing. May God preserve our city from their rule [*Idio ne guardi la nostra città dalla loro signoria*]."[23]

As I have argued elsewhere,[24] Bruni's condemnation of the Ciompi revolution as an eruption of irrational and even criminal impulses latent in "poor guildsmen and men of base condition" heavily conditions his treatment of both the guilds and the social bases of Florentine

---

[22] Leonardo Bruni Aretino, *Historiarum florentini populi libri XII*, ed. E. Santini, in *Rerum italicarum scriptores*, vol. XIX, part III (Città di Castello, 1914–26), 224 (my translation).

[23] Giovanni di Pagolo Morelli, *Ricordi*, ed. V. Branca (Florence: Felice Le Monnier, 1969), 256 (my translation).

[24] John M. Najemy, "*Arti* and *Ordini* in Machiavelli's *Istorie fiorentine*," in *Essays Presented to Myron P. Gilmore*, vol. I: *History*, ed. Sergio Bertelli and Gloria Ramakus (Florence: La Nuova Italia, 1978), 161–91.

politics in the *Histories*.[25] In a work that (beginning with book II) surveys the history of Florence from the middle of the thirteenth century to 1402 – the century and a half in which the guilds were at the center of Florentine political and constitutional developments – the only context in which Bruni acknowledges their leading role is the revolution of 1378 that he presents as the most dangerous moment of the city's turbulent history. Otherwise he ignores them, even in discussing the events of the 1290s and 1340s in which they had a decisive part. His purpose in this strategy was, clearly, to dissociate the guilds and their propensity to challenge the authority of the elite from what he wished to represent as the mainstream tradition of respectable politics dominated by the upper-class families: a "tradition" – still quite precariously in the process of consolidation around 1400 – of civic unity and social consensus, of deference toward the republic's "natural" leaders from those same upper-class families, and of a political morality in which a citizen's worthiness was a function of dutiful acceptance of this leadership, and not of the promotion of the interests or rights of any group. Bruni sought to delegitimate the older guild republican notion that accepted the existence of different and legitimately contrasting social, economic, or political interests. It was because the guilds had sustained such a conception of politics in Florence that they had to be written out of Florentine history.

Bruni's recasting of Florentine history no doubt reflected the attitudes of the elite families that loathed the memory of 1378. But it also served the more complex needs of the class of nonelite major guildsmen that had been frightened away, by the same memory of 1378, from its former attachment to guild republicanism into a posture of awkward submission to the very elite families that they (or their fathers and grandfathers) had tenaciously opposed for over a century. In the generation after the last guild government of 1378–82, these nonelite major guildsmen finally and definitively chose alliance with the elite as preferable to what they now saw as the unacceptable risks of further revivals of the guild republic in coalitions with minor guildsmen and with all those workers who still wanted guilds – and thus a voice – of their own. As the political reforms of the 1380s, 1390s, and beyond eliminated the artisan and working classes from any significant role in communal politics,[26] diminished the political

---

[25] On Bruni's *Histories* and their contribution to the formation of an ideology of state sovereignty, see Riccardo Fubini, "La rivendicazione di Firenze della sovranità statale e il contributo delle 'Historiae' di Leonardo Bruni," in *Leonardo Bruni cancelliere*, 29–62.

[26] See Brucker, *Civic World*, chap. 2, 60–101.

clout of the guilds,[27] and consolidated the leadership of the elite families,[28] the nonelite major guildsmen were offered in effect an unofficial compact according to which they would be included, collectively, in larger numbers than ever before, in the ranks of communal office-holders in return for renouncing, once and for all, any temptation to ally with the rest of the guild community in movements of opposition to the elite. They thus accepted occasional election to prestigious offices as the reward – or consolation prize – for relinquishing any real share of power.[29]

Participation without power was the central feature of the compact that overturned traditional assumptions about the nature of political participation in Florence. It thus needed, and engendered, a justification and rationalization that in due course became the ideology of civic humanism. From this perspective, civic humanism did not originate in this or that text of Coluccio Salutati or Leonardo Bruni. It had its beginnings in the changing attitudes toward political participation in the class of nonelite major guildsmen, the class whose deferential acquiescence in the hegemony of the elite was the foundation of the new configuration of Florentine politics and society in the decades around 1400. The elite of course welcomed and applauded these attitudes, but the true believers in the civic humanist ethic of citizenship came not so much from the ruling class as from the nonelite members of the office-holding class over several generations from the late fourteenth to the mid-fifteenth century: from men like Marchionne di Coppo Stefani (1336–85?), Gregorio Dati (1362–1435), and Giovanni di Pagolo Morelli

[27] See my *Corporatism and Consensus*, chap. 8, 263–300.
[28] The best profile of this elite in the first and second decades of the fifteenth century is in Brucker, *Civic World*, chap. 5, 248–318. Dale Kent provides an analysis of comparable value for the 1420s and 1430s in "The Florentine *Reggimento* in the Fifteenth Century," *Renaissance Quarterly* 28 (1975): 575–638.
[29] The numbers of citizens nominated for the Signoria rose from approximately 3,500 in the mid-fourteenth century to 5,350 in 1382, 6,310 in 1391, and 6,354 in 1433 (even though the city's population was significantly lower in the early fifteenth century than it had been in the second half of the fourteenth century). The results of the scrutiny process that approved candidates were an official secret, a feature of the system that allowed hundreds, perhaps thousands, of citizens to nourish the hope that they had been or would some day be approved. In fact, after a slight decline in the 1390s, the numbers of those approved in the scrutinies also rose dramatically in the early fifteenth century: approximately 875 in 1382; 677 in 1391; 619 in 1393; 1,069 in 1411; and 2,084 in 1433. But even before this explosion in the number of approved office-holders, the policy of a wide distribution of offices within the upper class is already apparent. Between March 1382 and the end of 1399 the 963 available posts in the Signoria (nine in each two-month term of office) were held by 898 individuals from 589 families. Eighty-four percent of the posts were held by 822 individuals who made only one appearance in the Signoria in these eighteen years. Never before in any period of comparable length were the seats in this office so widely distributed. For these data and the electoral reforms that produced them, see my *Corporatism and Consensus*, chap. 8, 263–300.

(1371–1444), and later figures like Matteo Palmieri (1406–75) and Marco Parenti (1422–97). Although some (like Dati) were merchants who achieved an imposing level of wealth, these were *not* men from the elite of great families. But they did rub elbows with the elite in the same guilds, and occasionally in the same offices of the republic, and even now and then married into the elite (although it is worth noting that in two cases – Giovanni Morelli's marriage to Caterina Alberti and Marco Parenti's marriage to Caterina degli Strozzi – the alliances were with exiled families of the elite). The ethic of civic duty and republican liberty to which these men subscribed functioned as a consolation for what they and their class had lost, as a rationalization for their submission to the elite, and thus as a legitimation of the elite's hegemony.

It has not been sufficiently recognized that the ideal of the *vita activa civilis* that we find both in these writers and in Leonardo Bruni was at its core an ethic of dutiful passivity. Far from encouraging the active pursuit of glory or political ambition, the image of the good citizen that they created was of one who suppresses his own ambition, who steadfastly exhibits deference toward the *reggimento* (or, simply, those who govern), whose willingness to cooperate borders on unquestioning obedience, and who has no ideas or policies or interests to promote or defend in the civic arena. On the occasion of his selection for one of the executive committees of government in 1412, Gregorio Dati commented as follows in his diary: "I feel I have received a very great favor, and I would have been satisfied if by some arrangement I could have been certain of being elected just once to one of the executive committees. If I had been able to know this for certain, I would not have wished for anything more. Therefore, in order not to appear ungrateful, and not wishing to stimulate an insatiable ambition [*appetito*] which, the more it gets, only wants still more, I have decided and resolved that from now on I must never implore the favors of anyone to secure [any office] . . . I will instead leave such matters to those who oversee them [*lasciare fare a chi fia sopracciò*], and let happen to me whatever may please God. Henceforth, whenever my name is drawn for any communal or guild office, I promise to obey and not to refuse the burden, and to do as well as I can and know how. In this way I will ward off the vice of ambition and presumption [*il vizio della ambizione e del presumere di me*], and I will live as a free man not bound by the necessity of seeking favors [*viverò libero e non servo per prieghi*]."[30]

[30] Gregorio Dati, *Il libro segreto*, ed. Carlo Gargiolli (Bologna, 1869), 72–3. Although portions of Dati's diary, including this passage, are excellently translated by Julia Martines in *Two Memoirs of Renaissance Florence: The Diaries of Buonaccorso Pitti and Gregorio Dati*, ed. Gene Brucker (New York: Harper and Row, 1967), I have here preferred to use my own translation. I have previously

As Dati saw himself, it was the stifling of his own ambition that made him a worthy citizen and free man and legitimated his selection for high office. All that he could offer in politics was his personal worth and virtue – his gratitude, lack of presumption, willingness to serve – and, of course, his submission to the will of "those who oversee" matters like scrutinies and elections. He had no point of view on political issues or policies; he represented no constituency or group; he did not come to office to shape or change things. He knew that he could advance in political life only by securing the favors of powerful patrons of the sort that he could never be, and he even admitted that to do so would make him a slave of ambition, a "servo per prieghi." So he resolved to steer clear of the hunt for patrons and to remain "free" – by his own definition, on the margins of the only kind of politics available to men of his class. But when Dati added that "should it happen that I do otherwise, I must penalize myself each time in the amount of two gold florins to be given to the poor," he must have been anticipating the impossibility of observing his own resolution and of not being a "servo" to the upper-class political bosses who are never directly mentioned, but are nonetheless very prominent, in this revealing passage.

Giovanni Morelli's advice about politics turns entirely on the necessity of playing the game that Dati wished he could avoid. Whether through marriage alliances or friendship, he thought it essential to "lean on someone in the ruling group [*fa . . . che tu t'appoggi a chi è nel reggimento*], some powerful Guelf who is well thought of and free of suspicion . . . Make him your friend by speaking well of him, helping him wherever you can, by going up to meet him and offering your services." One should cultivate such powerful men by asking their advice and inviting them to one's home. "Beyond this, always stand by those who hold and possess the palace and the rule of our city [*tieni sempre con chi tiene e possiede il palagio e la signoria*], and obey and follow their wishes and commands. Keep yourself from denouncing or speaking evil of their undertakings and actions, even if they are harmful. Stay silent, and depart from your

commented on Dati's reflections on his election to office in *Corporatism and Consensus*, 301–3. On Dati and his political ideas, see Claudio Varese, "Una 'Laudatio Florentinae Urbis': La 'Istoria di Firenze' di Goro Dati," in Varese's *Storia e politica nella prosa del Quattrocento* (Turin: Einaudi, 1961), 65–91. And on Dati's *Istoria di Firenze*, which recounts the Florentine war with Milan in a very patriotic key, see Baron, *The Crisis* (1966), 167–88; Louis Green, *Chronicle into History: An Essay on the Interpretation of History in Fourteenth-Century Florentine Chronicles* (Cambridge: Cambridge University Press, 1972), 112–44; Andrew P. McCormick, "Toward a Reinterpretation of Goro Dati's *Storia di Firenze*," *Journal of Medieval and Renaissance Studies* 13 (1983): 227–50; and Antonio Lanza, *Firenze contro Milano (1390–1440)* (Anzio: De Rubeis, 1991), 86–96. Lanza very usefully reprints (ibid., 211–98), but with some changes, the text of Dati's *Istoria* from the older edition of L. Pratesi (Norcia, 1904).

silence only to praise them." Morelli thinks it advisable even to refuse to listen to anything spoken "contro a chi regge," and to avoid the company of anyone who is "male contento." One should immediately and without second thoughts report to the government authorities any words that one hears spoken against them.[31] His loyal support for the leadership of the "buoni uomini antichi di Firenze" was accompanied by an expression of frank dislike of "parvenus, guildsmen, and people of modest stature [*gente veniticcia, artefici e di piccolo affare*]," for whom he wished "wealth, peace, and happy concord," but whose "reggimento" he did not like – an allusion to the regime of 1378–82 – "although having them to a certain degree mixed in is good for restraining excessively ambitious spirits."[32] After recounting the suppression of the anti-government conspiracy of 1400, Morelli adds: "I have recalled these events... so that every descendant of ours may take this as an example and never do anything against any *istato o reggimento*, being happy instead to support the wishes of our rulers, and especially to place himself in the hands of men of worth from old Guelf families [*sendo nelle mani degli uomini da bene, antichi e guelfi*], for you see the harm and the shame that follow one who seeks to do otherwise."[33]

These are the very qualities that Bruni will associate with the ideal of virtuous citizenship in the *Life of Dante* – an ideal that even Bruni's Dante falls short of. According to Bruni, Dante "left aside nothing of cultural and civic affairs" and "was frequently employed in affairs of the Republic." He emphasizes in particular that Dante "fought valorously for his native land" at the battle of Campaldino, which Bruni initially presents as a struggle between Florentines and Aretines (until he has to admit that Ghibellines from both cities were fighting Guelfs from both cities). The effect is to make Dante a man of no faction or party. The only policy or opinion that Bruni attributes to him in the factional wars of 1300–1302 that led to Dante's exile is that the priors sought to defend themselves against the armed bands of both factions. Bruni suggests that Dante was trying to remain neutral between the parties, even as circumstances began to identify him more closely with the faction of the White Guelfs.

The account that Bruni gives of Dante's exile is especially telling. At first, here too he gives us Dante the model citizen, who was in Rome as

---

[31] Morelli, *Ricordi*, 274–6.
[32] Ibid., 196: "ma non gli piacque in tutto il loro reggimento, ma sì in alcuna cosa mescolato, ch'è buono per raffrenare li animi troppo grandi."
[33] Ibid., 377.

an envoy to the pope "in order to offer the agreement and peace of his citizens," while back in Florence Black Guelf partisans were destroying his house and property. Then came the order of banishment, promulgated under "a perverse and iniquitous law." But in exile Dante began to engage in riskier kinds of conduct. Although "he tried with good works and good behavior to win the favor that would allow him to return to Florence [*cercando con buone opere e con buoni portamenti racquistar la grazia di poter tornare in Firenze*]," when the new emperor Henry VII came to Italy to restore imperial power, "Dante could not maintain his resolve to wait for favor, but rose up in his proud spirit and began to speak ill of those who were ruling the land [*cominciò a dir male di quei che reggevano la terra*], calling them villainous and evil and menacing them with their due punishment through the power of the emperor ... Then Henry died ... and Dante entirely lost all hope, since he himself had closed the way of a change of favor by having spoken and written against the citizens who were governing the Republic [*perocchè di grazia lui medesimo s'aveva tolta la via per lo sparlare e scrivere contro i cittadini, che governavano la repubblica*], and there remained no force to support his desires."[34]

In this way Bruni makes Dante himself responsible, despite the injustice of the original decree of banishment, for the fact that the exile became permanent. The implicit assumption behind the judgment that his error consisted in having "spoken ill of those who were ruling the city" is that even in exile, even in an unjust exile, the citizen owed respect, deference, and obedience not only to his republic, but also to those who ruled it.[35] Here again the good citizen is passive, loyal even to the point of turning a blind eye to the injustices perpetrated against himself by those in power. Bruni's Dante failed to follow the advice of Giovanni Morelli and thus brought on himself the indefinite extension of his exile. Bruni seems to imply that the Florentine ruling class need not have felt any guilt over the fact that the city's greatest poet died in exile. The *Vita di Dante* dates from 1436, and the passage on Dante's exile may have been intended as a cautionary tale for the new generation of exiles created by the victory of the Medici faction in 1434. Palla Strozzi,

---

[34] Text in Hans Baron, *Leonardo Bruni Aretino: Humanistisch-Philosophische Schriften* (Leipzig: Teubner, 1928), 50–69, and 57–8 for the passages on Dante's exile; translation by Alan F. Nagel in *The Humanism of Leonardo Bruni: Selected Texts*, ed. G. Griffiths, J. Hankins, and D. Thompson (Binghamton: Medieval and Renaissance Texts and Studies and the Renaissance Society of America, 1987), 85–95 and 90–1.

[35] For an illuminating discussion of the development of Stoic attitudes of resignation in the "art of accepting exile," in the wider theater of fifteenth-century Italian politics, see Randolph Starn, *Contrary Commonwealth: The Theme of Exile in Medieval and Renaissance Italy* (Berkeley: University of California Press, 1982).

one of the most notable of these exiles, became legendary for his absolute loyalty to the rulers of Florence and for his refusal to utter a harsh word against the government or the Medici in thirty years of patiently suffered injustice.[36]

The characteristic posture of civic humanism's dutiful and subservient citizen is one of respectful distance from those who exercise power – the factions, patrician families, and patrons – and of isolation from all the many others like himself who must try to win the favor of the powerful or at least minimize the capacity of the latter to inflict harm on him. The good citizen never belongs to, or represents, a group. He is sometimes figured as representing the entire community – as in the case of Dante in war or diplomacy – but never as a spokesman for others like himself. His claim to a role in politics comes therefore to rest entirely and exclusively on his personal worth – on his virtue – and not on the extent to which he represents the voices or interests of some constituency. The growing emphasis on the link between virtue and political participation – one of the central ideas of civic humanism and a crucial point of intersection between the civic traditions of the medieval communes and the *studia humanitatis* grounded in Roman moral philosophy – needs to be understood as a crucial substitution of the operative criteria for the distribution of honors and offices. In place of the older guild republican idea that citizens merited their offices because they were elected by their constituencies and because they represented the collective interests of the latter, civic humanism embraced the idea that citizens became worthy of election when they demonstrated a sufficient level of personal virtue. The importance of this for the class relations underlying the configuration of political power in Florence is clear: the ruling elite had recognized the necessity of expanding the ranks of the office-holders in order to broaden the consensus around their hegemony, but they were willing to do so only if the hundreds and eventually thousands of nonelite office-holders accepted their posts as a recognition of, and reward for, personal merit and thus loyalty to their patrons, and not as an opportunity to represent the interests of their class. The politics

[36] See the portrait of Palla in the *Vite* of Vespasiano da Bisticci, ed. A. Greco, 2 vols. (Florence: Istituto Nazionale di Studi sul Rinascimento, 1976), II: 139–65. Vespasiano recalls that when other Florentine rebels or exiles went to visit Palla, "he dismissed them, did not wish to speak with them, and wanted no one to speak of the city in his house except with respect [*et della sua città non voleva che se ne parlassi in casa sua, se non onoratamente*]." A Florentine ambassador who visited Palla in exile was astonished "at his courage and to see him in good spirits and never complaining about the exile or the misfortunes he had suffered. He hardly seemed a man exiled from his country [*de la sua constantia lo viderlo istare di bonissima voglia, et mai dolersi dello esilio né di cose averse ch'egli avessi, ma pareva ch'egli non fusse quello exule della sua patria*]"; ibid., 161.

of virtue delegitimated and supplanted the politics of class and collective interests.

The connection between virtue and the taming of class antagonisms can be seen in a revealing passage in book 3 of Matteo Palmieri's *Vita civile*.[37] Palmieri defines his overall purpose as that of "showing the approved way of life of virtuous citizens [*monstrare l'approvata vita de' civili virtuosi*]."[38] In book 3, following several pages on the importance of civic unity and the evils of factional divisions, Palmieri's spokesman Agnolo Pandolfini begins a discussion of distributive justice. Among the tasks of this kind of justice, he says, the first is that of "equitably conferring offices in the public sphere [*Questa in publico prima gl'honori equalmente conferisce*] . . . It is according to the dignity of each man that public honors should be distributed." Realizing perhaps that this needed more definition, Palmieri acknowledges that contrasting concepts of dignity have been held by different social groups. In language that evokes Florence's tumultuous political past, he writes that "It is a difficult thing in a republic to prove who has more dignity, since among the people there has been much disagreement on the matter. The nobles and the powerful say that dignity resides in great wealth and in ancient and magnanimous families. The *popolari* [say that it consists] in the civility and friendly sociability of free and peaceful life [in a community]. Wise men say it consists in active virtue. Let those whose responsibility it will be to distribute offices in the city follow the most approved advice and give these offices to the most virtuous persons. For . . . nothing is more worthy among men than the virtue of those who work for the public good."[39] Palmieri is here clearly alluding to the long struggle between the elite families and the *popolo*. He quickly summarizes their contrasting views of the "dignity" that renders citizens worthy of high office: the patrician emphasis on wealth and ancient lineage, and the popular preference for the collective values of broadly shared sociability. But

---

[37] For an extensive and up-to-date bibliography on Palmieri, see Alessandra Mita Ferraro's introduction to her edition and translation of the *De captivitate Pisarum* in Matteo Palmieri, *La presa di Pisa* (Naples: Istituto Italiano per gli Studi Storici and the Società Editrice Il Mulino, 1995), vii–xxxiii. Mita Ferraro dates the composition of the *Vita civile* to the years 1434–7: ibid., xvii.

[38] Matteo Palmieri, *Vita civile*, ed. G. Belloni (Florence: Sansoni, 1982), 7.

[39] Ibid., 136: "Difficile cosa è in ella republica provare di cui [=chi] sia la degnità magiore, però che di quella infra il popolo variamente si dissente: e nobili et potenti dicono la degnità essere posta nelle abondanti facultà et nelle famiglie generose et antiche, i popolari nella humanità et benigna conversatione del libero et pacifico vivere, e savi dicono nella operativa virtù. Coloro che nella città aranno a distribuire gl'honori, seguitando il più approvato consiglio, quegli sempre ne' più virtuosi conferischino, però che . . . niuna cosa sarà mai più degna fra gl'huomini che la virtù di chi per publica utilità se exercita."

Palmieri decides for neither of these opinions; to do so would be to take sides in the greatest of the "civil discords" that had, as he believes, plagued Florence. Instead he opts for the third opinion represented by those "wise men" who claim that "virtue" ought to be the decisive criterion for identifying the sort of dignity that merits elevation to high office.

Palmieri's approach implies that a proper appreciation of virtue, and of the way it qualifies citizens for political office, can make the social conflicts of the past irrelevant. He takes a dim view of citizens from aristocratic families who claim a right to public honors on the basis of their ancestors' accomplishments. Although he allows that where "the claims of virtue are equal, the man from a distinguished family is to be preferred [*preponendo sempre la nobiltà, quando sono pari virtù*]," Palmieri insists that "the man who seeks glory through the virtues of his forebears denudes himself of any claim to honor, and the man who uses up the fame of his ancestors is certainly wretched. Let him who merits honor give proof of himself, not of his family members." But he devotes the next two pages to examples from Roman history of men, not from the nobility but from the lower ranks of society, who rose to positions of great power and won the respect and admiration of their social betters: "The very wise ancients, who extended their empires so greatly, raised foreigners, workers, and men of the lowest condition to the highest positions of rulership when they recognized in them noteworthy excellence in virtue . . . Let no one disdain being governed by virtuous men from humble beginnings and unknown family origins . . . It would take a long time to recount those in Rome who, although humbly born, through their virtue alone gained the most honored ranks and splendidly adorned the republic."[40] The special pleading offered on behalf of the lowborn who attained great heights makes it clear that, in the moral economy of political virtue, those who rose from humble origins to achieve political power and glory, even if there were many of them, were and always would be the noteworthy exceptions. Given the context of class antagonism with which Palmieri introduces this subject, the force of the claim that virtue ought to be the defining element of eligibility to office, and that many lowborn men achieved prominence in Rome in this way, is that virtue is the *only* legitimate avenue to political participation for citizens of the popular classes. The lowborn gain office and honors exclusively through the recognition, by their

[40] Ibid., 137-8.

"natural" superiors, of their exceptional personal qualities. Such a definition of the relationship of virtue to political participation fits the purposes of the Florentine ruling elite quite nicely, even as it was a consoling fiction that helped the nonelite office-holders *not* to see their own political emasculation. Bruni had written something very similar just a few years before in the 1428 *Oration for the Funeral of Nanni Strozzi*: "The hope of attaining office and of raising oneself up is the same for all, provided only one put in effort and have talent and a sound and serious way of life. Virtue and probity are required of the citizens by our city [*Virtutem enim probitatemque in cive suo civitas nostra requirit*]. Anyone who has these two qualities is thought to be sufficiently well born to govern the republic."[41]

By the early fifteenth century both the elite and the *popolo* felt the need to deny the old history of their conflict: the elite, because they were winning the long struggle and needed the passive support – the consensus – of the nonelite to make their victory more secure; and the *popolo* because they had lost an old war and needed the favor of their new patrons in order to hold on to the consolation prize; and both, because they feared and loathed the working classes. The discourse of political virtue was a crucial element of this denial. Its purpose was to buttress the myth of civic unity, to promote the notion of the republic as a single harmonious entity, and thus to suppress the legitimacy of claims of separate collective interests – of class, difference, dissent, and political conflict. Everywhere in the civic humanist texts we find the insistence on the fundamental homogeneity and unity of the republic. Here too the roots are in the characteristic assumptions of the politics of the 1380s and 1390s: for example, in the declaration by the *balìa* of 1382 – the plenipotentiary body that dismantled the popular regime of 1378–82 – that "the things that need to be done can in no way be carried out without the full, total, and absolute power and authority of the whole Florentine people . . . and that this authority cannot legally be obtained, nor the will of the people requested, especially given the custom observed by the Florentine people in the past, except by a *parlamento* and convocation to the same of the whole Florentine people and by a general assembly."[42] As I

---

[41] Translation by Gordon Griffiths in *The Humanism of Leonardo Bruni*, 124. The Latin original of this passage is provided by Baron, *Crisis* (1966), 556.
[42] Florence, Archivio di Stato, Balìe, 17, f. 5: "et quod ea que expediunt nullo modo exequi valent sine plenaria, libera, totali et absoluta potestate et auctoritate totius populi florentini . . . et quod huiusmodi auctoritas juridice haberi non valet nec voluntatis exquisitio, maxime considerato more in populo florentino hactenus observato, nisi per viam parlamenti et convocationis ad parlamentum totius populi florentini et per adunantiam generalem."

have noted elsewhere,[43] general assemblies of the "whole Florentine people" had not in fact been part of the popular movement's constitutional program, which was grounded instead in the corporate representation of the guilds. The emphasis on the wholeness and oneness of the people, which gained strength toward the end of the fourteenth century, aimed at undermining the popular vision of the republic as a federation of independent parts and separate collective voices.

The assumption of a fundamental unity among all Florentines was of course wishful thinking, but the kind of wishful thinking that powerfully affects political behavior. Commenting on the electoral scrutiny of 1404, Giovanni Morelli noted that the results of the balloting displeased some members of the ruling group, "because of the suspicions they had of many *popolani* whom they did not consider their friends." The suspect *popolani* to whom he refers may have included Morelli himself, who, after many years of being passed over in the scrutinies, was at long last approved for high office in the 1404 scrutiny, and subsequently drawn for the executive college of the Sixteen Gonfalonieri in 1409.[44] They "need not have such suspicions," Morelli continues, "because the only reason one becomes an enemy of, or dislikes, the ruling group is if one does not belong to that good that is [held in] common [or, that good that is the commune: *se non perché e' non fa parte di quello bene che è comune*]. I do not mean one who takes it [the office] for his own evil purposes, but one who has conducted and continues to conduct himself well [*chi ha fatto e fa buoni portamenti*]. Such a person should not be held in contempt nor deprived of his honor. If you do these things to him, he will have every reason to hate you."[45] Morelli refused to see his exclusion from office before 1409 as the result of larger political or social conflicts. He could not imagine himself as representing interests or ideas opposed to those of the oligarchy. He saw his misfortune as personal, as the result of a marriage alliance[46] that deprived him for a time of his part in "quello

---

[43] "The Dialogue of Power in Florentine Politics," in *City-States in Classical Antiquity and Medieval Italy*, ed. A. Molho, K. Raaflaub, and J. Emlen (Ann Arbor: University of Michigan Press, 1991), 279–80, n. 23.

[44] On the 1404 scrutiny, see Renzo Ninci, "Lo 'Squittino del Mangione': il consolidamento legale di un regime (1404)," *Bullettino dell'Istituto Storico Italiano per il Medio Evo e Archivio Muratoriano* 94 (1988): 155–250. Morelli records his election to the Sixteen in *Ricordi*, 532.

[45] Morelli, *Ricordi*, 430.

[46] He married Caterina d'Alberto di Luigi Alberti in 1395, two years after the Alberti had suffered a major political defeat at the hands of the Albizzi faction. He comments: "I believe that this marriage alliance has deprived me of much honor which I might have had from the commune if I had married into another family as I could have [*Credo che 'l detto parentado m'abbia tolto assai onore per avventura arei avuto dal mio Comune, se avesse imparentato con altre famiglie, come arei potuto*]"; ibid., 341.

bene che è comune." In any case, he believed that his "buoni portamenti" had finally proven his worth and rewarded him with his small place in the political sun. The conclusion he drew from this experience was not about the abyss that separated him from the powerbrokers in the *reggimento*. It was rather about the importance of being a team player and the victories that the acceptance of such a role makes possible: "I have recalled this in order to inform you of the methods one should employ to acquire the honor that the commune accords its citizens: doing good, obeying the laws, paying honor to the officials of the commune, to particularly respected citizens, to men of ancient families, and to persons of worth. The good deeds of your ancestors will make you known to such persons, will recommend you to them, and will keep you in their memory."[47] This is the very stuff of the consensus politics at the center of civic humanism. Morelli wants to see only the harmonious whole, and his "good conduct" – his political quiescence, his willingness to pay honor to the very oligarchs who had kept him on the sidelines – proved to him that virtue would in the end merit honor.[48]

Such attitudes underlie civic humanism's horror of political conflict. The texts abound with denunciations of factionalism and praise of civil concord. In the *Vita civile* Palmieri says that a citizen elected to any office must know that he is no longer a "privata persona": he now "represents the universal person of the whole city and has become a living republic [*rapresentare l'universale persona di tutta la città, et essere facta animata republica*]." He must know that the "public dignity has been entrusted to him and the common good left to his good faith." He must imprint in his mind Plato's admonition, as reported by Cicero in the *De officiis*, to preserve the "whole body of the republic in such a way that, as he defends one part, he does not abandon the others ... The condition and stability of every republic rest in civic unity [*Lo stato e fermamento d'ogni republica è posto nella unione civile*]." And "anyone who departs from this [precept] and attends to the well-being of individual citizens, and abandons the rest, sows scandal and grievous conflicts in the city, from which, with the citizens often divided amongst themselves, strife and civil wars result ...

[47] Ibid., 431: "Di questo ho fatto memoria none ad altra fine se non per informarvi de' modi si vogliono tenere 'acquistare l'onoranza dà il Comune a' suoi cittadini: cioè con fare bene, ubbidire alle leggi, rendere onore agli ufficiali del Comune, a' cittadini molto onorati, agli uomini antichi e alle persone da bene: e a loro ti dà a conoscere, a loro ti raccomanda e ricorda l'operazione buone de' tuoi passati."

[48] On Morelli, see Claudio Varese's two essays, "I 'Ricordi' di Giovanni Morelli," I and II, in *Storia e politica*, 37 64; Christian Bec, *Les marchands écrivains à Florence, 1375–1434* (Paris: Mouton, 1967), 53 75; and Richard C. Trexler, *Public Life in Renaissance Florence* (New York: Academic Press, 1980), 159 86.

The end brings exiles, insurrections, slavery, and final destruction." Palmieri cites examples of ancient states that came to ruin because of civil conflicts, and about Florence he says that, although "it would perhaps be better to pass over in silence rather than recount the afflictions and miseries that have accompanied our city because of civil conflicts and quarrels," it is in fact useful to recall such things in order to ward off similar evils in the future. The brief history he provides of Florentine partisan conflicts, from the Guelfs and Ghibellines in the thirteenth century to the Black and White Guelfs in the early fourteenth century, proves, he says, that internal conflict has too often led to appeals by one or the other party to foreign princes for protection and to the loss of "la libertà, lo stato, et publica maiestà." Thus, those who possess "la dolce libertà" – the independence of Florence from foreign control – should learn from the examples of states that have been ruined by internal conflicts to resist and repair their own.[49] Liberty, understood as independence from foreigners, is here invoked to strengthen the frequent warnings against class conflict and to make even more urgent the exhortations to social harmony and civic unity. The argument that class and factional conflicts at home made the republic more vulnerable to foreign tyrants underscored the virtues of civic unity and social consensus as the standards by which good citizens were identified and measured. Here indeed was one of the links between foreign policy and civic humanism.

Bruni similarly emphasized unity and consensus. We have already seen his ferocious denunciation in the *Histories* of the conflicts of 1378. Many years earlier in the *Laudatio*, he had acknowledged that even the best governed cities have some "evil men." But "the perversity and evil of a few ought not to deprive an entire nation of being praised for its virtuous deeds." He distinguishes between "public and private crimes": the latter result from the "intentions of the individual wrong-doer," the former from the "will of the entire city [*universe civitatis voluntas*]." Here again is the assumption that an entire city has a single will, which is found by "following what has been hallowed by law and tradition [*legibus ac moribus sancitum sit*]," and "usually the entire city follows what the majority of the citizen-body would like. While in other cities the majority often overturns the better part, in Florence it has always happened that the majority view has been identical with the best citizens [*Sed in aliis quidem populis maior pars sepe meliorem vincit; in hac autem civitate*

---

[19] Palmieri, *Vita civile*, 131–6.

eadem semper videtur fuisse melior que maior]."[50] The force of Bruni's assertion that "the majority view" is "identical with [that of] the best citizens" is that the "best citizens," which he of course identifies with the ruling elite, are the ones responsible for shaping that view. Bruni merges the "single will" of the city with "what has been hallowed by law and tradition," and both of these with the views of the "melior pars" of leading citizens. His mistrust of the lower orders ("the good qualities of a few men cannot really free the foolish and perverse mob from its infamy"[51]) leads him to privilege the authority of the republic's "natural" leaders from good patrician families.

A similar fear of the lower classes had earlier led Stefani to idealize the order and rationality, and thus the inevitable leadership, of the elite families. His reaction against the unwelcome sight of organized workers led him, not only to deny that artisans and laborers were capable of any political order or rational decision-making, but also to praise the "wisdom, gentility, and order" of those he called the *grandi*. He particularly admired the way (he thought) they arrived at decisions among themselves: "it is easy to bring about agreement among the great families of wisdom, gentility, and order, who revere the wisest person of their line or, at the most, the wisest few [*li Grandi di senno, di gentilezza, d'ordine e le famiglie, che hanno sempre reverenza a uno il più savio del loro legnaggio, o a pochi, è poco accordare*]." Precisely because there were "fewer of them to be convened and consulted," they were able to discuss their affairs and bring into harmony "la volontà degli appetiti."[52] Upper-class lineages may not in reality have made their common decisions in quite so orderly and hierarchical a fashion,[53] but the importance of Stefani's opinion is that in it we see the beginnings of a tendency to idealize the patrician families of Florence as models on which citizens could construct an ideological image of the communal constitution. In the minds of nonelite members of the political class, like Stefani, the elite families began to represent even in their private

---

[50] *Laudatio Florentinae urbis*, in Hans Baron, *From Petrarch to Bruni* (Chicago: University of Chicago Press, 1968), 250; translation by B. G. Kohl in "Panegyric to the City of Florence," in *The Earthly Republic: Italian Humanists on Government and Society*, ed. B. G. Kohl and R. G. Witt (Philadelphia: University of Pennsylvania Press, 1978), 158.
[51] *Laudatio*, in Baron, *From Petrarch to Bruni*, 250; "Panegyric," in *The Earthly Republic*, 158.
[52] Stefani, *Cronaca*, 194.
[53] At least not in the thirteenth century: see Carol Lansing, *The Florentine Magnates: Lineage and Faction in a Medieval Commune* (Princeton: Princeton University Press, 1991). But F. W. Kent believes that in the fifteenth century some of the patrician families may have held frequent meetings to discuss matters of common interest; see his *Household and Lineage in Renaissance Florence* (Princeton: Princeton University Press, 1977), 238–46.

behavior an alternative vision of the political community based on the assumption that power should be held by the experienced few and confirmed by the passive but willing consensus of those who recognize those few as benevolent fathers to the whole civic family. In civic humanist thought, the family replaces the guild, or corporation, as the conceptual model for the republic. The republic is no longer a fraternity of equals, whose task is to create authority out of equality. Increasingly the republic is now seen as a kind of family, even a lineage, in which authority naturally belongs to experienced elders, which is to say, to the fathers of the best families.

Again, Bruni appropriates these themes and transforms them from a set of political attitudes into a moral and educational program. In the *Laudatio* he writes of the Florentine constitution that "under these magistracies this city has been governed with such diligence and competence that one could not find better discipline even in a household ruled by a solicitous father [*Sub his igitur magistratibus ita diligens et preclara est huius urbis gubernatio ut nulla unquam domus sub frugi patre familias maiori disciplina fuerit instituta*]."[54] This family-like republic is to be judged by the standards of the kind of paternal discipline that one expects to find in the household of a "solicitous father." Bruni's republic is a family writ large, in which "discipline" – culture, learning, and education – serves the program of virtue by preparing the individual to assume his place as a citizen. But it also serves the needs of power by reinforcing the authority of fathers and patricians. As the son is formed in the image of the father, so the citizen is to be shaped in the mold of "what has been hallowed by law and tradition." Education, and thus citizenship, have become theaters of socialization in the consensus that sustains the hegemony of the ruling elite. In the *Life of Dante* Bruni underscores the social dimension of education. When Dante devoted himself to studies, he "left aside nothing of cultural and civil affairs. It is a marvelous thing that although he was studying continuously, yet it would never have seemed to anyone that he studied, because of his pleasant habits and youthful conversation." Bruni further insists that the "studious life" is also fully compatible with marriage and family, as are both with the responsibilities of citizenship. What particularly irritates Bruni is the suggestion that the life of study ought to be conducted in "solitude and leisure . . . hidden away and removed from conversation with men."[55] It is not difficult to surmise that, for Bruni, the danger

---

[54] *Laudatio*, in Baron, *From Petrarch to Bruni*, 262; "Panegyric," in *The Earthly Republic*, 173.
[55] Text in Baron, *Leonardo Bruni Aretino*; translation by Nagel in *The Humanism of Leonardo Bruni*, 87.

posed by such isolated intellects is that they will not be properly socialized into the cultural and political consensus that sustains the structures of power. There is a sense in which Bruni's main point in the *Life* is that exile eroded Dante's participation in the "discipline" and thus the consensus that his studies, his family life, and his political role had earlier inculcated into him. He then became a critic, a dissenter from the very traditions of both culture and power that had created him, and, as such, a threat to the polity.

The family was the obvious and ideal metaphor for a republic that assumed the natural and benevolent leadership of experienced fathers, tolerated no opposition from its citizen/children, and conceived of citizenship in terms of training, education, and socialization into the virtues of the whole community as represented by its revered elders. Not for nothing, therefore, did Palmieri introduce his main speaker in the *Vita civile*, Agnolo Pandolfini, as an "older and well-educated citizen [*antico et bene admaestrato cittadino*]" who will hold forth on virtue and the civic life "quasi con dimestico ragionamento"[56] – which is to say, with an almost domestic, or family-like, kind of discourse or conversation. The elder Pandolfini answers the questions of two younger men. Seeking to inquire into the "arti" (skills) and "discipline" with which it is possible to secure the good life of "some fine republic," Palmieri proposes to collect from the literature of antiquity the "precepts appropriate for teaching [*precepti accommodati a admaestrare*] the best life of citizens."[57] The *Vita civile* is dedicated to Alessandro degli Alessandri, and at the end of the preface Palmieri explicitly weaves together citizenship, education, the moral authority of the paternal example, and the nobility and power of great families: "You [Alessandro] are born of noble stock, offspring of an excellent father, trained in the study of the good arts, adorned with good manners ... your good habits clearly show in you the firm intention to strive with merited praise to become an honored and excellent citizen."[58] Good son; good student; good citizen – the terms are almost interchangeable.

Bruni had already suggested in the *Laudatio* that the Florentines were both the sons of their city and of their Roman founders. The terms in which he does so point to certain anxieties embedded in the family romances (or dramas) into which the civic humanists were fond of inscribing their vision of Florence. "As we may see several sons with so great a resemblance to their parents [*tantam habere cum parentibus simili-*

---

[56] Palmieri, *Vita civile*, 7.   [57] Ibid., 4 5.   [58] Ibid., 9.

tudinem] that they show it obviously in their faces, so the Florentines are in such harmony with this very noble and outstanding city that it seems they could never have lived anywhere else. Nor could the city, so skillfully created, have had any other kind of inhabitants."⁵⁹ Cities do indeed shape their inhabitants, but this passage makes the Florentines sound like so many identical cookie-cutter citizen/children who could in no way have been different from one another or have been other than they were. Other anxieties emerge in passages that make the Florentines the sons of the Romans: "The fact that the Florentine race [*genus*] arose from the Roman people is of the utmost importance. What nation in the entire world was ever more distinguished, more powerful, more outstanding in every sort of excellence than the Roman people?" Such thoughts may indeed have stimulated a sense of pride, but what reaction could Florentines have had to Bruni's claim in the next sentence that the "deeds [of the Romans] are so illustrious that the greatest feats done by other men seem like child's play [*pueriles ludi*] when compared to the deeds of the Romans"? The civic humanist insistence on the Roman origins of Florentine republicanism (and in general on the Romans as the perfect model in all things for the Florentines) merges with the sense of the republic as a patrilineal family writ large in which the elders (or the elite) shape citizen/sons in their own image: "Now if the glory, nobility, virtue, grandeur, and magnificence of the parents can also make the sons outstanding, no people in the entire world can be as worthy of dignity as are the Florentines, for they are born from such parents who surpass by a long way all mortals in every sort of glory."⁶⁰ But how does one ever escape the tutelage of such perfect parents? And what if the sons do not measure up? Later in the text Bruni, perhaps not fully aware of just how much this vision of Roman fathers and Florentine sons exposes the element of oppressive patriarchy in the metaphor that made of the republic a patrilineal family, writes: "The same dignity and grandeur of the parent also illuminate its sons, since the offspring strive for their own virtue. And you may be sure that if the descendants had been cowardly or dissolute or had in any way fallen from virtue, the splendor of the ancestor would not so much have hidden their vices as it would have uncovered them. The light of parental glory leaves nothing unhidden; indeed, the expectation that the virtues of the parent will be reduplicated in the son

---

⁵⁹ *Laudatio*, in Baron, *From Petrarch to Bruni*, 233; "Panegyric," in *The Earthly Republic*, 136.
⁶⁰ *Laudatio*, in Baron, *From Petrarch to Bruni*, 244; "Panegyric," in *The Earthly Republic*, 149–50.

focuses all eyes on the offspring."⁶¹ Do such ideas unintentionally register the insecurities and anxieties of the politically infantilized nonelite members of the office-holding class who were, as I have suggested, the true believers of civic humanism?

Civic humanism was, I think, deeply conservative in its denial of the legitimacy of class interests and conflict and in its affirmation of a natural leadership of patrician fathers over their citizen/children. It may also have served as the intellectual foundation for a regime of conformity and surveillance⁶² in which the individual was allowed the status of citizen only insofar as he suppressed dangerous tendencies toward dissent or critical views of the ideological consensus. My answer to the question about whether the ideas of the civic humanists were rooted in the realities of Florentine politics and society would therefore begin with the observation that civic humanism was *not* a restatement of the central values of the popular republicanism of the thirteenth and fourteenth centuries. It was a new ideology that provided cultural, educational, historical, and moral buttressing for both the newly established hegemony of Florence's elite families and for the subordinate political and social status to which the middle ranks of Florentine society were now relegated. In this vision of things the elite families produced the wise fathers of the republic, devoted guardians of the best interests of all; the irony of their fate is that, in trying to make themselves *patres conscripti*, they made a *pater patriae*, and ultimately a prince. The middle-rank Florentines became their client/children, deprived, as the recent and well-illuminated example of Marco Parenti shows was still the case in the middle of the fifteenth century,⁶³ of any political voice and able only to go on repeating the platitudes of civic humanism: the fate also illustrated for us by the character Microtoxus in Alamanno Rinuccini's *De libertate*.⁶⁴ Civic hu-

⁶¹ *Laudatio*, in Baron, *From Petrarch to Bruni*, 248; "Panegyric," in *The Earthly Republic*, 155.
⁶² This notion is explored by Andrea Zorzi and Michael Rocke in two intriguing treatments of the proliferation in the early fifteenth century of government agencies with the power to investigate the private life of Florentines; see Zorzi's *L'amministrazione della giustizia penale* (Florence: Olschki, 1988), and Rocke's *Forbidden Friendships: Homosexuality and Male Culture in Renaissance Florence* (Oxford: Oxford University Press, 1996). See also my forthcoming article, "The Politics of Sex in Civic Humanist Florence."
⁶³ See Mark Phillips, *The Memoir of Marco Parenti: A Life in Medici Florence* (Princeton: Princeton University Press, 1987).
⁶⁴ *Dialogus de libertate*, ed F. Adorno, in *Atti e memorie dell'Accademia toscana di scienze e lettere "La Colombaria"*, 22 (1957): 270–303. English translation by Renée N. Watkins, in her *Humanism and Liberty: Writings on Freedom from Fifteenth-Century Florence* (Columbia, S.C.: University of South Carolina Press, 1978), 193–224.

manism was not merely professional rhetoric from the chancery. It was a whole complex of attitudes, assumptions, and values that, to be sure, did not simply mirror the "realities" of Florentine life. But it had a huge part in a profound transformation of Florentine politics and social relations from the late fourteenth century through the middle of the next century and beyond.

CHAPTER 4

The two myths of civic humanism

Mikael Hörnqvist

In the preamble to the new statutes of the Guelf party, composed around 1420, Leonardo Bruni solemnly proclaims that liberty is a value "without which no republic can survive, and without which wise men do not think life worth living."[1] The statement attests to the overriding importance of the idea of liberty within the Florentine republican tradition. Cherished as the heart and nerve of the public ethos animating the political life of the Italian city-states of the fourteenth and fifteenth centuries, liberty has, during the last thirty years, probably also been the most discussed and analyzed concept in Italian Renaissance studies.[2] Ever since the publication of Hans Baron's seminal work, *The Crisis of the Early Italian Renaissance* in 1955, scholarly orthodoxies have come to conceive of Florentine republicanism largely as an ideology of

I am grateful to James Hankins and Ken Gouwens for their advice and comments on the typescript.

[1] Quoted from *The Humanism of Leonardo Bruni: Selected Texts*, ed. G. Griffiths, J. Hankins, and D. Thompson (Binghamton: Center for Medieval and Early Renaissance Studies, 1987), 48.
[2] On the meaning and use of the term *libertas* or *libertà* in the Florentine Renaissance, see Nicolai Rubinstein, "Florentina Libertas," *Rinascimento*, n.s. 2 (1986): 3–26; Quentin Skinner, *The Foundations of Modern Political Thought*, 2 vols. (Cambridge: Cambridge University Press, 1978), I: 3–84, esp. 7 and 77–8; Skinner, "The Idea of Negative Liberty: Philosophical and Historical Perspectives," in *Philosophy in History: Essays on the Historiography of Philosophy*, ed. R. Rorty, J. B. Schneewind, and Q. Skinner (Cambridge: Cambridge University Press, 1984), 193–221; Skinner, *Liberty before Liberalism* (Cambridge: Cambridge University Press, 1998); J. G. A. Pocock, *The Machiavellian Moment: Florentine Political Thought and the Atlantic Republican Tradition* (Princeton: Princeton University Press, 1975), 142–3, 232 and passim. Pocock's view is summarized and synthesized in *Virtue, Commerce, and History: Essays on Political Thought and History Chiefly in the Eighteenth Century* (Cambridge: Cambridge University Press, 1985), 39–41. These accounts should be compared to Gennaro Sasso, "'Florentina libertas' e rinascimento italiano nell'opera di Hans Baron," *Rivista storica italiana* 69 (1957): 250–76; Marvin B. Becker, *Florence in Transition: Studies in the Rise of the Territorial State*, 2 vols. (Baltimore: Johns Hopkins University Press, 1967–8), II: 203–4; Ronald Witt, "The Rebirth of the Concept of Republican Liberty in Italy," in *Renaissance Studies in Honor of Hans Baron*, ed. A. Molho and J. A. Tedeschi (Florence: Sansoni, 1971), 175–99; Riccardo Fubini, "La rivendicazione di Firenze della sovranità statale e il contributo delle 'Historiae' di Leonardo Bruni," in *Leonardo Bruni, cancelliere della repubblica di Firenze*, ed. P. Viti (Florence: Olschki, 1990), 29–62; Paolo Viti, *Leonardo Bruni e Firenze: Studi sulle lettere pubbliche e private* (Rome: Bulzoni, 1992), 14–42. See also Alison Brown's contribution to this volume (chapter 6).

105

liberty.³ The political theorizing of early fifteenth-century Florentine humanists, the general argument goes, was centered around the ideal of republican liberty and the question of how it could best be promoted and preserved in the face of external aggression and threats from within. In order to relate the ideology to the historical context in which it is alleged to have developed, the image of Florence as a small and vulnerable city-state, bravely defending her liberty and free republican constitution against an outside world of powerful predatory states, has been forged. While most scholars today reject Baron's claim that this republican ideology – which he in a stroke of genius named *Bürgerhumanismus* or civic humanism – was born in Florence around 1402 in the immediate aftermath of the city's protracted war against Giangaleazzo Visconti of Milan, the great majority share his view that the republican liberty promoted by the Florentine prehumanists and civic humanists was purely, or mainly, defensive in character.⁴

The problematic nature of Baron's definition of civic humanism as an ideology of self-defense and peaceful coexistence became immediately apparent, though, when in the *Crisis* he was forced to comment on the Florentine republic's unprovoked assault and subjugation of Pisa in 1406.⁵ In this context, Baron contrasted the views of two politically noncommitted humanists, Roberto de' Rossi and Niccolò Niccoli, to those of the civic-minded Leonardo Bruni, the great promoter of the new movement Baron claimed to have discovered. Whereas Rossi on that occasion had voiced complaints about the vanity of political activity in general, and Niccoli condemned the Florentine aspiration for territorial expansion as a form of "childish madness" that eventually would bring ruin to the republic, Bruni was later to celebrate the triumph in his *Historiae Florentini Populi* (begun in 1415) as a milestone in Florence's rise

---

³ Hans Baron, *The Crisis of the Early Italian Renaissance: Civic Humanism and Republican Liberty in an Age of Classicism and Tyranny* (Princeton: Princeton University Press, 1966).
⁴ For this view of the republican tradition, see especially Quentin Skinner, *Foundations*, I: 3–189; Skinner. "The Vocabulary of Renaissance Republicanism: A Cultural Longue-durée?" in *Language and Images of Renaissance Italy*, ed. A. Brown (Oxford: Clarendon Press, 1995), 87–110; Nicolai Rubinstein, "Florentina libertas"; William J. Bouwsma, "Italy in the Late Middle Ages and the Renaissance," in *The New Encyclopedia Britannica*, 29 vols. (Chicago: Encyclopedia Britannica, 1987), XXII: 210–11; Maurizio Viroli, *From Politics to Reason of State: The Acquisition and Transformation of the Language of Politics, 1250–1600* (Cambridge: Cambridge University Press, 1992), 2–177. For Viroli's partial retraction of this view, see his *For Love of Country: An Essay on Patriotism and Nationalism* (Oxford: Clarendon Press, 1995), 29.
⁵ For Baron's claim that the idea of peaceful coexistence among free city-states was a Florentine and a civic humanist ideal, see Baron, *The Crisis*, 25–6, 30, 35, 45, 174, 185–6 and 368; Baron, *In Search of Florentine Civic Humanism: Essays on the Tradition from Medieval to Modern Thought*, 2 vols. (Princeton: Princeton University Press, 1988), I: 46 and 81–2.

to imperial greatness. In commenting on Bruni's and the merchant historian Gregorio Dati's view of the conquest of Pisa, Baron wrote: "Works like Dati's *Istoria* and Bruni's *Historiae Florentini Populi*, which took their initial inspiration from the consciousness that Florence by this act had finally made herself a region-state with its own coast and ports, show the important role which this experience played in the growth of a politically-minded civic Humanism with historical interests."[6] It seems that Baron was here, unwittingly and in open contradiction to his self-professed zeal for liberty and peaceful coexistence between independent states, defining civic humanism not only as a republican, but also as an imperialist project, albeit limited in scope. If Florence was to constitute itself as a competitive territorial state, Pisan liberty and the independence of other Tuscan city-states had to be sacrificed. Baron was thus legitimizing Florentine aggression without acknowledging that Florence on this occasion had acted towards Pisa in a way equivalent to the way Milan, according to Baron's own account, had acted towards Florence only four years earlier.[7]

Since Baron's idealistic and rather naïve conception of the political culture of fourteenth- and fifteenth-century Florence met early opposition from leading Renaissance historians, there is no need for us to rehearse here what are now tired controversies.[8] But while Baron's views of the political realities of the day should be allowed to rest in peace, we have all the more reason to examine how later scholarship has tried to reconcile his understanding of Florentine liberty with the indisputable facts of Florentine expansionism and imperialism. The most authoritative attempt in this direction has been furnished by Nicolai Rubinstein, whose discussion of the subject can be seen as representative of the prevailing view within the field today. According to Rubinstein, the idea of *Florentina libertas* was characterized by three distinctive features: freedom of speech, rule according to justice, and civic equality, understood both as equality under the law and as the chance for all citizens to take an active part in the government under which they live. In Rubinstein's view, this ideology of liberty should not be seen as an

[6] Baron, *The Crisis*, 324-5.
[7] Concerning Baron's failure to recognize the imperialist side of Florentine republicanism, see James Hankins, "The 'Baron Thesis' after Forty Years and some Recent Studies of Leonardo Bruni," *Journal of the History of Ideas* 56 (1995): 323.
[8] For a general overview of the early controversy surrounding Baron's thesis, see Albert Rabil, Jr, "The Significance of 'Civic Humanism' in the Interpretation of the Italian Renaissance," in *Renaissance Humanism: Foundations, Forms, and Legacy*, 3 vols. (Philadelphia: University of Pennsylvania Press, 1988), I: 141-74.

accurate or objective representation of Florentine political culture at the turn of the Quattrocento, as Baron had argued, but as a distant, and perhaps unrealizable, ideal. This ideal of true liberty had received its fullest articulation during the Visconti wars in the writings of the Florentine humanists in general, and in Leonardo Bruni's *Laudatio Florentinae urbis* (c. 1403–4) in particular. This latter work constitutes, in Rubinstein's view, "the first exhaustive presentation of the concept *Florentina libertas*."[9] How are we then to understand the fact that humanists like Coluccio Salutati, Leonardo Bruni, and Matteo Palmieri all served oligarchic regimes and refused to see a contradiction between the Florentine liberty they celebrated in their works and the city's expansionist policy? Rubinstein resolves the problem by arguing that the civic humanists, like most other citizens of Italian city-states of the time, simply considered territorial expansion to be a "natural political ambition of their state."[10] The idea of liberty can be weakened or corrupted by oligarchic or imperialist misuse, Rubinstein concedes. But since the civic humanists' unreflective and conventional acceptance of imperialism had little to do with their views on liberty, the Florentine republic's pursuit of empire did not compromise their ideological commitments. The burden of this argument, it seems, is that the relationship between liberty and empire in the Florentine context should be understood in terms of a conflict between ideology and political reality, between the high and lofty ideals of civic humanism and the low and messy world of policy-making and power politics. In Rubinstein's view, Florentine liberty and expansionism were, in other words, two different and theoretically unrelated phenomena.[11]

The present essay takes issue with this view of civic humanism as either opposed or unrelated to expansionism and the pursuit of empire. By arguing that the civic humanist notion of *Florentina libertas* was not

---

[9] Rubinstein, "Florentina libertas," 12.   [10] Ibid., 17.
[11] The view that Baron gave a correct definition of the civic humanist ideology but failed to account for the underlying political realities is also expressed in Gene Brucker, "Humanism, Politics and the Social Order in Early Renaissance Florence," in *Florence and Venice: Comparisons and Relations*, 2 vols., ed. S. Bertelli, N. Rubinstein, and C. H. Smyth (Florence: La Nuova Italia, 1979), I: 3 11; Ronald Witt, *Coluccio Salutati and His Public Letters* (Geneva: Librairie Droz, 1976), 42 88; Witt, "The Crisis after Forty Years," *American Historical Review* 101 (1996): 110 18. Baron's definition of Florentine liberty is also accepted in Nancy S. Struever, *The Language of History in the Renaissance: Rhetorical and Historical Consciousness in Florentine Humanism* (Princeton: Princeton University Press, 1970); Eugenio Garin, "Leonardo Bruni: politica e cultura," in *Leonardo Bruni, cancelliere della repubblica di Firenze*, 3 14; Antonio Lanza, *Firenze contro Milano: Gli intellettuali fiorentini nelle guerre con i Visconti (1390–1440)* (Rome: De Rubeis, 1991). Most of the articles collected in *Machiavelli and Republicanism*, ed. G. Bock, Q. Skinner, and M. Viroli (Cambridge: Cambridge University Press, 1990) also adhere to this basic view.

only compatible with Florentine territorial ambitions but inherently imperialist, it also moves beyond the claim that the concept was merely a propagandistic device designed to disguise Florentine aggression.[12] To put it simply, most Florentine humanists of the early Quattrocento were republican imperialists (or imperialist republicans) who subscribed to the idea of liberty at home and empire abroad. The reason why they did not see a contradiction between their love of liberty and their support for Florentine expansionism was not because they failed to relate them, as Rubinstein seems to imply, but because they considered them to constitute two interconnected and complementary sides of their republicanism, each aspect reinforcing the other. They had strong historical motives for thinking in this way. The powerful and extremely influential paradigm of the Roman republic taught that love of liberty, justice, and the common good could coexist comfortably with the pursuit of empire within a single ideological frame. In a quest for security, peace, and justice, the Romans had defended their liberty and conquered the world under the command of their gods.[13] This Roman perspective, which we find fully developed in Livy, Sallust, and Cicero, was transmitted to the Renaissance and appropriated by the Florentine humanists at the turn of the Quattrocento.

I will in the following argue that Florentine republicans from the Dugento to the early Cinquecento came to regard Florence, through a strong and intensely felt identification with the ancient Roman republic, as destined for imperial greatness and hegemonic rule over Tuscany, Italy, and, on occasion, even the entire world. A discussion of how liberty and empire are related in the thought of the leading civic humanists of the early Quattrocento will lead to the claim that the concept of civic humanism is in need of revision. The redefinition of civic humanism, I will argue, must be based on a radical rethinking of the meaning of Florentine liberty as well as a reevaluation of the role

[12] For the argument that the proclamations in the writings of the civic humanists should be dismissed as deceitful propaganda, see Peter Herde, "Politik und Rhetorik in Florenz am Vorabend der Renaissance," *Archiv für Kulturgeschichte* 47 (1965): 141–220; Herde, "Politische Verhaltensweisen der Florentiner Oligarchie, 1382–1402," in *Geschichte und Verfassungsgefüge: Frankfurter Festgabe für Walter Schlesinger* (Weisbaden: Steiner, 1973), 156–249; Michael Seidlmayer, *Wege und Wandlungen des Humanismus: Studien zu seinen politischen, ethischen, religiösen Problem* (Göttingen: Vandenhoeck and Ruprecht, 1965), 47–74.
[13] On the imperialism of the Roman republic in general, see Ernst Badian, *Roman Imperialism in the Late Republic* (Ithaca: Cornell University Press, 1968); William V. Harris, *War and Imperialism in Republican Rome 327–70 B.C.* (Oxford: Clarendon Press, 1979). For a brief account, see also Michael Crawford, *The Roman Republic* (London: Fontana, 1978), 46–48. On the Roman military triumph, see H. S. Versnel, *Triumphus: An Inquiry into the Origin, Development and Meaning of the Roman Triumph* (Leiden: Brill, 1970).

played by the Roman legacy in the Florentine tradition in general. In the second part of the essay I call for an intellectual history of Renaissance Florence which, instead of insisting on situating individual works and writers within abstract ideological traditions divorced from the political, social, and personal contexts of the day, concentrates its efforts on a study of the dynamic process of myth-making.[14]

The Renaissance idea that the republic had two ends – one internal, centered around the classical concept of liberty (*libertas*), and one external, aspiring to acquisition of dominion (*imperium*), material goods, greatness, and glory – went back to the revival of Roman republicanism in the fourteenth century. During the early Trecento Roman historians, primarily Livy and Sallust, began to exert a profound influence on the intellectual life of the Italian city-states. In Livy's history of Rome, republican theorists encountered the fullest and most detailed history of the Roman republic ever written. Livy relates how Rome rose from her obscure and humble beginnings to become the mistress of the world, and how the early kingship developed into a strong and vigorous republic based on citizenship, liberty, the common good, simple and austere mores, piety towards the ancestral gods, and an ardent and uncompromising pursuit of personal glory.[15] From Sallust derived the notion that republican government, expansionism, and imperial authority were not only compatible but also closely related and mutually supportive phenomena.[16] The idea that freedom-loving republics are more acquisitive and more vigorous than monarchies and principalities underlies his widely read *Bellum Catilinae*, where Rome's exceptional growth under the republic is contrasted to her more hesitant progress under the kings and the stagnation and decline that followed the loss of liberty.

Inspired by their reading of Aristotle, Cicero, and Roman historians, medieval theorists of communal self-government began to view the life enjoyed under a free republican form of government as distinct from the

---

[14] On civic humanism as myth-making, see also John Najemy's contribution to this volume (chapter 3). While Najemy deals with the oligarchic or domestic side of the civic humanist myth, this essay concentrates on its external and imperialist aspects.

[15] The enormous impact of Livy on Italian Renaissance thought is attested to by the fact that at least four of the major works of the period, Petrarch's *Africa* and *De viris illustribus*, Bruni's *Historiae Florentini Populi*, and Machiavelli's *Discorsi sopra la prima deca di Tito Livio* are all based on Livy.

[16] On Sallust's importance for Italian intellectuals from the Trecento up to Machiavelli, see Skinner, "The Vocabulary of Renaissance Republicanism"; Patricia J. Osmond, "Sallust and Machiavelli: From Civic Humanism to Political Prudence," *Journal of Medieval and Renaissance Studies* 23 (1993): 408–38; Osmond, "Princeps Historiae Romanae: Sallust in Renaissance Political Thought," *Memoirs of the American Academy in Rome* 40 (1995): 101–43.

servitude experienced under the corrupt and tyrannical rule of a prince or *signore*. In order to provide an ideological defense against the aspirations of the emperor, the pope, the aggressive principalities emerging in northern Italy, and the ever-present threat of internal tyranny, apologists for the Italian city-states during the Dugento and the early Trecento came with increasing frequency to invoke the term liberty (*libertas* or *libertà*). Employed in the dual meaning of political independence and republican self-rule, the concept constituted – together with other classically inspired values like the common good, justice, greatness, peace, civic concord, and the pursuit of virtue – the cornerstone of the new republican ideology that began to develop at the turn of the fourteenth century.[17]

But *libertas*, or *libertà*, was a complex term in the political vocabularies of the day. On the one hand, it was used in a juristic context to denote a negative form of liberty: the right to live one's life free from external interference under the protection afforded by the law. This form of liberty was compatible both with princely and republican rule. On the other hand, the term was employed by vernacular poets and humanists within a civic context, where it was given a more positive meaning, signifying the independence and self-rule of the republic and the citizen's right to participate in the government of the city. Used in this way, liberty came to be seen as an exclusive property of the republic, which was at times also referred to as a *vivere libero*, *vivere politico*, or *vivere civile*. On a purely theoretical and ideological level, the contest for supremacy in the chaotic political landscape of Trecento Italy could therefore be said to oppose two well-defined ideologies based on two distinct sets of values. Whereas a prince or a monarch was traditionally conceived of as ruling over friends (*amici*), assisting him in his government, and subjects (*sudditi*), who were allowed passively to enjoy the protection afforded by the laws and the stewardship of their ruler, republics like Florence took pride in their self-rule, free way of life (*vivere libero*), and collective form of government.

But matters were complicated to a considerable degree by the fact that only a minority of the inhabitants living within the territory controlled by an Italian republic could call themselves citizens and enjoy the special prerogatives that went with that designation. In Florence, one of the most popular and broadly based republics of the day, approximately 3,000 of the city's total of 20,000 male inhabitants were qualified to hold

---

[17] On the use of the term "liberty" in the medieval tradition, see note 2 above.

public office at the beginning of the fifteenth century.[18] This meant that republics, like princes, ruled over subjects who lacked the privileges and positive rights that full citizenship carried. In the case of Florence, the subjects of the republic could be divided into two principal categories: on the one hand, the disenfranchised workers living within the city proper; on the other, the people of the dominion, which traditionally was divided into the countryside (*contado*), and the outlying district (*distretto*). To this second category belonged also the inhabitants of subject cities like Pistoia, Arezzo, and Pisa after they had been brought under Florentine control.[19]

By the middle of the fourteenth century, when the Florentine republic began to emerge as an imperialist state in its own right aspiring to Tuscan hegemony, the terms *libertas* and *libertà* were often coupled with the concepts *imperium* and *signoria*, denoting dominion over internal or external subjects. A Florentine document from 1353 states, for example: "Signory and liberty, for mortal men nothing is more dear, nor more welcome than these two things."[20] Internal liberty enjoyed by free citizens and external growth and acquisition of foreign lands were by most Florentine republicans of the day not conceived of as contradictory concepts. Since the republic, understood as a community of free men, ruled over internal subjects in a legally binding relationship of domination and submission, there was basically nothing incongruous in its desire to extend its *imperium* and to incorporate more lands and more subjects in its dominion. Imperialism was not an external or additional element to the republican ideology. It was an integral and essential aspect of the tradition. Freedom, for some, entailed oppression or control of others.

In order to reexamine the civic humanism Baron uncovered but failed to understand, we need to return to the Florentine crisis of the early Quattrocento, which in his view gave rise to the new ideology. The

---

[18] See Nicolai Rubinstein, "Oligarchy and Democracy in Fifteenth-Century Florence," in *Florence and Venice*, I: 107.

[19] On Florence's rule of the *contado* and the *distretto*, see Guidubaldo Guidi, *Il governo della città-repubblica di Firenze del primo Quattrocento*, vol. III: *Il contado e distretto* (Florence: Olschki, 1981). See also Marvin B. Becker, "The Florentine Territorial State and Civic Humanism in the Early Renaissance," in *Florentine Studies: Politics and Society in Renaissance Florence*, ed. N. Rubinstein (London: Faber and Faber, 1968), 109–39; Giorgio Chittolini, "The Italian City-State and Its Territory," in *City-States in Classical Antiquity and Medieval Italy*, ed. A. Molho, K. Raaflaub, and J. Emlen (Stuttgart: Franz Steiner Verlag, 1991), 589–602.

[20] Quoted from Jerrold E. Seigel, "'Civic Humanism' or Ciceronian Rhetoric? The Culture of Petrarch and Bruni," *Past and Present* 34 (1966): 24.

historical facts are well known and can easily be summarized. Sometime around 1395, the Milanese court humanist Antonio Loschi wrote an anti-Florentine pamphlet in which he challenged the Florentines' right to call themselves the champions of Italian liberty as well as their longstanding claim to a direct Roman descent. During the following decade, a series of Florentine intellectuals and humanists took upon themselves to refute Loschi's allegations, among them the humanist chancellor, Coluccio Salutati; the teacher of rhetoric at Santa Maria in Campo, Cino Rinuccini; and the young aspiring humanist, Leonardo Bruni. Three of the texts produced by these writers attracted Baron's particular attention and came to serve as the foundation-stones for his civic humanism: Salutati's *Invectiva in Antonium Luschum Vicentinum* (c. 1403), Rinuccini's *Risponsiva alla Invettiva di messer Antonio Lusco*, and Leonardo Bruni's *Laudatio*.[21] For various reasons, Baron added to his canon of early civic humanist texts the wealthy silk merchant Gregorio Dati's *Istoria di Firenze*, a chronicle of the recent wars composed shortly after Florence's acquisition of Pisa in 1406, perhaps as early as 1407.[22] Since the exact dates of most of these works are uncertain and subject to scholarly controversy, and since their chronological order has little or no bearing on my argument, I will treat them as contemporary, conditioned not so much by particular historical events as by the principal issues at stake. For the purpose of analytical clarity, I shall address the two points raised by Antonio Loschi in his *Invectiva* one by one, beginning with Florence's right to call itself the defender of Italian liberty and then with her claim to a Roman legacy and the right to empire.

The roots of the Florentine republic's self-assumed role as the defender of Tuscan and Italian liberty must be sought back in the mid-Trecento, when the city entered a series of aggressive wars designed to subjugate

[21] *Invectiva Lini Colucii Salutati in Antonium Luschum Vicentinum*, ed. D. Moreni (Florence, 1826). The essential part of the text has been published in *Antologia della letteratura italiana*, vol. II: *Il Quattrocento e il Cinquecento*, ed. A. Asor Rosa et al. (Milan: Rizzoli, 1966), 50 54My references are to this latter edition (henceforth cited as Salutati, *Invectiva*). For Rinuccini's *Risponsiva*, I have used the contemporary Italian translation of the lost Latin original, *Risponsiva alla Invettiva di messer Antonio Lusco* (hereafter quoted as Rinuccini, *Risponsiva*), published in Antonio Lanza, *Firenze contro Milano*, 187 97. The original text of Leonardo Bruni's *Laudatio Florentinae urbis* is in Hans Baron, *From Petrarch to Leonardo Bruni: Studies in Humanistic and Political Literature* (Chicago: Chicago University Press, 1968), 232 63; English translation, "Panegyric to the City of Florence," trans. B. G. Kohl, in *The Earthly Republic: Italian Humanists on Government and Society*, ed. B. G. Kohl and R. G. Witt (Philadelphia: University of Pennsylvania Press, 1978), 135 75. References will be to these two editions.

[22] Gregorio Dati's *Istoria di Firenze* has recently been republished in Lanza, *Firenze contro Milano*, 211 300.

the surrounding cities and establish Florentine hegemony in Tuscany. The acquisitions resulting from these campaigns – Colle Valdelsa in 1338, Prato and Pistoia in 1351, San Gimignano in 1354, and Volterra in 1361 – were generally justified on the grounds that they had been carried out for the sake of territorial security and in order to protect Florentine and Tuscan liberty in the face of Milanese aggression.[23] But this expansionist program needs also to be seen in the context of the traditional Guelf ideology, according to which the liberty of the individual commune was conceived as subordinate to the *libertas* of Christendom at large. Expansionism in the name of Guelf *libertas* was consequently conducted primarily for the sake of the *Respublica Christiana*, secondly for the papacy, and only in the third place for the commune itself. Matteo Villani could thus in the middle of the Trecento complain about the Church's unwillingness to assist Florence in spite of the many acquisitions the republic had made on her account.[24]

The breakdown of the Guelf league during the second half of the Trecento meant that Florence had to find a new role for herself in the ongoing struggle for supremacy in central Italy. During the War of the Eight Saints (1375–8), the republic openly defied papal leadership and claimed to be acting on its own as the champion of liberty against tyranny, Good against Evil, and true Christianity against its perverted form embodied by the Roman Church. In the patriotic poetry, religious writings, and political debates of the 1370s and 1380s, Florentines rehearsed their city's elect status as the blessed center of the future Christian *renovatio* and the eternal daughter of Rome, and prophesied that Florence would emerge as the new leader of Italy, bringing renewal, peace and *libertas* in her train.[25] Under such proclamations, the republic took it upon herself to defend the sacrosanct liberties of Arezzo (acquired by Florence in 1384), Montepulciano (annexed in 1390), Perugia, Bologna, and other cities allegedly under threat from the advancing Visconti dukes of Milan.

In the so called *missive*, the republic's official correspondence, composed by Coluccio Salutati during his tenure as chancellor from 1375 to his death in 1406, Florence was frequently represented as the champion

---

[23] Another reason frequently adduced by the Florentines to legitimate the subjugation of neighboring cities was that they had come under tyrannical rule. For examples, see Rubinstein, "Florentina libertas," 8; Gene A. Brucker, *The Civic World of Early Renaissance Florence* (Princeton: Princeton University Press, 1977), 304.
[24] Brucker, *The Civic World*.
[25] Becker, *Florence in Transition*, II: 201–4; Donald Weinstein, *Savonarola and Florence: Prophecy and Patriotism in the Renaissance* (Princeton: Princeton University Press, 1970), 42–43.

of Italian liberty opposing foreign domination and domestic tyrants.[26] In his letters to other free communes, Salutati often appealed to love of liberty and to the principle of republican self-government as a common cause uniting all free city-states in their defense against princely or signorial aggression. Writing to the Sienese at a time when the Visconti of Milan were aspiring to greater dominion in central Italy, Salutati sought to establish such a bond between the two republics:

> If you wish, as is your duty, to leave your old enemy [i.e. Milan], who pretends to be a friend and protector only in order to be able to command you ... and to return to the friendship of your old, true and eternal brothers in order to defend together with us your liberty and that of the others, as was the custom of your ancestors, we are ready to embrace you.[27]

It is tempting to see in passages such as this confirmation of Baron's thesis that the civic humanists, and Salutati among them, supported the idea of creating a system of independent city-states in central Italy. But such a reading of the *missive* ignores the rhetorical and strategic aspects of Salutati's invocations of Italian liberty, and the hidden motives we have reason to believe were concealed behind the Florentines' claim to Italian and Tuscan leadership. The implications of Salutati's appeals to the common cause and the Florentines' protestations of good will were rarely lost upon the city's neighbors, who had learnt from hard-won experience to view Florentine motives with suspicion. On this particular occasion the Sienese, who were anxious to curb Florentine influence in neighboring Montepulciano, currently under Sienese jurisdiction, saw little reason to accept the Florentine embrace and decline the Milanese offer of assistance.

It is against this background that we need to understand the attempt by Antonio Loschi to refashion Florence as the disturber of Italy's peace, and the efforts of the Florentine humanists to demonstrate that it was Milan, and not Florence, who was the aggressor in the conflict. In his *Risponsiva*, Cino Rinuccini met Loschi's challenge by extolling Florence as the defender and head of Italy's liberty and by stressing how just and liberal Florence's rule of her subject cities had always been. While the Visconti had always acted like tyrants in relation to their own city and to foreign lands, Rinuccini argued, the Florentines had not only defended their own freedom but had also treated their subject peoples in a just

---
[26] On the *missive* in general, see Ronald Witt, *Coluccio Salutati*; Herde, "Politik und Rhetorik"; Daniela De Rosa, *Coluccio Salutati: Il cancelliere e il pensatore politico* (Florence: La Nuova Italia, 1980).
[27] Quoted from De Rosa, *Coluccio Salutati*, 103.

and fair manner. Referring to Florence's recent purchase of Arezzo from the French, which in reality had been one of the factors provoking the war, Rinuccini claimed that internal divisions had brought the Aretines to the verge of destruction before the Florentines had moved in and restored order. Having found their neighbor "despoiled of goods and almost consumed," the Florentines had "recomposed her, so that the good men of both the contending parties could rest in sweet tranquillity, affirming on both sides that they had never been in such repose." The same could also be said of the city of San Miniato, Rinuccini claimed, which the Florentines had liberated from the excessive pride of its nobles and a very cruel tyrant.[28]

It is evident that Loschi's criticism had touched a sore spot. What was at stake in this paper war, the Florentine responses reveal, was Florence's right to exercise dominion over subject cities, while continuing to claim to be the defender of Italian liberty. The problem facing the Florentine humanists on this occasion was by no means unique. Working within an ideological framework based on the fundamental distinction between the dominant city and its subject territory, they were often forced to express themselves in terms that revealed a princely set of mind within a generally republican outlook. In his reply to Loschi's claim that the subjects of the Florentine republic were suffering under the tyrannical yoke of the Tuscan city, Coluccio Salutati consequently had to resort to the rather dubious claim – dubious at least from a republican point of view – that the subject cities in the Florentine dominion were quite satisfied to enjoy the sweet liberty of living under the law and being protected by it:

[Are you saying] that Florentine subjects, whom our city has established and made or snatched and taken back from the hands of tyrants, have been suffocated by tyranny or despoiled of their ancient dignity? Those who were either born with us in liberty or recalled to the sweetness of liberty from the distress of a wretched servitude? Do they long to throw off a yoke they do not have, or exchange the sweet restraints of liberty [*dulce libertatis frenum*] – which is to be free from arbitrary power and live according to the law [*iure vivere legibusque*] to which everyone is subject – for the tyrannical yoke of your lord, as you pretend to believe?[29]

The definition of liberty Salutati offers here is not the positive, participatory form of freedom Baron, Rubinstein, Pocock and others have come to identify with Florentine republicanism. Salutati does not concede to

[28] Rinuccini, *Risponsiva*, 190. [29] Salutati, *Invectiva*, 52.

the subjects of the Florentine dominion the liberty of self-government and political participation. The juristic understanding of the concept contained within the term *iure vivere* only in practice means that Florentine subjects have the privilege of living under Florentine laws instead of under those of the duchy of Milan. If we are to retain the traditional distinction between a juristic and a civic humanist definition of *libertas*, we must thus acknowledge that two different types of liberty coexisted within the Florentine republic, one for citizens and one for subjects.

Florence's role as the defender of Tuscan liberty is also one of the main themes in Bruni's *Laudatio*. According to him, the Florentines had always shown great discretion in their conduct of war and had never taken up arms other than in self-defense and in order to avenge received injuries. Having made this clear, Bruni goes on to claim that each time the city has "taken to the offensive," it has been transformed "by its amazing desire for praise and glory." Because of her love of liberty and sense of dignity, Florence has in the course of her history also been forced to defeat and subjugate many of her neighbors. Among the "almost innumerable trophies" the republic has captured, Bruni singles out Siena, Pisa, and the "ancient and noble town" of Volterra for special mention. Florence has also "suffered many dangers for the freedom and security of other states," as on the occasion when she came to the rescue of her ally, the city of Lucca, which had been besieged by the Pisans, "a nation rarely at peace with Florence."[30]

Perhaps the most elaborate attempt to legitimate Florentine expansion in the name of liberty, however, is to be found in Gregorio Dati's *Istoria*, which was one of the first in a long series of Florentine chronicles narrating the events of the Pisan war. The two most striking features of the *Istoria* are its celebration of Florentine republican liberty and its persistent and generous attempt to justify the city's aspiration to achieve Tuscan hegemony. The brief and fragmentary outline of Florentine history the work offers is organized in terms of republican liberty understood as self-government and independence from foreign domination. Following the tradition from Matteo Villani's *Cronica*, Dati emphasizes the importance of Florence's past adherence to the Guelf cause. From Villani he also borrows the definitions of the Ghibellines as men of "an imperial and lordly spirit," and the Guelfs as defenders of liberty and the Church.[31] During the War of the Eight Saints, which saw Florence and the papacy on opposing sides, the Florentines are said to

---

[30] Bruni, *Laudatio*, 254 6 (Eng. trans., 163 5).
[31] Dati, *Istoria*, 266. Cf. Matteo Villani, *Cronica* 4.77.

have defended their liberty against those "haughty and evil pastors" who were attempting to subjugate them and "dismantle their liberty."[32] In more recent times, Florence had acted as the bulwark of Italian liberty by opposing and defeating Giangaleazzo Visconti after the Milanese ruler had seized control of all the cities surrounding Florence in his quest to become "lord and king of Italy."[33] In Dati's view, the Florentines had always throughout their history fought their wars in self-defense and in order to preserve their liberty in the face of external aggression.

Florence's reluctance to engage in warfare is seen by Dati as a direct consequence of the peace-loving nature of her inhabitants, who are said to live by friendly trade and to take up arms only as a last resort and in order to restore peace. This benign mentality manifested itself after the death of Giangaleazzo, when Florence without further ado could have acquired new territory on the other side of the Apennines but refrained from doing so, being content to remain within her secure borders. To the Florentines' love of liberty and peace, moderation and restraint, Dati adds their devotion to the principles of justice and the rule of law. When they undertook their recent campaign against Pisa, which Dati describes as a "just enterprise," they did so after having first established the legitimacy and lawfulness of their purchase of the city.[34]

Whereas Dati holds love of liberty and the devotion to justice and peace to be the cornerstones of Florentine republicanism, he insinuates that the other Tuscan cities' envy (*invidia*) of Florentine prosperity had swayed them to forsake their own liberty in order to destroy or hurt their rival. An example of this occurred in the course of the Trecento, when the Aretines "acted against themselves" by submitting to the duke of Anjou and appointing him lord of their city in the hope that he would subjugate "the liberty of Florence and her Commune." The Pisans are similarly said to have subjected themselves to the lordship of the duke of Milan in order to bring down the Florentines. This readiness to accept princely rule on the part of Florence's neighbors bespeaks, in Dati's view, a fundamental defect in their commitment to republicanism. The shortcomings of Pisan liberty, he implies, were also partly due to the way the city was ruled before falling under Florentine domination. Although it claimed to be a free commune in which all magistracies were filled by Pisan citizens, its form of government was ambiguous since it included a Captain of the People for life "who could almost be called a lord

---

[32] Dati, *Istoria*, 267.   [33] Ibid., 244.   [34] Ibid., 227, 235, 255 and 271 2.

[*signore*]." As long as this office was vested in the virtuous Pietro Gambacorta, who stood on friendly terms with the Florentines, this constitutional flaw remained hidden, but as soon as he withdrew from politics and was replaced by his former chancellor, the ambitious Jacopo d'Appiano, the way to tyranny lay open. After Jacopo had seized control of the city and placed himself under the protection of the duke of Milan, the people of Pisa, compelled by fear, granted him unlimited power and appointed him *signore libero con vero e misto impero*.[35]

Due to Dati's representation of the internal developments in Pisa prior to Florence's purchase of the city, the conflict came to appear to stand not between two free and independent city-states, but between Florentine liberty and Pisan servitude under Milanese tyranny. It is only by ignoring a series of less flattering circumstances that Dati can come up with this black-and-white account. In reality, the Pisans had, before the outbreak of the war, revolted against the purchase of the city, overthrown their tyrant Gabriel Maria Visconti, the illegitimate son of Giangaleazzo, and reclaimed their liberty. At this point, the Florentines, anxious not to let the acquisition slip through their fingers, had sent troops to Pisa in an attempt to rescue Gabriel Maria who had taken refuge in the fortress. Having passed over this development in next to complete silence,[36] Dati could go on to claim that Florentine domination actually had come as a blessing to the Pisans, since it had put an end to the horrendous sufferings inflicted by the war and the long siege. It also meant, he argued, that the Pisans would now be free to participate in the growth and expansion of Florence, and become prosperous in their own right, since they would no longer run the risk of being sold or afflicted by war.[37] The fact that the peace-loving Florentines had been compelled to bestow these benefits on Pisa by force was, from Dati's point of view, a regrettable but inevitable consequence of the Pisans' own obstinacy and failure to understand their own good.[38]

Although Dati towards the end of the *Istoria* expresses his anxiety over the future and urges the Florentines to show restraint and refrain from further expansion,[39] his position must be considered expansionist. Florentine hegemony in Tuscany is seen by him as a natural conse-

[35] Ibid., 222, 230 and 236-7.
[36] The episode is related in passing by Dati, see ibid., 260. Compare Matteo Palmieri, *La presa di Pisa*, ed. Alessandra Mita Ferraro (Naples: Mulino, 1995), 14-18.
[37] Dati, *Istoria*, 258-9.
[38] In this regard, the willingness of the people of Montepulciano to accept Florentine rule offers a sharp contrast to Pisan resistance, see ibid., 220-1.
[39] Ibid., 276.

quence of the city's moral superiority. In his view it is exactly because the Florentines are so imbued with the love of liberty, justice, and peace that they have been chosen to exercise dominion over Tuscany. Baron's attempt to excuse the darker side of Dati's republicanism by claiming that he was not "thinking of conquests outside Tuscany" does little to alter this fact.[40]

The other main head in Loschi's critique of the Florentine mythology concerned the city's claim to a Roman descent. Since the Roman legacy had been an important source of civic pride in the Florentine tradition from the very outset, this was an emotionally charged question that touched the very core of the collective Florentine identity. According to the oldest extant chronicle of the city, the thirteenth-century *Chronica de origine civitatis*, Florence had been founded during the reign of Julius Caesar "from the flower of Roman manhood," and she had early on, as a token of her privileged status within the empire, received the name "little Rome [*parva Roma*]."[41] The ties between Florence and her great ancestor were loudly proclaimed at the turn of the fourteenth century, when an inscription was placed on the recently erected Communal Palace, celebrating Florence as the leader of Tuscany, a city enjoying good fortune and full of wealth, and a fearsome warring nation comparable to triumphant Rome.[42] The Roman heritage continued during the Trecento to constitute an essential element in Florentine Guelfism, and Roman civic ideals and *exempla* began towards the end of the century to be invoked in public and private writings with a frequency that suggests a strong influence from the emerging humanist culture. Volgare poets like Fazio degli Uberti, Franco Sacchetti, and Braccio Bracci celebrated Florence's greatness during the period by comparing the city to ancient Rome, though within a markedly Christian framework.

A crucial role in the introduction of the new humanist culture to Florence was played by Coluccio Salutati. Salutati contributed to strengthening and deepening the city's Roman identity in his public letters by inserting quotations and examples from classical authors and by drawing close parallels between the Florentine republic and her ancient Roman forebear. The Roman idea that love of liberty and the

---

[40] Baron, *The Crisis*, 174.
[41] Weinstein, *Savonarola and Florence*, 36 7; Nicolai Rubinstein, "The Beginnings of Political Thought in Florence: A Study of Mediaeval Historiography," *Journal of the Warburg and Courtauld Institutes* 5 (1942): 198 227.
[42] Ibid., 213.

pursuit of empire are not only compatible but closely related is also a frequent theme in the *missive*. Addressing the peoples of Cesena, Spoleto, and Recanati, for example, Salutati argued that the servitude in which the Italian peoples presently found themselves was particularly humiliating given "the Italic race's" innate desire for liberty, which in the past had inspired it to "obtain liberty at home after innumerable victories," and to "exercise empire over the whole world."[43] In Salutati's laudatory account of the Italian peoples' Roman past, which constitutes a continuous theme of the *missive*, empire abroad comes to appear as a natural extension of liberty at home rather than as a betrayal of the values of the *res publica*. According to him the ancient Romans had acquired their world-wide empire by fighting for their own liberty and by defending their allies and confederates. In an inspired moment he even went on to claim that it was "the desire for liberty alone that brought forth the empire, the glory and all the dignity of the Roman people."[44]

After Florence's Roman descent had been called into question by Antonio Loschi, Salutati researched the archives and classical sources in order to muster support for the city's Roman myth of origin. As a result of these investigations, he came to the conclusion that the city had indeed been founded by the Romans – but not under the auspices of Julius Caesar as had traditionally been assumed, but by a group of veterans from Sulla's army.[45] The importance of this affirmation is evident from Salutati's response to Loschi's challenge in the *Invectiva*. Here he claimed that Florence's Roman heritage and love of liberty gave the city a natural right to dominion and lordship over Tuscany and the rest of the peninsula. While the Florentines, who were Roman citizens both by blood and legal right, had received their love of liberty as a divine gift and gradually acquired the habit of hating servitude, the Milanese and the Lombards lived under the deception that "the highest liberty and the inestimable dignity" were to obey the unrestrained will of a tyrannical patron like the Visconti duke. To live under the constraints of law appeared to them instead as "a grave yoke and a horrendous servitude." Whether or not they would be able to rise to liberty, now that ancient virtue was being revived under Florentine auspices, only

---

[43] Quoted from De Rosa, *Coluccio Salutati*, 92.
[44] Quoted from Witt, "The Rebirth of the Concept of Republican Liberty," 196.
[45] For Salutati's contribution to the reinterpretation of Florence's origins, see Ronald G. Witt, *Hercules at the Crossroads: The Life, Works, and Thought of Coluccio Salutati* (Durham: Duke University Press, 1983), 246–52.

time could tell. The outcome would depend entirely, Salutati argued, on whether they would prove themselves to belong to the servile Lombard race of transalpine origin, or to "the glorious Gallic race" which formerly had inhabited Cisalpine Gaul and had been imbued with the freedom-loving Italic spirit. In the latter case also the Lombards would be able to claim a place of privilege within the new emerging political order based on liberty and Florentine hegemony.[46] Needless to say, it does not take much to read the traditional paradigm of Roman imperialism into Salutati's defense of Florentine republicanism and expansionism in the *Invectiva*.

The close ties between Florence's claim to a Roman legacy and the city's imperialist aspirations are also evident from Cino Rinuccini's *Risponsiva*. Having laid down that a popular form of government was superior to rule by a single man, Rinuccini brought up the example of the ancient Roman republic in connection with Florence: "Have you never read about how Rome under the kings grew only a little, but under the senate in a short time acquired the empire over the world [*lo 'mperio del mondo*], and then was reduced to almost nothing under the emperors?" The general applicability of this ancient Sallustian theme, Rinuccini argued, had been confirmed by modern experience: "This you must also have observed in beautiful Italy, if you are not utterly blind: that the free cities are the greater, that is, Florence, Venice and Genoa."[47] When Rinuccini later returned to the subject of Florence's Roman heritage, he articulated the imperialist perspective with even greater emphasis as he appropriated the Roman legacy for Florence: "So much intellect is there in us that in the same way as we in the past have been the defenders of beautiful liberty, we will in the future be its enlargers [*ampliatori*]; it is very well known that we do not lack prudence, industry, eagerness and riches; these things will give our republic power, and when this has been acquired, we will, as the legitimate sons of the Romans, and as imitators of their virtue, maintain it."[48] In the light of this invocation of the hegemonic Roman republic and the coupling of liberty and expansion (the term *ampliatori* also carries territorial connotations), Baron's characterization of Rinuccini's *Risponsiva* as a treatise written in defense of "city-state independence," must be dismissed as highly misleading.[49]

The influence of Salutati's and Bruni's understanding of the connection between Roman liberty and the Roman republic's rise to world

---

[46] Salutati, *Invectiva*, 52.   [47] Rinuccini, *Risponsiva*, 192.   [48] Ibid., 193.
[49] Baron, *The Crisis*, 96.

rule is also evident from the link Gregorio Dati forges between the modern Florentines and the ancient Romans. According to Dati, the Florentine people's love of liberty can be explained by the fact that they "were born as the descendants of those Romans who, by rule of liberty, had acquired the lordship of the world [*con reggimento di libertà, avevano acquistata la signoria del mondo*] and established Rome in a state of greater peace, tranquillity and honor than there ever was."[50] Like Salutati, Bruni, and Rinuccini before him, Dati thus viewed the Roman republic's "rule of liberty" as a direct cause of its acquisitiveness and its rise to world supremacy.

There can be no doubt, though, that the fundamental early civic humanist text when it comes to situating the modern Florentine republic within the tradition of Roman liberty and imperialism is Leonardo Bruni's *Laudatio*. According to Bruni, it was an indisputable fact of "utmost importance" that "the Florentine race arose from the Roman people,"[51] the most virtuous and glorious people ever to have existed. The right to lordship over the world, which God had originally bestowed upon the Romans, had now, Bruni proudly declared, been passed on to the Florentine people. This epochal event allowed him, the self-styled new Cicero, to address his Florentine audience as a race of reborn and resurrected Romans, to whom belonged the right to exercise "dominion over the entire world." According to Bruni, all Florentine wars were thus by definition legitimate and just, since they were either fought in defense of Florentine liberty or in order to regain land that belonged to the free Florentine people by "a certain hereditary right."[52]

In order to explain how the rights and privileges which the Romans had originally received by divine decree or acquired through display of virtue had come to pass into the possession of the Florentines, Bruni offered a historical perspective on the Florentine people's Roman descent. Taking his cue from Salutati's discovery that Florence had been founded under the late Roman republic and not during the early days of the empire, Bruni claimed that the city had been born "at the very moment when the empire of the Roman people was most flourishing" (*populi Romani imperium maxime florebat*) and "very powerful kings and warlike nations" were being brought under Roman sway. After centuries of warlike activities, the Roman people had finally put the world around them to rest: "Carthage, Spain, and Corinth were

---

[50] Dati, *Istoria*, 266. [51] Bruni, *Laudatio*, 244 (Eng. trans., 149). [52] Ibid., 244 (Eng. trans., 150).

leveled to the ground; all lands and seas acknowledged the rule of these Romans, and these same Romans suffered no harm from any foreign state."[53]

Although the liberty and the military virtue of the Roman people had been destroyed at the hands of the emperors, the republican spirit had not completely vanished. It had survived in the little Roman colony of Florence and in the heart of the Florentine people. This little Roman offshoot had now grown to maturity and brought about a revival of the virtues of its great forebear. By successfully emulating their Roman ancestors, the modern Florentines had come to gain might and glory, and through their achievements in all kinds of activities they had proven themselves to be without equals.[54] What remained for them to do now? Bruni asks. The answer he gives is as straightforward as it is revealing: "What greater thing, what more outstanding feat could this city accomplish, or in what way could it better prove that the virtue of its forebears was still alive than by liberating the whole of Italy, by its own efforts and resources, from the threat of servitude?"[55] Florence is thus set to repeat what her Roman ancestors had accomplished in the past: Italian liberty under the auspices of a strong, vigorous and hegemonic republic. In this section of the *Laudatio* Bruni establishes with great clarity and force the connections which according to him existed between republican liberty and the move toward empire, growth and expansion, on the one hand, and between monarchy, the loss of liberty and the decline and demise of empire, on the other.

All the texts we have been considering so far subscribe in one way or another to the idea that the republic has two ends: to preserve its liberty at home and to pursue empire abroad. The notion is in fact such a salient feature in these works that it suggests itself as one of the dominant themes – if not *the* dominant theme – of a Florentine patriotic tradition that both precedes and extends beyond civic humanism.[56] At the same time as this observation allows us to redefine civic humanism as a republican *and* imperialist ideology, it begs the question about civic humanism's place within the Florentine tradition at large. Differently put, what distinguished early Quattrocento humanism from the Guelfism of the preceding century, and what made it into a unique moment or a specific trend within Florentine republicanism? Since defense of

[53] Ibid., 245 (Eng. trans., 151).   [54] Ibid., 251 (Eng. trans., 159).   [55] Ibid., 258 (Eng. trans., 168).
[56] On the Florentine tradition, see Weinstein, *Savonarola and Florence*, 27–66; Mark Hulliung, *Citizen Machiavelli* (Princeton: Princeton University Press, 1983), 3–30.

liberty and pursuit of territorial expansion were tenets the civic humanists held in common with earlier Florentine writers outside and within the Guelf tradition, this cannot be the distinguishing mark of civic humanism. In order to determine what was distinctively new about this version of republicanism, we need to examine how the meaning the civic humanists gave the concept of liberty differed from that of their predecessors, and in what sense their view and their use of the Roman legacy constituted a departure from the earlier tradition.

Although the Florentine chroniclers and patriotic poets of the Trecento frequently celebrated Florence for her Roman ancestry and conceived of her love of liberty as a Roman inheritance, they rarely – if ever – claimed that this was a special or exclusively Florentine inheritance. In their view, Florentine liberty did not exclude the existence of other equally legitimate liberties.[57] While this mitigating feature can still be discerned in the works of Salutati, Rinuccini, and Dati considered above, it has been completely effaced from the triumphalist vision of Bruni's *Laudatio*. In this imperialist myth, the Florentine republic appropriates in the name of *Florentina libertas* the universalist claims of the Roman imperial tradition and assumes the role as leader of the free Italian peoples formerly vested in the Church. The Florentines are here not represented merely as one among many Italian peoples with a rightful claim to a Roman descent, but as Rome's first-born sons and principal heirs. As a consequence, *Florentina libertas* comes in this simplistic but powerful vision to constitute a supreme form of freedom, morally superior, more authentic and more refined than all surrounding "liberties." Such an exclusive and utterly patriotic view of liberty can ill afford to respect the sovereignty of other cities, states, and peoples. On the contrary, it entails a commitment to empire understood as a defense and militant extension of true liberty in a hostile world of threatening warlords and tyrants. In concrete terms, it translates into a pursuit of territorial security which justifies intervention in the political life of neighboring states and the subjugation and annexation of foreign lands. Whereas Guelfism had been based on a network of free communes or city-states exercising *de facto* sovereignty under papal overlordship, Bruni's republicanism is centered around the idea of the *imperium populi Romani* and the asymmetrical relationship of patronage and *clientela* which in the ancient past had characterized the relations between the Roman people and its allies.

[57] See, for example, Matteo Villani, *Cronica* 3.1 and 4.77.

In a world largely dominated by the paradigm of Roman law and the idea that all legitimate government originated in the will of the Roman emperor and ultimately in the Roman people, Bruni's appropriation of the Roman legacy on behalf of the Florentine people was bound to provoke angry reactions outside Florence. But although the work later gave rise to a heated debate between Bruni and leading Milanese and Roman humanists,[58] the circumspect way in which he couched his argument in the *Laudatio* strongly suggests that his intention at the time was not to provoke or to offend non-Florentine readers. Trained in civil law as he was, Bruni took care not to upset the jurists by unequivocally attributing the prerogatives of the *princeps* to the Florentine people. Instead, he opted for the less-than-committed statement that the right to empire over the whole world belonged to the Florentines "by a certain hereditary right [*iure quodam hereditario*]." Here, the meaning of *quodam* is so evasive that it threatens to cancel the whole statement. Bruni's prudence also shows when he addresses the non-Florentine listener and credits him with having discovered that the Florentines are worthy of world rule instead of claiming this controversial view for himself or the Florentines. Everyone who has experienced the architectural wonders of the city, he maintains, "immediately comes to believe that Florence is indeed worthy of attaining dominion and rule over the entire world."[59] Bruni's frequent use of such cautious rhetorical strategies in the *Laudatio* gives us reason to believe that he was not writing exclusively for a Florentine audience but also for external consumption. This impression is also strengthened by his way of shaping his reader partly as an outsider, who is either seen visiting Florence for the first time, or lacking first-hand experience of the Arno city.[60]

As a schooled rhetorician, Bruni had been trained to think in terms of context and to adapt his rhetorical performance to the audience and the circumstances involved. This fundamental fact allows us to expect from Bruni a capacity to calculate the effects of his text upon its intended readers. In order to understand the rhetorical performance of the *Laudatio* we need therefore to identify the implied readers of the work. Although we cannot with any certainty determine who they were, a qualified guess would include among them fellow humanists like Niccolò Niccoli and Coluccio Salutati, the ruling elite and the leadership of Florence, as well as policy-makers and potential pro-Florentine elements in neighboring cities under Florentine rule or within the Floren-

---

[58] See James Hankins' essay in this volume. See also Baron, *In Search*, I: 49.
[59] Bruni, *Laudatio*, 239 (Eng. trans., 143).
[60] See especially ibid., 235–9 (Eng. trans., 138–44).

tine orbit of influence.[61] As a native of the recently acquired subject city of Arezzo, Bruni was uniquely qualified to address this latter kind of audience; in a sense, it could even be claimed that he belonged to it himself. This is also to suggest that at issue here was not only Florence's claim to sovereignty and empire, but Bruni's own status as intellectual and imperial subject as well.

If the *Laudatio* offers itself as a mobilizing and unifying myth and a sort of mirror-for-cities for its Florentine audience, how does it represent Florentine claims and aspirations to the outside world? On the basis of how the city's relationship to neighboring peoples is represented in the *Laudatio*, one could argue that Bruni's remaking of Florence in the image of republican Rome was intended primarily for the non-Florentine reader. When external relations are treated in the *Laudatio*, one is often in doubt whether Bruni is actually describing the Florentine republic or its ancient Roman predecessor. In his discussion of cities that are either allied to or on friendly terms with the Florentines, he uses, for example, the terms *socii* and *amici*, which recalls the *socii et amici populi Romani*, a phrase which in ancient times was employed to denote free states under Roman overlordship. The policy of friendly and disinterested patronage *vis-à-vis* their neighbors, which he attributes to the Florentines, is also taken directly from Roman republican propaganda.[62] The Romans had also prided themselves on their hospitality towards foreigners who wanted to take up residence in their city and on their generous policy of extending Roman citizenship to subjugated peoples. Consequently, Bruni has the Florentines follow their lead by claiming that they too were in the habit of giving refuge to exiles and offering citizenship to other peoples: "Hence there is no one in the whole of Italy who does not consider himself to possess dual citizenship [*duplicem patriam*], the one of the city to which he naturally belongs, the other of the city of Florence."[63] This picture of Florence as the second homeland of every Italian – modeled on the ancient idea of Rome as the *communis patria* of all Italy – contains, of course, a great deal of deceitful propaganda, fanciful fiction, or wishful thinking on the part of Bruni. For as the author, who was not a Florentine citizen at the time, was bound to know, the Arno republic was extremely restrictive in granting citizen-

---

[61] In chapter 5, James Hankins identifies foreign elites as the intended audience of the work (see p. 178), and in chapter 3 John Najemy argues that the civic humanist ideology was crafted with a view to Florentine nonelite guildsmen (see p. 86f.).
[62] Bruni, *Laudatio*, 252 (Eng. trans., 160–1).
[63] Ibid., 251 (Eng. trans., 159).

ship to its subject peoples.[64] It is telling that Matteo Palmieri, when he later wanted to represent the Florentines in the *Vita civile* (c. 1435) as practicing the same open and receptive policy as the Romans, could do no better than to bring up the people of the tiny hamlet of Figline in the upper Arno valley, who, he claimed, had been embraced by the Florentines and offered citizenship after having surrendered to a Florentine force.[65]

Insofar as the *Laudatio* exaggerates Florence's resemblance to the ancient Roman republic, which had expanded its empire by incorporating foreign peoples through treaties and extension of citizenship, it is evident that it contains an exhortation to the Florentines to follow the example of their ancient forebears, and a criticism of the republic's current ways.[66] But we could also read the *Laudatio* with an eye to its non-Florentine audience. For at the same time as the work is busy shaping the image of Florence as the New Rome, it seeks to fashion future roles for the other Italian peoples as well. From this point of view the *Laudatio* presents itself as a script in which Florence's neighboring cities are invited to accept Florentine protection and patronage, just as the Romans in antiquity had assumed the responsibility for the security of surrounding peoples in exchange for deference and obedience. The language of fiction is appropriate here since what the *Laudatio* explicitly proposes is a Florentine restaging of the history of the rise of Rome in which the Florentines themselves were to be cast in the leading role of the Romans, while the other Italian peoples would perform the minor parts of the *socii et amici populi Romani*.

To accept the Florentines' special claim to the Roman legacy and their self-proclaimed destiny of expansion and conquest would, for other Italians, not necessarily mean giving up their cherished liberties. It had, after all, been one of the central tenets of Guelfism that the Italian peoples during antiquity had remained free even under Roman domination. According to Matteo Villani, the Italian communes had in ancient times "participated in the citizenship and the liberty of the Roman people," in contrast to foreign nations, who had been tributaries and "subjected to the people, the Senate and the Commune of Rome."[67] Salutati had similarly claimed that the Italians, by submitting to Roman imperial overlordship, had given up part of their own liberty,

[64] Bruni acquired Florentine citizenship in 1416; see *The Humanism of Leonardo Bruni*, 36.
[65] Matteo Palmieri, *Vita civile* (Florence: Sansoni, 1982), 130.
[66] On this aspect of the *Laudatio*, see Harvey C. Mansfield's essay (chapter 8 in this volume).
[67] Matteo Villani, *Cronica* 4.77.

but in return acquired the right to call themselves Romans and to "exercise empire over all nations [*omnibus nationibus imperare*]."[68] Implicit in the script Bruni held out to Florence's potential allies was also the promise that they would not forfeit their liberty or be reduced to servitude if they subjected themselves to the Florentine people. Instead, they would be allowed to enjoy the same free and semi-independent status under Florentine overlordship as they had in antiquity under the Romans.

There was, after all, in Bruni's view no contradiction between being free and accepting Roman overlordship: "Who is there among men who would not readily acknowledge themselves subjected to the Roman people?"[69] The words refer to Florence's Roman descent, but since the Florentines themselves had inherited the Roman prerogatives, this cheerful view of how willing everyone is to accept Roman domination has less bearing on the Florentines than on their Italian neighbors and potential satellites. If you accept our script, our protection and our rule, Bruni's argument goes, you will be allowed to participate in an exciting new imperial adventure and together we will revive ancient culture and reenact the history of the Roman people. You will have to accept our leadership and renounce part of your own precarious autonomy, but your liberty will be subsumed under a higher, more elevated and expansive form of freedom, *Florentina libertas*. Such is the seductive language of the *Laudatio*. And such, it seems, was the self-assurance of the Florentine republic at a time when it saw itself as the heir of Rome and expected its neighbors to acknowledge this fact, giving up their own independence to embrace the Florentine cause. On a more personal level, it could be argued that the role the Aretine Bruni was outlining for the subject peoples of Florence, he was also fashioning for himself.

The rhetorical reading of Bruni's *Laudatio* presented above raises questions about the relationship between civic humanist representation and myth-making, on the one hand, and the social and political reality in which they evolved, on the other. For Hans Baron, who accepted civic humanism on its own terms after having cleansed it of what he found unacceptable, this problem simply did not exist. Nicolai Rubinstein solves the difficulty, as we have seen, by divorcing the ideology of "true" *Florentina libertas* from the political reality of oligarchic rule and imperialism. In the approach of Quentin Skinner and Maurizio Viroli, who

[68] See De Rosa, *Coluccio Salutati*, 93.   [69] Bruni, *Laudatio*, 244 (Eng. trans., 150).

study ideologies and their vocabularies and define the meanings of texts by situating them in ideological traditions, the question is, if not immaterial, at least not one of central importance.[70] Does the failure of this historiographical tradition to make sense of the relationship between civic humanist representation and the reality within which it was produced mean that we are hopelessly trapped within the myths the civic humanists created? I do not think so.

In order to move beyond the civic humanist paradigm which today conceals more of Florentine Renaissance culture than it explains, I propose that we should study the dynamic and open process of civic humanist myth-making instead of the ideology as a self-contained and detached system of values and beliefs. Such an approach would have to be rhetorical by definition and based on a recognition of the relational, local, and historically contingent status of the civic humanist ideology. Since it could be claimed that this ideology was used not only to legitimate the political interests of Florence's ruling elite and to justify Florentine imperialism, but also to define and, to a certain extent, shape these policies and practices, civic humanism should, in my view, be studied as a process of myth-making or as a system of representation. Such an approach would allow us to view the ideology as a rhetorical construct in continuous interaction with the various institutional, judicial, ritual, and symbolical systems and practices contributing to promote and reinforce the policies and interests served by the civic humanists.

In order to live up to such a grandiose design for a study of civic humanism and Florentine imperialism, we would have to take into consideration the roles played by institutions such as the Florentine chancery, which produced and disseminated much of the propaganda justifying the expansion; the Monte, the state-funded debt necessary to finance the costly wars; the various political offices in the *contado* and the *distretto* responsible for the administration of the subject territory; and different power groups in neighboring cities in collusion with whom the Florentines sought to expand their influence beyond their territorial borders. We would also have to pay attention to the many legal and

---

[70] Skinner's lack of attention to the rhetorical aspects of the writings of the Florentine civic humanists is surprising in the light of the importance he attaches to agency, intentionality, and the illocutionary force of texts in his methodological works; see especially "Meaning and Understanding in the History of Ideas," in *Meaning and Context: Quentin Skinner and his Critics*, ed. J. Tully (Cambridge: Polity Press, 1988), 29–67. For a related criticism, see Victoria Kahn, *Machiavellian Rhetoric: From the Counter-Reformation to Milton* (Princeton: Princeton University Press, 1994), 243–8.

ritual practices contributing to define the relationship between the city and its dominion, and the numerous visual symbols used by the Florentines to manifest and articulate their claim to empire. By studying civic humanist imperial myth-making within such a broad political, social and aesthetic context, and by focusing on the various processes and practices by which these myths were created and reproduced, we should be able to enlarge our understanding of how the Florentine republic was establishing, consolidating, and expanding imperial power at the turn of the Quattrocento. Since myth-making and political manipulation were important aspects of Florentine Renaissance culture, such an approach might also provide important new insights into the historical context in which these practices took place. While Richard Trexler has dealt with this side of Florentine political culture extensively and in some depth in his studies of the public and ritual life of the Florentine republic, very little has as yet been done in this direction within the field of textual criticism and the study of humanism.[71]

Since this is not the place to initiate such an ambitious enterprise, I shall here confine myself to one example showing how the study of civic humanist myth-making can help us to recover the meaning and rhetorical power of important texts – texts which for different reasons have become marginalized in the ideology-centered scholarly tradition on civic humanism. The text I have chosen, Matteo Palmieri's Latin chronicle describing Florence's acquisition of Pisa in 1406, *De captivitate Pisarum* (*c.* 1450), offers an example of myth-making where the representation of a specific political reality does not so much depend upon as call into being a relationship of domination and subordination. Such a text, I hope to demonstrate, is possible to interpret even with only a marginal knowledge of the immediate context in which it was produced. Having subjected the text to a rhetorical reading, we may then go on to surround it with meaningful and illuminating contexts in order to determine its relationship to historical reality, mode of interac-

---

[71] Richard C. Trexler, *Public Life in Renaissance Florence* (Ithaca: Cornell University Press, 1980). Two studies that spring to mind in this connection are Kahn, *Machiavellian Rhetoric* and Wayne A. Rebhorn, *The Emperor of Men's Minds: Literature and the Renaissance Discourse of Rhetoric* (Ithaca: Cornell University Press, 1995). But both Kahn and Rebhorn deal mainly with a later period and are more interested in studying how Renaissance rhetoricians understood their own practice than inquiring into how rhetoric was used for political and other ends. For studies of myth-making outside the field of Florentine Renaissance studies, see Paul Zanker, *The Power of Images in the Age of Augustus*, trans. A. Shapiro (Ann Arbor: University of Michigan Press, 1990); Stephen Greenblatt, *Shakespearean Negotiations: The Circulation of Social Energy in Renaissance England* (Oxford: Clarendon Press, 1988); Greenblatt, *Marvellous Possessions: The Wonder of the New World* (Oxford: Clarendon, 1991); Edward W. Said, *Orientalism* (New York: Pantheon Books, 1978); Said, *Culture and Imperialism* (London: Chatto and Windus, 1993).

tion, and place within the broader context of political, social, and cultural practices.

While the imperial myth of Bruni's *Laudatio* addresses cities not yet firmly under Florentine control but within the Florentine orbit of power, Matteo Palmieri's Latin chronicle *De captivitate Pisarum* focuses on the republic's relation to the conquered and subjugated city of Pisa. In contrast to Palmieri's *Vita civile*, which has come to receive its fair share of scholarly attention recently and is generally considered to offer a solid, mainstream version of civic humanism, *De captivitate* remains one of the least studied and most misunderstood major works of the Florentine Renaissance.[72] The perplexity and embarrassment modern Renaissance scholars have experienced before this work are understandable. As a piece of undisguised imperialist propaganda, *De captivitate* sits uncomfortably next to the idealistic teaching of the *Vita civile*.[73] Since the text not only resists being classified according to the facile categories of civic humanist historiography, but also goes a long way to question and subvert many of the general assumptions underlying this scholarly tradition, one can easily understand why it has come to be written out of the civic humanist canon. Scholarly attempts to come to grips with *De captivitate* have been confined to investigations into Palmieri's use of contemporary sources and classical historiographical models, vague remarks about the roles of fortune and moral and psychological qualities in the text, and complaints about the work's failure to live up to the standard for humanist historiography set by Bruni's *Historiae*, with which it often circulated in the manuscripts of the period.

The difficulties we experience when dealing with *De captivitate* arise largely from our problem of defining a proper or meaningful context for the work. It is not easy to see how *De captivitate* fits into Palmieri's intellectual development, for example, which is supposed to have evolved from the civic humanism of the *Vita civile* to the disillusioned Platonism of the *Città di vita*. Although we have reason to believe that the text was composed around 1450, we do not have, and will probably

---

[72] The text in Latin with Italian translation is in Palmieri, *La presa di Pisa*. References are to the Latin original, referred to here as *De captivitate*. For general introductions to Palmieri's thought, see George M. Carpetto, *The Humanism of Matteo Palmieri* (Rome: Bulzoni, 1984); Claudio Finzi, *Matteo Palmieri dalla "Vita civile" alla "Città di vita"* (Rome: Giuffrè, 1984). For a concentrated account of the republicanism of Palmieri's *Vita civile*, see Viroli, *From Politics to Reason of State*, 82–5. On *De captivitate*, see Donald Wilcox, "Matteo Palmieri and the 'De captivitate Pisarum liber'," in *Renaissance Studies in Honor of Hans Baron*, 267–81; Alessandra Mita Ferraro, "Introduzione," in Palmieri, *La presa di Pisa*, vii–xxxiii.

[73] For a reading of the *Vita civile* that questions this prevailing view, see John Najemy's essay (chapter 3 of this volume).

never have, any way of knowing what prompted Palmieri to chronicle the Pisan war in Latin more than forty years after the event. We know, moreover, that *De captivitate* draws heavily upon Neri Capponi's vernacular *Commentari della guerra o dell'acquisto di Pisa*, and one modern historian has even claimed that the concluding speeches of the work are mere translations from Capponi.[74] But as to why Palmieri would have engaged in the unusual practice of translating from the vernacular into Latin, we are completely in the dark. However, in spite of these interpretative problems, *De captivitate* is a highly readable text which offers fascinating insights both into the relationship between the Florentine republic and its subject territory, and also into the mentality that fueled and was fostered by the city's territorial expansion.

The text opens with a declaration about the purpose of writing history, followed by a fairly conventional account of the background to the Florence–Pisa conflict. The war of 1405–6 is narrated in great detail, with much attention paid to the resistance of the Pisans and the hardships they suffered during the final siege. The circumstances of Pisa's capitulation and the Florentine army's entry into the city are accounted for. Two long speeches delivered on the occasion follow, the first by the Florentine commissioner Gino Capponi, the father of the work's dedicatee, Neri Capponi, and the second by a Pisan representative, a certain Bartolomeo da Piombino. Palmieri goes on to describe how the triumph was celebrated back in Florence. In closing, he relates how a Pisan delegation was received in Florence and there handed over the city's formal submission to the Florentine authorities.

While Gregorio Dati had viewed the conquest of Pisa as a just punishment for the support the Pisans had given the Visconti during the recent Milanese War, Palmieri defines the conflict in terms of a final showdown in a longstanding contest over Tuscan hegemony: "Everyone was hoping for spoils, because one was fighting not only to maintain possession of one's own, but also to establish empire over Tuscany, because it seemed as if fortune now was going to let arms decide which of the two cities should rule."[75] In this regard, his view of the war closely resembles that of Leonardo Bruni, who in the preface to the *Historiae* compared Florence's recent conquest of Pisa to Rome's ultimate victory over Carthage.[76] Initially, Palmieri represents the conflict between Pisa

[74] Wilcox, "Matteo Palmieri," 268.   [75] Palmieri, *De captivitate*, 8.
[76] "The siege and final conquest, fought with equal obstinacy by victors and vanquished, includes deeds that are so worthy of memory that they appear in no way inferior to the greatest deeds of the ancients that we read about" (quoted from *The Humanism of Leonardo Bruni*, 191). Cf. Mita Ferraro, "Introduzione," xxv.

and Florence as a contest between equals. The relationship between the two cities is symmetrical: what holds good for one of them is also true of the other. This basic equality is grounded in certain general assumptions about human nature and the nature of war expressed in the work. It is said, for example, that all living beings have a natural inclination to look after their own interests and to protect themselves and their own. Conquerors and conquered are also expected to behave in a certain way. After their defeat, the Pisans thus step forward to acknowledge that they would have acted in exactly the same manner as the Florentines had the victory fallen to them instead: "to keep what one has conquered is in accordance with human nature, and if we had been the victors, we would have tried to do the same."[77]

These observations lead us, unexpectedly, back to Palmieri's discussion of Roman military conduct and his treatment of conquered peoples in the *Vita civile*. Roman military history instructs us, we are told by Palmieri's mouthpiece Agnolo Pandolfini, that combatants who give up the fight and seek the protection of their opponents should be accepted even if they have defended themselves bravely and with great spirit. Inversely, it teaches that even though spirited men are urged by nature to fight vigorously when there is still hope of victory, they should also be able to endure with equanimity the fate of the defeated.[78] These brief comments on how victors and defeated ought to conduct themselves after the cessation of hostilities seem to provide a context within which *De captivitate* could, and perhaps should, be interpreted. For there can be no doubt that the Florentines and the Pisans are represented in *De captivitate* in the roles of exemplary victors and vanquished. While the Florentines show great mercy towards the surrendered city by distributing bread among the starving population and guaranteeing that the city's commercial liberties will not be infringed, the Pisans respond by welcoming the Florentine conquest as a relief and a promise of a new, bright future.

Although the passage describing the exemplary conduct of victors and vanquished in the *Vita civile* provides us with an important key for unlocking the meaning of *De captivitate*, the work cannot be understood merely as an attempt on Palmieri's part to illustrate or elaborate upon

---

[77] Palmieri, *De captivitate*, 64.
[78] Palmieri, *Vita civile*, 130: "Chi vuole ricorrere alla fede di chi il combatte, sempre debbe essere acceptato, non obstante che con animo franco et gagliardamente si sia difeso. L'animo bene informato dalla natura sempre debbe fortemente combattere per vincere quando si conviene et, se pure la fortuna lo supera et stringe a essere perdente, con patientia sopportare."

these general principles. *De captivitate* is not a self-contained, autonomous text or a harmless humanist exercise that can be detached from the extraliterary reality in which it was conceived. It must instead be read in the wider context of Florentine territorial expansion and imperial domination over Pisa. But it does not suffice to say that *De captivitate* was shaped by the imperial relations of domination and subordination in which it was caught up. As I hope to demonstrate, we cannot understand this text properly without acknowledging that it was participating actively in the preservation and reinforcement of the imperial context that produced it. *De captivitate* is, in short, a text designed to produce submission and to establish and legitimate the principal divide between rulers and subjects which separated Florentines and Pisans in the middle of the fifteenth century.

While the symmetrical and formal view of the Florence–Pisa conflict adopted at the outset of *De captivitate* had the effect of placing the two combatants on equal terms before the war, its consequences for the status of the defeated Pisans, once the war has been concluded, are, to put it mildly, grim. The iron law of victory which places the surrendered city at the complete mercy of the conqueror is in *De captivitate* seen as the basis for all ensuing dealings between the two peoples. This fundamental fact is also acknowledged by the Pisans, when they, through their spokesman Bartolomeo da Piombino, express their gratitude for the way they have been treated after the capitulation: "Our crimes, whatever they may have been, have certainly been exceeded by the clemency of the Florentines, and we should therefore rejoice at having been defeated by such victors. In fact, if we, according to the law of victory, are obliged to obey the victors, in whom should we put our complete confidence if not in those victors who now wish our salvation, although it lies in their power to destroy us?"[79] As a consequence of the Florentine triumph, the once reciprocal relationship between the two cities has undergone a radical transformation and become polarized and radically uneven: from having been rivals, Florence and Pisa have now become ruler and ruled. From now on, it is understood, all Pisan possessions should be conceived of as gifts of grace from their Florentine rulers.

Far from betraying Palmieri's tragic awareness of the fact that everything is transitory and that Florence one day may suffer the same cruel fate as Pisa, as has been suggested,[80] the representation of Florence and Pisa as interchangeable at the outset of the conflict, is, I will claim,

[79] Palmieri, *De captivitate*, 64.   [80] Mita Ferraro, "Introduzione," xxviii.

designed to create a framework within which the conditions of Florentine domination over Pisa can be worked out in principal terms and with great effect. One of Palmieri's chief concerns in *De captivitate*, it seems, is to define and establish the appropriate relationship between conqueror and conquered, between ruler and subject and, more particularly, between Florence and Pisa after the Florentine conquest in 1406 – and to do so in absolute terms and once and for all.

This intention is evident from the narrative point of view adopted by Palmieri, which enables him to impose an oppressively monolithic perspective on the conflict. Although many voices are recorded in the chronicle, a massive uniformity of opinion is buried under the polyphonic surface of the text. Everyone who comes forward to speak in the work – the Florentine commissioner, Gino Capponi, the Pisan representatives, Bartolomeo da Piombino, Giovanni d'Appiano, and the delegation of people from Campi Bisenzi who call on the Pisans in an attempt to solicit their surrender – express the same basic view of the conflict: since Pisa's fate is to come under Florentine domination and since the city will benefit from this development, the Pisans should accept their new status as Florentine subjects with equanimity.[81] An analysis of how the key concepts of civic humanism – justice, the common good, and liberty – are played out in the text will reveal the imperial double standard Palmieri seeks to establish as the basis for the relationship between the two cities.

Like most other theorists of republican self-government, Palmieri defines justice in the *Vita civile* as the most excellent of all virtues and the very foundation upon which a well-ordered republic rests.[82] In *De captivitate* this view is articulated by the Pisans as they, shortly after the revolt provoked by the selling of the city, dispatch a delegation to Florence to clarify their position. In an oration closely modeled on the teaching of the *Vita civile*, the Pisan representatives appeal to the Florentines' innate sense of justice:

If nature had allowed men to remain satisfied with what they have as they are satisfied with their own knowledge, justice would seldom be violated . . . We are

---

[81] For this reason, it makes little difference if the orations at the end of *De captivitate* are mere translations of speeches found in Neri Capponi's *Commentari della guerra o dell'acquisto di Pisa* as Donald Wilcox has claimed; see "Matteo Palmieri," 280. Instead of considering *De captivitate* derivative due to these borrowings, we should ask what purposes the quotations serve for Palmieri. To insert extensive translations from existing texts is also one of the main textual strategies of the *Vita civile*, where Palmieri translates from classical Latin authors into the vernacular.

[82] Palmieri, *Vita civile*, 104.

of the opinion that you Florentines are wise and discriminating enough to understand how inhumane and contrary to all sense of justice it is not only to desire the things of others but, having acquired them through fraud, to try to maintain possession of them by force of arms.[83]

Towards the end of the speech, the Pisans claim that nothing more befits a well-ordered state than to maintain justice. Since justice gives to each his due and no one can be said to give according to justice unless he does so willingly, Florence should now, they argue, return to them what they consider to be rightfully theirs, including the strongholds of Ripafratta and Santa Maria still in Florentine possession.[84]

Although the oration makes a strong appeal to principles central to republicanism in general and Florentine civic humanism in particular, the Florentine authorities remain inflexible. In fact, they consider the speech to be so provocative that even the most cautious among them now see no other option than to declare war on the Pisans. Although Palmieri never informs us whether this strong reaction was provoked by the principles invoked in the speech or merely by their application in this specific case, it is evident that he viewed the Florentines' own claim to justice to be of a different order.[85] In *De captivitate* justice is on the side of the victors. Far from being an independent and disinterested principle by which both sides in the conflict might judge each other, it is the reward and the responsibility of the conqueror.

The chronicle gives the same rhetorical twist to the common good, another cornerstone of the civil philosophy of the *Vita civile*. In that work Palmieri argued that a magistrate or ruler of a republic should care for the city as a whole and at all times act in the interest of the common good.[86] In the preface to *De captivitate*, he similarly claims that men should devote their learning and skills to serve the good of all people, or, as we would say today, humanity. If this is not possible, they should instead work for the good of the majority of people, or at least for the good of their own republic.[87] This is also the explicit motivating factor behind Palmieri's own enterprise in writing *De captivitate*, as well as the principle underlying Florence's policy vis-à-vis Pisa, with which the author finds himself in complete agreement. This noble and generous attitude contrasts sharply with the Pisan approach, at least as it is presented in the self-denunciatory speech delivered by Giovanni

[83] Palmieri, *De captivitate*, 18. [84] Ibid., 20.
[85] Shortly afterwards a Florentine embassy was sent to the king of France to argue that the war they were fighting was a *bellum justum*; see ibid., 46.
[86] Palmieri, *Vita civile*, 131–2. [87] Palmieri, *De captivitate*, 2.

d'Appiano, the former Pisan ruler, on the occasion of the consignment of his city to the Florentines. According to Giovanni, the Pisans have during the conflict attended exclusively to their own interests and in so doing come to neglect the common good. He now urges the Florentines to assume responsibility for the common good (the common good of whom, we are never told), since it is "a precious thing that concerns the whole of Italy."[88] While the Florentine conception of the common good in *De captivitate* is represented as inclusive and expansive, potentially embracing the good of the whole of Italy, the Pisan view is seen as restrictive and exclusive, as a form of self-interest rather than as the common good properly understood. It is therefore only appropriate, one is led to conclude, that the good of the Pisans should now be absorbed, incorporated and made part of the common good of the Florentines. The logic of this conceptual annexation is made explicit in Gino Capponi's speech before the defeated Pisans, in which he forecasts that the Florentine domination will prove beneficial not only to the Florentines but to the Pisans as well.[89]

The traditional republican value of liberty too takes on different guises in *De captivitate*, depending on which side of the conflict it appears. Palmieri relates, for example, how the Pisan citizenry, after having overthrown their tyrant, assembled in a public ceremony to swear solemnly that they should all defend their liberty and their popular government against the Florentines.[90] This account of the Pisans' heroic commitment to the republican values cherished by the civic humanists may tempt us into believing that Palmieri's real purpose is to criticize the ruthless imperialist policy of the Florentine regime. This expectation is at first also nourished by Palmieri's way of reporting how the news of the Pisan revolt was received in Florence. For at the same time as the whole Florentine citizenry is said to have lamented the dishonor inflicted on the republic, we learn that discussions arose all around the city, in which "some accused the guards of the fortress, others extolled the audacity and virtue of the Pisans, and not a few people condemned the neglect of the magistrates who had been entrusted with the running of the war."[91] It seems that Palmieri is here open to the possibility that the Pisans' recovery of their liberty should be viewed with respect, and perhaps even admiration.

But as the narrative of the war unfolds, we are made painfully aware that such a reading is utterly untenable, based as it is on a set of

[88] Ibid., 54.   [89] Ibid., 62.   [90] Ibid., 22.   [91] Ibid., 18.

erroneous assumptions about Palmieri's republicanism. In reality, the Florentines' reaction to the news of the Pisan revolt is a rare, if not unique, moment when the fresh air of referential meaning can be sensed in *De captivitate*. It offers itself as a crack in the rhetorical armor of the text, when Palmieri, for reasons unknown to us, is made to say something that does not serve, but goes completely contrary to, his rhetorical purpose. As the text progresses, it becomes abundantly clear that the Pisan people's devotion to the ideals of republican liberty does not constitute a source of respect or admiration in the eyes of the Florentine authorities or in those of their chronicler. If Pisan love of liberty has a purpose to serve in *De captivitate*, it is to enhance the glory of the Florentine triumph by underscoring the ferocious nature of the Pisan people's resistance.

Again, we are made to witness how the Pisans are brought before their conqueror to solemnly renounce their former commitments. According to their spokesman Bartolomeo da Piombino, the recently concluded war should not be understood in terms of Florentine aggression or as a defense of Pisan liberty, but as the unfortunate outcome of a great misunderstanding. The whole episode, the final siege included, had taken place only because the Pisans had failed to acknowledge the great humanity and generosity of the Florentines. Only after the Florentines had entered the starving city and liberated the Pisans from famine had they become aware of their mistake.[92] The good will of the Florentines had ultimately been demonstrated by their resolve not to destroy Pisa, but to keep her markets open and to grant immunity to the whole population so that everyone would be free to continue to live and work in the city.[93] In reality, Bartolomeo went on to argue, Pisan liberty would benefit from the surrender, since the city under Florentine rule would no longer risk falling prey to tyrants as in the past.[94]

Having painted this rosy picture of Florentine domination, Bartolomeo goes on to exhort his compatriots to seize the opportunity offered by the Florentine conquest: "Go therefore and attend to your affairs and trades in security and liberty and with good hope, and work so that your population and your affairs will increase, as we hope."[95] Needless to say, the freedom – *libertas* – frequently referred to in Bartolomeo's speech is not the participatory liberty celebrated by modern historians of civic humanism, but the negative form enjoyed by subjects living under the protection of the law. The ultimate fixing of the

[92] Ibid., 66.   [93] Ibid.   [94] Ibid., 64.   [95] Ibid., 62.

Pisans in their new status as Florentine subjects is achieved as Bartolomeo's final words are met with the acclaim of the assembled Pisan citizenry: "Let us hope that, having obtained our safety and such great favor, that the Pisans shall always be obedient, faithful, and most beloved of the Florentine people."[96]

It should be clear by now that Palmieri's *De captivitate* is not an innocent text that can be read in isolation from the historical context of Florentine domination and imperialism within which it was written. The work can, consequently, not be dismissed as a mere literary exercise or exculpated as a failed attempt in the developing genre of humanist historiography.[97] Instead, we have reason to believe that one of Palmieri's principal aims in writing *De captivitate* was to establish and consolidate the conceptual relationship between Florentines and Pisans as one between rulers and subjects.

It has always been the privilege of conquerors and rulers to command obedience, to reshape the identities of conquered peoples, and to impose their fictions on the world. Instead of dealing with this complex process, Palmieri's *De captivitate* represents what had by the mid-fifteenth century become the founding event and defining moment of Florentine–Pisan relations: the moment of conquest and surrender which had brought Pisa under Florentine control and established a relationship of domination and subordination between the two cities. The rhetorical enactment of imperial power performed in *De captivitate* cannot be abstracted from the development of similar ideas and practices of imperial control in the political, social, and cultural context in which the text participates. We know, for example, that Florentine authorities, immediately after the acquisition of Pisa, sought to impose a law prohibiting mixed marriages between Florentines and Pisans. This law soon proved impossible to implement, but other judicial regulations and cultural practices remained in force to remind the Florentines and the Pisans of the radical divide separating them.[98] Shortly after the conquest, Pisan representatives were accordingly required to participate alongside Florence's other extra-urban subjects in the feast of St. John the Baptist, Florence's patron saint, and to give obeisance to the republic through offerings and

---

[96] Ibid., 66. The eternal nature of the event is also referred to in Gino Capponi's speech; see ibid., 54.

[97] Cf. Wilcox, "Matteo Palmieri"; Mita Ferraro, "Introduzione."

[98] On Florence's rule of Pisa in the fifteenth century in general, see Michael Mallett, "Pisa and Florence in the Fifteenth Century: Aspects of the Period of the First Florentine Domination," in *Florentine Studies*, 403–41.

tributes.99 The *marzocco*, the Florentine lion and the very emblem of the violent potency of the Florentine people, began in the meantime to show up on palaces and bridges all around Pisa. As a measure to prevent rebellion, leading Pisan citizens were in times of external peril deported to Florence and kept in custody there. On the Pisan side, tax concessions and rent-free housing were introduced in order to attract Florentine settlers to the city. Up until the Pisan rebellion of 1494, Florentines continued to go to Pisa as conquerors and rulers, and Pisans to come to Florence as conquered subjects.

Palmieri's and the Florentine authorities' attempts to fix the Pisans in the role of the obedient subject were later to meet with failure. When Charles VIII of France descended on Italy in 1494, the Pisans rose in rebellion and reclaimed their liberty. The *marzocchi* on the bridges over the Arno were destroyed and thrown into the river, Florentine citizens were attacked and their houses sacked. The uprising came as a complete surprise to the Florentine commissioner, who is recorded to have said only a few days before the revolt that he had no reason to doubt the loyalty of the Pisans, since he could not imagine that anyone among them, after having been subject to Florentine rule for so long, would be able to recall the city's past liberty any more. He was spectacularly wrong, of course. The night after the French had entered Pisa, the streets of the city resounded to the ancient cry "libertà! libertà!"100 A Pisan notary wrote around this time in his *Ricordi*: "The Pisans have always been a free and generous people. The wars they have fought against the Ligurians and the Genoese since the commencement of the Pisan name have demonstrated their worth . . . Liberty has always been dear to our people, because it was given to us by our ancestors and betters."101 This was one of the simple facts of life, which no judicial discrimination, ritual discipline, or Florentine myth-making had been able to alter.

While Hans Baron, who was bold enough to claim that his civic humanism reflected the political realities of early fifteenth-century Florence, made the serious mistake of accepting civic humanist propaganda on its own terms, other scholars have been more modest when they, on Baron's behalf, have claimed that civic humanism was only an

---

[99] See Dati, *Istoria*, 253. On the feast of San Giovanni in general, see Cesare Guasti, *Le feste di S. Giovanni Battista in Firenze* (Florence, 1884); Heide L. Chretien, *The Festival of San Giovanni: Imagery and Political Power in Renaissance Florence* (New York: Peter Lang, 1994); Trexler, *Public Life*, 257-8.

[100] Piero Vaglienti, *Storia dei suoi tempi 1492–1514*, ed. G. Berti, M. Luzzati, and E. Tongiorgi (Pisa: Nistri-Lischi e Pacini Editori, 1982), 11 and 17.

[101] "Ricordi di Ser Perizolo da Pisa dall'anno 1422 sino al 1510," *Archivio storico italiano* 6 (1845): 391.

ideology, but a good, peaceful, and liberal one. Reexamining in the course of this essay the texts on which Baron and his sympathizers base their claims, we have found that they contain carefully couched myths and fictions designed to justify and promote Florentine expansionism and aspirations to imperial rule. If civic humanism was born out of the controversy between Antonio Loschi and a group of Florentine intellectuals at the turn of the Quattrocento, as Baron claimed, it was from the very outset articulated as a defense, not only of Florentine liberty, but also of the city's claim to a special Roman heritage and right to empire.

This observation leads us to the question of how civic humanism should be defined. In order to approach this issue we need to understand that civic humanism comes to us as a double myth: on the one hand, as a modern mediating myth created by Baron and elaborated on and modified by later scholars; on the other hand, as a Renaissance myth produced for a different age and for different ends by the Florentine civic humanists of the early Quattrocento. To understand how these two myths relate to each other and to the different realities in which they were conceived is to understand what constitutes civic humanism. For the modern and the Renaissance myths are not unrelated. They share many values, beliefs, and preconceived ideas about man and human society and they also participate in the same myth-making mechanisms. But the modern myth-makers have preferred to cleanse the original myth of some of its less attractive features – from a modern point of view – particularly the oligarchic manipulation hiding behind the policy of consensus and civic unity analyzed elsewhere in this volume by John Najemy, and the aggressive imperialism pursued under the cloak of Florentine, Tuscan, and Italian liberty, discussed in this essay.

By having defined civic humanism in this way, I hope to have cleared the ground for new approaches. I have in this essay proposed that we should shift our focus from a study of ideologies to a study of myth-making. Such a move would allow us to leave the modern civic humanist myth behind and to concentrate our energies on the study of how power was established, maintained, and expanded in Renaissance Florence, how it was analyzed, questioned, and contested, how myths and ideologies were produced and staged, from what materials and for what ends, and how they interacted with other cultural practices and were played out in personal, political, social, and cultural relations. Such a new approach would have to be based on a rhetorical reading of texts; a broad, open and pluralistic form of contextualism; and good, solid, old-fashioned scholarship.

CHAPTER 5

*Rhetoric, history, and ideology:
the civic panegyrics of Leonardo Bruni*

James Hankins

Dum patriam laudat, damnat dum Poggius hostem,
Nec malus est civis, nec bonus historicus.
Jacopo Sannazaro, *Epigr.* I.20

I am afraid I shall have to bore the reader slightly by relating, in the first part of this essay, some dull but necessary information about the context, content and reception of two orations by Leonardo Bruni: the *Laudatio Florentinae urbis* and the *Oratio in funere Ioannis Stroze*. As is well known, these are the two most widely cited texts in modern discussions of Florentine civic humanism. Together with the *De militia* (*On Knighthood*), they are practically the only texts by Bruni read by historians of political thought. After that I hope things will get rather more interesting. I want to show in some detail the relationship between the rhetorical form and the historical (or rather unhistorical) character of these texts. My contention will be that both texts have been misunderstood because modern readers have not sufficiently appreciated the rhetorical conventions they assume and have not troubled to situate them in the context of Bruni's other works. This done, it will be clear, I believe, why the old dichotomy, "civic humanist or professional rhetorician?" that has bedeviled Bruni scholarship since the 1960s is fundamentally anachronistic.[1] In closing, I shall question whether "civic humanism", at least as it has been defined by Hans Baron and J. G. A. Pocock, is the best term to describe Bruni's humanism.[2]

[1] The dichotomy emerged from the well-known controversy between Hans Baron and Jerrold Seigel in the 1960s (see below, 160).
[2] For Baron's conception of civic humanism, see A. Rabil, Jr., "The Significance of 'Civic Humanism' in the Interpretation of the Italian Renaissance," in *Renaissance Humanism: Foundations, Forms, and Legacy*, 3 vols. (Philadelphia: University of Pennsylvania Press, 1988), II: 141–74; for Pocock's, see his *The Machiavellian Moment: Florentine Political Thought and the Atlantic Republican Tradition* (Princeton: Princeton University Press, 1975), esp. chapter VII.

The literature on the *Laudatio Florentinae urbis* is of course extensive, and many of the fundamental issues regarding the text have now been satisfactorily addressed. We have two adequate critical editions and an English translation.[3] Baron has established beyond reasonable doubt the date of the oration as summer 1403 or summer 1404; the present writer has argued for 1404 as the preferable date between these two alternatives.[4] Baron has also studied the historical context of the *Laudatio* in great detail; indeed the so-called "Baron thesis" might be described as an elaborately contextualized reading of the oration.[5] Antonio Santosuosso has written a detailed analysis of the structure of the oration and its relationship to its model, the *Panathenaicus* of Aelius Aristides.[6]

But other aspects of the text still require comment. The first is Bruni's motivation in composing the oration. Jerrold Seigel suggested over thirty years ago that the *Laudatio* was a kind of exhibition piece intended to promote Bruni's candidacy to succeed Salutati as chancellor of Florence.[7] This is an attractive proposal. In 1404, Bruni had dropped out of law school a second time – probably he could not afford the expense of taking his degree – and was casting about for gainful employment. Salutati was an elderly man nearing the end of his career, and Bruni would surely have had his eye on his post. We know that Bruni was put up for the chancellorship after Salutati's death in 1406, and that Bruni refused the position, but by this time (since March 1405)

[3] The text is edited in V. Zaccaria, "Pier Candido Decembrio e Leonardo Bruni (Notizie dall'epistolario del Decembrio)," *Studi medievali*, ser. 3, 8 (1967): 504 54, at 529 54, and H. Baron, *From Petrarch to Leonardo Bruni: Studies in Humanistic and Political Literature* (Chicago: University of Chicago Press, 1968), 232 63. An English translation may be found in in B. G. Kohl and R. G. Witt, *The Earthly Republic: Italian Humanists on Government and Society* (Philadelphia: University of Pennsylvania Press, 1978), 135 75; part IV only is translated in *The Humanism of Leonardo Bruni*, trans. G. Griffiths, James Hankins, and D. Thompson (Binghamton, New York: Center for Medieval and Early Renaissance Studies, 1987), 116 21. Stefano Baldassari is preparing a new critical edition of the oration, to be published in Florence by the Società Internazionale per lo Studio del Medioevo Latino.
[4] See J. Hankins, *Plato in the Italian Renaissance*, 2 vols. (London and Leiden: Brill, 1990), II: 367 78 (appendix 1), with references to the earlier literature on the dating controversy.
[5] H. Baron, *The Crisis of the Early Italian Renaissance: Civic Humanism and Republican Liberty in an Age of Classicism and Tyranny*, 2 vols. (Princeton: Princeton University Press, 1955; revised edition in one volume, 1966).
[6] A. Santosuosso, "Leonardo Bruni Revisited: A Reassessment of Hans Baron's Thesis on the Influence of the Classics in the *Laudatio Florentine urbis*," in *Aspects of Late Medieval Government and Society. Essays Presented to J. R. Lander*, ed. J. G. Rowe (Toronto: University of Toronto Press, 1986), 25 51. On the *Laudatio* see also N. Rubinstein, "Il Bruni a Firenze: retorica e politica," in *Leonardo Bruni cancelliere della repubblica di Firenze, convegno di studi*, ed. P. Viti (Florence: Olschki, 1990), 15 28, and P. Viti, *Leonardo Bruni e Firenze: studi sulle lettere pubbliche e private* (Rome: Bulzoni, 1992), esp. 3 91.
[7] J. E. Seigel, "'Civic Humanism' or Ciceronian Rhetoric? The Culture of Petrarch and Bruni," *Past and Present* 34 (1966): 3 48, at 16, note 33.

he was firmly established in his position as papal secretary and high in the favor of Innocent VII. We also know that, in 1404, Bruni was closely identified with the circle of Niccolò Niccoli – indeed, Bruni was Niccoli's alter ego in this period – and that Niccoli's group had acquired a reputation for unpatriotic and snobbish sentiments. The *Laudatio* would have been a perfect instrument for establishing Bruni's devotion to Florence and improving his standing with the ruling oligarchy. A passage in the *Laudatio*, where Bruni states that he runs a personal risk of offending Florence's enemies by his panegyric, has the appearance of a clumsy effort to emphasize his loyalty to the city.[8] Another passage holds out to his readers the tempting prospect of a history of Florence, written by Bruni, celebrating her great deeds.[9] Just how tempting the prospect was would become clear a decade later, when the Florentine government gave Bruni citizenship and a tax privilege in perpetuity in return for his services as official historian. From this point of view, the *Laudatio* might be considered a kind of prospectus for the *Florentine Histories*, with which it shares a number of themes and narratives.

The *Laudatio* of course needs to be seen in the context of Florentine history as well as of Bruni's biography. The brief period between 1402 and the conquest of Pisa in 1406 was probably the moment when Florence exercised more power in Italy than at any other time in her history. The Milanese empire had collapsed like a punctured balloon with the death of Duke Giangaleazzo Visconti in September of 1402, and Lombardy was quickly reduced to a state of internecine strife. Ladislaus of Durazzo had not yet begun his rise to power; the Papal States were a shambles owing to the effects of the Schism. Genoa was smarting from maritime defeat and racked by civil war. Only Venice could be considered a serious rival, and Venice had yet to turn her attentions seriously to the *Terrafirma*. The Florentines were riding high, and dreams of empire were in the air. When Florence captured her ancient rival, Pisa, in 1406, Bruni and his friends saw in the victory the beginnings of a new Roman empire, based in Florence. Bruni exulted with his friend Niccoli over the new Florentine acquisition, joking that he would now have to revise his *Laudatio* to take account of recent developments. He did not mention that Florence's victory had been won less by *bellica virtus* than by starvation and bribery. Nor did he describe how the Pisans had been reduced to cannibalism and necrop-

---

[8] Baron, *From Petrarch to Bruni*: 249–50.
[9] Ibid., 254–5: "But now is not the occasion to relate so many different battles and such great deeds; they require their own work, and a large one at that, which I hope I shall someday attempt."

hagy by the siege, nor how the Florentines had stood by while the Pisan faction they supported slaughtered their enemies in the streets.

The *Laudatio* was born in this heady atmosphere of imperialist triumph and expansionism. The oration, indeed, is essentially an imperialist tract, a celebration of Florence's potentiality to be the center of world empire. The theme is stated unambiguously and repeatedly throughout. The opening section, containing the physical description of Florence, plays repeatedly on the theme of centrality and *aurea mediocritas*. Florence's central position in the Italian peninsula makes her highly defensible, yet a crossroads with excellent communications. As though queen of Italy (*quasi regina quedam Italie*), she is seated midway between the Tyrrhenian and the Adriatic seas. Port cities, by contrast (we are surely meant to think of Venice), are unhealthy and difficult to defend; Bruni spends three pages of a thirty-page text showing with a wealth of historical examples why an inland is better than a coastal situation.[10] Florence's hilly terrain, moreover, is a mean between the mountains and the plains, her climate is perfectly balanced and her hinterland fruitful. The section culminates with Bruni's declaration that anyone who beholds the greatness and beauty of Florence will cease to be amazed at her great and wide-ranging deeds, and will aver that she is capable of attaining dominion and empire over the whole world (*sufficientem autument ad totius orbis dominium imperiumque adipiscendum*).

The second part of the oration, which deals with the origins, character, institutions, and mores of the Florentines, continues the imperial theme. Florence is the daughter of Rome and inherits her empire: "To you, men of Florence, belongs dominion over all the earth by a kind of hereditary right, as a paternal inheritance." To those who might object that Florence's constitution is republican, not monarchical, and hence inappropriate for imperial rule, Bruni points out that the greatest period of Rome fell under the Roman republic. Rome's republican virtues and civilization declined when it came under the rule of the wicked Caesars, and this decadence led ultimately to the fall of Rome, but Florence preserved intact her ancient constitutional forms and therefore her virtues and cultural brilliance. She was now ready to take over leadership in Italy. She has deserved empire by her virtues, which are superior to those of all other cities. For instance, her liberality towards exiles from other cities has made her in effect the common

---

[10] More extensive treatment was probably required on rhetorical grounds, since to praise a city for its inland situation would count as *admirabile* or paradoxical from the point of view of classical rhetoric; in antiquity, it was more usual to praise cities for their maritime situation (see Quintilian, *Institutio oratoria*, 3.7.27).

patria of all Italians (*hec communis quedam sit patria et totius Italie certissimum asilum*); her liberality towards neighboring cities in distress has made her their patron. Her spotless behavior in war and diplomacy rivals that of Rome. She is, finally, the cultural center of Italy. Her tongue is the purest, clearest, sweetest and most elegant in Italy; she has the greatest poets; humane letters, which have always flourished among princely peoples (*que in omni principe populo semper floruerunt*), in her alone have achieved their greatest vigor. She is thus in every way worthy to inherit the empire of Rome.

One might expect a text of this kind to have had little appeal outside Florence itself, but the information we now have on the *fortuna* of the *Laudatio* in the Renaissance belies this expectation.[11] The present writer's survey of Bruni manuscripts has turned up forty-three codices of this text in the original Latin, and one manuscript containing an Italian translation of the work.[12] There were no printed editions of the text in the Renaissance. This would be a respectable circulation for most early Renaissance texts, but, given Bruni's status as the best-selling author of the Quattrocento, it hardly amounts to overwhelming popularity. In fact, the text was among the less popular of Bruni's published works. By way of comparison, his translation of Aristotle's *Ethics* survives in 225 manuscripts and 31 printed editions; his version of St. Basil's *Epistula ad adolescentes* (Bruni's most popular work) survives in over 440 manuscripts and 91 printed editions; his own *Isagogicon moralis disciplinae* exists in 186 manuscripts and 70 printed editions. Many of Bruni's works were extremely popular in vernacular translations; the Italian translation of his *Commentaries on the First Punic War*, for example, circulated in over 150 manuscripts and a dozen printed editions. So the single manuscript containing Fra Lazaro da Padova's volgare version of the *Laudatio* is not a very impressive witness to the text's appeal outside the world of Latin readers.[13]

---

[11] A brief sketch of the *fortuna* of the text is found in Baron, *From Petrarch to Leonardo Bruni*, 152.

[12] J. Hankins, *Repertorium Brunianum: A Guide to the Writings of Leonardo Bruni*, Fonti per la storia dell'Italia medievale, Subsidia 3 (Rome: Istituto storico italiano per il medio evo, 1997), *ad indices*. Zaccaria, "Pier Candido Decembrio," and Baron, *From Petrarch to Leonardo Bruni*, had between them identified seven manuscripts of the text. Stefano Baldassari has now found an additional manuscript of the work.

[13] Fra Lazaro da Padova was a Dominican theologian who worked primarily in the court of Sixtus IV, but had spent some part of his youth in Florence, when he had acquired an admiration for the city. The text was published with a learned introduction in a rare imprint *per nozze* by F. P. Luiso, *Le vere lode de la inclita et gloriosa città di Firenze, composte in latino da Leonardo Bruni e tradotte in volgare dal frate Lazaro da Padova* (Florence, 1899) (copy at the Biblioteca Riccardiana, Florence); the Lazaro text was republished with Baron's edition of the Latin text in Leonardo Bruni, *Panegirico della città di Firenze: Testo italiano a fronte di Frate Lazaro da Padova*, presentation by G. De Toffol (Florence: La Nuova Italia, 1974).

The manuscript tradition also gives us an impression of the contemporary readership of Bruni's text. We have good information about the date and provenance of about three-quarters of the manuscripts. The survival pattern resembles that of most other humanistic literary texts. The bulk of the manuscripts can be dated to the middle decades of the fifteenth century, with the numbers dropping off rapidly after the introduction of printing; only five copies are securely datable to before 1440. As for geographical distribution, ten copies were written in Florence or owned by Florentines; another twelve are about evenly distributed between Lombardy, Rome, and the Veneto. A third of the manuscripts come from princely libraries and are generally the work of professional scribes; the rest are split between curial officials, notaries, lawyers, and Florentine patricians (including the Medici, Pandolfini, and Gaddi). *Habent sua fata libelli*, but we can sum up by saying that the *Laudatio* was a moderate success in Italy, though unpopular in northern Europe and Spain; within Italy, its readership was fairly typical for a Quattrocento humanistic text.

The one slightly unusual element is the large number of copies that can be associated with notaries, lawyers, and chancery officials. But contemporary testimonia give us some clues to the text's appeal in these quarters.[14] The earliest record we have of the *Laudatio* being read outside Bruni's immediate circle goes back to 1409, when it is quoted by the Bolognese jurist, Marcus de Canetulo, in a speech before the Council of Pisa. In a section of the speech labeled "de laudibus Florentie", Marcus praises Florence for its wisdom, prudence, and generosity in protecting other cities from tyrants like Giangaleazzo Visconti. He then cites Bruni, who was probably in the audience. "But why go on? How can I embrace all the praises of this city briefly, when that poet of our times, Aretinus, was not able to do so in his great work?"[15] In other words, Marcus found the *Laudatio* a useful store of commonplaces in praise of Florence. Other Renaissance orators used the *Laudatio* in the same way. It was, it seems, regularly quoted or paraphrased by visiting *podestà* whose duties included making ceremonial speeches at the beginning

---

[14] Some of the testimonia will be collected in vols. II and III of my *Repertorium* (forthcoming).
[15] The speech is preserved in a number of manuscripts, e.g., Biblioteca Apostolica Vaticana, MS Vat. lat. 3477; Florence, Biblioteca Riccardiana, MS 784, ff. 123r–124r (the "Coronula Parisina," a sermon collection); and London, British Library, MS Harl. 2268, ff. 30v–32v. In ancient rhetorical theory there is a close relationship between poetry and panegyric, which may help account for why Marcus calls Bruni a "poet": see T. C. Burgess, "Epideictic Literature," *Studies in Classical Philology* 3 (1902): 89–261. A letter of Ognibene Scola to Lorenzo Faledro preserved in Vat. lat. 5223, f. 147v, attests that Bruni's *Laudatio* was circulating in Padua as early as 1409.

and end of their tenure; the *Laudatio* is present in this way in a number of speeches by the *ufficiali forestieri* Giannicola Salerno da Verona and Stefano Porcari.[16] I have also found it cited in university orations, for example, in an anonymous oration for the doctorate of laws granted by the University of Florence to Lucas de Belmonte, a Florentine patrician, and in a speech by the jurist Gaspar of Perugia on his election as rector of the University of Florence.[17] These examples are all from the 1420s. Later in the century, the text was still being mined for topics of praise. When the *rimatore* Antonio Cornazzano was trying to acquire the patronage of the Medici in 1464, just before Cosimo de' Medici's death, he wrote an Italian poem in *terzine*, still unpublished, entitled "De Florentine urbis laudibus"; this poem freely pillaged Bruni's *Laudatio* for suitable commonplaces in praise of Florence.[18]

Cornazzano had been a courtier of Francesco Sforza, the duke of Milan, and his poem contained a kind of ideal comparison of Florence and Milan, praising the benefits that had accrued to Italy by the happy alliance between Sforza and Cosimo de' Medici. A quarter-century before, however, Florence and Milan had still been mortal enemies, rivals on the field of battle and in the realms of culture and diplomacy. In the later 1430s the *Laudatio* had become the center of an ideological struggle between the two powers.[19] The conflict began in 1435, when the duke of Milan's secretary, Pier Candido Decembrio, fell into talk with

---

[16] Giannicola Salerno's oration is preserved in many manuscripts; I consulted London, British Library, MS Harl. 2268, ff. 32v–34r: "Oratio habita per dom. Iohannem Nicolai de Silernis de Verona militem clarissimum dum esset capitaneus in Florencia, ad laudes urbis et suorum functorum officiorum"; Stefano Porcari's orations are published by Giambattista Carlo Giuliari, *Prose del giovane Buonaccorso da Montemagno inedite alcune da due codici della Biblioteca Capitolare di Verona*, Scelta di curiosità letterarie inedite o rare dal secolo XIII al XIX, Dispensa 141 (Bologna: Gaetano Romagnoli, 1874; repr. Bologna: Commissione per i testi di lingua, 1968); Giuliari mistakenly attributes the speeches to Buonaccorso. A manuscript of the *Laudatio* in the Regenstein Library of the University of Chicago was copied by Laurentius de Terenzis of Pesaro while he was *podestà* of Florence (*Repertorium*, I: 28, no. 324).

[17] See London, British Library, MS Harl. 2268, ff. 39v–41r: "Oratio domini Guasparis de Perusio legum doctoris pro rectore universitatis magistratum assumente; ff. 20v–21r: anon., "Pro doctoratu".

[18] See D. Zancani and R. L. Bruni, "Antonio Cornazzano, la tradizione manoscritta," *Bibliofilia* 90.3 (1988): 217–22, and Zancani and Bruni, *Antonio Cornazzano: La tradizione testuale* (Florence: Olschki, 1992), 56–62 (listing five manuscripts).

[19] See E. Garin in *Storia di Milano*, vol. VI (Milan: Fondazione Treccani degli Alfieri, 1955), 581f.; Baron, *From Petrarch to Leonardo Bruni*, 152. The Archivio di Stato in Turin has a manuscript of the *Laudatio* and the Strozzi oration (J a VI 35) with the subscription: "Leonardus Arretinus edidit feliciter MCCCCXXXIIII," an indication that Bruni may have republished the orations in this year, possibly for the information of those attending the Council of Basel; see P. O. Kristeller, *Iter Italicum* (London and Leiden: Brill, 1967), 177. The same subscription is found in Giannozzo Manetti's copy (Hankins, *Repertorium*, I: 194, no. 2644).

Lorenzo Valla (then in Milan) about Bruni's panegyric. Valla was severe: the work was "trifling and inert" (*plenam levitatis et supinitatis*) and stylistically corrupt; "he speaks as though he thought no one could reply and no one could not agree with his nonsense"; "he would have it that Florence is the heir to the empire of the Roman people, as though Rome herself were extinct; and [he says] Florence was descended from the best Romans, as though later Romans did not trace their origins from those early ones." He then went on to encourage Decembrio to "flatten" Bruni, and "stab" him with the knifelike sharpness of his wit.[20]

Decembrio did not heed Valla's call to literary violence, but he did write a reply, in the form of an oration of his own, the *Panegyric of the City of the Milanese*. The speech treats Bruni respectfully, but firmly rejects his arguments for the preeminence of Florence. "[Bruni] writes so brilliantly and elegantly that, unless you pay very close attention, you might easily be led to believe that what he is saying is true." Milan is in fact superior to Florence on every count. Following Plato's *Republic* (which he was in the midst of translating),[21] Decembrio sees Milan as a "timocracy," a polity ruled by the desire for honor. It was honor that moved Giangaleazzo Visconti and his grandson Filippo Maria. Florence, by contrast, is an oligarchy ruled by the desire for wealth, and therefore, by Plato's analysis, constitutionally inferior to Milan. Florence, far from having been ennobled by her origins in republican Rome, ought to be shamed by them. Her founder (Bruni says) was Sulla, but Sulla (says Decembrio) was the wickedest of tyrants; it was no surprise that Catiline went to Fiesole to find recruits for his criminal conspiracy. Decembrio even suggests, rather mischievously, that the Florentines must have originally moved down to the Arno valley from Fiesole in order to escape the ignominy of their origins. Certainly their beginnings as a Roman colony give them no right to claim the empire as their special inheritance. Livy reports that Piacenza was the fifty-third Roman colony founded in Italy. Does then Piacenza, do those other fifty-two colonies, have an equal right to claim the empire, too? Much better, like Milan, to have been founded by a Celtic king than by the soldiers of a tyrant.

Decembrio's *Panegyric*, though it aims to refute the *Laudatio* point for point, nevertheless shares many assumptions with Bruni's speech. Indeed, were we not still dazzled by the Baronian dichotomy between Florentine "civic liberty" and Milanese "tyranny," we might be able to

---

[20] Edited in L. Barozzi and R. Sabbadini, *Studi sul Panormita e sul Valla* (Florence, 1891), 75 6.
[21] Hankins, *Plato*, I: 117 54.

see that the text really belongs to the same world of "civic humanism" as does Bruni's oration. As students of English republicanism in the seventeenth century have begun to notice, classical republicanism is not defined by its opposition to monarchy and by no means excludes monarchical constitutions.[22] But I shall have to return to this issue on another occasion.[23]

Until recently, Bruni's *Oration for Nanni Strozzi* was much less studied than the *Laudatio*, and scholars had to rely on an inadequate text published in Baluzius' *Miscellanea* of 1681. Thanks to Dr. Susanne Daub, however, we now have a reliable critical text with a valuable commentary on the speech's models and sources.[24] The dating of this text, too, seems secure: Baron's arguments dating the oration to March/May 1428, correcting Sabbadini and Bertalot, are generally accepted;[25] while Paolo Viti's recent attempt to argue that the speech was actually delivered in public by Bruni has been decisively rejected.[26] Baron also analyzed some aspects of the context and content of the oration; indeed this analysis forms the peroration, as it were, of his *Crisis of the Early Italian Renaissance*. Yet Baron and most subsequent commentators have focused primarily on the first third of the oration, describing Florence and its republican institutions and culture. The latter two-thirds, praising the deeds of Nanni Strozzi, have been mostly ignored by students of Renaissance political theory.

The textual tradition of the Strozzi oration closely resembles that of the *Laudatio*.[27] It survives in about sixty-five manuscripts; there are no

---

[22] See Blair Worden, "English Republicanism," in *The Cambridge History of Political Thought, 1450–1700*, ed. J. H. Burns (Cambridge: Cambridge University Press, 1991), 443–75 at 443, 446–7. Quentin Skinner has been so struck by this circumstance that he now seems to prefer the term "neo-Roman" to "classical republican"; see his recent *Liberty Before Liberalism* (Cambridge: Cambridge University Press, 1998), 54–5. The use of the term "republican" as the opposite of "monarchical" goes back only to Montesquieu; in the older republican tradition "republican" means simply commonwealth, and its opposites are tyranny or mob rule.

[23] The thesis has yet to be demonstrated for the Italian fifteenth century, but see my forthcoming article on "Civic Humanism under the Visconti," to appear in the proceedings of a conference *I Decembrio e la tradizione della "Repubblica di Platone" tra Medioevo e Umanesimo*, Pavia, 24–27 May 2000, and, in the meantime, my recent remarks in "The Baron Thesis after Forty Years and Some Recent Studies of Leonardo Bruni," *Journal of the History of Ideas* 56 (1995): 309–38 at 327–30.

[24] Susanne Daub, *Leonardo Brunis Rede auf Nanni Strozzi: Einleitung, Edition, und Kommentar* (Stuttgart and Leipzig: Teubner, 1996). The first part of the speech is translated in *The Humanism of Leonardo Bruni*, 121–7.

[25] Baron, *Crisis* (1955), II: 430–9.

[26] Viti, *Leonardo Bruni e Firenze*, 397–8; rejected by Hankins, "The Baron Thesis," 334–5, and Daub, *Nanni Strozzi*, 351–5.

[27] See Hankins, *Repertorium*, ad indices.

Renaissance printed editions or translations. The text did not therefore enjoy the mass audience enjoyed by many of Bruni's works. The slightly greater number of manuscripts, compared with the *Laudatio*, may be owing to the inclusion of the work in the main Florentine bookstore collection of Bruni's works, a collection made almost certainly by Bruni himself. The *Laudatio* was not included, probably because (as we shall see) Bruni later became slightly ashamed of this juvenile work. The Strozzi oration was also much better, indeed brilliantly written, and this undoubtedly contributed to its relatively larger readership. It has been possible to establish the provenance of some thirty of the manuscripts. Slightly over half (sixteen) were copied in Florence or in Florentine Tuscany or by Florentines, eight were copied in Lombardy, two in Venice, one in Rome, and there are three manuscripts of non-Italian provenance. The book seems to have been less popular in the curial milieu than the *Laudatio*, probably because it was composed after Bruni had ended his career as papal secretary. The surviving codices come from the usual assortment of princely libraries, ecclesiastical institutions, notaries, merchants, *condottieri*, and one doctor of theology. In short, "fit audience though few." The contemporary testimonia, which will be mentioned in due course, make it clear that the book was intended for foreign as well as domestic consumption.

The text "descends as though by golden steps" (as Bruni says) from praise of Nanni's city, Florence, to praise of his family, of his father, and finally of Nanni himself. Though inspired in a general way by Pericles' funeral oration in Thucydides, the number of formal correspondences between Bruni and Thucydides is few. Certainly the text uses a much freer style of imitation than Bruni had employed in the *Laudatio*.[28] The greatest and most significant difference, of course, is that, while Pericles' speech praises together all the citizen-soldiers fallen in Athens' recent battles with Sparta, Bruni's praises a single individual, a close relative of one of Florence's mightiest oligarchs, who is represented as a citizen-soldier. We shall return to this point later.

The speech begins by invoking the law of Solon whereby those who have fallen in battle for their country are to have a funeral oration spoken over them, and their orphaned children are to be maintained at the expense of the state. Bruni himself is discharging the first of these obligations by his present speech, and he trusts that "those who can and

---

[28] On Bruni's models and sources see now the excellent study by Daub, who has identified Thucydides and Plato's *Menexenus* and *Crito* as Bruni's most important models; other important sources are Aristotle, Livy, Sallust's *Catilinarian Conspiracy*, and Cicero's *De officiis*.

should" will discharge the second. He states clearly that the oration is a literary composition, secondary rhetoric, not an actual speech intended for public delivery. The first section of the speech, following Thucydides in general structure, praises Nanni Strozzi's Florence as a topic of praise for Nanni himself. The greatness of a man is inseparable from the greatness of his city. Nanni was fortunate in being born in a rich and powerful city. Florence was founded by mighty and virtuous ancestors, the Etruscans and the Romans. Florence has been, time out of mind, the chief city of Etruria. (The Etrurian ancestry was a relatively new theme with Bruni, first enunciated in book I of the *Florentine History*, written *c.* 1415; it was obviously embraced as reinforcement for Florence's imperial claims.)[29] The ancestral virtue of the Romans and Etruscans has been preserved in Florence in her holy laws. These are an example of right living for other races (*ut exemplo ceteris gentibus bene vivendi essent*), a phrase that recalls Pericles' famous praise of Athens as *tes Helladou paideusis*, an "education for Greece." Her excellence is shown in her recent martial vigor, and Bruni praises the oligarchy for its military successes. "The present-day citizens also deserve praise, for they have greatly extended the power they received from their fathers, adding Pisa and certain other great cities to the empire by virtue and arms."

Florence is great because of her liberty and equality. Bruni compares Florence's republican government and mores with those of monarchy. Significantly, the comparison with oligarchy is limited to a single sentence: "oligarchies have roughly the same weaknesses" (*Nec multo secus accidit in dominatu paucorum*).[30] The great difference between a signory and a republic is that the latter allows for social mobility, or, as Bruni puts it, "equal hope for all of attaining office and raising oneself" – an unsurprising emphasis for a *novus homo* like Bruni. Bruni represents Florence as a meritocracy, where virtue and ability make one "noble enough to govern the republic"; this is the old humanist theme that virtue is true nobility. Florentine liberty consists in equality before the law and, thanks to her laws and institutions, freedom from the arbitrary behavior of the powerful. Florence even has a kind of reverse affirmative-action program called the Ordinances of Justice which keep the powerful from exercising too much influence in government. Florentine meritocracy

---

[29] See G. Cipriani, "Il mito etrusco nella Firenze repubblicana e medicea," *Ricerche storiche* 5 (1975): 257–309.
[30] The near silence about oligarchy is all the more significant in that the passage of Pericles' funeral oration on which Bruni's discussion is based was directed against oligarchy rather than against monarchy.

has the further effect of "firing up the intelligence of its citizens." Monarchies, on the other hand, are inferior because kings cannot allow their subjects to become too successful, lest their own power be undermined. Bruni goes so far as to say that monarchies are illegitimate forms of government, employing the Aristotelian definition of legitimacy, i.e., that rule be exercised in the interests of the whole, not just a part, of the citizen body. As no king who ever lived acted entirely for the sake of his subjects, praise of monarchy has something "fictive and shadowy" about it. Bruni goes on to praise (1) the size of Florence's population, which he says is the greatest in the world; (2) her military skill (a short section); (3) her cultural brilliance – a section which includes some ill-concealed self-praise; and (4) her wealth, which "as though from some divine source" seems to "sprout up daily" in the city.

The second and shortest section of the speech deals with Nanni Strozzi's family and parentage. These are praised in much the same terms as Bruni used to praise Florence. The ancient lineage of the Strozzi is celebrated; their numerous offices; the size of the family, its connections and its military glory. Its wealth is so great as to exceed the normal measure of citizen wealth, and makes them like little kings. The same topics are used to praise Nanni's father, Carlo Strozzi.

The third and much the longest section of the speech is devoted to praise of Nanni himself. Bruni describes admiringly how Nanni chose a military career over less noble and glorious occupations such as trade and agriculture, how he attached himself to the Este princes and was ultimately knighted by them on the field of battle. There follows a long section on true knighthood, which recapitulates several of the themes in Bruni's treatise *De militia* (1421).[31] This sets up a new topic: Nanni as the perfect embodiment of knighthood. Bruni praises his knowledge of military affairs, his leadership abilities, his fine though unostentatious appearance, his continence and frugality, his modesty and truthfulness, his humane treatment of enemies, and finally his courage and devotion to the fatherland. Bruni then illustrates Nanni's virtues by describing his exploits in the Second Milanese War against Giangaleazzo Visconti as well as in the most recent war, just ending, against Giangaleazzo's grandson Filippo Maria Visconti. The *narratio* culminates in a dramatic account of Nanni's last battle, the battle of Gottolengo. Bruni presents Nanni as the key figure in the encounter, a kind of Horatius at the

---

[31] The best edition available is that of Paolo Viti, ed., *Leonardo Bruni: Opere letterarie e politiche* (Turin: U.T.E.T., 1996), 651–701, with an Italian translation; an English translation may be found in *The Humanism of Leonardo Bruni*, 127–45.

Bridge who singlehandedly turns the tide of battle, inspiring others with his feats of arms, his valor and love of country. Bruni does not lose the occasion to comment on the superiority of citizen-soldiers to mercenaries: while the latter, thinking only of their own safety, had turned tail *primo impetu*, Nanni fought on heroically when all was seemingly lost, turning a rout into a victory. Finally, amid many wounds he fell gloriously and was carried off the field of battle at the same moment that the enemy was broken and driven off from the walls of Gottolengo. Had it not been for Nanni's courage, the enemy would have dealt the League a stunning blow that would have led to total victory for the Milanese. This observation leads to a speech within a speech where Bruni movingly addresses the spirit of the dead soldier, praising his courage and self-sacrifice; Nanni is represented as replying in a short speech on the theme *dulce et decorum est pro patria mori*. The speech ends with a peroration on the topic of the rewards of virtue. Bruni extracts from the usual humanist stew of Stoic, Aristotelian, and Platonic commonplaces the sentiments that virtue is its own reward, and the consciousness of virtue is enough for noble minds, yet Nanni also deserves and has won immortal glory and heavenly beatitude. In a remarkable outburst of what is now called "civic religion", Bruni declares that, since every man's *patria* is to him most holy and deserves the greatest piety, there can be no doubt that those who have fallen in battle for her safety and liberty have eternal rewards reserved for them in heaven.

As in the case of the *Laudatio*, some observations on the biographical and historical context of the speech are in order. When Bruni wrote the *Laudatio*, he was a penniless and unknown young man; by the time he composed the Strozzi oration he had become one of the seventy wealthiest men in the richest city in Europe, he was the chancellor of Florence, and he was the most famous living man of letters in Italy, perhaps in the world. But while Bruni's personal status had risen dramatically, that of Florence had declined. In 1404 she had had no effective rivals on the mainland of Italy; now she was confronted in Filippo Maria Visconti with a young, active, and resourceful enemy; in Venice with an untrustworthy and powerful ally with ever-increasing territorial ambitions; and with a resurgent and hostile papacy. She was on the point of ending a long war with Milan in which she had expended incredible sums for no territorial benefit. The war had been a series of military disasters for Florence; she had saved herself only by her alliance with Venice. It had never been popular, and it had divided the citizenry while fatally undermining the regime. The fact that the popular councils had consistently tried to block the regime's war legislation indicates class tensions between the oligarchs and the lower orders had become serious. Bruni's friend Nicola di Vieri de' Medici thought that civic discord had reached the highest levels in the regime's history.[32] Taxes had ruined some families and had made economic refugees of many others; so strong was tax resistance that a year before the end of the war the regime had had to prescribe the death penalty for nonpayment of assessments. Plots and conspiracies were in the air and the regime was forced to take vigorous steps to suppress them. The Medici were using the widespread dissatisfaction with the regime to build up their party.[33] In short, Bruni's speech was composed at a time when he was the spokesman for a faltering regime whose very existence was under serious threat, a regime that only six years later would be swept away by the Medici.

It is against this background that we must try to interpret Bruni's motives for composing the oration. He seems to have had both public and private aims in view. Privately, we know that Bruni had close ties with the Strozzi family. Carlo Strozzi had been a close political ally of Michele Castellani, the great-grandfather of Bruni's daughter-in-law; the Castellani were minor members of the Albizzi regime with whom Bruni had a variety of business dealings.[34] Palla Strozzi was Bruni's banker, and we have a letter from Palla to his factor Orsino Lanfredini in which he describes Bruni as "a me come fratello."[35] Palla had been Bruni's fellow student under Chrysoloras and he remained a friend and correspondent until Palla was exiled by the Medici. Palla was also a prominent member of the regime responsible for the Milanese War and had served as Florence's ambassador when the unpopular peace treaty was being negotiated.[36] He may well have felt that the public image of

[32] G. Brucker, *The Civic World of Early Renaissance Florence* (Princeton: Princeton University Press, 1977), 472; the situation described in the rest of the paragraph is summarized from this work.

[33] D. Kent, *The Rise of the Medici: Faction in Florence, 1426–1434* (Oxford: Oxford University Press, 1978).

[34] For the Castellani family, see Francesco di Matteo Castellani, *Ricordanze. I. Ricordanze A (1436–1459)*, ed. G. Ciappelli (Florence: Olschki, 1992); on Bruni's marriage alliance with the Castellani, see L. Martines, *The Social World of the Florentine Humanists, 1390–1460* (Princeton: Princeton University Press, 1963), 199–210; for his business dealings with them see vol. III of my *Repertorium* (forthcoming).

[35] The letter of Palla to Orsino Lanfredini (dated 6 January 1424, i.e. 1425) is in Florence, Biblioteca Nazionale Centrale MS Naz. II V 10, f. 218r (reference found in the Baron papers, Duke University Archives; original reference to Baron from Gene Brucker). For Bruni's business dealings with Palla, see Heather Gregory in *Patronage, Art and Society in Renaissance Italy*, ed. F. W. Kent and P. Simons (New York: Oxford University Press, 1987), 212.

[36] The diplomatic correspondence between the ambassadors and the Signoria, written partly by Bruni, is preserved in Florence, Biblioteca Mediceo-Laurenziana, MS Martelli 8.

the Strozzi needed some polishing. There was also the issue of Nanni Strozzi's orphaned children. The exordium of the speech itself suggests strongly that an important aim of the work was to encourage the state to provide for the upbringing of Nanni's children. In the oration it is not clear whether Bruni wanted them looked after by the Este or by a public grant from the commune of Florence. The latter would not have been unprecedented. The historian Giovanni Cavalcanti reports that the city of Florence about the same time supplied dowries to the orphaned children of Tommaso Frescobaldi, a Florentine captain who had been captured by the Milanese and had died under torture.[37] Bruni may have had something of this sort in mind. But a recently published document, a letter of presentation from Matteo Strozzi (probably drafted by Bruni himself) to Niccolò III d'Este accompanying a copy of the oration, implies that Bruni and the Strozzi expected Niccolò to provide for the orphans.[38]

The speech must also have been motivated by Bruni's concern for the stability of the regime. A number of passages in it read like justifications of the regime's war policy. When the war began to loom on the horizon in 1422, there had been a large party – Brucker calls it "the party of detente" – which opposed reacting militarily to what the regime chose to interpret as Visconti's provocations. The party of detente believed that the regime was seeking targets of opportunity for its expansionist program, or trying to buttress its popularity by foreign adventures. As usual, given the imperialist aims of both sides, the identity of the true aggressor was hard to discern once the elaborate dance of provocations and mobilizations and diplomatic feints had begun. The position of the regime, especially after things had begun to go badly, was that the war was a purely defensive one for the preservation of the republic. Filippo Maria alone had been responsible for provoking it. Florence's failures sprang from his treachery and that of Florence's own *condottieri* and hired troops, not from errors made by the regime and its military commissioners. This is also Bruni's interpretation of events; the *Oratio* mirrors precisely the views of Rinaldo degli Albizzi and other members of the regime as reported in the Consulte e pratiche. The desire to defend the regime's policies also helps explain why Bruni omitted here the theme of Florence's imperial destiny, so prominent in the *Laudatio*. Instead, he implicitly exonerated the regime's military policies by fusing moral

[37] Giovanni Cavalcanti, *Istorie fiorentine*, 2 vols. (Florence: Tipografia all' insegna di Dante, 1838-9), I: 17 (IV.4).
[38] See Hankins, "The Baron Thesis," 334-6.

outrage at Visconti's behavior and the cowardice of mercenaries with pride in Nanni Strozzi's glorious deeds. Brucker tells us that between 1426 and 1429 the leadership launched "a massive campaign to stimulate patriotism", which took the form of "a veritable orgy of civic celebration."[39] Bruni's oration must surely be seen as part of this campaign.

Another problem for the regime was the growing polarization of the city by class. Rinaldo degli Albizzi and the other great oligarchs were believed to harbor secret designs to exclude the lower orders from government. The political class was seen as increasingly elitist, its interests increasingly at odds with those of the minor guildsmen, its tastes and mores increasingly aristocratic, its actions increasingly high-handed. In this context, Bruni's ringing reaffirmation of Florence's traditional political values – equality, liberty, the defense of the weak against the powerful, and the rule of law – would have had a special meaning. Bruni himself, the poor boy from the provinces who had become Florence's wealthy and honored chancellor, was a powerful symbol of the system's openness to outsiders. His intimate association with the republic's leadership must have reassured Bruni's readers that the values he had so powerfully affirmed were still shared by the regime. Indeed, Bruni several times at the beginning of the speech stresses its character as an official publication.[40] Bruni's influence should not be underestimated: he was always a great culture hero to the notarial class and it formed a great part of his audience. It was also a class, as Dale Kent has shown, critical to the stability of the regime.[41]

Finally, the oration must have been intended to serve a propagandistic function abroad. We have evidence of this in a remarkable letter of 9 April 1429 from Bartolomeo Capra (an old friend of Bruni from his curial days) to the private secretaries of the duke of Milan. Capra, the archbishop of Milan, was serving as Filippo Maria's governor in Genoa, a city Visconti had captured at the beginning of the Third Milanese War. Genoa was a city with a strong republican tradition; a few years later it would revolt from Milan and reestablish its republican government. The letter was written to encourage the duke to hire Antonio Beccadelli, "il Panormita", as his court poet. Capra pointed out that all

---

[39] Brucker, *Civic World*, 481.
[40] Daub, *Nanni Strozzi*, 282. Bruni says: "This most important public task [*munus*] has been committed to me"; and "though fully aware of the [rhetorical] difficulties of the task, my good will towards the man *and the command and authority of my country* have compelled me to take it up to the best of my ability" (my italics). The speech was also seen as an official Florentine pronouncement by Bartolomeo Capra, the Visconti governor of Genoa, in the letter quoted immediately below.   [41] Kent, *Rise of the Medici*, 119 20.

Filippo Maria's glorious deeds would be forgotten unless he found some great writer to celebrate them in Latin letters. He then invoked the example of the cities Filippo Maria hated above all others.

The Florentines have recently caused their deeds to be published in six books;[42] the Venetians are also composing their own writings and poems to commend themselves and their cities to immortality. And to the degree that they extol their own deeds, to that degree are they trying to obscure our own deeds, both recent ones and older ones. Leonardo of Arezzo has just written a funeral oration for the Florentine knight Nanni Strozzi; those who have read it know how much it lowers the estimation of our prince and our fatherland . . . In my view, since we don't have a man whose talent, devotion and literary skill are equal to watching out for and answering the detractors of our prince, we should bring one from the ends of the earth, even if it costs no small sum.[43]

We shall soon see how Bruni's distortion of the historical record disparaged the achievements of Filippo Maria. In any case, it is clear why the *Oration for Nanni Strozzi* would make an effective propaganda vehicle. "Opinion leaders" around Italy would naturally be trying to estimate the fallout from Florence's failures in the Visconti wars and her current war potential. Would the regime fall? Would the revolts against the *catasto*, within and outside of Florence, reduce the city to civil strife? Would she be an ally worth having, or would she fall easy prey to her enemies? Bruni's speech represents the Florentines as united, confident, firm in their patriotism, loyal to their leaders, ready to resist any power who might infringe on their liberties. Though the war had cost them nearly three and a half million florins, "men were readier now, at the end of the war, to pay their assessments than they were at the beginning," indeed, the city was bursting with wealth and warlike virtue. Visconti, on the other hand, was tyrannical, treacherous, and militarily ineffective.

A major problem in interpreting these two orations is the question of Bruni's sincerity. The problem was raised, or perhaps created, by Hans Baron in his *Crisis of the Early Italian Renaissance*, first published in 1955. Baron wished to establish that his civic humanists 'during the early fifteenth century produced a code of civic values not found among [non-civic humanists] who were essentially courtiers or *literati*, unat-

---

[42] This refers to the first six books of Bruni's *Historiae Florentini populi*, presented to the Signoria on 16 May 1428, on the occasion of the peace treaty with Milan; see my *Repertorium*, vol. II (forthcoming).

[43] Published by R. Sabbadini, "Come il Panormita diventò poeta aulico," *Archivio storico lombardo*, ser. 5, 3 = 43 (1916): 27 8. The need for a Milanese version of recent history was met a few years later by Andrea Biglia (see below).

tached to the life of an active, political citizenry."[44] Bruni was for Baron the ideal type of the civic humanist, so it seemed important to him that Bruni should have meant what he said, most of all in these two speeches which appeared to Baron to sum up the central beliefs of the "civic humanists". These could not be the work of a "professional rhetorician," a hired gun who would spout republicanism, or anything else, for the appropriate sum.[45]

Later I shall argue that the dichotomy civic humanist/professional rhetorician is not a very useful one, but first we shall need to look more closely at the issue of Bruni's sincerity in these two orations. Baron always recognized that both speeches contained exaggerations and inaccuracies, *suggestio falsi* and *suppressio veri*, but his admiration for Florentine republicanism and his personal tenderness for Bruni prevented him from examining the issue too closely. For Baron, whatever rhetorical exaggerations Bruni may have indulged in, his fundamental commitment to the larger vision of the civic life enunciated in these works could not be questioned. Yet when one begins to attend more carefully to the various statements and claims Bruni makes in the two panegyrics, and especially when one compares them with what Bruni says elsewhere in his writings, the problem of Bruni's sincerity is not so easily dismissed.

We may begin with the well-known letter Bruni wrote in 1440 to Francesco Pizolpasso, the archbishop of Milan and an old friend of Bruni's from curial days. Francesco had reported to Bruni some criticism he had heard of the *Laudatio* as a clumsy and untruthful work. In response, Bruni does not say that he had been elegant and honest but rather excuses himself by pointing out his youth and the nature of the genre he had been employing.

> The oration was written when I was young, fresh out of Greek class. It was a boyish trifle, a rhetorical exercise . . . The rhetorical genre (for a critic should consider this, too) in panegyrics of this kind calls for boastfulness and winning applause . . . In civic panegyrics the speech is directed to those whom you wish to praise; the genre demands an audience, and brings together a multitude of people, not for the purpose of hearing legal cases or deciding on public policy [i.e., it is different from judicial or deliberative oratory, which according to ancient theory was obliged to respect the truth], but in order to reap applause

---

[44] Baron, *From Petrarch to Leonardo Bruni*, 102 3.
[45] On the quarrel between Baron and Jerrold Seigel on this point, see Hankins, "The Baron Thesis," 317 18. For Baron's passionate belief in Bruni's "ethical purity," see the interesting remarks of Najemy in "Baron's Machiavelli and Renaissance Republicanism," *American Historical Review* 101 (1996): 119 29.

and pleasure from hearing its own praises sung . . . History is one thing, panegyric another. History must follow the truth, panegyric extols many things above the truth [*supra veritatem*].⁴⁶

It is striking to place this passage next to another one from the *Laudatio* itself:

> No doubt a few fools will suspect that I am trying to capture some popular favor from this panegyric of mine, and that in the process of winning your good will and disposing your minds favorably towards me as much as possible, I am trespassing on the limits of truth, mixing false things with true for the sake of rhetorical embellishment [*ornandi causa*]. Let me teach such persons, or rather unteach them, to stop thinking such things and put aside all suspicions of this sort. For though I wish to be loved and accepted by everyone – a thing I admit I really wish for and long for – I have never been brought to the point where I should wish to achieve this through flattery and adulation. I have always thought that I should be loved for virtue, not vices, nor do I expect or demand any favor from this panegyric.⁴⁷

This looks very much like a wink of the eye towards the more knowledgeable members of Bruni's audience – those who understood the genre requirements of epideictic rhetoric and the state of Bruni's career in 1404. This would not be the only instance of Bruni's using private jokes to convey different messages to different parts of his readership.⁴⁸ Not surprisingly, the passage comes near the beginning of the most mendacious section of the *Laudatio*.

For in fact, the *Laudatio* and the *Oration for Nanni Strozzi* are both full of the most shameless exaggerations, embellishments, fictions, and untruths. In the *Laudatio*, Bruni claims that Florence excels all other cities in every topic of praise. She has never refused to take in any exile from another city. She has never injured another city, she has always helped cities in distress, protecting them from tyranny. All her wars are just wars. She has always defended the weak against the powerful, sacrificing her own interests selflessly while battling for others. She has never broken her faith, even with her bitterest enemies, nor violated any treaty. She has won battle after battle thanks to her martial valor and military skill. (One would never guess from reading the *Laudatio* that Florence had ever employed mercenary soldiers.) Yet her successes have

---

⁴⁶ *Leonardi Arretini Epistolarum libri VIII*, ed. L. Mehus, 2 vols. (Florence: Paperinius, 1741), II: 111–12 (Ep. VIII.4).
⁴⁷ Baron, *From Petrarch to Leonardo Bruni*, 249.
⁴⁸ For example, David Quint argues that the *Dialogi ad Petrum Histrum* are directed simultaneously to an esoteric and exoteric audience; see his "Humanism and Modernity: A Reconsideration of Bruni's *Dialogues*," *Renaissance Quarterly* 38 (1985): 423–45.

not made her arrogant; she has always displayed clemency amid her triumphs. Her government is ideally ordered to prevent the powerful from exercising undue power or putting themselves above the law. No injury goes unredressed, the law is the same for everyone.

None of the above statements is strictly true, of course – indeed, a hundred counter-examples could be cited[49] – but we are plainly dealing with crowd-pleasing, Land-of-Hope-and-Glory jingoism that could not then and should not now be taken too seriously. The situation is rather different with the historical illustrations Bruni provides of Florence's military prowess. They are of special interest as they allow us to compare Bruni's treatment of the same events in the differing genres of history and panegyric.[50] In one example, Bruni describes vividly the failure of Henry VII's siege of Florence in 1312. "That monster" had encamped beneath the walls of Florence "like Hannibal at the Porta Collina," thinking that Florence, struck with terror, would immediately capitulate. Instead, the city carried on its normal life as if nothing were happening; the shops and stalls remained open, public works continued, courts of law remained open. When Henry found out about this, he raised the siege, marveling at the city's greatness of spirit. At least, that is the version in the *Laudatio*. In Bruni's *History of Florence*, the story is told rather differently. Here, it was Florence's allies, gradually reinforcing her, which enabled her to resume her normal life and eventually forced the withdrawal of Henry's forces.

Even more striking is Bruni's account of Florence's capture of Volterra in 1254. In the *Laudatio* version, the Florentine troops had been trapped in a narrow mountain defile leading up to the walled hill-town of Volterra. They had forced their way through a hail of spears and a volley of huge rocks the Volterrans had sent thundering down the cliffs until finally they were able to storm the city walls and capture it in a single day. In the *History*, this rhetorical *ornatio* is considerably toned down. That version has a disordered mob of Volterrans make a sortie outside the city walls, where they are turned to flight by the Florentines. As the beaten Volterrans enter the portal of the city, the pursuing Florentines are able to force an entrance at the same time at the undefended gate. The *History*'s version is considerably less heroic than

---

[49] To give but one example, only a year or two before the *Laudatio* was written Florence had ignored calls for help from Cremona, Crema, Brescia, and Parma, all formerly cities in Giangaleazzo's empire which after his death were reduced to subjection by local warlords.

[50] For the two examples which follow, cf. Baron, *From Petrarch to Leonardo Bruni*, 154, 254–5. Baron does not choose to note the discrepancy between Bruni's two accounts of the end of the Visconti wars.

the *Laudatio*'s, yet both versions may tell less than the full story. That at least is what one (probably Volterran) reader of Bruni's *Laudatio* thought. He was so incensed at Bruni's account that he wrote the following note in the bottom margin of the page:

Everything the orator says here about Volterra is totally false and entirely contrary to the truth of the matter. The Florentines did not capture the city of Volterra at that time by their strength, but by fraud and deceit, since treaties had been entered into which then in those times were violated. Nor did the Florentines get possession of the city by physical courage, but rather owing to the betrayal, baseness and poverty of the Volterrans and the Florentines' power, standing and wealth.[51]

The note reminds us what Florence's "defense of Tuscan liberties" meant for those whose liberties were being defended.

Most shameless of all, because the event was fresh in everyone's recollection, was Bruni's account of the end of the recent war with Giangaleazzo Visconti. This, Bruni gave his readers to understand, had ended in a great military victory for Florence; Italy had been saved singlehandedly from the tyrant of Milan by the courage and sacrifices of the Florentines.

The city being thus animated [by love of honor and liberty] she courageously joined battle with this most powerful and wealthy of enemies; and he who but a little before had threatened all Italy and was thought to be irresistible was compelled to choose peace and to tremble within the walls of Pavia, and finally to give up the cities, not only of Tuscany and Umbria, but even the best part of Gaul [i.e. Lombardy].[52]

In fact, Florence's last battle with Giangaleazzo, the battle of Casalecchio outside Bologna on 26 June 1402, had been a crushing defeat for the Florentines and their Bolognese allies. As Bruni himself writes in his *History*, the only Florentines who escaped were those who dashed back in time to the protecting walls of Bologna.[53] After the disaster at Casalecchio, Giovanni Bentivoglio, the tyrant of Bologna whom the Florentines had been maintaining in power, was deposed and a free Comune was established with the support of Giangaleazzo. Two weeks

---

[51] Florence, Biblioteca Mediceo-Laurenziana, MS Ashburnham 1918, f. 21v: "Totum hoc quod de Vulterris hic dicit orator falsissimum est, et penitus contra rei veritatem. Non enim eo tempore capta est a Florentinis civitas Vulterrana vi, sed dolo atque fraude, cum ea fuerunt federa init[i]a que tunc istis temporibus violenter fracta fuerunt, nec virtute corporea eam Florentini adepti sunt, sed proditione, vilitate et paupertate Vulterranorum et Florentinorum potentia[e], statu[s] et divitia[e]."
[52] Baron, *From Petrarch to Leonardo Bruni*, 258.
[53] *Historiarum Florentini populi libri XII*, ed. E. Santini, *Rerum italicarum scriptores*, n.s., vol. XIX, part 3 (Città di Castello: Lapi, 1914), 287.

later the communal government chose Giangaleazzo as their *signore*.[54] Florence escaped the Visconti threat in 1402, not owing to any great military victory, but to Giangaleazzo's sudden death from the plague on 3 September 1402. Nor had she ever been entirely alone in standing up to Giangaleazzo, as Bruni tries to make out; she had been aided at various times during the previous twelve years of war by Venice, the pope, Francesco Carrara, Giovanni Bentivoglio, the French, Ladislaus of Hungary, Rupert of Bavaria, Paolo Guinigi of Lucca, and sundry other potentates. This is something almost all of Bruni's contemporary readers must have known. And Bruni himself gave an accurate account of the true situation at the war's end in book XII of his *Florentine Histories* (composed after 1440).

Bruni was even bolder in bending history to his purposes in the *Oration for Nanni Strozzi*.[55] Indeed, the oration comes close to being historical fiction. As in the *Laudatio*, there are plenty of questionable assertions: that the Florentines were happily paying their war taxes, that they were not subservient to an oligarchy, that all great poets past and present have been Florentines, that Florence singlehandedly revived eloquence and Greek and Latin letters, etc. But in the case of the Strozzi oration, the whole premise of the speech and the key narrative in it are fictional. Bruni presents Nanni Strozzi (1376–1427) as a model citizen of Florence who lived and died in the service of his *patria*. But Nanni was not in fact a Florentine citizen at all. He was a citizen of Ferrara; the *patria* he served and for which he died was not Florence, but Ferrara.[56] Nor is it the case (as Baron claimed[57]) that Florence and Ferrara were so closely allied during Nanni's lifetime that service to the one could be seen as service to the other.[58] Ferrara was occasionally but by no means always allied with Florence between 1390 and 1427. Indeed, in the last few years of

[54] D. M. Bueno de Mesquita, *Giangaleazzo Visconti, Duke of Milan (1351–1402): A Study in the Political Career of an Italian Despot* (Cambridge: Cambridge University Press, 1941), 279.

[55] Daub, *Nanni Strozzi*, 357, notes simply: "As the inquiry has shown, Bruni adopted in his account of Nanni's life the freedom permitted to a panegyrist."

[56] On Nanni's life see Baron, *Crisis* (1955), II: 430 9, and Daub, *Nanni Strozzi*, 357 83 (with a collection of the testimonia). Baron was mistaken in believing that Nanni was born outside of Florence, as Daub shows (357, note 540). If Bruni intended to deceive his readers that Nanni was a Florentine, he seems to have succeeded in the case of Bartolomeo Capra, who in the letter quoted above (154) describes Nanni as a "Florentine knight."

[57] Baron, *Crisis* (1955), II: 438: "The state of the Este . . . was Florence's constant ally through the whole era of the Visconti wars." Contrast Bueno de Mesquita, *Giangaleazzo Visconti*, 234, 239 41, 264, 274 8, 284 6, and W. L. Gundersheimer, *Ferrara: The Style of a Renaissance Despotism* (Princeton: Princeton University Press, 1973), 72 4.

[58] Baron, *Crisis* (1955), II: 437 8: "The life and death of this Strozzi had been in the service of a foreign prince, it is true; but in effect, and in Nanni's own intention, he had lived and died for Florence." It is not clear from which sources Baron recovers "Nanni's own intention."

Florence's war with Giangaleazzo Visconti, Niccolò III d'Este, the marquis of Ferrara, was actually leaning towards the Milanese. His preferred stance during the period in question was that of a neutral. Nanni Strozzi was the son of Carlo Strozzi, a leader of the oligarchic party in Florence and a Guelf *ultra* who had left Florence in 1378, after being declared a magnate by the populist regime. Nanni himself was raised in Ferrara and became a professional soldier, diplomat, and courtier in the service of the Este; in the 1390s he was put by Niccolò III's regents in charge of the young prince's military education. We know of only two occasions when he made (brief) visits to Florence. He certainly did not take part in any military action against Giangaleazzo after the capture of Bologna in 1402, as Bruni gives the reader to understand;[59] the only record we have of him in the last few years of that war relates how he accompanied Niccolò d'Este in September of 1401 on a hunting party with Giangaleazzo in Milan;[60] nor do we know of any occasion when he planted 'our standard practically on the doorstep of the hostile city' (i.e. Milan).

The story of Nanni's heroic death at the battle of Gottolengo, too, was almost entirely a fabrication. The battle at Gottolengo was not a great and decisive Florentine (or Ferrarese) victory which prevented Filippo Maria Visconti from winning the Third Milanese War. Most accounts see the battle as little more than a bloody skirmish, on balance a victory for the Milanese, but less decisive than it might have been thanks to the bravery of the Ferrarese and Venetian forces.[61] The encounter took place after the League and the Milanese had already signed a peace treaty; contemporary historians regarded Visconti's surprise attack as an attempt to improve the terms of the peace settlement in his favor by scoring a quick victory. No other Florentines besides Nanni participated in the battle, which was fought entirely between professional soldiers.

Two contemporary accounts of the battle allow us some further control over Bruni's tale. In Giovanni Cavalcanti's pro-Florentine

[59] Daub, *Nanni Strozzi*, 295-6.
[60] During this trip Niccolò seems to have assured Visconti of his friendly neutrality. Throughout the siege of Bologna Niccolò allowed Giangaleazzo to bring troops and supplies through the Modenese. See Daub, *Nanni Strozzi*, 363 and Bueno de Mesquita, *Giangaleazzo Visconti*, 275.
[61] In the *Storia di Milano*, VI: 237, the battle is dismissed in a single line: "Il 29 maggio il Carmagnola [the Venetian commander] dopo aver tentato di riprendere Montichiari, attaccò Gottolengo, ma fu respinto dal Piccinino con gravi perdite." Gino Capponi in his *Storia della Repubblica di Firenze*, 3 vols. (Florence: Barbèra, 1875), I: 483, sees it as a minor clash, "inutile ma sanguinoso." For other authorities on the battle, see Daub, *Nanni Strozzi*, 366. The decisive battle of the Third Milanese War took place four months later, at Maclodio. Andrea Biglia (see below) saw the battle of Gottolengo as a great Milanese victory.

account, the true hero of the battle on the Ferrarese side was identified as the *condottiere* Niccolò da Tolentino (later captain-general of the Florentine mercenaries).[62] In Cavalcanti's telling, it was Niccolò who played the part Bruni assigned to Nanni Strozzi in his oration.[63] It was Niccolò who had thrown himself into the middle of the fray, rallied the Ferrarese troops and prevented a total rout. Nanni, on the other hand, who was in late middle age, was said to have fallen owing to dehydration, hyperthermia, and the dust of battle.[64] On the other hand, Andrea Biglia's pro-Milanese version of the battle, written between 1431 and 1435 (and therefore possibly in response to Bruni's oration), gives Nanni credit for putting up brief resistance in a battle that was otherwise a total rout for the Venetian-Ferrarese forces.

> When Niccolò [Piccinino, the Milanese commander] noticed [the unprepared state of the Venetian forces], having readied his forces he charged the enemy and put Carmagnola's army to flight with his sudden attack. Nanni Strozzi, a Florentine citizen and a famous knight, put up some slight resistance. He had been married a few days before in Ferrara, and had been sent to camp to help the Venetians by the Marquis [Niccolò III d'Este] in command of about forty cavalry lances; he had offered his services voluntarily for the expedition from partisan motives. He withstood the attack to a certain extent, and while exerting himself in the battle somewhat more bravely from partisan motives, he was crushed among the slaughtered horses, having either overestimated his strength or being unused to effort of this kind. The rest [of his troops] were put to flight in the same attack.[65]

[62] Bruni wrote a panegyric of Niccolò in Italian, the *Sermone detto al magnifico capitano Niccolò da Tolentino* (1433). The text was much more popular than either the *Laudatio* or the Strozzi oration, surviving in about ninety manuscripts.
[63] Cavalcanti, *Istorie fiorentine*, 209 13: "Niccolò al tutto ogni ozio aveva sbandito; e, come uomo che morte non conoscesse altro se non il perdere, dov'erano le maggiori presse si metteva. Tutti gli antichi uomini contro ai nemici metteva, e dopo a loro, i giovani gagliardi; e tutto faceva perche ai vecchi è tolta la speranza del fuggire, ed ai giovani dato l'ardire dello star fermi alla battaglia. Questo Niccolò dall'uno e l'altro esercito fu detto che quel dì fosse il più valente dei due campi: per le quali laudi, finita la guerra, il duca con solenni patti il soldò."
[64] Ibid., 115. "Messer Nanni per la patria combattendo, il caldo grandissimo, il polverio serrato, e la sete senza rimedio il fece trafelare."
[65] Andrea Biglia, *Historiae patriae libri IX*, in L. A. Muratori, *Rerum italicarum scriptores*, vol. XIX (Milan, 1731), cols. 98 9. On Biglia, an Augustinian hermit (*c.* 1395 1435), see the bibliography in P. O. Kristeller, *Medieval Aspects of Renaissance Learning*, ed. E. P. Mahoney, second edn. (New York: Columbia University Press, 1992), 131. This testimonium is overlooked in Daub's collection. Daub, following a number of late Ferrarese accounts, prefers to assign a decisive role in the battle of Gottolengo to Nanni, but it is clear from her collection of testimonia that all these later accounts are dependent on book V of Poggio's *History of Florence*, which is in turn dependent on Bruni. See Poggius Bracciolini, *Opera Omnia*, ed. R. Fubini, 2 vols. (Turin: Bottega d'Erasmo, 1966), II: 340 1. Cavalcanti and Biglia are the only fully independent contemporary witnesses. On the question of Cavalcanti's reliability, see Najemy, "Baron's Machiavelli," 122 3, with further bibliography.

In any case, it is clear that Bruni's story – modeled on the death of the Theban hero Epaminondas in Plutarch – that Nanni fell wounded in battle, regained consciousness, then expired upon hearing news of the victory, is pure fantasy.[66] The whole speech, indeed, looks very much like a strained attempt to reflect some military glory onto the Strozzi family at a time when its head, Palla Strozzi, was deeply unpopular.

Should the crown jewels of Florentine civic humanism, then, be written off as impudent fabrications, worthless propaganda written by a "professional rhetorician," telling us nothing either about Bruni's real beliefs or about political realities in early Renaissance Florence? This, I think, would be an anachronistic response. It would amount to a failure to recognize the rhetorical conventions Bruni and the humanists of his time had inherited from the ancients and particularly from their idol, Cicero. For the Romans, history like oratory was a branch of rhetoric. In the *De oratore* Cicero had made telling the truth without flattery or animosity the first law of the historian, it is true;[67] but in practice he recommended that the historian learn the art of embellishment, *ornatio*. A simple account of the naked facts would not serve the purpose of the historian, which was to teach through example and inspire his readers to perform similar acts of virtue. Thus in the dialogue *Brutus* Cicero demonstrates his technique of embellishment by freely inventing numerous details in his *comparatio* of Themistocles and Coriolanus. Atticus responds by joking, 'Well, *you* can say this; orators are allowed to lie about the facts of history so as to let some truths stand out more clearly.' Atticus criticizes Cicero good-humoredly for his highhanded attitude to historical truth, but he is tolerant of Cicero's practice, knowing it to be normal behavior for an orator.[68] In Cicero's *Epistulae familiares*, the text on which Bruni formed his style, Cicero actually asked his friend, the historian L. Lucceius, to write a monograph on the Catilinarian conspiracy with Cicero in a starring role.

I'm well aware how impudent it is for me, first, to lay this burden on you – I know how busy you are – and then to demand that you embellish my actions. Now what if you think my actions don't deserve embellishment at the cost of

---

[66] He died three days later in Asola near Mantua, not on the battlefield; see Daub, *Nanni Strozzi*, 367.
[67] Cicero, *De oratore* II, 15 (62). For a discussion of Cicero's attitude to the distortion of historical fact for rhetorical and moral ends, see T. P. Wiseman, *Clio's Cosmetics* (Leicester: Leicester University Press, 1979); and P. G. Bietenholz, *Historia and Fabula: Myths and Legends in Historical Thought from Antiquity to the Modern Age* (Leiden: Brill, 1994), 58ff., to which my discussion is particularly indebted. [68] Cicero, *Brutus* 10.42 11.44.

such labor? But the man who has once crossed the border of modesty might as well be impudent into the bargain. So let me openly beg you to embellish my deeds with even more conviction than perhaps you feel, and in that respect to disregard the laws of history.[69]

As the subsequent passage makes clear, Cicero felt that the facts of history should be adjusted so as to paint his virtues and the vices of Catiline in the strongest possible colors. Only in this way would the moral ends of history be served. It was like a case of law versus equity. Historical truth could be at war with moral truth, and the historian had to balance the two. Fiction had an important role to play in achieving the ends of history. As Cicero said in the *Partitiones oratoriae* (11.40), "The greatest sense of trust is created [in the orator's audience], first, by an *exemplum* in the likeness of a truth, then by bringing in something plausible; sometimes even a fable, though incredible, will impress people." And what is true for history is true *a fortiori* for panegyric; as Quintilian wrote, à propos of epideictic rhetoric, *proprium laudis est res amplificare et ornare*; "when praising it is appropriate to amplify and embellish the subject."[70]

So account must be taken of the tradition within which Bruni was working. The borders between fact and fiction, truthful history and untruthful, have shifted over time. As I have argued, Bruni must have been actuated by a variety of practical motives in composing his civic panegyrics, but the element of fiction in these works should not mislead us into thinking he had no higher motives as well. Sincerity and honesty are not the same thing, after all. To compare great things with small, modern political "spin-doctors" are nearly always, presumably, devoted to the politicians they serve; the fact that their pronouncements are a tissue of lies and distortions does not permit us to doubt their sincere attachment to their parties and their causes. Such behavior is expected of them by their employers and by knowledgeable "news consumers." But no sane historian would think of writing the biography of a president from the statements of his press secretary.

As a representative of the classical rhetorical tradition, Bruni must have believed that the best way to arouse patriotism and the generous emulation of virtue was to embellish the facts of history. Historical reality is, after all, rarely inspiring, and the humanists sought above all else to inspire. That is why there is, in practice, no real contradiction between the "civic humanist" and the "professional rhetorician"; rhet-

[69] Cicero, *Epistulae familiares*, V, 12, 2 3.   [70] Quintilian, *Inst.* 3.7.6.

oric is simply a tool whereby the humanist may compass his ends, many of them no doubt good and admirable. That is why it can still be a moving experience to read texts like the Strozzi oration even though we may recognize that they are largely fictional. A humanist can have had a sincere desire to reform and ennoble his age, as many humanists undoubtedly did, and still have employed methods that, nowadays, seem morally questionable. We may leave it to the philosophers to decide whether the moral heteronomy between truth and eloquence perceived by premodern thinkers is a necessary one; we may leave it to the moralists to decide whether a cause can or should be discredited by the means used to promote it. Historians need only recognize that Bruni's culture tolerated greater latitude with the truth in the interests (at least sometimes) of edification. This may save them from creating useless and anachronistic dichotomies between "civic humanism" and "rhetoric."

But no sane historian would think of writing the intellectual biography of Leonardo Bruni or the history of Renaissance political thought from a pair of civic panegyrics. These texts can only be used as sources with the greatest circumspection. They must be situated in their context, account must taken of their genre requirements, and they must be carefully compared with other works by the same author. For present purposes, the most serious interpretative issue arising from these texts are two passages which might suggest to the unwary reader that Bruni was indeed the populist ideologue of Hans Baron's *Crisis*. Read without a proper understanding of the rhetorical and historical situation, they appear to be robust affirmations of populism, and therefore problematic for the modern interpretation of Bruni as an apologist for the Florentine oligarchy.[71] But there are good reasons to question whether, in this case, the most literal reading is the correct one.

The first passage occurs in part III of the *Laudatio* where Bruni is arguing that one should make a distinction between private vices and public vices.[72] This is in aid of his larger point that, though individual Florentines might behave wickedly, the Florentines when acting as a public body are always virtuous.

In private delicts the mind of the agent must be considered; in public ones the will of the whole city. In the latter case one should not worry about whether what particular individuals feel is sanctioned by laws and customs; what the

---

[71] See my "Baron Thesis," 321-3, and Najemy's essay (chapter 3 in this volume).
[72] For a different reading of this passage, see Najemy's essay, 98, above; my reading is closer to that of Mansfield (chapter 8 below, 237).

greater part of the people has done is what the whole city seems to have done. But in other cities the greater part always overcomes the better part; in this city the greater part and the better part always seem to be one and the same [*in hac autem civitate eadem semper videtur fuisse melior que maior*].⁷³

This is a rather extraordinary statement by the lights of the classical republican tradition. It was always assumed by ancient republicans like Aristotle and Cicero that there were natural differences of rationality and virtue in any people, and that the highest levels of rationality and virtue were by natural necessity restricted to a small group of aristocrats. Much of classical political theory is about how to bring together the few and the many ("quality and quantity" as Aristotle put it) in a just whole. But to claim that the many could possess virtue and rationality, as Bruni in effect does here, seems to contradict bedrock assumptions of ancient political anthropology, especially the assumption that there existed a natural hierarchy of virtue and intelligence within the human race. If we take Bruni seriously, we might even suspect that he was anticipating a modern political anthropology like that of Rousseau, where goodness resides in the whole *qua* whole rather than in any part. Even if one were not willing to go so far, Bruni's statement might still be taken to legitimate notions of consent and majority rule – to warrant, in other words, a kind and degree of popular rule unusual if not unexampled in Renaissance political life.

But we should not take Bruni seriously. In the first place, he is clearly not making any general statements about human nature; the "greater part" is to be identified with the "better part" only in Florence. More to the point, it is clear from Bruni's *Florentine Histories* that he was far from holding a high opinion of the prudence of the Florentine *multitudo*. Indeed, many passages in the *Histories* are meant as object lessons showing the ill effects of allowing the common people to make decisions without the guidance of prudent and virtuous aristocrats.

To take one example of many, in book II Bruni presents the great defeat of the Florentines at the battle of the Arbia in 1260 as a result of the failure of the *popolo* to take the advice of "military experts." "Plebeians ignorant of the art of war" ("the sort who tend to predominate in magistracies," he adds) were so eager for glory and plunder that they failed to appreciate the overwhelming advantages of the enemy's position and to see through the Ghibellines' disinformation campaign. So, foolishly, they decided to march out and face the enemy. At this point a group of *nobiles*, led by Teggiari Aldobrandi de'Adimari, tried to per-

---

⁷³ Baron, *From Petrarch to Leonardo Bruni*, 250.

suade the magistrates of their error, laying out carefully all the advantages and disadvantages – classic Florentine *ragione*. But all for nought. After his speech there arose a certain "Expeditus" ("Ready-For-Action," surely a fictional character), "the sort of person unrestrained liberty can sometimes produce":

> For some time he had barely been able to contain himself as he listened to this good advice. As soon as Teggiari finished, he shouted – his voice shaking with passion – "What are you after Teggiari? Have you turned into a filthy coward? This magistracy isn't going to pay any attention to your fears and quakings. It's going to consider the dignity of the Florentine people. If you're paralyzed with fear, we'll let you off military service."
>
> Teggiari defended himself with dignity, but the die had been cast.
>
> Then the rest of the magistrates fell to grumbling and began to defend their decision, fixing a fine for anyone who debated the matter further. The rashness of the magistrates was assisted by a fierce people, proud of its many victories. They wished to expose themselves to battle, not so much out of concern for their allies' perils, nor led by any particular goal, but simply to avoid the appearance of fearing their enemies. So the best course having been shouted down, the expedition was prepared with resolve.[74]

The result, of course, was the disaster at the Arbia, the return of the Ghibelline exiles and the temporary eclipse of the *popolo*.

As many similar passages in the *Florentine History* and in the *Commentary on the Events of My Lifetime* attest, Bruni never really questioned the classical republican belief that, in matters of policy and government, the rudderless and passionate many needed the guidance of the wise and virtuous few. His apparent statement to the contrary in the *Laudatio* is surely rhetorical exaggeration, a sophistical argument intended to cement his rhetorically "amplified" thesis that all the acts of the Florentine people were virtuous, and that it was therefore worthy of empire.[75]

The second disputed passage occurs in the Strozzi oration where Bruni declares all forms of government other than the popular to be illegitimate.

> This is true liberty, this is fairness [*equitas*] in a city: not to have to fear violence or injury from any man, and for the citizens to be able to enjoy equality of the law and equal access to the commonwealth [*paritatem rei publice adeunde*]. But

---

[74] Bruni, *Historiae*, 36–8. The translation is from my forthcoming edition and translation of Bruni's *Florentine History*, to appear in the I Tatti Renaissance Library.

[75] As James Blythe shows in the second essay in this volume, for Ptolemy of Lucca and Marsilius of Padua, and presumably other medieval writers as well, 'exceeding virtue' was in effect a title to empire.

these conditions cannot be maintained under the rule of one man or a few. For those who prefer royal government appear to ascribe a virtue to the king that they concede was never present in any man.[76] What king has there ever been who would carry out all the acts involved in government for the sake of his people, and desire nothing for his own sake beyond the mere glory of the name? This is why praise of monarchy has something fictitious and shadowy about it, and lacks precision and solidity. Kings, the historian says,[77] are more suspicious of the good than of the evil man, and are always fearful of another's virtue. Nor is it very different under the rule of a few. Thus the only legitimate constitution of the commonwealth left is the popular one [*Ita popularis una reliquitur legitima rei publice gubernande forma*], in which liberty is real, in which legal equality is the same for all citizens, in which pursuit of the virtues may flourish without suspicion.[78]

This passage has been cited countless times in the modern literature to show the depth of Bruni's ideological commitment to republicanism. Yet it is the only place in Bruni's writings where he asserts that a popular constitution is the *only* legitimate form of government. (Indeed, with the possible exception of Ptolemy of Lucca,[79] I am unaware of any medieval or Renaissance writer who denies legitimacy outright to monarchical constitutions.) To be sure, if the remark is taken *au pied de la lettre*, as representing Bruni's innermost convictions, it would change radically the view we have of Bruni from other sources. It would make him into a ideologue almost of the modern sort, a partisan committed to a single political ideology to the exclusion of all others. At the same time, since Bruni spent his entire life as the faithful servant of non-populist and even anti-populist regimes, it would make him into a hypocrite, a penthouse populist. It is possible to imagine such a character – numerous modern analogues spring to mind – but it is not necessary to read Bruni this way.

In fact, all Bruni's other relevant works show him to have possessed the cool and detached attitude to politics of the Aristotelian analyst.[80] For Bruni as for Aristotle a government was legitimate when it ruled for the sake of all, when its rulers were virtuous; it was (strictly speaking) irrelevant to the issue of legitimacy whether a city was ruled by one man, by a few, or by many. In the letters relating to his translation of

---

[76] Cf. Aristotle, *Politics*, III.17.   [77] Cf. Sallust, *Bellum Catilinae*, 7, 2.
[78] Daub, *Nanni Strozzi*, 285 6; I have slightly modified Griffiths' translation in *The Humanism of Leonardo Bruni*, 125.
[79] But even Ptolemy says only that popular governments are the only good governments; he does not seem to take the further step of denying legitimacy to monarchical constitutions; see Blythe's analysis in this volume, 56, above.
[80] In *Epistola* IX.4 (ed. Mehus, II: 144 7), Bruni explicitly declares himself to be a follower of Aristotle.

Aristotle's *Politics* (dedicated first to Duke Humfrey of Gloucester, and later to the pope), Bruni never dissents from Aristotle's view that, given the right circumstances, monarchy is the best form of government, followed by aristocracy, and that a purely popular form of government is illegitimate.[81] Take, for example, his summary of Aristotle's constitutional theory in book III of the *Politics*, addressed to Flavio Biondo in 1438:

> But the special thing about [Aristotle] is his admirable power of analysis. He thinks that the good kinds of commonwealth [*respublica*] are three in number: either one person governs for the public benefit, and he is a king [*rex*]; or a few do, and are optimates, or a multitude composed of both wealthy [*mixta ex opulentis et popularibus*] and this last is called a republic [*respublica*] in the proper sense of the word. To these legitimate kinds there correspond three illegitimate kinds, which he refers to variously in terms of perversion, excess or error. For the royal government is perverted into tyranny, that of the optimates into oligarchy, and the republic into the popular state. The popular state, therefore, is not a legitimate species of government, nor is oligarchy nor tyranny. All three of these are cases of excess and perversion. Of the legitimate species the most excellent of all is kingship; next in dignity and goodness [*bonitas*] is that of the optimates; and after the optimates comes that of the republic. In the perverted species, however, the order is reversed. For the popular state [*popularis status*], which is the perverted form of the republic, comes immediately after the republic. Oligarchy, which is the perverted form of the rule of the optimates, follows after the popular. Tyranny, which is the perversion of kingship, is put in sixth place. Thus kingship falls from the highest to the lowest form, that is, from the best of all the good to the worst of the perverted species. The other forms fall from a lesser height, since they are less perfect than royal government.[82]

This is precisely the view he appears to be attacking in the Strozzi oration, though there (significantly) he leaves out Aristotle's name. In the *Epistola ad magnum principem imperatorem* of 1413, where Bruni emphasizes the popular character of the Florentine constitution, he nevertheless endorses the orthodox view of Aristotle that kingship, aristocracy and *popularis status* are all legitimate forms of government.[83] Nor does he ever question the legitimacy of kingship as such in his *Histories* or in his public and private correspondence. Like most Renaissance humanists, Bruni's political analysis – outside propagandistic contexts – is a pruden-

---

[81] See *The Humanism of Leonardo Bruni*, 154–70.
[82] *Epistola* VIII.1 (ed. Mehus, II: 205–6). I have modified Griffiths' translation slightly in *The Humanism of Leonardo Bruni*, 160–1.
[83] Edited most recently in my article, "Unknown and Little-Known Texts of Leonardo Bruni," *Rinascimento*, n.s., 38 (1998): 125–61. Bruni's authorship of this text is not entirely certain; see my discussion in the article cited.

tial analysis, conducted in terms of better or worse, not right and wrong.[84]

Bruni's late treatise in Greek *On the Constitution of the Florentines* (1439), I would argue, provides the clearest glimpse of his personal view of Florentine politics.[85] The treatise is a brilliant piece of analysis in the Aristotelian manner, written in the plainest possible style, without rhetorical embellishment of any kind. It was addressed to members of the Greek delegation attending the Council of Florence, most of whom would be prejudiced against popular governments. This, it might be argued, could have discouraged Bruni from bringing contempt on his city by describing its government as popular. On the other hand, Bruni was by that time himself a powerful member of the *reggimento* – he was then serving as a member of the Ten of War – and he would also have had powerful motives for concealing any inclinations he had towards elitism. It should further be noted that there was something esoteric and cipherlike in the way the early humanists used Greek; one can find many examples in the letters of Guarino, Filelfo, and other humanists of Greek being used as a kind of secret code. In the treatise Bruni describes Florence as having a mixed constitution:

The Florentine constitution is not completely aristocratic or democratic, but a kind of mixture of the two. This is quite clear from the fact that certain noble families are forbidden, because they have too great a power of numbers and of force at their command, to hold the chief offices in this city; and this rule is anti-aristocratic. On the other hand, mechanics and members of the lowest class do not participate in the political life of the community; and this seems to

[84] I have made a rhetorical argument here, but one might as easily make a "grammatical" argument against taking "legitimate" in its modern sense. Bruni uses the term "legittimus" (also in the *Epistola ad magnum principem imperatorem*), but Aristotle distinguishes between good and bad regimes on the basis of justice. Unlike "legitimate," justice is a term that admits of degrees and is therefore amenable to a prudential analysis, whereas a language of "legitimacy" being dichotomous is necessarily more ideologically heated. It is true that "legitimus" in medieval civil law can mean "what is in accordance with legally enacted rules and the right of those elevated to authority under such rules to issue commands" (one of Weber's three kinds of legitimacy). But Bruni cannot mean that here; his meaning is moral rather than legal. In general the whole problem of political legitimacy, of course, belongs to a modern (post-Rousseavian) discourse about the justified exercise of power. See P. Bastid et al., *L'Idée de légitimité* (Paris: Presses universitaires de France, 1967), especially the essays of A. P. Passerin d'Entrèves and Dolf Steinberger. Bruni's use of the term here is close to its tropical sense, that is, a laudatory term meaning something like "real" or "genuine," as opposed to praises of kingship, which are "fictitious and shadowy [*ficta et umbratilis*]." Compare Bruni's description of Romulus' institution of knighthood in the *De militia*: "Hec fuit institutio Romuli circa militiam, hec forma civitatis ab eo constitute, non iam *ficta et umbratilis, sed vera et solida*" (ed. Viti in *Opere letterarie e politiche*, 672; my italics).

[85] The text has been critically edited in A. Moulakis, "Leonardo Bruni's Constitution of Florence," *Rinascimento*, n.s. 26 (1986): 141–90; see also R. Dees, "Bruni, Aristotle and the Mixed Regime in *On the Constitution of the Florentines*," *Medievalia et Humanistica*, n.s. 15 (1987): 1–23.

be anti-democratic. Thus, avoiding the extremes, the city looks to the mean, or rather to the best and the wealthy but not [to the] over-powerful [i.e., the magnates].[86]

Later in the treatise Bruni lists in detail aristocratic and democratic features of the constitution and manifests a clear sense, without giving any sign of disapproval, that Florence had become more aristocratic in recent times. Bruni shrewdly attributes the aristocratic tendency to the introduction of mercenary troops in place of citizen levies, owing to which "political power [came . . .] into the hands of the aristocrats and the wealthy, because they contributed so much to the community [i.e., they paid for the soldiers], and had counsel to offer in the place of arms." And, as Bruni's account of the Ciompi revolt in his *Florentine Histories* makes clear, Bruni entirely approved of keeping "arms and political initiative" out of the hands of the multitude.[87]

Bruni's view of Florence in *On the Constitution of the Florentines* is usually seen as a late development in his thought, a departure from his earlier populism, a sign of his increasing disillusionment with Florentine government owing to the advent of the Medici regime.[88] But there is no reason to assume that this is really the case. To Cosimo de' Medici, with whom Bruni had always been on cordial terms, Bruni owed, after all, his elevation to the *reggimento*; this was an extraordinary honor for a provincial and a *novus homo*, and Bruni was always a man who rewarded favor with loyalty.[89]

In short, the only instances when Bruni adopted the stance of a fiery populist occur in the two panegyrics whose tendency to flattery and

---

[86] Trans. G. Griffiths in *The Humanism of Leonardo Bruni*, 171.
[87] *Historiarum Florentini populi*, ed. Santini, 224; see also the remarks of Najemy in this volume, 85 above.
[88] Griffiths in *The Humanism of Leonardo Bruni*, 115–16; this is also the view of Dees, "Bruni, Aristotle and the Mixed Regime," Viti, *Leonardo Bruni e Firenze*, and Pocock, *Machiavellian Moment*, 89–91.
[89] See my article, "The Humanist, the Banker and the Condottiere: An Unpublished Letter of Cosimo and Lorenzo de' Medici written by Leonardo Bruni," in *Renaissance Society and Culture: Essays in Honor of Eugene F. Rice, Jr.*, ed. J. Monfasani and R. G. Musto (New York: Italica Press, 1991), 59–70. I remain unconvinced by arguments recently advanced against this view by Arthur Field, "Leonardo Bruni, Florentine Traitor? Bruni, the Medici, and an Aretine Conspiracy of 1437," *Renaissance Quarterly* 51.4 (1998): 1109–50. I am also reluctant to accept as valid the evidence of the document (published and learnedly annotated by Field, 1140–5), purporting to show that Bruni supported a conspiracy to overthrow the Medici, reestablish the Albizzi oligarchy under the protection of the duke of Milan, and establish a signory in Arezzo. The absence of any corroborative evidence of such a conspiracy outside the document itself, combined with the tendency of diplomatic *fondi* to be full of the most egregious conspiracy theories (as I have been reminded by Edward Muir), and Bruni's generally prudent reserve in the face of purely political conflict, suggest that a verdict of *non liquet*, in the absence of further documentation, is the correct one.

rhetorical exaggeration has already been illustrated. It would fit much better what we know of Bruni's character and opinions from other sources, as well as his own explicit statements about epideictic rhetoric, if we assumed that it was the Aristotelian treatise, and not the two panegyrics, that represented his considered views of Florentine politics.

That Bruni was more sympathetic to the Albizzi oligarchy and later to the Mediceans than to populist forms of government should not really come as a surprise. Bruni spent his entire adult life as a loyal servant of the *signore* of the Papal States, the post-Ciompi oligarchy and ultimately the Medici party. Originally a deracinated and ambitious intellectual from the provinces, he eventually became devoted to his adopted city, if not to any one political party in it. But he always retained a certain detachment and realism in his view of the Florentine political tradition, a detachment sharpened by his study of history and Aristotelian political theory. If one reads the whole of his works – the histories, the letters, the treatises, and prefaces – and not just the two or three texts most commonly studied by historians of political thought, it becomes much harder to maintain that he was a genuine populist, or that his humanistic activities in general were motivated and shaped by a strong ideological preference for a particular regime or constitution.

Two negative proofs help make the point. If Bruni's humanistic activities had been *au fond* instrumental to a "civic humanist" ideology, one would have expected his treatise and letters on education to have promoted some species of political education, some nurturing in republican traditions. Instead, Bruni's *De studiis et literis* and his letters on education are all in the Isocratean tradition of cultivating personal distinction and virtue; they do not subordinate education to civic ends in any way.[90] Secondly, as an Aristotelian one would have expected Bruni to have subordinated ethics to politics; to have made full human flourishing in the active life dependent upon participation in civil and military affairs. But Bruni's *Isagogicon moralis disciplinae* (1424), a summary of Aristotelian ethics, nowhere mentions self-rule or participation in politics as a condition of the Good Life.[91] Though the use of this particular argument for participation was apparently rare among late

---

[90] See *The Humanism of Leonardo Bruni*, 240–54. The exception that proves the rule in this case is Bruni's letters to the kings of Castile and Aragon, and to Duke Humfrey of Gloucester (ibid., 155, 167), where Bruni says the *studia humanitatis* are necessary to the craft of kingship as well as to personal *ornatus*. On the other hand, in his letter presenting the Signori of Siena with his translation of the *Politics* (ibid., 166), Bruni recommends his own translation as a proper work for citizens to study.

[91] Ibid., 267–82; the Latin text is in Viti's collection, *Leonardo Bruni*, 195–242.

medieval Aristotelians,[92] its omission in Bruni's writings is a striking symptom of his discomfort with anything that might entail a particular constitutional form. On the one occasion Bruni does mention in passing the basis of human association, he subordinates the Aristotelian model based on human flourishing or perfection to the Ciceronian model of association based on mutual need.

Since man is a weak animal and must get the sufficiency and perfection he lacks in himself from civil society [*ex civili societate*], no branch of philosophy can be more appropriate to him [than the study of politics].[93]

As James Blythe points out in chapter 2 of this volume, such a formulation "shifts the emphasis from a natural need to participate in government to a natural need to live together in communities."[94]

If Bruni cannot be described as a man with a deep ideological commitment to a republican constitution, it may well be asked whether it is appropriate to describe Bruni's humanism as "civic humanism." If we mean by this only that Bruni was part of a movement to revive the political and moral excellence of the ancients in the urban elites of his day, the term could be used without embarrassment. Indeed, in this sense it presents certain advantages over its rivals, "classical republicanism" and "neo-Roman ideology." But if it is meant to suggest that Bruni considered that the aim of his efforts as a humanist – as a historian, translator, moralist, and man of letters – was to promote an antimonarchical form of republicanism and to disparage other political constitutions, the term would be, in my opinion, highly misleading. Elsewhere in this volume, Paul Rahe writes: "The classical republicanism of Aristotle and Cicero was not an ideology blindly dictating partisan regime preferences; it was a way of thinking about human association that left ample room for the exercise of political prudence."[95] This description applies perfectly to Bruni as well. If Bruni had found employment with the *condottiere* prince Carlo Malatesta, or with the Visconti ally Giovanfrancesco Gonzaga – as at different points in his life he attempted to do[96] – it is not implausible to suppose that he could have adapted the major themes of his humanism to suit those princely regimes, just as he had done when he had served as apostolic secretary to the pope in the first decade of his professional career.

[92] See Blythe in chapter 2, above, 63.
[93] Leonardo Bruni, *Humanistisch-philosophische Schriften*, ed. H. Baron (Leipzig: Teubner, 1928), 73; I have adjusted Griffiths' translation in *The Humanism of Leonardo Bruni*, 162.
[94] Blythe, chapter 2, above, 59, 64.   [95] See chapter 10, below, 289.
[96] Viti, *Leonardo Bruni e Firenze*, 368 70. The evidence is circumstantial but persuasive.

In the end, Bruni, like Dante, was a man with a universalist point of view, and his humanism had universalist aims. That is one reason why it was so popular everywhere in Europe in the fifteenth and sixteenth centuries: with kings, princes, curials, and *condottieri* as well as with citizens of republics. Like that of most early Quattrocento humanists, Bruni's humanism was about the need for virtue and eloquence and the value of the classical past as a model for modern societies. It was a message aimed primarily at ruling elites who were his patrons, not at broad, popular audiences.[97] To be sure, Bruni while chancellor of Florence was an able defender of republican government. But constitutional forms, for him, were far less important than nurturing an aristocracy of virtue, patriotism, and devotion to the common good.[98] This hard truth may make the real Bruni a less attractive figure in the "century of the common man" than was the Bruni of Hans Baron's imagination. But (whatever Cicero and the humanists may have thought) historical truth is not the rival, but the precondition, of true edification.

[97] John Najemy in chapter 3 of this volume argues that the target audience of Bruni's civic humanism was made up of "politically infantilized nonelite office-holders." But while Bruni surely had many nonelite readers in Florence, especially notaries, the evidence of the manuscript tradition reminds us that at least three-quarters of his contemporary readership consisted of elite non-Florentines. We should also remember that Bruni's professional writings as chancellor were overwhelmingly directed to non-Florentines.

[98] An attitude which is now seen as characteristic of English "classical republicanism" in the seventeenth century; see Steve Pincus, "Neither Machiavellian Moment nor Possessive Individualism: Commercial Society and the Defenders of the English Commonwealth," *American Historical Review* 101 (1998): 705–36, esp. 708ff.

CHAPTER 6

De-masking Renaissance republicanism

Alison Brown

"The city of Florence was always much more enthusiastic for liberty than other cities – in fact, as you know, the name of Liberty can be seen written in gold letters among her public emblems"; "liberty is no less engraved in men's hearts than it is written on our walls and banners."[1] The survival of the blue shield crossed with the word "liberty" on the Palazzo Vecchio in Florence seems to confirm the proud boast of the Florentines Alamanno Rinuccini and Francesco Guicciardini. But in fact by the time they were writing in the late fifteenth and early sixteenth century, the republican ideal was already losing credibility. Belief in the values described by Quentin Skinner – which are depicted so graphically on the walls of the Sala del Buon Governo in Siena – was being replaced by skepticism about the claims made for liberty. Yet because liberty was (and remains) an empowering word in republican political vocabulary, it is not so easy to put one's finger on the moment when the slow process of disbelief begins, engendered by a perceived gap between political reality and the rhetoric of liberty. In fact, it is the very men I

Originally delivered at the Joint Conference on "Representations" of the Australian and New Zealand Medieval and Renaissance Historians in Hobart, Tasmania, in 1994, subsequently at seminars in London and Cambridge, and also in Siena, at the conference *La teoria repubblicana del governo civile*, whose proceedings are to be published in Italian by the Istituto storico italiano per il Medio Evo. I am grateful to participants in these seminars for their helpful comments, as well as to Mikael Hörnqvist for his apposite remarks on this paper. In the notes that follow, the abbreviation ASF stands for Archivio di Stato, Florence.

[1] Alamanno Rinuccini, *De libertate dialogus*, ed. F. Adorno, *Atti e memorie dell'Accademia Toscana di scienze e lettere "La Colombaria"* 22 (1957): 274; trans. R. N. Watkins in *Humanism and Liberty. Writings on Freedom in Fifteenth-Century Florence* (Columbia, S.C.: University of South Carolina Press, 1978), 197: "Florentinam civitatem semper libertatis avidam, semper studiosam prae caeteris extitisse, adeo ut inter publica signa aureis, ut nosti, litteris inscriptum libertatis nomen ubique conspicatur" (Microtoxus); Francesco Guicciardini, *Dialogo del reggimento di Firenze*, in *Dialogo e discorsi del reggimento di Firenze*, ed. R. Palmarocchi (Bari: Laterza, 1932), 25, 37 100; trans. A. Brown, *Dialogue on the Government of Florence* (Cambridge: Cambridge University Press, 1994), 16 17: "perché in Firenze non è manco scolpita ne' cuori degli uomini la libertà che sia scritta nelle nostre mura e bandiere" (Pagolantonio Soderini). On the shield, see note 12, below.

179

begin by citing, Rinuccini and Guicciardini, who go on to undermine it by warning us that "these exotic signs and words clash with the facts," for liberty is no more than a "name" whose "appearances and image" are used as a pretext to deceive people and to "dazzle" them.[2] Are their dialogues simply rhetorical exercises in putting the truth on either side, *in utramque partem*, or do they represent a serious attempt to alert us to change?

All the contributors to this volume agree on the difficulty of defining not only the meaning of the word liberty in the Renaissance but also its iconic status, whether it functioned as a myth, an ideology or a realistic depiction of political institutions. Because of its long history as part of the language of classical republicanism and the ancient rhetorical tradition, it is self-referential to answer these questions by studying only the texts themselves and their classical sources. In coupling words with visual signs and images, both Rinuccini and Guicciardini suggest there may be another approach through a different tradition, the tradition of visual representation and the theater, which played an equally important part in transmitting republican ideas in the Renaissance. Using these writers as our guides, we can perhaps begin to trace the process that undermined belief in liberty in the course of the fifteenth and early sixteenth centuries through images as well as words – a sequence of appropriation and de-masking that uses not only the familiar language of classical republicanism but also the much less familiar language of the theater and role-playing in Florence.

There was a long history in Florence, as in other Italian cities, of public festivals and displays. Initially providing the opportunity for private citizens to dress up as lords and gather in courts, these festivals were gradually transformed into civic ceremonies by means of which rival groups were integrated in a single community.[3] They helped to

---

[2] Rinuccini, *De libertate dialogus*, ed. Adorno, 274 (trans. Watkins, 197): "haec enim ipsa exotica signa et verba longe e rebus ipsis dissonare meo iudicio videntur" (Alitheus); Guicciardini, *Dialogo*, ed. Palmarocchi, 25, 37 (trans. Brown, *Dialogue*, 23, 35 6): "el nome, le dimostrazioni e la immagine di essere libera," "preso più presto per colore e per scusa . . . gli uomini si lasciono spesso ingannare tanto da' nomi che non cognoscono le cose . . . abagliati da ['l nome di libertà]"; cf. his *Ricordi*, C 66, ed. R. Spongano (Florence: Sansoni, 1951), 76 (trans. Brown, *Dialogue*, 172). Cf. also my earlier re-reading of republicanism in "City and Citizen: Changing Perceptions in the Fifteenth and Sixteenth Centuries," in *City-States in Classical Antiquity and Medieval Italy*, ed. A. Molho, K. Raaflaub, and J. Emlen (Stuttgart: Steiner Verlag, and Ann Arbor: University of Michigan Press, 1991), 93 119; reprinted in A. Brown, *The Medici in Florence* (Florence: Olschki, and Perth: University of Western Australia Press, 1992), 281 303.

[3] R. C. Trexler, *Public Life in Renaissance Florence* (New York: Academic Press, 1980), esp. 215 47. On the tradition of religious and secular plays produced by confraternities and guilds, see N. Newbigin, "The Word Made Flesh: The *Rappresentazioni* of Mysteries and Miracles in Fifteenth-

give visual expression to the civic ideology that, according to Baron, was so clearly articulated in humanist writings. However, as I shall argue, the republicanism of festivals and public shows or "representations" was no less ambiguous than the written republican tradition is now seen to be. For this reason, just because visual images present the same problems of interpretation as written texts, they may provide useful insight into the use and appropriation of republican ideology more generally.

In the Renaissance, as now, the word "representation" had a double meaning. It meant both a symbol for an abstract concept like liberty, and also a play or a show in which actors "represent" or play the role of characters, the word *rappresentazione* being used to describe the religious and the secular plays produced in public places in Italy by confraternities and guilds. In a socially mobile city like Florence, the language of shows and role-playing also came to be used to describe the political process by which citizens dressed up in the regalia of political office and military service, only to "drop their masks" when they returned to civilian status two or three months later.[4] Francesco Vettori used the same image to describe how Maximilian Sforza's initial elation at the French defeat in 1513 was followed by the dawning realization that he was now instead in the hands of the Swiss: he was, Vettori wrote, like "our kings of festivals, who as evening draws on think about having to return to being those men they were before."[5] So does Francesco Guicciardini, in a *Maxim* that underlines the social mobility implied by the republican process. For if life itself is "like a comedy or a tragedy," in which "we don't rate the person playing the

---

Century Florence"; C. Barr, "Music and Spectacle in Confraternity Drama of Fifteenth-Century Florence"; and P. Ventrone, "Thoughts on Florentine Fifteenth-Century Religious Spectacle," all in *Christianity and the Renaissance*, ed. T. Verdon and J. Henderson (Syracuse: Syracuse University Press, 1990), 361–75, 376–404, 405–12, respectively. P. Ventrone, "Lorenzo's *Politica festiva*," and N. Newbigin, "Politics in the *Sacre Rappresentazioni* of Lorenzo's Florence," both in *Lorenzo the Magnificent: Culture and Politics*, ed. M. Mallett and N. Mann (London: Warburg Institute, 1996), 105–16 and 117–30, respectively; and P. Ventrone, *Gli Araldi della commedia. Teatro a Firenze nel Rinascimento* (Pisa: Pacini, 1993).

[4] Leonardo Bruni, *De militia*, trans. G. Griffiths in *The Humanism of Leonardo Bruni*, ed. G. Griffiths, J. Hankins, and D. Thompson (Binghamton, New York: Center for Medieval and Early Renaissance Studies, 1987), 145; cited by Patricia Simons in an unpublished paper, "Separating the Men from the Boys: Masculinities in Early Quattrocento Florence," which she kindly allowed me to read.

[5] Francesco Vettori to Niccolò Machiavelli, 20 August 1513, in *Machiavelli: Lettere*, ed. F. Gaeta (Milan: Feltrinelli, 1961), 284: "para essere come li nostri re delle feste che pensono la sera haversi a tornare quelli uomini erano prima." The correspondence of these months is discussed by John Najemy, *Between Friends. Discourses of Power and Desire in the Machiavelli–Vettori Letters of 1513–1515* (Princeton: Princeton University Press, 1993), chap. 4, esp. 156–67.

role of the master and the king higher than the person playing the role of the servant," what counts – as he says – is not social status or hierarchy, but "simply who performs better."[6]

Used like this, these images have republican connotations, in encouraging social fluidity and equality by role-playing and the frequent change of office-holders. As Salutati wrote, when congratulating the city of Bologna for evicting the papal governor and replacing him with a popular government of merchants and artisans, these are the people in every state who love liberty, equality and justice and "who rule the republic in turn when called to power and when they return to being private citizens obey the government without reservation."[7]

However, representation and masques also have less egalitarian connotations: far from openness, they also imply duplicity and concealment. In the theater, as Stephen Greenblatt points out, the distance between the actors and their role is essential for separating the theater from the reality outside. But although an illusion, playwrights rely on it to exercise power over their audiences – like politicians, as Machiavelli realized, when he advised a new prince that political success depends on his ability to manipulate the distinction between appearances and reality, because "men in general judge more with their eyes than with their hands" and are taken in by appearances.[8] From early on, ritualized ceremonies in Florence were knowingly used to convey duplicitous messages to foreign powers. Sometimes victory celebrations were canceled and sometimes they were instigated to create a false impression of good will, "like those who masquerade in silk and gold and appear rich

---

[6] Guicciardini, *Ricordi*, C 216, ed. Spongano, 228 (trans. Brown, *Dialogue*, 174). Cf. Machiavelli, *Il Principe*, ed. S. Bertelli (Milan: Feltrinelli, 1960), chap. 18, 74: "Ognuno vede quello che tu pari, pochi sentono quello che tu se," and F. Vettori, "Viaggio in Alamagna," in *Scritti storici e politici*, ed. E. Niccolini (Bari: Laterza, 1972), 32: "con quante astuzie, con quante varie arte, con quale industria uno uomo s'ingegna ingannare l'altro . . . Et in effetto tutto il mondo è ciurmeria." Cf. E. Raimondi, *Politica e commedia. Dal Beroaldo al Machiavelli* (Bologna: Mulino, 1972), 188; W. A. Rebhorn, *Foxes and Lions: Machiavelli's Confidence Men* (Ithaca: Cornell University Press, 1988), 12. On this and what follows, see also A. Brown, "Lorenzo and Guicciardini," in *Lorenzo the Magnificent*, ed. Mallett and Mann, 282, 294. And on the use of art "to disseminate political messages," see *Artistic Strategy and the Rhetoric of Power: Political Uses of Art from Antiquity to the Present*, ed. D. Castriota (Carbondale: Southern Illinois University Press, 1986), the reference to which I owe to Lucas Burkart.

[7] R. G. Witt, "The *De tyranno* and Coluccio Salutati's View of Politics and Roman History," *Nuova rivista storica* 53 (1969): 455.

[8] Machiavelli, *The Prince*, ed. Bertelli, chap. 18, 74: "li uomini in universali iudicano più alli occhi che alle mani." On the Renaissance theater, see Stephen Greenblatt, *Shakespearean Negotiations: The Circulation of Social Energy in Renaissance England* (Oxford: Clarendon Press, 1988), chap. 1, and Alison Brown, "Representation and the Renaissance Theatre," in her *The Renaissance*, second edn (London: Longman, 1999), 91–6.

and powerful, yet when the mask and the garment come off... are the same persons they were before."9 But when abroad, Florentines professed themselves to be disconcerted by the secrecy and duplicity of princely courts, claiming that their decisions were not only unpredictable but also more irrational than those reached by open debate in a public assembly. Since it is impossible to know the secrets of princes, Vettori wrote to Machiavelli, and yet it must be supposed that all princes have an objective (or "intention"), "we must estimate it from their words, from their appearances [*dimostrazioni*] and even to some extent imagine what it is."10

Dimostrazioni is also the word used by Guicciardini to warn against being deceived by the name and outward appearances of liberty, alerting us to its role-playing function in representing – or misrepresenting – the image of "liberty" in Florence. Since the display of the word on the facade of the Palazzo Vecchio also served to symbolize the abstract concept of freedom, it usefully illustrates both senses of the word "representation", as a symbol and as a show, that constitute its potential meaning. In order to unwrap this meaning, we need to understand its position and function in the wider republican "system of representation." As Roger Chartier reminds us, no official or state systems of representation are ever politically neutral; and as instruments of power, they can be appropriated, and they can also be "stripped bare" (or "expropriated") – as they were by Pascal in France in the seventeenth century, when he described the clothes of magistrates as dressing up, or make-believe, which created respect through illusion, as though life itself was a charade.11 Pascal's language of dressing up and illusion suggests that Florentine writers may have been engaged on a similar

---

9 Trexler, *Public Life*, chap. 9, esp. 279 90, and 286, citing G. Cambi, *Istorie*, in *Delizie degli eruditi toscani*, ed. Isidoro di San Luigi, 24 vols. (Florence: Gaetano Cambiagi, 1770 1789), XXII: 2: "chome quelli che vano in maschera, che quello ch'è vestito di seta e d'oro pare ricco et potente, di poi chavatosi la maschera et la vesta, è pure poi quel medeximo che prima."
10 Vettori to Machiavelli, 12 July 1513, in *Lettere*, 267, 269, discussed by Najemy, *Between Friends*, 148 9: "Noi habbiamo a pensare che ciascuno di questi nostri principi habbia un fine, et perché a noi è impossibile sapere il segreto loro, bisogna lo stimiamo dalle parole, dalle dimostrazioni, et qualche parte ne immaginiamo."
11 R. Chartier, *Cultural History: Between Practices and Representations* (Oxford: Polity Press, 1988), introduction, at 5 and 8, quoting *Œuvres de Blaise Pascal*, ed. Leon Brunschvicg and Pierre Boutroux, 11 vols. (Paris: Hachette, 1904 14), II: 7-8, *Pensées*, no. 82, "Imagination"; cf. Chartier, "Le monde comme répresentation," *Annales E. S. C.* 44 (1989): 1505 20, and his recent defense against the criticism of "idealism," "Rappresentazione della pratica, pratica della rappresentazione," *Quaderni storici* 92 (1996): 487 93. On "appropriation" and "expropriation," see J. G. A. Pocock, "The Concept of Language and the *métier d'historien*: Some Considerations on Practice," in *The Languages of Political Theory in Early-Modern Europe*, ed. A. Pagden (Cambridge: Cambridge University Press, 1987), 24.

stripping-bare enterprise. To find out, we need first to describe the imagery and the language of republicanism before we can understand its appropriation and de-masking in late fifteenth- and early sixteenth-century Florence.

FLORENTINA LIBERTAS

In its clearest and least ambivalent representation, *Libertas* was written out in bold capitals on banners and on a shield in the center of the facade of the Palazzo Vecchio, just as it had been "written on the turrets of the city of Lucca in great characters" from the fourteenth to the seventeenth century, when Hobbes espied it there.[12] In both cities the slogan proclaimed political independence and freedom from external domination, as it did in 1375–8, when a banner crossed "with letters saying LIBERTY" was used to identify all the cities who joined Florence in her war against the papacy.[13] As a result of Florence's part in this war and in later wars against Giangaleazzo Visconti, the banners and shields crossed with the word "liberty" came to signify Florence's role as champion of liberty, as we can see from the republican voices in dialogues like Rinuccini's *Dialogue on Liberty* and Guicciardini's *Dialogue on the Government of Florence*.[14] But we also know that this insignia was associated by Florentines with their open republican system of government, not simply with the city's independence, from the evidence of a political debate in 1465, during a brief interlude of more open government after the death of Cosimo de' Medici. In the first consultative meeting held by Niccolò Soderini, newly drawn as head of state by lot, not election, one citizen rose to his feet to propose that "the shield of liberty should be placed on the rostrum [of the council chamber] as a sign of restored liberty."[15] And another incident demonstrates that even

---

[12] Thomas Hobbes, *Leviathan*, ed. M. Oakeshott (Oxford: Blackwell, 1946), chap. 21, 140. The shield on the facade of the Palazzo Vecchio is illustrated in G. Brucker, *Florence, 1138–1737* (Berkeley: University of California Press, 1998), 138; cf. note 27, below.

[13] N. Rubinstein, "Florentina libertas," *Rinascimento*, n.s. 26 (1986), 7–8; on Florentine republicanism, see also the essays by Rubinstein, Giovanni Silvano, and Quentin Skinner in *Machiavelli and Republicanism*, ed. G. Bock, Q. Skinner, and M. Viroli (Cambridge: Cambridge University Press, 1990), 3–16, 41–70 and 293–309, respectively. See also note 18, below.

[14] See note 1, above. In Rinuccini's *Dialogue*, Eleutherius ("the lover of liberty") represents the author himself, who responds in book II to the critical analysis of liberty in Medicean Florence by Alitheus ("the truthful") and Microtoxus ("the short-range shooter") in book I; in Guicciardini's *Dialogue*, Pagolantonio Soderini and Piero Capponi present the republican argument.

[15] Giovanni Giugni: "Scutum libertatis suggestui imponendum ut esset id signum restitute libertatis," ASF, Consulte e practiche 57 (3 November 1465), ed. in G. Pampaloni, "Fermenti di riforme democratiche nelle consulte della Repubblica Fiorentina," *Archivio storico italiano* 119

as late as 1512 it still symbolized political republicanism, or the active freedom of citizens to participate on an equal basis in government; for after the Medici's return from exile in that year, the newly-elected Gonfalonier of Justice, Guglielmo de' Pazzi, immediately declared that the Medici must live as citizens, "and unfurled from the window of the Palace the old blue banner with the inscription of LIBERTY."[16]

Liberty was also personified, as we know from references to her "shadow," and we must imagine that her figure became elided in the popular imagination with that of Florence herself, who was described in the fourteenth century as a beautiful woman, "the Flower of Flowers."[17] So when the image of Florence bearing an olive or laurel branch with the legend *Pax libertasque publica* appears on Medici medals in the fifteenth century, we can guess that the woman is intended to represent the concept of the free city, Florentia/*libertas*, in a joint personification.

This is not the place to discuss in detail the other images that represented Florentine liberty, the most virile of which was the heraldic lion or *marzocco*, as well as Hercules and David.[18] The *marzocco* was represented on banners and as a figure – Donatello's freestanding statue

---

(1961): 251. On the debate, N. Rubinstein, *The Government of Florence under the Medici, 1434–1494*, second edn. (Oxford: Clarendon Press, 1997), 164–5; P. C. Clarke, *The Soderini and the Medici* (Oxford: Clarendon Press, 1991), 80–1; V. Beamish, "The *Practiche* Debates of the Florentine Deliberative Assembly, 1465–1466" (M.A. dissertation, University of Leeds, 1993), esp. 27–36, 38–47; the last three writers point out that Soderini was in fact much less radical than Pampaloni represents him to be.

[16] Jacopo Pitti, *Dell' Istoria fiorentina*, in *Archivio storico italiano* 1 (1842): 108: Guglielmo de' Pazzi "non prima entrato Gonfaloniere, predicava che i Medici dovevano stare da cittadini . . . e trasse fuora alla finestra del Palagio la bandiera vecchia turchina, con l'iscrizione della libertà." "LIBERTY" was also inscribed "in big letters" on the new banners of the militia established in 1528; see F. W. Kent, "Ties of Neighborhood and Patronage in Quattrocento Florence," in *Patronage, Art and Society in Renaissance Italy*, ed. F. W. Kent and P. Simons (New York: Oxford University Press, 1987), 90.

[17] Piero Parenti, *Storia fiorentina*, ed. A. Matucci (Florence: Olschki, 1994), I: 87: "Feciono, in ombra di libertà, Richiesti"; cf. F. Guicciardini, *Del modo di assicurare lo stato ai Medici*, in *Dialoghi e discorsi*, ed. Palmarocchi, 281: "sotto questa ombra di civilità e di libertà"; Convenevole da Prato, *Regia carmina dedicati a Roberto d'Angiò, re di Sicilia e di Gerusalemme*, ed. C. Grassi, 2 vols. (Milan: Silvana, 1982), I: 71 (43c, line 1), illustrated in Brucker, *Florence, 1138–1737*, 15: "Flos florum flore, Florentia crescit honore."

[18] The symbols representing *Florentina libertas* are discussed by Luca Gatti, "The Art of Freedom: Meaning, Civic Identity and Devotion in Early Renaissance Florence," (Ph.D. dissertation, University of London, 1992); Gatti, "The *Comune Studio Libertatis* of Florence and Venice, and the Political Implications of the pre-Medicean Restoration of the Convent of San Marco," *Quaderni di storia dell' architettura e restauro* 13–14 (1995): 36–47, and note 51, below; Monica Donato, "Hercules and David in the Early Decoration of the Palazzo Vecchio," *Journal of the Warburg and Courtauld Institutes* 54 (1991): 83–98; H. W. Janson, *The Sculpture of Donatello* (Princeton: Princeton University Press, 1963), 3–12, and the articles of H. Spurling and F. Caglioti referred to in note 35, below. Lions were also kept by the commune in a cage at the rear of the Palazzo Vecchio, the present Via de' Lioni; they are represented in Leo X's 1519–20 antiphonary (see note 47, below).

in front of the communal palace – whereas Hercules was used on the communal seal and as a painted image or statue in the Palazzo Vecchio.[19] Donatello also produced a marble statue of David, which was transferred in 1416 from the cathedral to the Palazzo Vecchio as a symbol of Florence's victory over Ladislas of Naples, with heraldic lilies added to the background and the inscription: "God helps those fighting against terrible enemies *pro patria.*"[20] But as symbols of liberty they were as ambiguous as the concept of liberty itself, with overtones of sovereignty and conquest as well as of freedom (the subject of Mikael Hörnqvist's contribution to this volume). So when the *marzocco*, for instance, was raised on banners above the ramparts of Colle Val d'Elsa "with great shouts of joy" in 1479, the lion signified support for Florence's fight for freedom against the enemy. But when in 1494, "the Pisans rebelled and cried 'liberty, liberty' and threw down the *marzocco* on a column on the Ponte Vecchio and another on a column in the Banchi," it clearly meant the opposite – the lion symbolizing Florentine imperialism, not freedom.[21]

The vocabulary of republicanism that underpinned these images of liberty was adopted initially from the writings of Cicero and Sallust,[22] to be enriched in the early fifteenth century by newly available Greek texts like Aristides' *Praise of Athens* and Pericles' *Funeral Oration* in Thucydides.

[19] See Donato, "Hercules and David," 84, note 4, quoting surviving written inscriptions: "as a baby I strangled the pair of serpents, I have brought down ungrateful cities and overcome cruel tyrants... Now Florence has offered me such a seat and holds me and keeps me in its seal." On the seal, see D. Marzi, *La cancelleria della repubblica fiorentina* (Rocca San Casciano: Capelli, 1910), 377-85. This use of Hercules as a republican symbol can be compared to the French revolutionary image of Hercules; see L. Hunt, "Hercules and the Radical Image in the French Revolution," *Representations* 1.2 (1983): 95-117, esp. 99-101.

[20] Donato, "Hercules and David," 90-8. For a broader interpretation of David's iconography based on the Hebrew version of the Psalms, which emphasizes his role as protector and defender of the homeland, see now A. Butterfield, "New Evidence for the Iconography of David in Quattrocento Florence," *I Tatti Studies* 6 (1995): 115-33.

[21] See Bartolomeo Scala and Piero Vettori to the Dieci di Balia in Florence, 20 October 1479, in Bartolomeo Scala, *Humanistic and Political Writings*, ed. A. Brown (Tempe, Ariz.: Medieval and Renaissance Texts and Studies, 1997), 73; the letter ends: "Idio con salveza della libertà et dello stato ci traghi dalle loro mani," referring to the enemy, King Ferrante of Naples and Pope Sixtus IV; Piero Vaglienti, *Storia dei suoi tempi, 1492-1514*, ed. G. Berti, M. Luzzatti, and E. Tongiorgi (Pisa: Nistri-Lischi e Pacini, 1982), 18.

[22] See most recently, Quentin Skinner, "The Vocabulary of Renaissance Republicanism: A Cultural *longue-durée?*" in *Language and Images of Renaissance Italy*, ed. Alison Brown (Oxford: Clarendon Press, 1995), esp. 101-10, insisting on the twelfth- and thirteenth-century origins of Renaissance republicanism, quoting Cicero (*De officiis*, II.vii.24, cf. II.xxii.87-9) on the contrast between living under tyranny and "in a free city." Cf. Charles Davis's earlier comments on Baron in his articles, "Brunetto Latini and Dante" (1967), "Ptolemy of Lucca and the Roman Republic" (1974), and "Roman Patriotism and Republican Propaganda" (1975), all reprinted in his *Dante's Italy and Other Studies* (Philadelphia: University of Pennsylvania Press, 1984), esp. 172-3, 229-30, and 258.

Both Latin and Greek sources contained the same ambivalence about liberty meaning the city's independence and/or imperialism, and liberty meaning an individual's free status within the city. Whereas in the fourteenth century liberty in Florence more usually meant political independence from an overlord, by the fifteenth it also came to mean a republican constitution that guaranteed freedom of speech and equality under the law, or *aequa libertas*.[23] So Leonardo Bruni declaimed in his Thucydidean *Oration for the Funeral of Nanni Strozzi*, delivered in 1428 after the soldier's death in the war against Milan:

> The constitution we use for the government of the republic is designed for the liberty and equality of all citizens. Since it is egalitarian in all respects, it is called a "popular" constitution. We do not tremble beneath the rule of one man . . . nor are we slaves to the rule of the few. Our liberty is equal to all, is limited only by the laws and is free from the fear of men.[24]

In Bruni's earlier and better-known *Praise of Florence*, which was modeled on Aristides' *Praise of Athens*, we can see how these republican concepts of liberty and equality were applied to Florence's political system. Liberty was said to consist in the right to attend assemblies and appoint foreign judges to ensure freedom under the law; and equality consisted in short-term offices to ensure a rapid turnover and fair distribution of offices, and in punishing the magnates more heavily than the commoners, in order to bring them down to the level of the poor. That these concepts remained integral to the Florentine definition of liberty we can see from Rinuccini's 1479 *Dialogue*. There freedom still means the freedom of speech, or "the right to say openly what [one] thinks," election by lot, and the right to attend public assemblies, summoned by the herald so eloquently praised by Demosthenes; and equality, which we are told is basic to the concept of liberty, consists in preventing "the rich from oppressing the poor and the poor, for their part, from violently robbing the rich."[25]

---

[23] See Rubinstein, "Florentina libertas," esp. 5–15.
[24] Translated by G. Griffiths in *The Humanism of Leonardo Bruni*, 124.
[25] *Laudatio*, trans. Griffiths, in ibid., 118–21. On Bruni's analysis, see N. Rubinstein, "Florentine Constitutionalism and Medici Ascendancy in the Fifteenth Century," in Rubinstein, ed., *Florentine Studies: Politics and Society in Renaissance Florence* (London: Faber and Faber, 1968), 442–55; and the essays of Hörnqvist, Hankins, and Mansfield in this volume. Rinuccini, *Dialogus*, ed. Adorno, 283–5 (trans. Watkins, 202–6): "priscam illam et in senatu et ad populum dicendi licentiam," contrasted with "hodierna taciturnitate"; "Quos in liberis civitatibus ex lectis quibusdam sorte instituit . . . Nunc . . . non sorte sed electione creari"; "praeclara illa in consiliis audire solita et tam multis verbis a Demosthene laudata praeconis vox qua, magistratus iussu, consulendi licentia volentibus datur, nunc plerunque siletur"; and on equality, Adorno, 283 (trans. Watkins, 204): "quis ignorat aequalitatem civium libertatis precipuum esse fundamentum? . . . ut ditiores inopes non opprimant, nec rursus a pauperibus divites vim patiantur."

This combination of ideas is summed up by another image, one that is both visual and verbal: *palazzo–piazza*. This alliterative image stood for Florence's open system of government in contrast to the secrecy of courts and princely states, which Machiavelli thought were "fuller of lies than piazzas."[26] It describes the close bond that existed between the Palazzo Vecchio, linked umbilically by its *ringhiera*, or raised platform, to the seat of people power in the open piazza outside. Summoned by bells and a herald, it was in the piazza that citizens participated in *parlamenti*, or plebiscites, which exercised supreme power in times of crisis; and it was there that they also attended the two-monthly induction of their government. Built in the late thirteenth century to house the new guild-based government, the battlements of the Palazzo and its later display of coats-of-arms – in the center of which was the blue shield crossed with the word LIBERTAS in gold – described its double role as a military bastion and a symbol of free government.[27] That it retained its ideological role as a bastion of communal liberty into the fifteenth and sixteenth centuries can be seen from the chancellor of Florence's riposte to Pope Sixtus IV in 1478, in the aftermath of the Pazzi conspiracy. Rejecting the pope's appeal to the Florentines to expel Lorenzo de' Medici as a tyrant, in order "to restore liberty to so famous a city," the chancellor Bartolomeo Scala retorted that it was the conspirators, not Lorenzo, who were the enemies of liberty in wanting to occupy the Palazzo della Signoria, which is "the citadel of our liberty" – or, as he described it two weeks later in his printed defense of Florence, the *Excusatio Florentinorum*, "the home of our government and of Florentine liberty."[28]

These images, of course, served as slogans, prescribing rather than describing freedom, and they had more to do with political sovereignty than with personal freedom. But Rinuccini's *Dialogue* reminds us that the

[26] Machiavelli, *Legazioni e commissarie*, ed. S. Bertelli, 3 vols. (Milan: Feltrinelli, 1964), III: 1187, from Mantua, 20 November 1509: "perché questo è uno luogo dove nascono, anzi piovono le bugie, e la Corte ne è più piena che le piazze."

[27] Rubinstein suggests that the coats-of-arms were added to the facade, with the *marzocco* on the *ringhiera* and four small gilded lions in the niches at the corners, after the fall of the duke of Athens, between 1349 and 1353; see Nicolai Rubinstein, *The Palazzo Vecchio, 1292–1532: Government, Architecture and Imagery in the Civic Palace of the Florentine Republic* (Oxford: Clarendon Press, 1995), 17; on the building, 5–17.

[28] "Arcem libertatis nostrae publicum palatium," Florentine Signoria to Sixtus IV, 21 July 1478, edited in Scala's *Humanistic and Political Writings*, 197; "status nostri et Florentinae libertatis domicilium," is in Scala's *Excusatio Florentinorum*, in ibid., 200; on its use as propaganda, Alison Brown, *Bartolomeo Scala, 1430–1497, Chancellor of Florence* (Princeton: Princeton University Press, 1979), 158–9. The pope's letter of 7 July is cited in ibid., 85, note 68 ("ut tam praeclara civitas in libertatem restituatur"); cf. Rinuccini, *Dialogus*, ed. Adorno, 302 (trans. Watkins, 221).

concept of liberty still included the active political activities defined by Bruni, despite the fact that, by 1479, the voice of the herald was "now silent."[29] By the early sixteenth century even the *palazzo–piazza* image was stripped of its republican connotations by Guicciardini, when he reflected that there was "such a dense fog, or thick wall, between the government palace and the piazza outside" that people knew and understood as little about what the rulers were doing "as they know about what goes on in India."[30] Nevertheless, since children were still erecting statues of Hercules during popular festivals in the late fifteenth century, it is perhaps true that liberty remained emotionally "engraved" on people's hearts – as it had been in 1409, when Florentines emerged after a massive snowfall to build not snowmen, but the civic insignia: "a great quantity of lions – and beautiful too, one on almost every corner, and in the loggias . . . and in the piazza of San Michele Berteldi they made a Hercules six foot tall."[31] According to Guicciardini, anyone who took away this image of liberty to reduce Florence to a principate would take away its life and soul.[32] Yet it was exactly this that the Medici did. How did they manage it?

THE APPROPRIATION OF *FLORENTINA LIBERTAS*

What the Medici did was to appropriate the republican images for themselves and for their own palace. That Cosimo was a skilled practitioner of republican rhetoric we can see from a speech he made in 1448. Announcing heavy extra taxes for the year, he simultaneously evoked liberty, equality, and justice to defend these arbitrary taxes – for, he declared, "although this is a bitter cup, we must nevertheless drink it to defend liberty . . . and since the taxes will be equaled out, all reason for discord will be removed justly."[33] So, paradoxically, arbitrary taxation

---

[29] See note 25, above.
[30] Guicciardini, *Ricordi* C 141, ed. Spongano, 153 (trans. Brown, *Dialogue*, 174): "spesso tra 'l palazzo e la piazza è una nebbia si folta o uno muro si grosso che . . . tanto sa el popolo di quello che fa chi governa o della ragione perché lo fa, quanto delle cose che fanno in India."
[31] Savonarola, *Prediche sopra Ezechiele*, ed. R. Ridolfi, 2 vols. (Rome: Belardetti, 1955), II: 208; Bartolomeo del Corazza, *Diario fiorentino, 1405–1439*, ed. R. Gentile (Rome: De Rubeis, 1991), 24, cited by Brown, "City and Citizen," 95.
[32] *Dialogo*, ed. Palmarocchi, 78 (trans. Brown, *Dialogue*, 75): "la anima sua, la vita sua."
[33] ASF, Consulte e pratiche 52, f. 35r, ed. E. Conti, *L'imposta diretta a Firenze nel Quattrocento, 1427–1494* (Rome: Istituto storico italiano per il Medio Evo, 1984), 224, note 5: "quod si amarum poculum sit, tamen pro tuenda *libertate* esse bibendum . . . Itaque tributa *aequanda*, ut *merito* omnis discordia e medio tollatur" (my italics). He was announcing extraordinary taxes of 100,000 florins; cf. N. Rubinstein, "Cosimo *optimus civis*," in *Cosimo "il Vecchio" de' Medici, 1389–1464*, ed. F. Ames-Lewis (Oxford: Clarendon Press, 1992), 15.

that is imposed equally on citizens ensures liberty as well as justice; and hen other citizens balked at using this money to buy peace from the enemy, since this – they argued – would sacrifice honor to utility, Cosimo again undercut their Ciceronian rhetoric by denying that liberty was at stake: if it were, no expense should be spared, but "as long as liberty is safe," concessions were not dishonorable.[34]

Subsequently he and his family cast themselves firmly in the role of defenders of liberty, using visual images as well as verbal rhetoric with equal dexterity. They commissioned their own bronze version of the marble *David* that Donatello had carved for the government, inscribed, "The victor is whoever defends the fatherland. God crushes the wrath of an enormous foe. Behold! A boy overcame a great tyrant. Conquer, o citizens!" And in 1464 they commissioned a bronze *Judith slaying Holofernes*, with the inscription: "Public safety [*Salus publica*]. Piero de' Medici, son of Cosimo, dedicated this statue of a woman to LIBERTY and FORTITUDE, so that the citizens might be induced again to defend the republic with an invincible and constant mind."[35] They modeled their new palace in Via Larga on the Palazzo della Signoria, subtly hinting at public authority by means of its rusticated exterior, its porphyry circle in the chapel and a *sala grande* decorated with a frieze of the communal coat of arms and the lily alternating with the Medici *palle*, and below, the *Labors of Hercules* painted by Antonio Pollaiuolo.[36] There, thanks to their chronic ill-health, Cosimo and Piero de' Medici often received public visitors, even when Piero was Gonfalonier of Justice and unable to reside in the Palazzo della Signoria, in this way confusing the boundary between the communal "liberty" represented by the public palace and the appropriated liberty represented in their own private space.[37]

[34] ASF, Consulte e pratiche 52, f. 62r, discussed by Rubinstein, "Cosimo *optimus civis*," 16–17: "nec esse turpe rei publicae si salva libertate aliqua ex parte Regi cedatur" (17, note 58). On the debate about *utile et honestum*, Cicero, *De officiis*, esp. II.iii.9–10 and III, passim.

[35] See H. Spurling, "Donatello's Bronze 'David' and the Demands of Medici Politics," *Burlington Magazine* 134 (1992): 218–24, quoting and translating the inscriptions from a manuscript (218–19); cf. F. Caglioti, "Donatello, i Medici e Gentile de' Becchi: un po' d'ordine intorno alla 'Giuditta' (e al 'David') di Via Larga," *Prospettiva* 75/76 (1994): 14–49, esp. 14; and ibid., 78 (1995): 21–55; and Butterfield, "New Evidence," 126.

[36] See F. W. Kent, "Palaces, Politics and Society in Fifteenth-Century Florence," *I Tatti Studies* 2 (1987): 51–2, 67; W. Bulst, "Die *sala grande* des Palazzo Medici in Florenz," in *Piero de' Medici, "il Gottoso," 1416–1469* (Berlin: Akademie Verlag, 1993), 89–97; A. Beyer, "Funktion und Repräsentation. Die Porphyry-Rotae der Medici," in ibid., 151–67; and A. Wright, "Piero de' Medici and the Pollaiuolo," in ibid., 129–49; Wright, "The Myth of Hercules," in *Lorenzo il Magnifico e il suo Mondo*, ed. Giancarlo Garfagnini (Florence: Olschki, 1994), esp. 325–6: "the great advantage to the early Medici lay precisely in [the canvases'] ambiguity."

[37] See Alison Brown, "Piero's Infirmity and Political Power," in *Piero de' Medici, "il Gottoso"*, 9–19.

Even before his death, Cosimo had been described as a republican *Pater Patriae*. And afterwards, when he was posthumously honored with this title in 1465, it became a formulaic device for claiming quasi-hereditary status for his descendants as leaders or fathers of their country. Tellingly, it was used not only publicly but also in small private notarial transactions, such as one in 1482 in which "the magnificent and generous man" Lorenzo is described as "the son of the late most outstanding man Piero, son of Cosimo de' Medici of honorable memory, who for his preceding and persisting merits and deeds for his patria won for himself the name of, and was declared by public decree to be, Father of his Country, as indeed he was and was famed to be."[38] But it is its public use that had greater impact at the time and now.

The title thus appears on Cosimo's tomb marker in porphyry in front of the high altar of San Lorenzo, where we know it carried political overtones from the fact that Cosimo's title *Pater Patriae* was twice ordered to be deleted after his family's expulsion from the city, "because he did not deserve such a title but rather that of tyrant."[39] But perhaps the most striking public use of the title of *Pater Patriae* to assimilate the Medici to Florence's republican liberty is on a medal cast within a decade of Cosimo's death, where the image of Cosimo and his written title *Pater Patriae* on the obverse, or "right" side, is conjoined with the image of Florence and the slogan *Pax libertasque publica* on the reverse. In this way, the medal's two faces employ both visual and written images to link Florence's "public peace and liberty" with the Medici name and face.[40]

The same function is served by the medals struck after the Pazzi conspiracy in 1478. Although the pope claimed that the attempted massacre of Lorenzo in the cathedral on Easter Day, and the successful murder of his brother, was tyrannicide, intended to restore liberty to Florence, the medals told another story by linking the Medici to Florence's freedom. On the obverse, Lorenzo is described as the "Savior of the People," *Salus populi*, and, on the reverse, the slaughter of his

---

[38] ASF, Notarile antecosmiano 14183, 33v (6 May 1482), "olim clarissimi viri Petri recolende memorie Cosme de Medicis qui suis precedentibus et persistentibus meritis et gestis in patriam Patris Patrie nomen sibi vendicavit et ita ex decreto publico declaratus extitit et nuncupatus"; cf. ibid. 9636, f. 57r (12 June 1482): "qui Cosma ex publico decreto pater patrie Florentie nuncupatur."

[39] In 1495 and 1527, see Susan McKillop, "Dante and the *Lumen Christi*," in *Cosimo "il Vecchio"*, 248 9 ("quia tale titulum non meruit sed potius tyrannus"); cf. 289 91 (appendix: "The Use and Meaning of Porphyry in the Early Medici Context") and 291 301 (the laws of 4 August 1464 and 18 March 1465 bestowing the title on Cosimo).

[40] See G. F. Hill and G. Pollard, *Renaissance Medals at the National Gallery of Art* (London: Phaidon, 1967), nos. 245 7.

brother Giuliano as the cause of "public," not private, "grief" (*Luctus publicus*). By evocatively portraying the brothers' faces above the scene of sacrilegious carnage before the high altar and the officiating priests (who include some of the conspirators themselves), the point is also effectively made that it was the Medici who protected Florence's liberty, not its archbishop or the priesthood.[41]

In the remaining years of his life, Lorenzo continued successfully to merge his public and private roles in the city, as we can see from both written and visual evidence. The mandate prepared for his mission to Naples in December 1479, for example, gave him *carte blanche* to conclude peace, "so that his private interest may be joined to the public, as it always was."[42] Similarly, because "the present regime to a large extent depends on Lorenzo's survival both in fact and in appearances [*dimostrazioni*]," special tax concessions were granted to him in 1482, "to preserve the public interest by preserving Lorenzo, since one can't survive without the other."[43] The same word *dimostrazioni* was used, as we saw, by both Guicciardini and Vettori to refer to the importance of "appearances" and show. It brings me back to my opening theme, the importance of role-playing and images in public life.

As we saw, there was a long tradition of public festivals and spectacles in Florence. Although it seems that Lorenzo de' Medici actively promoted such shows only in the last years of his life, it is difficult not to attribute political significance to the veiled imperial and patronal themes of the *Rappresentazione di San Giovanni and San Paolo* and the two San Giovanni pageants of 1490 and 1491, the *Seven Triumphal Pageants of the Seven Planets* and the *Triumphs of Paulus Emilius*.[44] In another public spectacle in 1490,

[41] Ibid., no. 252, discussed by J. Draper, *Bertoldo di Giovanni, Sculptor of the Medici Household: Critical Reappraisal and Catalogue Raisonné* (Columbia, Mo.: University of Missouri Press, 1992), 86–95.

[42] Dieci di Balìa, Mandate of 12–13 December 1479, in Bartolomeo Scala, *Humanistic and Political Writings*, 204: "ut esset cum re sua privata etiam coniuncta publica, ut semper fuit." Scala wrote to Lorenzo on 1 January 1480: "Se non a voi, non si sarebbe obtenuta di tanta cosa si libera commissione. Ecci et de' primi che l'hanno baptezata el foglio bianco," ibid., 83.

[43] ASF, Miscellanea repubblicana 109, f. 80r, ed. A. Brown, "Lorenzo, the Monte and the Seventeen Reformers," appendix II, in *Lorenzo de' Medici Studi*, ed. G. C. Garfagnini (Florence: Olschki, 1992), 145, reprinted in Brown, *The Medici in Florence*, 190: "et pendendo la salute del presente stato in gran parte dalla preservatione di decto Lorenzo et in facti et in dimostratione . . . per fare el bisogno publico con la preservatione di decto Lorenzo, che l'uno sanza l'altro stare non può."

[44] For two interpretations of the political element in Lorenzo's own plays and *rappresentazioni*, see Ventrone, "Lorenzo's *Politica festiva*" and Newbigin, "Politics in the *Sacre Rappresentazioni*"; see also A. Brown, "Platonism in Fifteenth-Century Florence," in her *The Medici in Florence*, 233–4, and Naldo Naldi's "Elegia in septem stellas errantes . . . per urbem Florentinam curribus a Laurentio Medice patriae patre duci iussas more triumphantium··," in Florence, Biblioteca Riccardiana, Edizioni rari 572, referred to in Ventrone, *Gli Araldi*, 42. On Lorenzo's image-making, see M. M. Bullard, in "Lorenzo de' Medici: Anxiety, Image-making, and Political Reality in the Renaissance," in *Lorenzo de' Medici Studi*, ed. Garfagnini, 3–40, reprinted in Bullard, *Lorenzo il Magnifico: Image and Anxiety, Politics and Finance* (Florence: Olschki, 1994), 43–79.

the ceremony inducting a new Signoria, Lorenzo was quite openly praised as a prophet who could control Florence's lot more prudently than the stars.[45] By being printed at the time, all these plays and the speech – like my final example of the Medici's appropriation of *Florentina libertas*, Cristoforo Landino's *Commentary on Dante's Commedia* – also reinforced the publicity value of these shows, wedding the transitory visual image to the permanent printed word.

It is the *editio princeps* of Landino's *Commentary on Dante*, printed in 1481, that demonstrates this process of appropriation most strikingly. Promoted by Lorenzo in a public ceremony which makes present-day publishers' launches pale by comparison, the presentation copy is richly adorned with Florence's communal symbols: the lily, the cross of the people, and the imperial eagle on the top margin, below them the *marzocco* and Hercules, and, on the bottom margin, the blue shield crossed with "Libertas" in gold.[46] A decade later, however, Hercules and *Florentina libertas*, encircled now with laurel and accompanied by the Medici coat of arms, reappear on the opening page of two magnificent volumes of St. Augustine copied for Lorenzo's grandiose public–private library – while the *marzocco* reappears in the antiphonary of Lorenzo's son Giovanni, together with the communal arms similarly encircled with laurel.[47] By the happy coincidence of sharing his papal name with the communal lion, Leo and the *marzocco* gambol with Medici *palle* in front of their communal cage.

Playful though this last image is, the Medici's success in appropriating these republican symbols was no joke, as can be seen from the speed with which the symbols were reappropriated after the Medici's expulsion from Florence on 9 November 1494. Just over a week later, on 17 November, the Florentines welcomed Charles VIII to their city with two giant figures "as high as a lance": a man with a shield bearing the king's coat-of-arms and a woman bearing a large sign, "on which was written in Roman letters of gold on blue, 'Libertas'."[48] On the same day

---

[45] See Brown, "Platonism," 233.
[46] Florence, Biblioteca Nazionale Centrale, MS Banco rari 341, described and illustrated in *Consorterie politiche e mutamenti istituzionali in età laurenziana*, ed. M. A. Morelli Timpanaro, R. M. Tolu, and P. Viti (Florence: Silvana, 1992), 115 17. It is decorated by Attavante.
[47] Florence, Biblioteca Mediceo-Laurenziana, Plut. XIII, 8 (St. Augustine, *Sermons*) and XIII, 5 (St. Augustine, *De Musica*), and Florence, Opera del Duomo, Archivio, Antifonario C 11, all illustrated in *Consorterie politiche*, nos. 8.9 and 8.10, on 231 5.
[48] "ung grant homme et una grande femme faintz de la hauteur d'una lance . . . et la dite femme tenoit ung gros escripteau ou avoit en escript en lettre rommaine d'or sur azur Libertas," cited by M. Plaisance, "L'entrée de Charles VIII à Florence," in *Problèmes interculturels en Europe XV–XVII siècles*, ed. E. Baumgartner, A. Fiorato, and A. Redondo (Paris: Sorbonne Nouvelle, 1998), 234 and note 28.

the people thanked God for their "recovered liberty," and seven weeks later measures were taken to protect Florence's "reacquired liberty" after the attacks on it during "the sixty years during which the Medici have tyrannized the city."⁴⁹ Harking back to an earlier image of Florence as a defenseless maiden or flower, the new government personified the city as an "orphan" who needed restitution for the damage done to her by her wards, from whom her lost possessions were to be reappropriated.⁵⁰ Foremost on the list for reappropriation was the city's liberty, represented visibly by the Medici's own statues of *David*, now placed in the courtyard of the Palazzo Vecchio, and *Judith and Holofernes*, first placed on the *ringhiera* and later removed to the Loggia, to make way for the republic's own vast *David* commissioned from Michelangelo in 1501. The Medici's Hercules panels painted by Antonio Pollaiuolo were also appropriated and hung inside the Palazzo Vecchio, again anticipating another (unfulfilled) public commission for a *Hercules* from Michelangelo.⁵¹

THE STRIPPING-BARE PROCESS

It remains in conclusion to return to Guicciardini and the "stripping-bare process." Even before the fall of the Medici in 1494, the reading of political images was beginning to be seen as problematic, or unstable. According to Alamanno Rinuccini in his *Dialogue on Liberty*, written in 1479 during the Pazzi War, at a low point of Lorenzo's popularity, "these exotic insignia and fine words" (of liberty) "clash with the facts."⁵² Shortly afterwards, two fables written in 1481 by the chancellor Bartolomeo Scala offer equally destabilized accounts of the political images of liberty and justice. In the fable titled "Liberty," a parrot, escaping from luxurious captivity into the talons of a hawk, exclaims, "Liberty costs too dearly that is bought with one's life!" In "Justice" we are told that the people had no difficulty (as we do not) in interpreting the meaning of two images of justice outside and inside the lawcourts:

⁴⁹ "e Dio si ringraziò della libertà riauta," Parenti, *Storia fiorentina*, I: 131; ASF, Signori e Collegi, Deliberazioni in forza di ordinaria autorità 96, f. 124r v (29 December 1494): "la casa de' Medici . . . contro la libertà habino tiranneggiata la città anni sexanta," "non possino nuocere alla reaquistata libertà."
⁵⁰ ASF, Provvisioni 185, f. 26r (13 January 1495): so that "la republica come pupilla ne fusse restituta."
⁵¹ L. Gatti, "Displacing Images and Devotion in Renaissance Florence: The Return of the Medici and an Order of 1513 for the *Davit* and the *Judit*," *Annali della Scuola Normale Superiore di Pisa*, ser. 3, 23 (1993): 349 73.
⁵² See note 2, above.

outside, a marble statue of Justice blind and handless, and inside Justice painted with a sword in her left hand, scales in her right, together representing her immunity to bribes and worldly things and her promise of tough justice combined with equity. So it is unsettling to be told in the fable that Verres (the corrupt Roman praetor who turned evidence against his co-governor) laughed cynically at these representations, "having very different thoughts" about justice himself.[53]

Equally unsettling is Machiavelli's image of David, one of Florence's icons of liberty as the victorious slayer of tyrants and patriot. David, we are now told, was "no doubt a very fine man, alike as soldier, teacher and judge"; but despite leaving a peaceful kingdom to his young son, he failed to be able to hand it on to his grandson, his own virtue being insufficient to ensure future peace and prosperity. Moreover, his success was in fact achieved by overturning established hierarchies, making the rich poor and the poor rich; for when David became king, as the Bible says, he "filled the hungry with good things and the rich he sent empty away."[54]

Are these all examples of "the stripping-bare process," in contrasting political reality with the ideal? If so, something similar may be at work in Guicciardini's *Dialogue on the Government of Florence*, as well as in his intimate *Ricordi*. In the *Dialogue*, it is the Medici protagonist of book I, Bernardo del Nero, who attacks the idealistic view of liberty as no more than a name, whose appearances and image were only intended to "dazzle" and deceive us about the true ambition of rulers; for "the powerful often use the name of liberty to deceive the rest," and "the majority of those who preach freedom" would "rush at top speed" to join a narrow or elitist regime if they thought they'd be better off there.[55] In this context, his references to "this pleasing title of liberty," and to its name, appearances, and image are surely intended to point up the difference between political reality and the ideal.

---

[53] "Libertas" and "Justitia," *Apologi centum*, nos. 42 and 84, in Scala, *Humanistic and Political Writings*, 319 ("'Quam nimio,' inquit, 'libertas constat, quae vita emitur'") and 334 ("Aliter longe sentiens, ridebat Verres").

[54] Machiavelli, *Discorsi*, ed. S. Bertelli (Milan: Feltrinelli, 1973), I, xix and xxvi, 184, 194; *Discourses*, trans. L. J. Walker (London: Penguin, 1998), 166, 176 (in fact the quotation is from Luke 1:53, reflecting on Kings 1:7); on David's exemplum in the fifteenth century, see Butterfield, "New Evidence," passim.

[55] *Dialogo*, ed. Palmarocchi, 37, 38 (tr. Brown, *Dialogue*, 35, 38–9) and *Ricordi* C 66, ed. Spongano, 76 (tr. Brown, *Dialogue*, 172): "vi correrebbono per le poste"; cf. note 2, above. The argument of the *Dialogo* and the problems of interpreting it, both on account of its dialogic structure and because of the time in which it was written, are discussed in the introduction to my translation, *Dialogue*, xiv–xxv.

This suggests that we should be chary of identifying either del Nero or Guicciardini too confidently with the idealistic image of liberty in book II as open government by patriotic men, ruling in the interests of the state as a whole. Republicanism, they remind us, is a system of representation – such as Chartier describes – and by "stripping it bare" they were helping to render it obsolete. Writing during the last Florentine republic, in 1528–9, Francesco Vettori agreed that there was little difference between a tyranny and what he had experienced or read about republics. Not only were the governments of France and Venice tyrannical in limiting power to a restricted minority of nobles, but so too was Florence's. For although Florence did not (yet) have a privileged nobility, the profits of office were similarly restricted to a few, because there were too many citizens who wanted "to share in the spoils and too few of them to distribute." So far from being a deserved reward for paying taxes, as Aristotle defined just government, honors and the rewards of office were restricted to one group, "and the other has been left on the side-lines to watch and comment on the game."[56]

After the fall of the republic in 1530, Guicciardini again attacked the "false name of liberty" but now on behalf of Duke Alessandro de' Medici. To the charge of the Florentine exiles in Naples that the emperor had broken his pledge to preserve "Florentine liberty" by suppressing "the Priors of Liberty," "since with the name, the form and essence of liberty" were also suppressed, Guicciardini countered that on the contrary, the emperor had preserved liberty by guaranteeing Florence's freedom from domination by a foreign power. By reverting to the earlier definition of liberty as freedom from external domination and condemning popular liberty as "dissolute license," Guicciardini shows how effectively he had undermined the old ideology.[57] This is not to say, of course, that the ideal of political liberty had lost its power to pull the heart-strings. The old battle cry, "Long live the People and Liberty" encouraged the crowds in

[56] *Sommario della storia d'Italia* in Francesco Vettori, *Scritti storici e politici*, ed. E. Niccolini (Bari: Laterza, 1972), 145: "sonvi di molti cittadini che arebbono a participare dello utile e vi sono pochi guadagni da distribuire. E però sempre una parte se è sforzata governare et avere li onori et utili e l'altra è stata da canto a vedere e dire il giuoco." Cf. his *Sacco di Roma, Scritti storici*, 277 8: "Perché io fo poco differenzia da quello stato che molti chiamano tirannico a questo che al presente molti chiamano populare o vero republica," cf. J. N. Stephens, *The Last Florentine Republic, 1527–1530* (Oxford: Clarendon Press, 1983), 253 4.

[57] *Risposta per parte della Duca alle querele de' Fuorusciti*, in *Opere inedite di Francesco Guicciardini*, ed. G. Canestrini, 10 vols. (Florence: Barbera, 1857 67), IX: 354 74, esp. 355 6, 358, discussed by D. Marrara, "Il problema della tirannide nel pensiero di Francesco Guicciardini e di Francesco Vettori," *Rivista storica del diritto* 39 (1996): 99 154, esp. 116 18. On Guicciardini and the later Medici, see Brown, "Lorenzo and Guicciardini," 295 6.

the piazza to expel the Medici in 1494 and afterwards "Liberty" firmly remained the slogan of the supporters of Savonarola and the anti-Mediceans.[58] So it was not the Mediceans but the ill-fated "Last Republic of Exiles" at Montalcino which used on their banner and their coins the communal emblem of a shield crossed with the letters LIBERTAS.[59]

Reading this image in the light of the earlier appropriations and the destabilization I have described, we must reevaluate not only Guicciardini's republicanism but the wider role of republicanism as a system of representation in the Renaissance period. To point out contemporaries' de-masking of liberty is not to deny its validity as an ideology or to dismiss all praise of liberty as empty rhetoric. As John Najemy argues, ideologies can be "inconsistent with the 'facts'" but nonetheless powerful and historically meaningful. There is no doubt that Machiavelli remained wedded to the ideal of liberty all his life, for – as Giovanbattista Busini recalled – despite his unpopularity and depravity in his last years, Machiavelli "loved liberty, most extraordinarily so, and only regretted that he got involved with Pope Clement VII."[60] His praise of free states and the benefits they confer in *Discourses* II.2 is unqualified and must reflect his own conviction, despite the fact that – as Quentin Skinner points out – the freedom he is talking about is personal in leaving the individual "free to pursue his own chosen ends."[61] Guicciardini, too, continued to sing the praises of liberty, but he no longer defined a free republic as one which enables "everyone to rule" and where there is "frequent changeover of offices," but negatively as one which ensures "that good laws and regulations are observed."[62] This is what Moulakis calls "realist constitutionalism" in his convincing analysis in chapter 7 of this volume of Guicciardini's *Logrogno Discourse* and his

---

[58] Tommaso Ginori, *Ricordanze*, in ASF, Carte Bagni (scaffale 43/III), filza 65 (inserto 15), f. 177r, ed. J. Schnitzer, *Quellen und Forschungen zur Geschichte Savonarolas*, 3 vols. (Munich: J. J. Lentner, 1902 4), I: 97: "E poi a dì 9 di detto mese a ore 20 incirca la cipta e il popolo si levò con l'arme [contro a detto Piero add. in marg.] e cominciò a correre in piazza e gridare 'Viva il popolo e la libertà'"; cf. Bartolomeo Cerretani, *Storia fiorentina*, ed. G. Berti (Florence: Olschki, 1994), 206. On this cry and its variants, see G. Brucker, *The Civic World of Early Renaissance Florence* (Princeton: Princeton University Press, 1977), 16 17.

[59] Illustrated in R. Starn, *Contrary Commonwealth: The Theme of Exile in Medieval and Renaissance Italy* (Berkeley: University of California Press, 1982), 148 49 and plate 14, reproduced from the *Corpus nummorum italicorum*, 20 vols. (Rome: Tipografia della R. Accademia de' Lincei, 1910 43), XI: plate 16.

[60] *Lettere di Giovanbattista Busini a Benedetto Varchi sopra l'assedio di Firenze*, ed. G. Milanesi (Florence: Le Monnier, 1860), 85, "infatti amava la libertà e straordinarissimamente, ma si doleva avere impacciatosi con Papa Chimenti."

[61] Q. Skinner, "The Republican Ideal of Political Liberty," in *Machiavelli and Republicanism*, 302.

[62] *Ricordi*, C 109, ed. Spongano, 120 (trans. Brown, *Dialogue*, 173); *Dialogo*, ed. Palmarocchi, 103, 111 (trans. Brown, *Dialogue*, 100, 108).

Dialogue on the Government of Florence, which entailed not the separation of powers but "a differentiation of functions," in that deliberation (by the senate) is separated from consent (by the people), freedom consisting in "freedom from arbitrary rule". Machiavelli did much the same thing in his 1520 blueprint for reform, which created a senate of 200 to replace all the existing councils, to be appointed initially by the Medici, and a popular council that elected to offices (except, initially, the senate and the executive, described below) but was deprived of legislative functions. Together these writings propose the creation of what Mansfield and Moulakis call "the beginnings of an impartial regime."[63]

To describe these blueprints as "prefigurations of modern constitutional thought," however, is to ignore the absence in them of any concept of the separation of powers or safeguards against despotism. What they have instead is a third force, the lifetime head of state. In Machiavelli's *Discourse*, this head of state was found in the Medici popes during their lifetimes and afterwards in an executive of sixty-five men, appointed for life – initially by the Medici ("all your friends and confidants") – and headed by a Gonfalonier of Justice, who together exercised *maestà* or sovereign majesty. In Guicciardini's *Dialogue*, the head of state was a lifetime Gonfalonier whom he described as "a boss or patron" and whom Guicciardini – like Machiavelli – also expected to acquire "a kind of majesty and the status of an oracle."[64] Since Machiavelli described his constitution "as a monarchy" during the lifetimes of the Medici popes, "because you are in command of the army and of the criminal judges, and you have the laws in your breast," it seems likely that the same powers would have devolved on to the executive of sixty-five after the Medici's demise. And although Guicciardini talked about the need to limit the powers of his three forces, in fact he failed to subject the executive and its area of competence to popular control – suggesting that it may not have been Montesquieu who was his heir as much as Bodin and Hobbes.[65]

[63] Niccolò Machiavelli, *Discursus florentinarum rerum post mortem iunioris Laurentii Medices*, in *Arte della guerra e scritti politici minori*, ed. S. Bertelli (Milan: Feltrinelli, 1961), 245–77; trans. A. Gilbert in *Machiavelli: The Chief Works and Others*, 3 vols. (Durham, N.C.: Duke University Press, 1989), I: 101–15.

[64] Machiavelli, *Discursus*, 269–70 ("tutti gli amici e confidenti sua"); trans. Gilbert, 108–9; Guicciardini, *Dialogo*, ed. Palmarocchi, 104, 109 (tr. Brown, *Dialogue*, 101, 106): "bisogna uno padrone," "diventerà come una maiestà ed uno oraculo." See my discussion of this third force in "City and Citizen," 109–10 (in the *Medici in Florence*, 300–24), and in my introduction to Guicciardini's *Dialogue*, xxiii–xxv.

[65] *Discursus*, 275; trans. Gilbert, 113: "ella è una monarchia; perché voi comandate all'armi, comandate a' giudici criminali, avete le leggi in petto"; cf. ibid., 271 (trans. Gilbert, 110): "avendo l'armi e la giustizia criminale in mano, le leggi in petto et i capi dello stato tutti sua." Cf. Guicciardini, *Dialogo*, ed. Palmarocchi, 143–4 (trans. Brown, *Dialogue*, 138–9).

These texts remain unclear and difficult to interpret. I began by saying that it is not easy to put one's finger on the moment when the slow process of disbelief in the ideal of liberty begins and the gap widens between realism and political idealism. Having examined the process by which the language and images of liberty were in turn appropriated and then de-masked by Florentine writers, we should perhaps take the hint they offer and not allow ourselves to take entirely at face value the language and emblems of liberty: were the Florentine realists more ready to embrace princely rule than we would like to acknowledge?

CHAPTER 7

Civic humanism, realist constitutionalism, and Francesco Guicciardini's Discorso di Logrogno

Athanasios Moulakis

Writing in the second decade of the sixteenth century, at the end of Florence's republican period, the historian and statesman Francesco Guicciardini gave systematic expression to a body of thought that had evolved out of the practice of Florentine oligarchic statesmen since the suppression of the Ciompi rebellion in 1378. In his early works such as the *Discorso di Logrogno* (1512) and the *Florentine Histories* (1508–9), but also in the more mature *Dialogue on the Government of Florence* (c. 1521–c. 1525), Guicciardini reflected upon and brought to a high degree of theoretical clarity this important strand of Florentine political opinion. Guicciardini's project was foreshadowed in the letters and hortatory writings of humanists like Leonardo Bruni, but it was rooted still more in the discussions and consultations on public matters that were a traditional part of Florentine political life. The records of such discussions disclose the attitudes behind the numerous efforts – some more successful than others – to change the legal, political, and institutional order of the city.[1]

This tradition expressed the aspirations of a social class that sought to consolidate its predominance by setting itself apart as a formally recognized political class, uniquely entitled to the higher offices of the state. As such it was resisted by a popular opposition that appealed to tradi-

---

[1] Athanasios Moulakis, *Republican Realism in Renaissance Florence: Francesco Guicciardini's Discorso di Logrogno* (Lanham, Md.: Rowman and Littlefield, 1998); Francesco Guicciardini, *Dialogue on the Government of Florence*, trans. Alison Brown (Cambridge: Cambridge University Press, 1994); Guicciardini, *Storie fiorentine*, in Guicciardini's *Opere*, ed. E. L. Scarano (Turin: U.T.E.T., 1970). I have borrowed, sometimes verbatim, from the introduction to my translation of the *Discorso di Logrogno*. For the significance of the Florentine political debates preserved in the Consulte e pratiche of the Florentine State Archives see Riccardo Fubini, "From Social to Political Representation in Renaissance Florence,' in *City States in Classical Antiquity and Medieval Italy*, ed. Anthony Molho, Kurt Raaflaub, and Julia Emlen (Stuttgart: Steiner Verlag, 1991), 223–39, esp. 224–5; the latter essay was republished in Italian in Fubini's *Italia Quattrocentesca: Politica e diplomazia nell'età di Lorenzo il Magnifico* (Milan: Franco Angeli 1994), 41–61.

200

tional mores and claimed the authority of the hallowed medieval civic statutes. Yet the ideas behind the oligarchic pursuit of power represent more than simply partisan views.

The development of this pattern of political thinking coincided with the decline of the commune and the rise of the territorial state.[2] It was linked to the passage from a corporate society to one ruled by elites.[3] It was closely interwoven with the transition from social to political representation and the concomitant assertion of sovereignty. Sovereignty in this context meant both the city's claim to complete independence from external authorities – however empty their universalist claims might be – as well as the internal concentration of authority in the hands of an ever more powerful executive center.[4] It was part of a far-reaching transformation of the self-understanding and symbolic representation of the Florentine polity, signaling a shift in the sources and meaning of political legitimacy.

What emerged in connection with these mutations, and was reduced to theoretical form by Guicciardini, was a considered constitutional project based on a functional analysis of political processes and institutions considered in their systematic relation to social forces. The realism of this program went beyond a pragmatic concern with the realities of power. The new ideas about government constituted a departure from medieval notions of universal order and natural law, and adumbrated a new, and distinctly modern, political anthropology. Power and will, on the one hand, structure and process, on the other, acquired foundational importance for the postulated political order. In seeking to overcome the tension between traditional norms that were untenable in practice, and a political practice in need of theoretical guidance and justification, Florentine statesmen elaborated a program that was more than a party platform. It was an original reflection on well-ordered government that I call "realist constitutionalism."

The most notable feature of realist constitutionalism was its startling modernity. Though its proponents made use of ancient sources, they did not revert to the model of the classical *polis* as theorized by Aristotle. On the contrary, far from conceiving the political community as part of nature, existing for a common moral purpose (such as

---

[2] Marvin B. Becker, *Florence in Transition*, vol. 1: *The Decline of the Commune*; vol. 2: *Studies in the Rise of the Territorial State* (Baltimore: Johns Hopkins University Press, 1967).

[3] John M. Najemy, *Corporatism and Consensus in Florentine Electoral Politics, 1280–1400* (Chapel Hill: University of North Carolina Press, 1982).

[4] Fubini, *Italia Quattrocentesca*, 28–32.

actualizing the rational goodness in man), they conceived it as a work of ingenious artifice – to use Jacob Burckhardt's phrase, they conceived the state as a work of art. The purpose of the state was security and liberty, and that required the judicious exercise of power, and indeed of dominion. Yet the freedom it sought to secure was freedom from arbitrary rule, to be achieved by means of observing due process: the *liberté des modernes*.

Guicciardini's theoretical exposition of the realist tradition in Florentine constitutional thought is a *terminus ad quem*. Republican speculation and the development of constitutional schemes became redundant with the final establishment of princely rule in Tuscany. Yet Guicciardini's constitutionalism is also, if not a direct source, at least a prefiguration of modern constitutional thought.[5] By the same token, due consideration of realist constitutionalism compels us to view continuities and discontinuities in the development of Florentine ideas, norms, and practices from a perspective different from that suggested by the historiographical topos of "civic humanism." Moreover, such a consideration leads us to reconsider the broader pattern of development of the republican tradition in Western political theory and practice.

Hans Baron drew attention to the fusion of humanist scholarship, patriotic action, and citizen participation in Florence, stimulated (if not caused) by the desire to resist the aggression of the Visconti rulers of Milan. He noted that Leonardo Bruni, the exemplar of civic humanism, acting in this spirit was the first to undertake a comprehensive description of the workings of the Florentine constitution, first in his *Laudatio Florentinae urbis* (1403/4) and later in other works.[6] Baron also pointed out that Bruni borrowed the terms of his analysis from Aristotle, whose *Politics* he translated in the 1430s. Baron thus saw in Bruni's work a retrieval of the ideals of the classical *polis* and a rebirth of the "echt griechischer Aristoteles," the authentic Greek Aristotle, as

---

[5] Maurizio Viroli is right to speak of a *forgotten* or *submerged* revolution in the case of Guicciardini, as the works in question remained unpublished for centuries: Maurizio Viroli, "Il significato storico della nascita del concetto di ragion di stato," in *Aristotelismo politico e ragion di stato*, ed. A. Enzo Baldini (Florence: Olschki, 1995), 67–81. Despite the impossibility of a direct literary influence on later thinkers, we find in Guicciardini intriguing intimations of Hobbes, Harrington, and Montesquieu. We cannot exclude independent intellectual developments in response to analogous challenges, but it is plausible to suppose a capillary influence, as it were, in response to the much denounced *politique à la Florentine*, perhaps via the entourages of the Medici queens of France.

[6] Hans Baron, *The Crisis of the Early Italian Renaissance: Civic Humanism and Republican Liberty in an Age of Classicism and Tyranny*, 2 vols. (Princeton: Princeton University Press, 1955), revised edition in one volume (Princeton: Princeton University Press, 1966).

opposed to the supposedly spurious reception of Aristotle by the scholastics.[7]

In his elaboration of Baron's thesis J. G. A. Pocock went even further in postulating a full-fledged revival of Aristotelian politics, even purging civic humanism's *vita activa* of the commercial activities that were still very much a part of the renewed civic life of the Renaissance as presented by Baron. Pocock asserted that the advent of civic humanism made it possible for an individual to feel that "only as a citizen, as a political animal involved in a *vivere civile* with his fellows, could he fulfill his nature, achieve virtue, and find his world rational," and that the distinctive strength of Aristotelian political philosophy, as recovered in the Renaissance, lay "less [in a] comparative study of institutions than [in] a science of virtue."[8]

Bruni certainly borrowed from Aristotle in his analysis of the Florentine constitution. But on closer examination we find that he borrowed from the more narrowly prudential (in the modern sense) and descriptive (i.e., comparative) part of Aristotle. Bruni wrote in the introduction to his translation of the *Politics* that "no science is more useful... than to know what a city is and what a commonwealth is, and to understand how society is maintained or destroyed."[9] Yet nowhere in Bruni's work do we find an inquiry into "what a city is" in the manner of Aristotle, i.e., an inquiry into the *physis*, the ontological foundation or moral teleology of the political association. There is, no doubt, an Aristotelian echo in his formula that "man is a weak creature and draws from civil society the self-sufficiency and capacity for perfection he lacks on his own," but this is not the beginning, but the sum of Bruni's philosophical foundation of politics.[10]

Bruni's understanding of the polity was not rooted in ethical theory, but depended rather on a typological classification and examination of structures and functions. In his *Constitution of Florence*, written in Greek, he remarked on its character as a mixed constitution, and he described its institutional features in language clearly indebted to Aristotle. But unlike Aristotle's political theory, Bruni's analysis was not grounded on general philosophical principles, such as the priority of the whole to the part or the natural determination of an action by its final cause. Indeed,

---

[7] *Leonardo Bruni Aretino: Humanistisch-philosophische Schriften*, ed. Hans Baron (Leipzig: Teubner, 1928), xviii.
[8] J. G. A. Pocock, *The Machiavellian Moment: Florentine Political Thought and the Atlantic Republican Tradition* (Princeton: Princeton University Press, 1975), 115.
[9] *Schriften*, 73.   [10] Ibid.

one might argue that Bruni's decision to translate Aristotle's moral philosophy in isolation from the rest of the latter's philosophical corpus was calculated to separate them from their ontological and metaphysical matrix.[11] His deliberate opposition to scholastic authority is thus hardly in the spirit of the classical original.

Just as Bruni's version of Aristotle's *Ethics* was directed against the *vetus interpres* (Robert Grosseteste) and the medieval tradition of scholastic philosophy,[12] so his *Constitution of Florence* was calculated to undermine the normative foundations of the traditional statutory order of the commune. In the latter text he promoted a view of the city that deliberately played down its communal, corporate character, and played up the public powers of the emerging state. The foreign officials of justice such as the *podestà* and the *capitano*, representatives of imperial authority and hence of the derived legitimacy of the commune, were disparagingly reduced to judges of mere private disputes. This textual suppression mirrored the actual changes in the role of the foreign officials as their independence was reduced by the Signoria in the course of the fifteenth century.[13] In the guise of a propagandistically modernizing description of Florentine government, Bruni sought to advance the cause of the oligarchic *reggimento*.

In the *Laudatio Florentinae urbis* Florence already appears in the title as an *urbs*, like Rome, laying down its own law, not as a mere *civitas* that can be inserted somewhere in the system of interlocking autonomies and overlapping dependencies of the medieval ecumenical order.[14] Such a conception of the city need not be incompatible with Aristotelian politics for the sake of virtue. There is, however, no evidence in Bruni's panegyric that the optimal polity rests on political friendship or on any such equivalent of Aristotle's understanding of the best regime's moral coherence. The emphasis in the *Laudatio* is instead on power (*potentia*), rule (*principatus*) and the entitlement of the Florentine *populus* to exercise dominion wherever it can.

Following the usage of Roman law, *populus* here signifies the repository of unfettered sovereignty. The Florentines, wrote Bruni, as the

---

[11] Riccardo Fubini, "Politica e morale in Machiavelli: Una questione esaurita" in *Cultura e scrittura di Machiavelli*, Atti del convegno di Firenze–Pisa, *27–30 ottobre 1994* (Rome: Salerno Editrice, 1998), 117–43, at 128.

[12] James Hankins, "Traduire *l'Ethique* d'Aristote: Leonardo Bruni et ses critiques," forthcoming in *Philosophie et philologie au Quattrocento*, ed. Fosca Mariani Zini (Lille: Presses universitaires du Septentrion).

[13] Athanasios Moulakis, "Leonardo Bruni's *Constitution of Florence*," *Rinascimento*, n.s. 26 (1986): 141–90 at 177.

[14] On the medieval order, see Paolo Grossi, *L'ordine giuridico medievale* (Bari: Laterza, 1995).

descendants and heirs of Rome, have inherited along with the prowess of their ancestors unqualified independence and the right to impose their rule wherever they can. All wars fought by Florence are *eo ipso* just, for everything the city can in fact subjugate already belongs to it by right.[15]

There is nothing like the ethos of an Aristotelian *polis* in any of this. Indeed, we learn from the *Historiae* that the purpose of political action, for the sake of which human communities hold together, the things that people consider (*putantur*) desirable, are "expanding borders, enlarging empire, to exalt the glory and splendor of the city, and to arrogate to it utility and security."[16] Such ends may have the ring of Roman grandeur about them, but are surely alien to the nature of political bonds as Aristotle understood them. If Bruni's political philosophy is a science of virtue, his *virtù* is a capacity to act and acquire, opposed to otiose inaction. It is what Aristotle would have called a *dynamis*, a capacity to act; not a *hexis*, a well-formed habit of mature moral judgment – not, that is to say, a virtue in the traditional sense.

Seeking for an adequate description of the emerging self-understanding of the Florentine political order, Bruni used the Greek word *politeia*. The Greek term had a useful elasticity: it could suggest "regime" in the Aristotelian sense, i.e., a form or mode of rule in a political society. But it could also serve as a classical republican cloak to cover, and thus legitimize, a regime in a very different sense: the established and recognized preponderance of a political class. Bruni's classicizing allusions were therefore also acts of advocacy aiming to promote the transformation of the polity, not merely to describe an existing state of affairs. Far from being a genuine revival of Aristotelian political philosophy, Bruni's use of ancient sources was eclectic and ideological.

The great servants of the Florentine state, its humanist chancellors, frequently portrayed as leading embodiments of civic humanism, were

[15] Leonardo Bruni, *Panegirico della città di Firenze*, ed. Giuseppe De Toffol (Florence: La Nuova Italia, 1974), 44: "ad vos . . . viri Florentini, dominium orbis terrarum iure hereditario ceu paternarum rerum possessio pertinet . . . ut omnia bella quae a populo Florentino geruntur iustissima sint, nec possit hic populus in gerendis bellis iustitia carere, cum omnia bella pro suarum rerum vel defensione vel recuperatione gerat necesse est."

[16] Leonardo Bruni, *Historiarum Florentini populi libri XII*, ed. E. Santini, in *Rerum italicarum scriptores*, vol. XIX.1 (Città di Castello, 1914), 140: "extendere fines, imperium augere, civitatis gloriam splendoremque extollere, securitatem utilitatemque asciscere." The sentence is placed in the mouth of Pino della Tosa, reputed a great warrior, arguing for the ever-popular enterprise of conquering Lucca.

in fact instrumental in subverting the juridical order of which, as the republic's chief notaries, they were the sworn guardians. Salutati more cautiously and implicitly, Bruni with increasing boldness, recast the republican order in terms of realist constitutionalism and acted to consolidate the oligarchic regime.

The subversion of the republican order by the Medici is well known. Modern historians understand it as that family's capacity to achieve *de facto* control by manipulating patronage, electoral procedures, and extraordinary commissions while preserving the external form of the constitution.[17] The underlying dynamic implicit in this scheme is that of dynastic ambition pitted against popular attachment to republican liberty. But this image is a simplification. The transformation of Florentine political life was both more complex and more far-reaching. The success of Cosimo, Piero, and Lorenzo de' Medici was due partly to their capacity to mobilize popular sympathies as well as elite support. They could maintain a "popular" posture (that is, in traditional Florentine terms, an anti-aristocratic tone) while simultaneously enjoying the standing of a princely house among the courts of Italy and Europe. This standing could be put to good use in domestic politics; it enhanced enormously the personal power of the preeminent citizen.[18] The Medici party cultivated a large popular clientele by means of patronage, protection, munificence, and magnificent display.[19] On the other hand they sought to co-opt the greater optimate families who considered themselves the Medici's peers. Other optimate families resented the Medici ascendancy, yet lived in a strange symbiotic relationship with it. To achieve high offices they considered their due against the resistance of the lower orders they needed the assistance of a political machine which only the Medici, with their immense resources and international connections, could provide.

But this pattern of machine politics did not originate with the Medici. The decisive turning-point had come in fact some fifty years earlier,

---

[17] Nicolai Rubinstein, *The Government of Florence under the Medici, 1434–1494*, second edn (Oxford: Oxford University Press, 1997).

[18] Riccardo Fubini, "Classe dirigente e diplomazia nella Firenze quattrocentesca," in *Ceti dirigenti nella Toscana del Quattrocento*, ed. Donatella Rugiadini (Impruneta: Papafava, 1987), 117–89, at 124.

[19] For the clientelistic rather than ideological aspects of allegiance or opposition to the Medici, see Dale Kent, *The Rise of the Medici: Faction in Florence, 1426–1434* (Oxford: Oxford University Press, 1978) and Kent, "Dinamica del potere e patronato nella Firenze dei Medici," in *Ceti dirigenti*, 411–62. For the threat posed by Lorenzo's personal and "princely" patronage to the traditional consensus and institutions, see William J. Connell, "Changing Patterns of Medicean Patronage," in *Lorenzo il Magnifico e il suo mondo*, ed. Giancarlo Garfagnini (Florence: Olschki, 1994), 87–107.

with the suppression of the Ciompi rebellion and the rise of the oligarchic regime. It is no accident that Guicciardini begins his *Florentine Histories* with the events of 1378.[20] Guicciardini went on to celebrate the regime of Maso degli Albizzi as "the wisest, most glorious and happiest government" the city had ever enjoyed. According to Guicciardini, from 1393, when the Albizzi takeover began, to 1420, the city was governed by *uomini da bene* and *savi*, and achieved internal concord, prosperity and military strength sufficient to conduct a successful war against Giangaleazzo Visconti and to conquer Pisa.[21] Guicciardini clearly sees in the Albizzi regime a prefiguring of his own constitutional preferences. Yet the Medici party, though more centralized in its decision-making, did not differ fundamentally from that of the Albizzi oligarchy in its manner of acquiring and exercising power.[22]

But in what, precisely, did the novelty of the oligarchic/Medicean system consist? One clear trend is towards codification of the Florentine constitution, indicating the assertion of a central, authoritative will.[23] Constitutionalism thus appears (in this context) as an oligarchic strategy to consolidate power. Before Bruni (who was himself instrumental in bringing about the new consensus politics), we find no systematic account of the various offices of state, the relations between them, or the rights and duties of citizens. The official statutes themselves do not contain a complete account of the institutions of government, nor any clear separation between what we would call constitutional matters, on the one hand, and civil and penal legislation on the other.[24] Instead, public records report statements of citizens to the effect that particular legal enactments or other public measures are, or are not, *secundum ordinamenta*, i.e., framed in accordance with the traditional statutes of the city and the laws consequent upon these general provisions. Such appeals to the *ordinamenta* rarely involve exact textual references to particular statutes or any ascent to first principles. They were, rather, somewhat generic and loose invocations of the strength of tradition in political controversy, usually invoked to accuse an opponent of subversive innovation.[25]

---

[20] Guicciardini, *Storie fiorentine*, 61.   [21] Ibid., 158.
[22] As John N. Stephens remarks: "Cosimo was heir not to the factionalism but to the leadership of Maso. The latter, in its turn, had been something new and it is to be explained by a new consensus which sprang up amongst the great 'popular' families to avoid the fratricidal ambitions which had led to the episode of the Ciompi"; see his *The Fall of the Florentine Republic* (Oxford: Clarendon Press, 1983), 12–13.
[23] Fubini, "Classe dirigente," 156; Fubini, "From Social to Political Representation," 231.
[24] Nicolai Rubinstein, "Florentine Constitutionalism and Medici Ascendancy in the Fifteenth Century," in his *Florentine Studies: Politics and Society in Renaissance Florence* (Evanston, Ill.: Northwestern University Press, 1968), 442–62.

We may usefully distinguish three salient characteristics of the medieval political tradition as expressed in the statutes: (a) the city's order was proclaimed to be a subordinate part of a more encompassing, overarching order of papal and imperial Christendom; (b) excessive concentration of power was prevented by an elaborate system of institutional balances and procedural controls, such as rapid rotation in office and the prohibition of close relatives serving together or in quick succession; and (c) the corporate identity of the body politic was understood as a coalescence of trades, neighborhoods, and clans.[26] And the temper of the medieval order can be illustrated by the preamble to the Statutes of 1355. These were promulgated, not in the name of a sovereign people, but in that of Christ, the Blessed Virgin, and all the saints. The preamble clearly proclaimed the city's allegiance to the pope, the emperor, the Angevin royal house and the Guelf party, and displayed Florence's self-conception as an association of trade and manufacturing corporations.[27]

By contrast, the regime that emerged in reaction to the Ciompi rebellion derived its legitimation from popular approval – however that approval was in fact contrived. Its title was proclaimed to derive from the "plenary, free, total, and absolute power and authority of the entire Florentine people."[28] The people, then, whether acting directly in a *parlamento* (general assembly) or by delegation to an appointed commission, was free to make what laws it willed, not only in matters of regular legislation but also (to use an anachronistic distinction) in matters of constitutional import. The people of Florence was proclaimed to be sovereign, *legibus solutus*, like a prince who recognizes no superior, and indeed possessed of what later constitution-makers would call *pouvoir constituant*.[29]

[25] Rubinstein, "Florentine Constitutionalism."
[26] Gene Brucker, *Renaissance Florence*, second edn (Berkeley: University of California Press, 1983), and Grossi, *L'ordine giuridico*.
[27] Statuti del Capitano del Popolo, 1355, cited in Fubini, *Italia Quattrocentesca*, 31, note 27: "ad honorem et reverentiam ipsorum, nec non sacrosancte ecclesie, domini nostri summi pontificis, illustri viri domini Karoli Romani imperatoris, serenissimi principis domini Loigii regis Jherusalem et Sicilie, et ad exaltationem et statum pacificum hominum et personarum ipsius augmentum, conservationem et gloriam populi et communis Florentie eiusque comitatus et districtus, sancte Partis dicte Romane ecclesie, que per totam urbem "Guelfa" vulgariter nuncupatur, nec non omnium et singulorum artificum et artium quarumcumque civitatis prefate."
[28] Najemy, *Corporatism and Consensus*, 268.
[29] See, for example, the document (Florence, Archivio di Stato, Balie 17, f. 70v) quoted by Riccardo Fubini, "La rivendicazione di Firenze della sovranità statale e il contributo delle *Historiae* di Leonardo Bruni," in *Leonardo Bruni cancelliere della Repubblica di Firenze, Convegno di studi, Firenze, 27–29 ottobre 1987*, ed. Paolo Viti (Florence: Olschki, 1990), 45: [Florence's legislative councils are declared] "soluta omnibus legibus . . . prohibentibus aliquid fieri vel disponi . . . et quilibet in eis

Some of the conditions contributing to the weakening of the communal tradition are obvious. From the later thirteenth century onwards, while Florence grew in wealth and power, the prestige of the authorities with universal claims – the papacy and the empire – declined. The War of the Eight Saints and the Great Schism led to a *de facto* reversal in the relationship of dependence between Florence and the papacy; until well into the fifteenth century, papal finances were kept afloat only with Florentine aid.[30] The Angevin–Florentine axis and active imperial power in Italy were now things of the past; Florence had her own tiny empire in Tuscany. Under the changed circumstances the idea of a delegated or derived legitimacy became implausible to people of good sense and intolerable to the city's pride.[31] Traditional Guelf ideals gave way before a habit of positing the city's own complete independence and unmediated authority. The powerful sentiment of dynamic and (in a sense) revolutionary pride was naturally articulated by the few. But it was broadly shared by the many who were, on the whole, more in favor of the city's wars of conquest than the rich, as they had less to lose. The notion that new orders, reflecting the factual realities of power, could be adopted or imposed, in defiance of traditional notions of legitimacy, became increasingly plausible.

The rejection of traditional forms of legitimation can be seen operating as well in Florentine internal politics. The post-Ciompi oligarchy vastly enlarged the degree of participation by ordinary citizens in public offices, while concentrating actual decision-making powers in the hands of the few.[32] The latter trend was aided by oligarchic control and corruption of the process of nomination to public offices. This naturally resulted in the growing importance of personal and family alliances, clientage relationships, and the exchange of favors among *amici*. At the same time, the traditional councils and advisory bodies were increasingly deprived of their powers of control and of any real authority in legislation. Government was frequently conducted by extraordinary commissions, *balìe*, that bypassed and overrode the traditional councils. Though these were regularly presented as temporary measures in re-

vel eorum altero proponens . . . intelligantur esse et sint libera et liberi et soluti."
[30] David S. Peterson, "The War of the Eight Saints and the Church in Florentine Memory and Oblivion," in *Self and Culture in Renaissance Florence*, ed. William J. Connell (Berkeley: University of California Press, forthcoming).
[31] Fubini, *Italia Quattrocentesca*, 91.
[32] David Herlihy, "The Rulers of Florence, 1282–1530," and John M. Najemy, "The Dialogue of Power in Florentine Politics," both in *City States*, ed. Molho, Raaflaub, and Emlen, 197–221 and 269–88 respectively; Herlihy's article is reprinted in *Women, Family and Society in Medieval Europe, Historical Essays, 1978–91*, ed. Anthony Molho (Providence, R.I.: Berghahn Books, 1995), 353–77.

sponse to emergencies and were generally appointed for limited periods, they were in fact staffed by the same small group of men who thus remained effectively in control.[33] The continuity of personnel was even more marked in the bodies concerned with finances and the administration of the public debt.[34]

The process was driven by two powerful and interrelated forces: the ever-present need to wage war and the related need to raise taxes. The necessity to prepare for war and raise money at short notice led to what was in effect a perpetual state of emergency. Given the unwieldy structure of its government as provided for in the statutes, the city could only meet such emergencies by extraordinary measures, forced loans, *ad hoc* committees, and officers with special powers. All this often went beyond, and indeed against, both the letter and spirit of the traditional statutes. Officers with great executive powers such as the Eight of Police and the Ten of War were created in response to internal or external crises, but then tended to become permanent. Such officers were elected or appointed by the Signoria or by special boards, adding another path of advancement for a select few, again bypassing and thus diminishing the authority of traditional institutions, while strengthening the executive center of the state and the narrow elites that controlled it.

Though in one sense functional, inasmuch as it met military emergencies and serviced the public debt, this system lacked both legal and sociological legitimacy. The oligarchs, themselves often divided by rivalries, were always faced by opposition from below. And the discrepancy between the *pays legal* and the *pays réel* was by no means superficial. Not only did the statutes not correspond to the actual practice of government, but that practice reflected choices made almost exclusively by a political class lacking full legitimacy. At the same time the lower orders of society no longer corresponded structurally to the corporate social order presupposed by the statutory tradition, hence the repeated efforts to make the regime coterminous with the institutions of the republic and to give the actual political system permanent, formal, and legal recognition, beyond the unremitting succession of "exceptional" and "temporary" grants of authority by which it lived.

In this way, under the pressure of events, the extraordinary and temporary in Florentine government became, in the course of the fifteenth

---

[33] Becker, *Florence in Transition*, II: 119.
[34] Anthony Molho, "L'amministrazione del debito pubblico a Firenze nel quindicesimo secolo," in *Ceti dirigenti*, 191–207.

century, the habitual and commonplace. Beyond partisan interest, the men responsible for governing Florence came to regard the medieval statutory order, in the light of experience, as a dysfunctional system of mutual mistrust that prevented the articulation and efficient execution of public policy. They therefore sought to refashion the system of government in accordance with political function and the effective exercise of power. As beneficiaries of the old, extrastatutory practices, they naturally sought to rationalize departures from the traditional order. Hence a body of thought emerged that, though hardly disinterested, was also analytical and constructive, representing a genuine effort to understand the underlying problems and principles, with a view of giving formal expression and direction to a new, coherent and effective constitution of the polity. Such efforts, guided by notions of competent administration, accommodation of interests, and expedient policy led to a new view of politics that could not but repudiate the customary conceptions of legitimate authority.

The result was realist constitutionalism, an important strand in Florentine political thought, best represented in the constitutional thought of Francesco Guicciardini. It was a constitutionalism *avant le mot*, which sought to understand the properly constituted body politic, not primarily in terms of ultimate foundations and normative postulates, but rather in terms of institutions and procedures capable of composing lucidly understood interests with a view to effective action. If, as the Florentine experience indicated, effective government could only be conducted under quasi-permanent abrogation of the statutory order, it seemed preferable to adapt the latter to the former rather than the other way around.[35] In that case, however, the normative sources of the old order would also have to be devalued. The polity would be posited by political will, rather than be understood as informed by, and subject to, a higher, ecumenical or transcendent norm.

In an order founded on will, consent (which was, of course, not absent from the medieval conception of legitimating public authority) assumed a new and much greater foundational significance. It became important to distinguish between consent, as a source of legitimacy, and deliberation as the condition of prudent policies, and to give each a distinct institutional embodiment. Political participation was accordingly conceived as two-tiered, divided between a deliberating elite, entrusted with making policy, and a broader public. This, at any rate, is the way

[35] Stephens, *The Fall of the Florentine Republic*, 16.

Guicciardini recommends ordering the Florentine constitution in his *Discorso di Logrogno*. In effect, he is giving constitutional shape to what had emerged in the previous century as the only effective way of transacting public business. As John Najemy shows elsewhere in this volume, starting with the reforms of the late fourteenth century, nonelite guildsmen were offered election to prestigious offices – "passive" participation – in return for relinquishing any real share in political decision-making. The latter was confined to the inner circle of the *reggimento*. But in Guicciardini's systematic discussion this structuring of the citizen body reveals a different quality – a quality that was probably not entirely absent from actual political practice for that matter.

In a republican regime the determination of courses of action and the adoption of important measures must enjoy the support – and must be seen to enjoy the support – of popular opinion. But the regime must also be guided by a constancy of purpose and an expert understanding of which only the few are capable. To achieve such a paradox the weight of the republic cannot rest safely on a broadly based legislative assembly and its shifting whims. The answer for Guicciardini seems to be not so much a separation of powers as a differentiation of functions. The aim is to bring about a form of government that was both effective and legitimate, i.e., capable of steering a prudent course and of responding swiftly to emergencies, while plausibly acting in the name of the whole political community.

The two functions in question were, first, the capacity to approve or withhold approval – the safeguard of liberty – and, second, the power to initiate, deliberate, and enact. Hence the intermediate council, placed between the plenary assembly of the enfranchised citizens and the executive board of government – the Signoria and Colleges – is the linchpin of the constitutional scheme advanced by Guicciardini. This council or senate is representative in the formal sense, resulting as it does from election and procedurally sanctioned appointment. Guicciardini goes to great lengths to ensure that selection does not depend on personal links of obligation that would vitiate the balance of the constitution in favor of a faction or a leading personality. In this respect it differs sharply from the Medicean Council of Seventy. The Medicean Seventy was for all practical purposes a senate, i.e., a permanent body of counselors with sweeping jurisdiction on all major affairs and appointments.[36] But it consisted of men hand-picked by Lorenzo as a reward for

---

[36] Rubinstein, *The Government of Florence*, 228–33.

their loyalty and in expectation of further alliance to his regime. Guicciardini proposes that some senators be elected by the Great Council for limited periods, so as to satisfy the 'lesser' men in such a way that the senate need not be saddled with them permanently. Others should serve for life, senatorial rank following *ex officio* on having occupied certain high positions in government. Still others should be co-opted by the body itself. Yet another group, finally, should be elected from shortlists of three, proposed to the Great Council by high-ranking magistrates.[37]

The composition of Guicciardini's senate is clearly oligarchic, as the greater number of its members pass through very selective procedures of election to and by the highest executive magistracies. But this is consistent with the senate conceived as a permanent *consulta*, analogous to the Venetian council of *pregati*. For the senate is also intended to be representative in a more substantive way: it is designed to include, and thus to co-opt, virtually all citizens of weight, influence and distinction. The various complementary nomination procedures are calculated to prevent the membership of the senate from being partisan, that is, beholden to a particular faction or personal clientele. Properly composed, the senate will enjoy the collective intellectual, social, moral, and material authority necessary to see that the law is enforced without fear or malice. Its composition is also meant to guarantee that it can apply universal law to particular cases without partisan distortions, and uphold equity without violating the principle that the law emanates from the people. The senate thus provides security, which means equal protection under the law. In the Florentine tradition equal protection implies the power to rein in powerful individuals, and this power too is entrusted to the senate. It is balanced by an equally important power of curbing the abuses to which volatile, vindictive, and rapacious mobs are inclined.

If security is the first essential element of liberty, popular consent is the other. Guicciardini proposes to establish (or rather continue) a Great Council whose membership constitutes a defined, sovereign *populus*. To be sure, the great majority of Florentine city folk as well as the inhabitants of the subject territories outside Florence's walls remain excluded from even the broadest *governo largo*. But the Great Council represents a virtual, but legally unambiguous whole, whose will legitimates the distribution of rewards and burdens in the republic.

This is not to say that Guicciardini trusts the good sense of the common people, or that he puts his faith in some natural tendency to

---

[37] Guicciardini, *Discorso di Logrogno*, in Moulakis, *Republican Realism*, 136 7.

moderation inherent in collective judgment. On the contrary, as he writes in his *Ricordi*, "Who says *people* really says 'insane animal, full of blunders and disorders by the thousand, without judgment, without discernment, without stability.'"[38] He believes, rather, that a measure of disorder is a price worth paying for the effective operation of an institution designed to express, and thus secure, the consensual legitimacy of public appointments, legal enactments, and tax measures. Members of the Great Council can be expected to act dispassionately if they have a right to vote, but no right to propose measures or stand for election themselves. Not being judges in their own cause, the people will not be moved by self-seeking motives to go against the natural inclination of men to do good if unhindered. A general reflection on human nature leads Guicciardini to advocate an institutional device modeled on legal procedure.

The people are too fickle and too many to articulate policy and see it through to execution. So liberty as public consent needs to be prevented from degenerating into plebiscitary license. This is accomplished by denying the larger assembly the right to initiate measures or introduce laws. On the other hand, a broad popular assembly, in Guicciardini's view, if properly hedged in by procedural rules, is likely to choose public officials reasonably well, based on their reputations, hence the decision to allow the Great Council to elect senators for limited terms, or senators for life from preselected shortlists.

Under such a system the many provide the audience for the agonal rivalry of the few, but must themselves be content with a marginal, passive role that John Najemy has aptly characterized as "participation without power."[39] At the same time, abstracting from the particularities of social antagonism in Renaissance Florence, we can see here, perhaps, an anticipation of modern representative government, or what Harvey Mansfield has called the "impartial regime."[40] As Mansfield points out, the mixed regime, which balanced elements of kingship, oligarchy, and democracy, had been Aristotle's remedy for the human partiality evident in every polity, manifest most clearly in the contrast between rich and poor, the nobles and the people. Yet the remedy was not a cure.

---

[38] Francesco Guicciardini, *Ricordi*, ed. Mario Fubini and Pietro Borelli (Milan: Rizzoli, 1977), 153 [B 140].
[39] See his essay in this volume; see also Pocock, *Machiavellian Moment*, 132 3.
[40] Harvey C. Mansfield, "The Unfinished Revolution," in *Three Beginnings: Revolution, Rights and the Liberal State: Comparative Perspectives on the English, American and French Revolutions*, ed. Stephen F. Englehart and John Allphin Moore, Jr. (New York: Peter Lang, 1994), 9 30.

To replace that conflict, the general formula for the modern impartial regime is to remove one of the two parties – the people – as a political actor, and then let the elite compete for its favor... The people, thereby, become the judge of all government. It does not form the government itself.[41]

Mansfield discovers the beginnings of the impartial regime in Machiavelli. But it is equally present in Guicciardini, who sets up the people as judges of reputations (and what else does any voter in a representative democracy judge?), if not the actual qualifications of the elite, even as he excludes the people from rule.

The exclusivity of Guicciardini's senatorial class stems, in part, from the old impulse towards institutional recognition of the Florentine governing elite as such. He did not conceive it, however, as rigorously sealed off in the manner of the Venetian aristocracy after the *serrata* of 1297, or the much broader but equally hereditary Savonarolan Maggior Consiglio. Though Guicciardini accepted the outer limits of citizenship defined by the Savonarolan settlement, he also wished to provide avenues of mobility within it. He produced a vigorous argument in favor of careers open to talent. For example, though it is evident that the chance of any one citizen achieving the highest office of Gonfalonier for life is very small, it is of the greatest importance to Guicciardini that access to the highest office should in principle be possible for all citizens.[42] Access to high office would undoubtedly be more arduous for *homines novi*, but Guicciardini welcomed the possibility for the renewal and continued competence of the elite. It is no accident that the protagonist of the later *Dialogue of the Government of Florence* is Bernardo del Nero, a man explicitly stated to be neither "of noble birth nor surrounded by relatives."[43] The well-established precedent for the rise of men outside the traditional optimate families involved the co-optation of individuals, by means of controlled scrutinies and participation in the *practiche*, on the basis of usefulness and loyalty to the regime of the moment. The ostensible reason, and the one adduced by Guicciardini in his treatises was, of course, merit.

For Guicciardini the expression *uomini da bene*, the standard term in partisan usage for the adherents of the *reggimento*, had meritocratic connotations.[44] The explicit recognition of individual merit, foreshadowed by Leonardo Bruni,[45] suggests an emancipation from a pat-

[41] Ibid., 13.   [42] *Discorso di Logrogno*, in Moulakis, *Republican Realism*, 131, 134.
[43] Francesco Guicciardini, *Dialogue on the Government of Florence*, ed. Alison Brown (Cambridge: Cambridge University Press, 1994), 9.
[44] Giovanni Silvano, "Gli *uomini da bene* di Francesco Guicciardini: coscienza aristocratica e repubblicana a Firenze nel primo '500," *Archivio storico italiano* 148 (1990): 845–92.
[45] Fubini, "La rivendicazione di Firenze," 49.

tern of office-holding laid down by the Ordinances of Justice which determined eligibility for office primarily by clan, neighborhood, and guild membership. As the studies of John Najemy suggest, Guicciardini's limited meritocracy had long precedents in Florentine political practice; in the post-Ciompi oligarchy a small number of men could rise from their class, but not with it. The ruling elite co-opted the intermediate classes by extending the ranks of office-holders, on condition that the lesser men understood such offices as rewards for individual merit, not as due them *qua* representatives of a constituency or corporate interest. In Guicciardini's constitutional projects, to advance corporate interests as such, allowing the social (or the private) to infringe on the public, was proscribed as factious.

What was gained, from a modern perspective, was a movement toward the individuation of citizenship. Public rank was achieved on political terms. Distinction became more directly linked to political office, for members of old families and new men alike, placing them all separately and immediately before the state. Hence meritocracy also meant that corporate loyalties and ascriptive attachments were rejected in favor of a universal reason of state, that bound individuals as such. The traditional network of medieval cross-cutting autonomies and obligations gave way to a self-willed, single collective subject, capable of upholding its sovereignty by force. But the gain for the autonomous political personality and the career open to talent seems also to open the way for Leviathan.

At the same time, the possibility, however limited, of rising to the highest office provides, in Guicciardini's thinking, a constitutional vent for high ambition and hence a stimulus for noble emulation in the service of the republic. It keeps the proud within the fold. It prevents sedition and enlists in the city's service the competitive energies of the best men. The resemblance here to the classical concept of magnanimity, however, is only superficial. Cicero, to be sure, had maintained that the magnanimous man who seeks to benefit his country performs great deeds which bring him deserved fame. When exercised in pursuit of selfish ends, however, and without regard for the public good, greatness of soul, no less than all the other intellectual and moral virtues, leads to abominable tyranny.[46] Cicero's example of tyranny was, of course, Caesar, whose magnanimity, intelligence, and culture were never in question. Cities, Guicciardini assures us, are made great by the deeds

---

[46] Cicero, *De officiis*, 1.14 ff.

performed by a few great men. The well-conducted *elatio animi* of spirited citizens is the motor of the city's greatness. But the elation of soul of these few is praiseworthy, not because it turns away from selfish goals towards an object of a different order, but because it is sublimated into a larger, collective selfishness. This is not the greatness of the Aristotelian *spoudaios*. On Guicciardini's criteria Alcibiades, if only an ungrateful city had not thrown him into the arms of the Spartans, would have had to be praised as a man of great virtue.

Mansfield writes that the modern "impartial regime" is actualized by lowering the moral standard for successful regimes. "Virtue comes to mean something closer to stability, or survival, because that is what the people can understand."[47] The lower standard is predicated on giving up the Aristotelian aspiration to a regime that would be virtuous for the sake of virtue, in the liberating knowledge that the regime, like ourselves, will not last forever. The modern impartial regime settles instead for the mediocre – the realistic – goal of its own survival. Virtue will, accordingly, be relative to the character of the regime.

This is not a goal to be despised. Montesquieu, who was, I believe, a clear beneficiary of the Florentine tradition, wrote at the very outset of his *Spirit of the Laws*:

What I call virtue in a republic is love of the homeland, that is love of equality. It is not a moral virtue or a Christian virtue, it is *political* virtue, and this is the spring that makes republican government move, as *honor* is the spring that makes monarchy move.[48]

Political virtue, in Montesquieu's sense, is a far cry from Aristotle's aristocratic self-perfection. It is a frame of mind or habitus, consonant with a certain form of government. It is a matter of sociological and psychological attunement to be achieved with the help of instrumental reason. It is distinct from religious duty to God or ethical duty to self.[49]

In modern republicanism, in which virtue is relative to the regime and subordinate to its duration, the classical view of the well-constituted polity is curtailed and reversed. For Plato, the city is legitimate and just because it is the image of a transcendent order, a microcosm, but also because it is man – in the good city the virtuous man – writ large. In the Florentine political tradition it is instead man who is micro-polis, for-

---

[47] Mansfield, "The Unfinished Revolution," 13.
[48] Montesquieu, *The Spirit of the Laws*, ed. Anne Cohler, Basia Carolyn Miller and Harold Samuel Stone (Cambridge: Cambridge University Press, 1989), xli.
[49] Ibid., 5 [part I, book I, chapter I].

med in the image of the city, which is itself not formed by the idea of the good, but as a response to the pressures of necessity and accident. The citizen and *a fortiori* the official is molded by the requirements of the regime. Matteo Palmieri wrote that a man elected to office came to "rappresentare l'universale persona di tutta la città, et essere facto animata persona."[50] The official is representative of a *persona ficta*, a figuration of its constitution and an agent of its will.

Guicciardini's plan for reform did not so much depend on the moral choices of individuals as on devising an institutional mechanism for channeling human passions and human pride in ways that would benefit the republic. Ordered liberty meant security against the arbitrary private will of individuals, and linked one's personal aggrandizement and fame to the greatness and glory of one's country. The novelty consisted in the attention paid to the institutional mechanisms whereby the appetite of the individual self is subsumed under the appetites of the collective. The *eros tyrannos* is neither suppressed nor converted, but absorbed by a larger yet no less immanent desire.

In the universe of realist constitutionalism, men engage in political activity driven by ambition, calculation, and a desire to excel. The city provides a frame for men – or some men – to show their worth, but not in the sense of a teleological unfolding of their rational political nature. Nature compels human beings into political society, but politics is not natural. Nature, in other words, is not understood as an Aristotelian *physis*, a principle of growth and perfection, but as a web of necessity pressing upon the human condition. The city is not constructed with a view to a final cause – virtue, justice, the good life – but from elementary conditions of possibility: first, the capacity to defend itself and to impose authority on its subjects, and second, to overcome internal disorder and secure prosperity and domestic tranquillity. Virtue becomes, accordingly, not the actualization of human potentiality, but the means of overcoming necessity. Government is ingenious artifice. The well-devised public order provides scope for virtues such as spiritedness and prudence and in turn relies upon their exercise. Upholding the republic requires the exercise of virtues, but the realization of virtue is not the republic's proper end.

This, clearly, is no revival of classical, Aristotelian politics. The point is a crucial one for understanding Florentine political thought from Bruni to Machiavelli. If it were recognized that the decisive novelty in Florentine republican thought is not the revival of ancient republican-

[50] *Vita civile*, ed. Gino Belloni (Florence: Sansoni, 1982), 131, cited by Najemy in chapter 3 of this volume.

ism but the advocacy of a new republicanism – a republicanism having much in common with other forms of the emerging modern state – it would no longer be necessary to explain away those parts of Machiavelli that cannot be integrated into the notion of ancient civic values of Aristotelian pedigree.[51]

In their attempt to free themselves from medieval norms, realist constitutional innovators, from Leonardo Bruni and Maso degli Albizzi to Francesco Guicciardini, invoked the ancient city as an authoritative prefiguration of their own project. The order they advocated was, however, quite unlike the Hellenic *polis*. To be sure, the ancient city excluded noncitizens, slaves, and metics, but the emerging Florentine polity posited differences of status *within* its own citizen body. A limited group of fully entitled and politically active citizens ruled over subjects with the approval, and sometimes the grudging support, of citizens of lesser right. Theorists like Guicciardini postulated a graduated citizenship, i.e., an explicit distinction between the principal actors and the broad public for whose approval the members of the elite competed, and whose consent they needed to secure.

Realist constitutionalism recognized the need for possibly tacit or muted, but nonetheless constant support of the many for the process itself. The express consent of the many to particular policies or to measures visibly affecting them was not enough. Validating laws and policies, not least those regarding the assessment of taxes, by the consent of those affected was, of course, nothing new. *Quod omnes tangit ab omnibus comprobari debet* was a well-established principle of medieval political theory.[52] But as this principle, which had originated in the private law of commercial transactions, was applied to a public sphere that was becoming ever more explicitly political and noncorporate, it was adapted to legitimize the distinction between (passive) approval and (active) initiative. It implied, furthermore, a change in the nature of political justification, for it provides a formal, procedural standard, much like modern majority rule, which takes the quantitative measure of will, independently of the rationality or intrinsic goodness of proposed courses of action.

---

[51] An approach exemplified, among others, by Hans Baron, "Machiavelli the Republican Citizen and Author of the Prince," in *In Search of Florentine Civic Humanism*, 2 vols. (Princeton: Princeton University Press, 1988), II: 101–51; Felix Gilbert, "The Composition and Structure of Machiavelli's *Discorsi*," in *History: Choice and Commitment* (Cambridge, Mass.: Belknap Press, 1977), 115–33; Pocock, *Machiavellian Moment*, esp. chaps. 6 and 7. On this problem in Quentin Skinner's interpretation of Machiavelli, see the essay by Paul Rahe in chapter 10 of this volume.

[52] See P. S. Leicht, "Un principio politico medievale," in *Scritti vari di diritto italiano* (Milan: Giuffré, 1943), I: 136–8.

Will is to decision as reason is to deliberation. Therefore, practical and historical considerations aside, Guicciardini's republic provides for a council of the people and for a senate. Volition and deliberation are assigned different seats – in the city as in the human psyche. In politics it is necessary to decide despite imperfect knowledge of matters of fact and – given the eclipse of traditional universal authorities – without the guidance of demonstrable, self-evident normative principles. In place of the medieval openness of relatively autonomous spheres of activity and organization with respect to an apprehended but ineffable transcendent order, we find in Guicciardini a new procedural openness, allowing decisive will to be guided by the plausible outcome of sensible adversarial reasoning.

What at first may appear to be a restoration of classical republican ideals is, in fact, a departure from it, as well as a departure from the medieval ecumenical order. And realist constitutionalism differs from the model of ancient republics, Roman as well as Greek, in yet another significant respect: the scope and mode of persuasion. Mansfield argues that one reason Aristotle's mixed regime had to give way to the modern impartial regime was that the former relied on the ability to persuade, which in turn required a citizen body that was persuadable, and that these are not empirically realistic expectations.[53]

This difference is reflected in the venues and style of debate in early modern Florence as opposed to the ancient city. The exemplary statesman of early modern Florence is not the Ciceronian *vir bonus dicendi peritus*. He is instead the *savvio*, the prudent man, capable of shrewd and reasoned judgment, informed by the worldly experience normally associated with high social standing. He will be guided in his public conduct more by procedural devices than by his character as *bonus*. The exclusive quality of government, the two-tiered structure of deliberation and consent, will give him no forum for emotional appeals calculated to move a broad public. In this, too, he is unlike the ancient orator who, in Rome as in Athens, needed to sway great assemblies.[54] Instead the *savvio* can converse, give his *parere* or informed opinion, to the rational few who are called together to deliberate.

The *savvio*'s political reason is instrumental and serves his desire for

---

[53] See Mansfield, "The Unfinished Revolution."
[54] Gary Remer identified a very similar pattern in Harrington and developed the difference between ancient and early modern republican oratory in his article, "James Harrington's New Deliberative Rhetoric: Reflections on an Anticlassical Republicanism," *History of Political Thought* 16 (1995): 532–57.

honor and gain. The well-constructed republic provides an institutional mechanism that encourages and induces individual concupiscence to coincide with and thus serve the ends of collective desire. Its reason is not like Plato's charioteer, who rules the horses of spiritedness and appetite with the reins of reason, but rather a modern coachman, a functionary serving the will of his master, an intimation of enlightened despotism's liveried "first servant of the state."

Guicciardini's skepticism does not indicate an abdication of reason but an awareness of its limits. Like Machiavelli, he separates the politically effective from the normatively valid and lets the contrast stand, rather than take refuge in specious mediation. To love one's country more than one's soul does not indicate indifference to one's spiritual and ethical integrity, but an awareness of being subject to incommensurable obligations.[55]

The realist constitutional project sought to create conditions of possibility for what *The Federalist* would come to call "the judicious estimate of our true interests."[56] But while the circumstances of the American founding gave considerable scope to reflection and choice, the Florentine development was very much shaped by force and accident.[57] It represents nonetheless a remarkable effort to grapple with the necessities of force and accident by explicitly recognizing their strength; it is an attempt, not to exclude them, but by introducing them into the very fabric of the regime, to exploit the tensions resulting from them. Machiavelli pointed to the virtue of disunion as an instrument to promote the liberty and power of the Roman people, thus breaking with a long tradition of pious appeals to unity.[58] Guicciardini sought instead to compose the tensions through the mediating and intermediate institution of a senate and by emphasizing procedural rather than substantive agreement.

Realist constitutional thought, as it developed against a background of Florentine historical experience, arrived at a comprehensive understanding of an articulated political whole, resistant to unlimited, arbitrary, despotic government. It advocated a sage and balanced distribution of powers. It sought to uphold the rule of law, to assure the security of persons and property, to provide for careers open to talent, and to distribute honors and burdens equitably. At the same time, it was designed to provide ideological cover for a regime with a specific, oligarchic, social content. It emerged, furthermore, as an ethically

[55] Guicciardini, *Ricordi*, 122 [B 48].   [56] *The Federalist*, no. 1 (Hamilton).
[57] Mansfield, "The Unfinished Revolution," 19.   [58] Machiavelli, *Discorsi*, I, iv.

agnostic, rational search for an efficient organization of power, a power most clearly manifest in the successful conduct of war and rule over subjects. Realist constitutionalism represents, then, a significant chapter in the history of reason of state, a move toward the definition of sovereignty and an attempt to tackle the characteristically modern problem of establishing good government in a corrupt society. It is a mistake, I think, to play down the instrumental hardness of its "humanism" in order to press it into line with an elusive, if not entirely factitious, "republican tradition."

CHAPTER 8

Bruni and Machiavelli on civic humanism

Harvey C. Mansfield

Civic humanism is not a new topic, but it is not a small one either. The term was coined by Hans Baron in 1925, writing in German, as *Bürgerhumanismus*, and it is elaborated in his chief work, *The Crisis of the Early Italian Renaissance* (1955, 1966). The "crisis" was the challenge to republican Florence in 1402 from absolutist Milan, which was resolved or at least met by "civic humanism," a movement of humanist orators, poets, and philosophers, hitherto unpolitical, or if political not thoroughly republican, into "civic" affairs, that is, republican partisanship. Of course the challenge had to be met in politics and on the field of battle by civic Florentines, but a "civic humanist" is, in the usage of historians, always a thinker or a writer who is shaped by, or gives shape to, the civic spirit of the city. Even though Baron tries to draw the closest connections between political or military events and the writers, thus implying that events come first, his interest is in the writers as expressions or interpreters – in those who come second.

Baron defines the advent of civic humanism, coming as it does after a crisis, as a "break" between Francesco Petrarch's uncivic humanism of the Trecento and Leonardo Bruni's civic humanism of the Quattrocento.[1] Almost immediately after speaking of a break, Baron refers to a "gradual process of fusion" leading from Coluccio Salutati and Filippo Villani to Bruni, and then immediately recoils from that concession, doubting that there could be fusion between citizens of a republic and aloof scholars or courtiers of a tyrant. Historians gain fame by creating periods in history, such as civic humanism, and they gain reputation by dissolving breaks into fusions, usually called "transitions." Baron was for the moment merely preserving his reputation at the expense of his fame.

My thanks to Bryan Garsten for help with this chapter.

[1] Hans Baron, *The Crisis of the Early Italian Renaissance* (Princeton: Princeton University Press, 1966), 3.

Other historians have followed his own suggestion by chipping away at the notion of a break, while not wishing or daring to abandon the concept of civic humanism.[2] After all, one cannot have a perpetual continuum of pure transition, because a transition goes from one thing to another, and one needs to establish definite things between which transitions may occur. The difficulty for historians is that they do not know any way history can proceed except gradually, out of antecedent conditions, through transitions that anticipate what is to come either entering into the period or coming out of it. At a certain indefinable point the historian, for example, will stop speaking of postscholasticism and, having edged his way past the mark, begin speaking of prehumanism. To be sure, the "pre" and the "post" presuppose the periods of history to which they are merely prefixes, and periods must be defined by breaks, by essentially new wholes. Historians do not like essences and cannot explain them, but they do find it necessary to make use of them.[3]

Baron appears to have designed "civic humanism" to modify, if not replace, Jacob Burckhardt's concept of Renaissance.[4] Whereas Burckhardt's Renaissance centered on "the state as a work of art," a work made of individuality linked with tyranny and absolutism,[5] Baron's civic humanism is a collective sentiment both republican and patriotic.

To define their periods, both Baron and Burckhardt feel obliged to call upon Machiavelli, who is the most compelling figure in the period containing him, whatever it may be called. Burckhardt sees Machiavelli as a patriot in the fullest sense, because "the welfare of the state was . . . his first and last thought."[6] Baron finds him also to be a patriot, but a promoter of active citizenship.[7] He is not attracted by patriotism for the modern state, having seen in Germany too much of what Nietzsche called the "cold monster."

---

[2] See James Hankins, "The 'Baron Thesis' after Forty Years and some Recent Studies of Leonardo Bruni," *Journal of the History of Ideas*, 56 (1995): 315 16. To the authors cited there one may add Marvin Becker, *Florence in Transition*, 2 vols. (Baltimore: Johns Hopkins University Press, 1968), II: 27.

[3] An example is Wallace K. Ferguson, in an article in which he admits the need for essences so as to define boundaries, but then defines the essence of the Renaissance as "the age of transition from medieval to modern civilization." "The Interpretation of the Renaissance: Suggestions for a Synthesis," *Journal of the History of Ideas* 12 (1951): 64.

[4] Baron, *Crisis*, 390.

[5] Jacob Burckhardt, *The Civilization of the Renaissance in Italy*, trans. S. G. C. Middlemore, third edn. (London: Phaidon, 1950), part 1. Burckhardt has a good Machiavellian sense of the link between individuality and illegitimacy: see 5, 82. On 132 he speaks of "the natural alliance between the despot and the scholar."

[6] Burckhardt, *Civilization*, 55.   [7] Baron, *Crisis*, 428.

Although Burckhardt and Baron speak of Renaissance and civic humanism, modernity is what they are reaching to describe. One might even say that modernity is what *all* historians seek to describe, directly or indirectly. It is the only historical period that set itself the ambitious task of controlling history. It is the period of periods, the absolute moment, as Hegel called it, when history becomes conscious of itself and peoples are no longer held in thrall by their pasts but are free to set their own courses. Today no historian is a Hegelian, and historians are more likely to consider men as prisoners than as commanders of large, impersonal forces. Indeed, the historical periods are thought to rule men's lives. But though not Hegelians, historians are post-Hegelian; they criticize the uniqueness of modernity, but they have not abandoned it. "Renaissance" and "civic humanism" are both attempts to trace the origins of what is characteristic of modern history. It is not that the two historians are merely preoccupied with the actions and troubles of their own times as if, despite their researches, they were unable to take a larger view. It is rather that their larger view still clings to the promise of modernity to control the future. Their own time has a prior right, and it is not merely parochial of historians today to try to define, however indirectly, the meaning of modernity. By the post-Hegelian constitution under which historians live today, all times are equal (none is "world-historical" as Hegel would have it), but that is because all are equally to be contrasted with the modern period when history becomes self-conscious. And when history becomes painfully self-conscious, and ironically aware of its own awareness, it becomes "postmodern," as we say. Postmodern historians doubt we can control the future but see no way out of the modern claim to do so; hence they cannot leave "modern" behind even in the name they accept for themselves.

Since modernity is aware of history, both Burckhardt and Baron speak of the discovery or refashioning of history in the periods they have established.[8] The appearance of history signals the demotion if not disappearance of the merely contemplative life, and both authors find in their periods new interest in the application of theory to practice, requiring the remaking of theory so that it can be exploited for practical application. They do not say so, but this change does not yet disclose the methodical or mathematical nature of modern science, but rather its fundamental drive toward a new kind of understanding that proceeds by manipulation of worldly things and results in mastery of them.

---

[8] Burckhardt, *Civilization*, 53, 145; Baron, *Crisis*, 66, 157–8, 170, 191, 350–1, 465–6.

When Baron corrected Burckhardt, therefore, it could appear, with elaboration and decoration, as something momentous. And so it did to contemporary political theorists who seized on civic humanism and used it for all it was worth, and more. They were particularly attracted by the possibility that republican virtue, the inspiration of civic humanism, might serve as an alternative to liberal individualism, and do so without obliging its present-day defenders to join the camp of socialism. The classic presentation of republican virtue is found in Montesquieu's *Spirit of the Laws*, in which it is described, praised, and then criticized and replaced by a version of liberal individualism. Montesquieu sees republican virtue as the sacrifice of one's own interest for the common good. He goes so far as to compare it to the renunciation of monks, who love the very order that deprives them of everything that self-interest ordinarily desires.[9] Thus defined, republican virtue is an antique not suitable for modern times.[10] Its noble ferocity demands too much loss of one's own interest and surrender of one's pride to be practicable now (if it ever was), and it could hardly serve as the principle of modernity. Then is there a way around Montesquieu's discouraging treatment of republican virtue?

The main political theorists of civic humanism have been J. G. A. Pocock and Quentin Skinner, particularly the former. Pocock makes republican virtue less exacting by not insisting on monkish frugality or dwelling on the element of sacrifice, and at the same time he makes it more fulfilling by introducing the element of participation. Montesquieu had seen participation as an excess leading to the corruption of republics, because it will be exercised at the expense of the people's chosen rulers, and will lead to their replacement by despots.[11] Pocock bases his impressive work, *The Machiavellian Moment*, on the political theory of Hannah Arendt.[12]

Arendt's work centers on political participation, which, for her, is the self-created essence of a human being. When entering into politics, man quits his private life of isolated, selfish contentment and leaps into common, transcendent meaning, passing from necessity to freedom and from animality to humanity. In her interpretation, Aristotle's "political

---

[9] Montesquieu, *Spirit of the Laws*, III 3; IV 1, 5, 8; V 2; VII 2.
[10] Montesquieu, *Spirit of the Laws*, V 6, where comical modern analogues of the ancient republic are found in William Penn and the Jesuits in Paraguay.
[11] Montesquieu, *Spirit of the Laws*, VIII 2.
[12] J. G. A. Pocock, *The Machiavellian Moment* (Princeton: Princeton University Press, 1975), 516 n. 15, 550; for Pocock on Montesquieu, see 491-2, 501; and for an epitome of Pocock's thesis, see chap. 7. For another example, see S. M. Shumer, "Machiavelli: Republican Politics and Its Corruption," *Political Theory* 7 (1979): 5-34.

animal" is not political "by nature," as Aristotle said, but humanly created by an assertive act, which in turn is either unprompted or obedient to some uncanny call beamed from the ontology of Martin Heidegger.[13] As a foundation for historical understanding, Arendt's formula has the solidity of an explosive gas, but Pocock used it nonetheless to carry civic humanism (the "Machiavellian moment") from the historiography of Hans Baron to that of Bernard Bailyn. His achievement is to have made a theme of the other modernity, one that does not reject the ancients, that does not take progress for granted, that rejects the manipulation of human selfishness, and that seeks to command the future without putting an end to history. His book shows stretch marks from his exertions, and it sets a record for dubious allusions and attempted brilliance, but it makes a point. Quentin Skinner's work is closer to historians than Pocock's, and perhaps to history; it is more flexible but more evasive. He is not sure whether his theme is the ancient–modern republic or "the modern state" *à la* Max Weber – which is neutral as to forms of government.[14] Like Pocock an enemy of essentialism, he vacillates between a groundless choice and choosing to be groundless, between venturing his preference for republics and returning to the safe haven of neutrality.

What the authors discussed so far have in common is a failure to come to terms with modernity. They all use the term "modern," and usually in a stronger sense than merely "current"; and they are generally if vaguely aware of the meaning of the term: it refers to the great design for submitting the world to rational control, which became visible to all in the thought of the Enlightenment and the events of the French Revolution. Its most complete expression, as said above, is in Hegel's rational state. This design was conceived before it became visible to all, but when? Did it begin in the Renaissance? The difficulty with which Burckhardt wrestles is that the Renaissance has modern features but appears as a rebirth of the ancients.[15] No Renaissance

---

[13] Hannah Arendt, *The Human Condition* (Chicago: University of Chicago Press, 1958), 23; *On Revolution* (New York: Viking-Penguin, 1990; first pub. 1963), 19. For my estimation, see Harvey C. Mansfield, Jr., *Responsible Citizenship Ancient and Modern* (Eugene, Oreg.: University of Oregon Humanities Center, 1994), 23–8.

[14] Quentin Skinner, *The Foundations of Modern Political Thought*, 2 vols. (Cambridge: Cambridge University Press, 1978), I: ix–x, xiv, 158–9.

[15] See Burckhardt, *Civilization*, 104–5. Ferguson says, with reason, that the Renaissance can be in general distinguished as "a sense of breaking new ground and of scanning ever-widening horizons"; "The Interpretation of the Renaissance," 70. But then what happens to the literal meaning of "Renaissance"? And the announced, deliberate, elaborated "sense of breaking new ground" applies only to Machiavelli.

writer calls for the conceiving of modernity by that name. Machiavelli proclaims his intent to bring "new modes and orders" but treats the ancients as strong and the moderns as weak, in which he contrasts markedly with Francis Bacon, who openly decries the authority of the ancients and vaunts the superiority of the moderns. With Bacon, one could say, the Renaissance is dead, because the meaning of Renaissance is an appeal to the authority of the ancients. The ancients are not the only authority, perhaps not even the principal authority to Renaissance authors, and the appeal to them may be made in many different ways and may not even be sincere; but it must be made.

The civic humanists of our day do not address Bacon's claim. They have no love for the bourgeoisie, whom they see as having profited from modernity more than anyone else. To replace the profit motive they want active citizenship and think they have found it in the ancient *polis*.[16] But in fact they would not want to live in the *polis* if it meant doing without clean underwear – which it does. The origin of modern comforts is in the modern rationality of which the civic humanists give no account. Is humanism Bacon's utopia devoted to the "relief of man's estate," or is it the rule of Aristotle's magnanimous man? These are two very different notions of "civic."

In this situation I shall make a modest attempt at clarification. Playing historian in reverse, and moving from thought to deed, I shall define a break between Bruni and Machiavelli through an analysis of Bruni's *Laudatio Florentinae urbis*. This is the very work Hans Baron most relied on to establish continuity between Bruni and Machiavelli, and between them and Aristotle.

In my showing Bruni is still very much within the Aristotelian tradition from which Machiavelli has definitely and intentionally departed. Machiavelli announces his departure, but conceals the extent of his amazing ambition. What he meant, I have suggested elsewhere, is to

---

[16] Quentin Skinner attempts to occupy a position intermediate between the profit motive and the *polis*, and denies that his classical republicans (from Machiavelli on) hold to an Aristotelian positive freedom. His attempt depends on the claim that corruption is "simply a failure of rationality." But does this mean that duty or virtue is in your self-interest – still the profit motive – or is it that corruption leaves the best part of your nature unsatisfied (which is a notion of positive freedom)? *Tertium non datur*. See Skinner, "The Republican Ideal of Political Liberty," in *Machiavelli and Republicanism*, ed. Gisela Bock, Quentin Skinner, and Maurizio Viroli (Cambridge: Cambridge University Press, 1990), 304–6. Yet in another chapter of the same volume, Skinner concludes, despite the differences he notes between Aristotle and Machiavelli, that the latter "presents a wholehearted defense of traditional republican values ... in wholeheartedly traditional ways": "Machiavelli's *Discorsi* and the Pre-humanist Origins of Republican Ideas," in ibid., 141. See also Maurizio Viroli, "Machiavelli and the Republican Idea of Politics," in ibid., 169.

overturn the judgment he appears to make between the ancients and the moderns, and to reveal that the ancients were weaker than they appear and the moderns can be much stronger.[17] Thus Machiavelli's Renaissance contains the promise of modernity. It is not truly a rebirth of ancient wisdom and ancient politics; on the contrary, it makes use of that rebirth, begun by others, to criticize them and to supplant the authority they place in the ancients with his own. From the standpoint of Machiavelli, the Renaissance is not so different from medieval scholasticism: both remain within the tradition of Aristotle, and both come to a compromise with Christianity. Perhaps, despite the differences, there is an affinity between Aristotle and Christianity in their common reliance on "imagined republics and principalities that have never been seen or known to exist in truth." When Machiavelli advanced his idea of "effectual truth,"[18] a phrase he made his own by using it only once, and when no one else had used it, he stepped out of his time and prescribed for the future. It was effectual truth that produced the Enlightenment, and effectual truth that it supplied at its retail outlets. All Machiavelli's praise and use of fraud, whatever they conceal, serve in the end to make truth effectual and thus visible in its effects, and thus to open the eyes of the unenlightened.

Let us see what Machiavelli might think of Bruni's *Laudatio*. We know that in later life Bruni himself referred to his speech as a "boyish trifle," but we also know that Hans Baron regarded it as the pioneer in a development leading through Bruni's later work to Machiavelli and the other great historians of the late Renaissance.[19] Let us put aside Bruni's remark, which may be no more than the ironic deprecation of his late maturity, and make the comparison that Baron suggests but did not carry out himself.[20] Machiavelli is too great a man to ignore as anomalous, yet too original to treat in a development including "other great historians." But Bruni is not lacking in subtlety. He is at least as subtle as Hans Baron. Baron laments the underestimation which Bruni's *Laudatio* has suffered, but we shall see that Baron rather continues than corrects this unhappy condition.

Like many historians, Baron is suspicious of rhetoric; so after choosing to raise the fortune of an avowed panegyric, indeed to make it the

---

[17] Harvey C. Mansfield, *Machiavelli's Virtue* (Chicago: University of Chicago Press, 1996), 8 13, 109 10, 258 63.
[18] Machiavelli, *The Prince*, chap. 15.
[19] Baron, *Crisis*, 191, 196 8. For Bruni's remark, see *Epistularum libri VIII*, ed. L. Mehus (Florence, 1741), II: 111 12, cited in Hankins, "The 'Baron Thesis,'" 325n.
[20] Baron compares Bruni with Donato Giannotti instead of Machiavelli; *Crisis*, 208.

original foundation of the period of his own manufacture or discernment, he incontinently goes about removing its "rhetorical guise."[21] But making sense of the rhetorical guise, or, which is the same thing, appreciating Bruni's irony, is the only way to see what Bruni is doing. Baron applies the standard of the modern historian to Bruni, seemingly unaware that the historian's preference for fact over rhetoric derives from Machiavelli's preference for guiding oneself by "how one lives" rather than by "how one should live."[22] For a difference over the place and value of rhetoric is the first point of contrast between Bruni and Machiavelli.

Bruni's *Laudatio* is an example of epideictic rhetoric, a form of speech for display in which the merits of the object displayed are brought to view and somewhat, or considerably, magnified. This might be done for an interested motive such as in modern advertising, but if the *Laudatio* initiates the time of "civic humanism," one should look for a civic or humane motive behind it. The motive Baron finds is Bruni's desire to support the cause of republicanism, which Baron believes is at stake in Florence's war against the duke of Milan.[23] Yet this motive, as Baron's critics have said, can readily be seen as the desire to flatter Florence with wartime propaganda – a charge that Bruni himself takes time to deflect.[24] Is there not some worthy motive for the exaggerated praise of panegyric? Aristotle supplies one in his *Rhetoric*, a work devoted to rescuing rhetoric from its evil reputation. In discussing epideictic rhetoric he remarks that praise and counsel can be interchanged: what you praise someone for is what you would counsel him to do, and vice versa.[25] Thus one can give counsel by praising, and by exaggerating the praise one can indicate a defect. The section on the virtues of Florence in Bruni's *Laudatio*, which Baron dismisses as "long and tedious," actually discloses the author's opinion that the Florentines are inferior to the Romans to whom they are said to be heir.[26]

In the second part of the *Laudatio*, preceding the praise of Florence's virtues, Bruni seeks to establish that Florence had its origin as a colony from Rome. He uses this fact to proclaim that Florence thereby inherits

---

[21] Ibid., *Crisis*, 199. [22] Machiavelli, *The Prince*, chap. 15. [23] Baron, *Crisis*, chap. 10.
[24] Leonardo Bruni, *Laudatio Florentinae urbis*, printed as appendix in Hans Baron, *From Petrarch to Leonardo Bruni* (Chicago: University of Chicago Press, 1968); English translation in *The Earthly Republic; Italian Humanists on Government and Society*, ed. Benjamin G. Kohl and Ronald G. Witt (Philadelphia: University of Pennsylvania Press, 1978); to be cited as *Laudatio*, English page/Latin page. *Laudatio*, 156 7/249 50.
[25] Aristotle, *Rhetoric* I 9. Aristotle shows here how to smuggle deliberative rhetoric into epideictic rhetoric a rhetorical guise for good advice.
[26] Bruni, *Laudatio*, 154 68/248 58. Baron, *Crisis*, 193.

dominion over the entire world by "a certain hereditary right" (*iure quodam hereditario*).[27] But, Bruni insists, Florence was a republican colony before the time of the empire, and therefore its inheritance is from republican virtue. Bruni names fourteen great republican families, as well as nine virtuous individuals, and contrasts them with execrable Roman emperors who destroyed the liberties of the republic, especially Caligula and Nero, but including also Caesar and the Antonines. He quotes Tacitus as saying that after the republic was subjected to the power of one, its outstanding geniuses (*praeclara illa ingenia*) were expelled.[28] But Tacitus made this celebrated caustic remark at the outset of his *Histories* in regard to historians like himself (and Bruni), those who serve truth, and not about men of political virtue.[29] Bruni uses it to give emphasis to the nobility of Florence's inheritance, which could be noble only if it was republican. After the republic, all genius disappeared except for Tacitus – and there was no virtue for Florence to inherit.

This exaggeration sets us up for a surprise – for the fact that no names of Florentine families or individuals are mentioned in the *Laudatio*. Bruni does indeed assure us that many of the greatest examples of Roman virtue could be recognized there,[30] but he does not specify any of them. Some of Florence's enemies are named, including the very duke of Milan Hans Baron believes to have been demonized, who is said to be a man of high qualities misused.[31] Why the omission? Before praising Florentine virtue, Bruni digresses on his own account, as we have noted; he wants to prove he is capable of praise because he is not flattering Florence. His praise is honest, he says, because it will earn him the hatred of Florence's enemies, who are envious of Florence and do not like to see her praised. But his failure to mention any Florentine names suggests that he fears the hatred he might incur from envious Florentines, which further suggests that Florence is not the harmonious city he says it to be. Bruni's denial that he is flattering his Florentine audience deflects its attention from his fear of flattering certain parts of it, lest other Florentines take offense. Bruni presents himself as taking the risk

---

[27] Bruni, *Laudatio*, 150/244. Bruni acknowledged that his *Laudatio* was based on the *Panathenaicus* of Aelius Aristides (*c.* 155 A.D.). But the obvious difference between them is that Bruni extols Florence's inheritance from Rome, while Aristides praises Athens for being itself the nurse or foster-father of all men. If Athens had an inheritance, it was the favor of the gods (*Panathenaicus*, 1, 33, 38). The gods are the equivalent of republican Rome in Bruni's oration.
[28] Tacitus, *Histories* I 1.
[29] The same phrase, *praeclara ingenia*, occurs in Sallust as describing writers rather than political men (*Bellum Catilinae*, 8.4). The Athenians, Sallust says, had writers who magnified their deeds, but the Romans lacked that advantage.
[30] Bruni, *Laudatio*, 155/249.   [31] Ibid., 166/257.

of standing up for Florence against her enemies, an action for which he does not praise any particular Florentine. He describes instances in which the Florentines stood up for themselves against the emperor Henry VII, against Volterra, and against Pisa; but he names no names in these glorious victories. Bruni addresses the men of Florence (*viri Florentini*) to exhort them, not any party or patron.[32] Such circumspection leaves him the friend of every faction and thus available, as has been suggested, to succeed Coluccio Salutati as chancellor of Florence.[33] But in this office, Bruni means to imply, he might do the city some good. By praising the Florentines as heirs of the Romans – in truth, a gross but prudent act of flattery – he counsels them to behave as if they were. He means, of course, that they should consider themselves heirs of the best Romans, and just what changes such self-regard may require are not immediately apparent. But the presumption of Bruni's rhetoric is that praise can be effectual for good. Praise uses a standard by which to praise, as Bruni uses Roman virtue to praise Florentine virtue; and the standard of praise has to be above the thing praised. Thus it is presumed that an invocation of behavior better than that we now witness can be the cause of improvement. High words can have an effect.

Machiavelli says quite the contrary. In his *Discourses on Livy* he quotes a Roman praetor asserting that one ought to consider more what to do than what to say, for once one decides, "it will be easy to accommodate words to things." Then Machiavelli pronounces for himself: "Without doubt these words are very true and should be relished by every prince and every republic."[34] Rhetoric for him has the character of rationalization: first do the deed, then the words to justify your action will come to you. Those who attempt the opposite, and try to accommodate their deeds to words, will come to grief. As Machiavelli says in *The Prince*: "For a man who wants to make a profession of good in all regards must come to ruin among so many who are not good."[35] A profession of good is a standard of conduct above "what is done" – which is just what Bruni's *Laudatio* offers. For behind and above the standard of Roman virtue dwells the "profession of good in all regards" – classical political philosophy as a whole – which Bruni spent his life in studying and translating, and in departing from which Machiavelli set out to "find new modes and orders."[36]

---

[32] Bruni uses *viri* twice in the vocative and then *homines* in the nominative; ibid., 150 51/244 5.
[33] Jerrold Seigel, "'Civic Humanism' or Ciceronian Rhetoric? The Culture of Petrarch and Bruni," *Past and Present*, 34 (1966): 3 48.
[34] Machiavelli, *Discourses on Livy*, II 15.1. [35] Machiavelli, *The Prince*, chap. 15.
[36] Machiavelli, *Discourses on Livy* I pr. 1.

Accommodating words to deeds does not amount to the abandonment of rhetoric, as we know sufficiently from the mordant grace of Machiavelli's prose. He wants to move us with speech, but not with fine words. His terse phrases are designed to produce a shock by the confrontation of morality with necessity, often with a comic reduction of serious evil to everyday calculation. The most effectual formulations, such as "men forget the death of a father more quickly than the loss of a patrimony,"[37] have become known as Machiavellisms whose fame is inseparable from infamy. In the last chapter of *The Prince* Machiavelli does not shrink from what he calls exhortation, urging Italians to an act of what he calls redemption; but the way to this seemingly unsupported "ought" has been prepared by the demonstration of necessary means in the rest of the book preceding the satirical exhortation.[38] Machiavelli's rhetoric is designed to instruct its hearers not to rely on words alone, which means not to rely on words regardless of necessities, for words not in accord with necessity are promises that will not be kept. Machiavelli is an unarmed prophet, but he will escape the ruin that awaits other unarmed prophets because his words appeal to human necessities.[39]

In appealing to necessities, Machiavelli brings up deeds or "examples," particularly of the ancients, that reveal necessity at work. He bemoans the fact that the ancients are imitated in law and medicine, not in politics, and he calls for "true knowledge of the histories" of the ancients.[40] Despite the honor accorded to the ancients in his time, he says severely, no sign whatever remains of ancient virtue. These remarks at the beginning of the *Discourses on Livy* constitute Machiavelli's most direct reference to what we, following Burckhardt, now call the Renaissance. In it Machiavelli claims to be the first to imitate the politics of the ancients. He ignores the claim made on Bruni's behalf by Hans Baron – to say nothing of possible claims for others – to have made a civic, or political, humanism. Machiavelli could not have been unaware of humanist political writings, but he ignores them, one may suppose, because they derive from rhetoricians and philosophers rather than historians. Their politics consists in precepts rather than deeds, in principles elaborated in imaginary republics and principalities rather than prompted by necessity. One does not have to read far in Machia-

---

[37] Machiavelli, *The Prince*, chap. 17; for how do you get your patrimony except by the death of your father?
[38] Especially *The Prince*, chap. 3, offering advice to the king of France on how to invade Italy. See Leo Strauss, *Thoughts on Machiavelli* (Glencoe, Ill.: The Free Press, 1958), 72–9.
[39] Machiavelli, *The Prince*, chap. 6.   [40] Machiavelli, *Discourses on Livy*, I pr. 2.

velli's *Discourses* to see that he sets the ancients' deeds against their precepts, the first example being the dissensions in Rome wrongly condemned by "many."[41] The many are writers like Bruni who presuppose an imaginary harmony in politics. While relying, or seeming to rely, on ancient historians, Machiavelli does not hesitate to proclaim in the first sentence of the *Discourses* that he is bringing "new modes and orders." The claim of novelty for himself is broadened to promote novelty in politics generally, since it provides more glory for the ambitious. New modes and orders in republics must be continuously new or renewed, and the new prince praised in *The Prince* must expect to be replaced by the next new prince.

In Machiavelli we suddenly have, without preparation by the humanists, a call for return to the ancients that is hostile not only to what is ancient but also to any notion of inheritance which might transmit the ancient to us. Machiavelli's Renaissance is a rebirth only insofar as it is a new birth, one lacking any imperative to return to better times. The ancients are praised at the same time that the precepts by which *they* praised are challenged. The ancients' deeds are held up for us to emulate, but their authority over us, which depends on their precepts, is denied. Machiavelli's rhetorical attitude supports the Renaissance and even urges it on to include politics. Yet since the ancients had no ancients, the consequence of imitating them is to leave them behind. I believe the consequence was intended. One should not say that Machiavelli was ambivalent about the Renaissance, as he was a man who was sure of his mind. But he was not quite straightforward in his support of the Renaissance. Conversing with the ancients as he did, he may have concluded that they would have endorsed his decision, in new circumstances, to depart from their "orders." In this sense, and in his opinion, the tradition remains intact despite his break with it.[42]

Novelty is one feature of Machiavelli's peculiar rhetorical stance; criticism is another. Bruni's *Laudatio* is a panegyric of Florence that makes it the heir of Rome; his rhetoric associates the modern city with the ancient republic. If his praise is exaggerated, as surely it is, the purpose is to give Florence a tradition to live up to. In this Bruni is typical of the humanists who like the scholastics, do not use the ancients

---

[41] Machiavelli, *Discourses on Livy*, I 4.1. Harvey C. Mansfield, Jr., *Machiavelli's New Modes and Orders* (Ithaca, N.Y.: Cornell University Press, 1979), 43.

[42] Machiavelli, Letter of 10 December, 1513 in Niccolò Machiavelli, *Lettere*, ed. F. Gaeta (Milan: Feltrinelli, 1961), 301–6, no. 140; *Discourses on Livy*, II 33. See also Mansfield, *Machiavelli's New Modes and Orders*, 293–6.

to embarrass the moderns. In particular, they do not make a point of the deepest and most obvious difference between ancients and moderns, the Christian religion – unless to count it a decisive advantage for the moderns. Whatever the private opinions of the humanists, they do not criticize Christianity. But Machiavelli openly and boldly attacks it. Instead of associating the moderns with the ancients, he contrasts them: the ancients are strong, the moderns are weak. And the cause of modern weakness is at least connected, in a famous and wonderfully misleading sentence, to what Machiavelli irreverently calls "the present religion."[43] Christianity, which he says brings weakness and "ambitious idleness," may thereby hinder the acquisition of "a true knowledge of histories," to which he apparently assigns the chief cause of modern weakness. For Christian doctrine teaches us that we live in an imaginary principality, St. Augustine's City of God, a belief Machiavelli rejects in favor of the effectual truth.

Machiavelli's rhetoric of nonreliance on rhetoric is only the first of his differences with Bruni. Going directly to the effectual truth requires him to speak quite differently about the beginnings of cities than does Bruni in his *Laudatio*. In the first part of his oration Bruni tells of the beauty and splendor of Florence, and having concluded that none is more blessed or happy (*beatior*), stops to consider an objection that Florence is defective because it is not on the sea. Bruni invokes the authority of Plato, "by far the prince of all philosophers,"[44] who argued at length, Bruni reports, that a city should not be too close to the sea. But Bruni does not report what Plato said, namely, that being close to the sea is bad for the acquisition of virtue, since it tempts a city into commerce and money-making while rendering the souls of citizens distrustful of itself and the rest of humanity.[45] So, without saying anything himself, Bruni leads us to Plato's statement of a fundamental criticism of commercial Florence. He goes on to discuss other disadvantages of a maritime site, but he says nothing about what, for Plato, is clearly the main point. Florence does not use its inland site to avoid commerce; it is commercial so to speak without being tempted. That Bruni does discuss virtue in Florence next,

---

[43] "[Failure to have recourse to the examples of the ancients] arises, I believe, not so much from the weakness into which the present religion has led the world, or from the evil that an ambitious idleness has done to many Christian provinces and cities, as from not having a true knowledge of the histories, through not getting from reading them that sense nor tasting that flavor, that they have in themselves." Machiavelli, *Discourses on Livy*, I pr. 2. See Mansfield, *Machiavelli's New Modes and Orders*, 26–7; Strauss, *Thoughts on Machiavelli*, 176–7.
[44] "omnium philosophorum longissime princeps," Bruni, *Laudatio*, 145/240.
[45] Plato, *Republic*, 421d-423c; *Laws*, 704b–705c. See also Aristotle, *Politics*, 1327a13–40; Cicero, *De republica*, II 3–5.

in the second part, only emphasizes his failure to connect it to the site, and in general to explain how, in the estimation of Plato and Aristotle, and the ancients as a whole, a commercial city can be virtuous. Here Bruni criticizes by the very character of his praise, which he reveals to be at least in part ironic.

Classical political philosophy raised the question of a city's site in order to explore in a city's beginnings the deeper question of choice and necessity. Assuming counterfactually that a founder could choose a site, and have what he liked, what sort would he prefer? The question gives human choice a range it is never given in fact, but the answer is illuminating nonetheless. It shows both what is most worthy of choice and what limits are set on choice by chance and nature. By considering the topic Bruni not only passes a surreptitious adverse judgment on Florence, but also shows that he remains within the classical tradition.

Machiavelli considers the same topic in the first chapter of the *Discourses* to show, by contrast, that he has broken with the tradition. His theme in regard to a city's beginnings is not choice but necessity. He sees not which site responds best to the needs of virtue, but rather which one is most in accord with human necessities. He too speaks of choice and virtue, but he subordinates them to necessity. Choice should be exercised for a fertile site that enables a city to become great, while harsh laws should be imposed on the inhabitants to keep them under the necessity of living virtuously, or at least not in idleness.[46] With these remarks at the very beginning of the *Discourses* Machiavelli signals his challenge to the foundations of classical political philosophy.

Founders must assume that choices are guided if not determined by necessity, and states must act under that assumption. To be free, they must deal with their own necessities rather than rely on others for protection. Machiavelli says that Florence did not have a free origin; it began under the Roman empire, built by those "trusting in the long peace that was born in the world under Octavian." Passing over the grave implication in that phrase, we note that Machiavelli disagrees with Bruni that Florence had a republican beginning, or better to say, he does not care.[47] What Florence inherited from Rome was not its republican spirit but the peace or security that kept it dependent on others,

---

[46] Machiavelli, *Discourses on Livy*, I 1.4 5. See Mansfield, *Machiavelli's Virtue*, chap. 2.
[47] Machiavelli, *Discourses on Livy*, I 1.3. In the *Florentine Histories*, he speaks of the "security that was born in Italy through the reputation of the Roman republic" (II 2), before stating that Florence was born under Sulla and under the Second Triumvirate. See Mansfield, *Machiavelli's Virtue*, 156 61.

unable or unwilling to make a beginning on its own. For him, states do not get their independence from a regime as in classical political science, in which the fundamental choice is which regime to establish, or which regime is best. Whereas Bruni, following Plato, considers the site as a place for a regime, Machiavelli considers it so as to bring out the necessities that override the choice of regimes.

Those necessities apply during the life of a state as much as at the beginning, since men are threatened as much by their fellows as by external nature. So a third difference between Bruni and Machiavelli concerns internal discords. In his *Florentine Histories* Machiavelli complains that Bruni's history is inadequate on this point, which Machiavelli takes for his theme. In the *Laudatio* Bruni maintains that Florence's virtue shone in its harmony. In other cities, he says, the greater part (*maior pars*) often overcomes the better (*melior*) part, but in Florence the two have always been the same. With that particularly unbelievable assertion Bruni makes it clear that he understands the political problem in classical terms as bringing together the few and the many – as Aristotle said, quality and quantity.[48] The few and the many are not the minority and majority of a collection of equal individuals, as in our modern view, but rather make different contributions to a whole, to a common good that is a whole.[49] That whole is defined by the end citizens aim at; it is always aspirational and is fittingly described as rhetorical – more harmonious than it is in fact, less so than it claims to be. A regime is a specious whole existing mainly, though not only, in what the citizens say about it. Even or especially in exaggeration, Bruni the orator describes the regime he might appear only to distort.

The harmony in Florence enables it to practice the virtue of liberality by welcoming exiles from disharmonious cities elsewhere, so that it has become "the fatherland and safest asylum of all Italy."[50] Bruni implies, very contrary to fact, that there were no exiles from Florence,

---

[48] Aristotle, *Politics*, 1296b17–24; see also 1279a23–1280a6; 1283a23–1284a3; 1290a13–27. The Aristotelian tone is more pronounced in Bruni's later work, *The Constitution of the Florentines* (1439), published by Athanasios Moulakis in "Leonardo Bruni's Constitution of Florence," *Rinascimento*, n.s. 26 (1986): 141–90, especially 147–52. See also Nicolai Rubinstein, "Machiavelli and the Florentine Republican Experience," in *Machiavelli and Republicanism*, 5.

[49] Toward the end of the *Laudatio* Bruni explains that in Florence a certain equity is produced from the diverse orders "since the greater [*maiores*] are defended by their power, the lesser [*minores*] by the republic, and both by the fear of punishment." *Laudatio* 173/262. Here the greater and lesser are defined by their power, not in regard to quality. The best, one assumes, will always be among the *minores*, while the poor and rich might be either *maiores* or *minores* according to circumstance. One cannot assume, as does Benjamin G. Kohl's translation, that the poor are always less powerful than the rich. See Aristotle, *Politics*, 1317b8–10.

[50] Bruni, *Laudatio*, 159/251.

a city quite without sedition and envy. When praising Florentine magnanimity, he describes the incident in 1312 when Florence stood fast and united, he says, against Emperor Henry VII, when he was camped at its gates. In fact, the emperor's army was reinforced with Florentine exiles, and the heads of the government in Florence used the expedient of inviting some of them to return so as to reduce and divide their number. Among those not invited to return was Florence's greatest and most renowned exile, Dante.[51] Machiavelli mentions this, Bruni does not – but again Bruni's praise leads us to its correction. In vaunting the noble origin of Florence he insists, as we have seen, on the superiority of the Roman republic to the empire which provided Florence with a worthy inheritance. In the passage considered above, he made Tacitus say that after the republic came under the power of one, its brilliant geniuses (*praeclara illa ingenia*) were expelled (*abiere*). But Tacitus, at the beginning of his *Histories*, was referring to authors (*auctores*), great geniuses who vanished (*cessere*) under the empire.[52] Dante is a genius and author expelled by the Florentine republic, Bruni points out to us in this unobtrusive way. Baron, who is not in the habit of making observations of this sort, uses the same passage to enthuse over Bruni's republicanism.[53]

Machiavelli's report on harmony in Florence could hardly be more different from Bruni's. Instead of proclaiming that Florence has a harmony not found in other cities, Machiavelli asserts: "From such divisions [as were in Florence] came as many dead, as many exiles, and as many families destroyed as ever occurred in any city in memory."[54] Putting aside any notion of harmony in republics, he contrasts the harmful divisions in Florence with the beneficial ones in Rome, which made "that republic free and powerful." One must recognize that in every republic or city there are "two diverse humors, that of the people and that of the great"; the great want to dominate, the people want only not to be dominated.[55] This diversity means that whatever common

---

[51] Machiavelli, *Florentine Histories*, II 24. Bruni later wrote a brief *Vita di Dante* (1436) in which Dante's exile is featured and Henry VII's encampment mentioned.

[52] Bruni, *Laudatio*, 154/247; the difference between Tacitus and Bruni's Tacitus vanishes in Kohl's translation.

[53] Baron, *Crisis*, 58–60. Of the humanists Anthony Grafton says finely, and more appreciatively than he believes: "They praised, they blamed, they concealed": "Humanism and Political Theory," in *The Cambridge History of Political Thought, 1450–1700*, ed. J. H. Burns (Cambridge: Cambridge University Press, 1991), 29.

[54] Machiavelli, *Florentine Histories*, pref.

[55] Machiavelli, *The Prince*, chap. 9; *Discourses on Livy*, I 4.1, 5.2. See Mansfield, *Machiavelli's Virtue*, 37–8, 75–6, 92–7, 237–8.

good may exist in a republic, there cannot be harmony. The people may be devoted to the common good but are incapable of achieving it, and the great are capable but not willing. Good effects (the effectual truth) come from a certain managed dissension between the two humors rather than from good will and cooperation.

In saying that the people do not desire to rule, Machiavelli implies that every popular regime is a hidden oligarchy. And in asserting that the great desire to dominate, he implies that every aristocracy is also an oligarchy. "The few were always ministers of the few."[56] A prince is merely one of the few who gets above the others, and a principality is caused either by the few, who to resist the people give that power to one of themselves, or by the people, who to resist the great choose one of them to dominate the rest.[57] Since only the few are political, and all the few desire to dominate, the political is essentially tyrannical; no one who rules acts for the common good. Tyranny may be mitigated by the presence, in a republic, of competing oligarchs, and in both a principality and a republic, by the need to keep the people happy. Many combinations are possible, and the distinction between republic and principality is far from meaningless, but effectually politics is acquisitive tyranny.

Machiavelli's deconstruction robs the few of any good intent and the many of capacity and good judgment. He knew that most people do not believe these derogations, and that despite his arguments and chilling examples, they never will. Life as "one alone" (*uno solo*) takes place in an atmosphere too thin to support any but the hardiest creatures.[58] Even natural-born criminals – Machiavellians *avant la lettre* such as Giovampagolo Baglioni – do not know how to be altogether bad.[59] So human beings in their weakness will continue to claim support for their moral notions and boastfully or pathetically to use the rhetoric which calls on such imaginary help. Even after the effectual truth has been set forth so winningly, fraud will not disappear from the scene. The common good to which we foolishly aspire will always accompany our selfish maneuvers like a cloud obscuring the sun. It prevents us from looking directly at the "common benefit of everyone," the selfish interests we have in common, the common good that divides us, which Machiavelli has a "natural desire" to teach each one of us.[60] The false, imaginary harmony of a city can be manipulated by clever princes because most

---

[56] Machiavelli, *Discourses on Livy*, I 49.3. [57] Machiavelli, *The Prince*, chap. 9.
[58] Machiavelli, *Discourses on Livy*, I 9. See Mansfield, *Machiavelli's Virtue*, xv, 312 14.
[59] Machiavelli, *Discourses on Livy*, I 27. [60] Ibid., I pr. 1.

people want to believe in it. They will not only *participate* in the common good, as our updated civic humanists demand, but even *sacrifice* for it. With his customary astuteness, Machiavelli notes that "the nature of men is to be obligated as much by benefits they give as by benefits they receive."[61] Republican virtue for Machiavelli is both sacrificial (as with Montesquieu) and fraudulent. He and Bruni do not disagree that the harmony of cities is false; the difference is that Bruni conceals this disagreeable truth and Machiavelli rubs our noses in it. Bruni thinks that the harmony we wish for points to the truth of man's perfection, a formal or teleological truth; Machiavelli believes that the effectual truth must eternally compete with our unfounded hopes.

That same difference is on view in the matter of just war, so prominent in Bruni's *Laudatio* that it has been called "essentially an imperialist tract."[62] Machiavelli said that a just war is a necessary one, and he added that one should never defer war to one's disadvantage, that it is foolish to remain neutral in war, that using fraud in the management of war is a glorious thing, that one ought to defend the fatherland in any way, "whether just or unjust, merciful or cruel, praiseworthy or ignominious," and that those who fight for their own glory are good and faithful soldiers. To top it off, he asserted that the hardest of all hard servitudes is to be conquered by a republic.[63]

Bruni's justification for imperialism, resting on excellence rather than necessity, is altogether opposed to Machiavelli's. For Machiavelli, it is either rise or fall, and if you fall, you cannot expect anyone to pick you up.[64] Although he does not speak of right, he implicitly grants the right to act on one's necessities to any power or anyone. But for Bruni, the right to rule depends on the virtue of the ruler and is reserved for the best. He therefore has to prove that Florence *deserved* to prevail. In a sense any power that follows Machiavelli's advice also deserves to win, so that he and Bruni agree that the best should rule. But then one would have to say that they understand "best" very differently: for Machiavelli, one who has the virtue to reject moral inhibitions; for Bruni, one who lives by those same inhibitions.

Bruni's position on imperialism can be found in Aristotle's *Politics* within a discussion of whether the active life is the most choiceworthy. Aristotle says that when another person is superior in virtue and power, then it is noble to follow him and just to obey him.[65] This reasoning

---

[61] Machiavelli, *The Prince*, chap. 10. [62] See the essay of James Hankins, 146, above.
[63] Machiavelli, *The Prince*, chap. 12, *Discourses on Livy*, III 12.2; *The Prince*, chap. 3; *The Prince*, chap. 21; *Discourses on Livy*, III 40; III 41; I 43; II 2.4.
[64] Machiavelli, *The Prince*, chap. 24. [65] Aristotle, *Politics*, 1325b10 12.

carries beyond national borders and does not respect what we would call the right of self-determination. It might even go so far as "authority over all [persons]," Aristotle says, a world imperialism of whoever is best, because this would be the widest authority and the noblest of actions – the active life indeed![66] The logic of superiority in virtue seems to lead to the conclusion of limitless acquisition that Machiavelli points out. Aristotle deflects it, however, with the thought that the activity of virtue is not so much in relation to others or for the sake of results as it is complete in itself and for its own sake. This kind of activity is study and thinking; it seeks independence or autarchy instead of superiority.[67] Thus imperialist politics does not come up against any barrier to its extension within politics, but rather finds its limit when contrasted with virtue that is superior because it is above politics. That virtue wants peace to enjoy its superiority; the other, political virtue wants war to establish its superiority (which it is postulated to possess). The lesson from Aristotle for civic humanists is that the *civic* remains moderate, hence truly civic, only when it acknowledges the superiority of the *uncivic* – of the private virtues in cultivating the liberal arts and humane letters. Civic humanism must not stray too far from simple humanism.[68]

Bruni describes the justice of Florentine imperialism as if he were looking forward to incurring the contempt of Machiavelli. The valorous Florentines, he says, never stooped to crimes and fraud in their wars;[69] they always kept faith (*fides*) with their promises.[70] All the wars they waged, therefore, were "most just," fought only for the defense or recovery of "their own things." But, since they were by "a certain hereditary right" from the Romans possessors of the whole world, every war they fought was necessarily defensive.[71] And being on the defensive did not prevent Florence from generously offering protection to weaker states when they needed it,[72] as, for example, the victims of Giangaleazzo Visconti.

That Florence did none of these things, or fell far short of them, was as evident to Bruni's contemporaries as to us. But in seeing that, they were judging Florence by the standard of Bruni's praise; and since the

[66] Ibid., 1325a35 6.   [67] Ibid., 1325b16 21.
[68] Hannah Arendt does not discuss this passage in her account of Aristotle's *vita activa*; see *Human Condition*, 15 16, 32n.
[69] Bruni, *Laudatio*, 155/248. The Florentines were not victims of fraud because, not being located near the sea, they did not suffer as the Trojans did from fraud by the Greeks; ibid., 146 7/241.
[70] Ibid., 161/253. The quotation from Cicero is misapplied; for Cicero seems to excuse false oaths to pirates as distinguished from legitimate enemies.
[71] Ibid., 150/244.
[72] Ibid., 160/252; or was it only "more often than not" that the Florentines were generous? Ibid., 164/255.

praise was high, the standard was high. It could be said that in his panegyric Bruni conflates Florence with the best regime. In accordance with what we have seen in Aristotle's argument on imperialism, he praises aspects of Florence that are essentially nonpolitical and that do not contribute directly to its civic life, though they adorn it. We have already discussed his mention of geniuses and his egregious omission of the greatest Florentine exile. His praise of the beauty of Florence shows how civic pride can arise from a desire or a love that is uncivic in origin.[73] The virtue of magnificence so surely associated with Florence makes one think about the relationship between uncivic and civic, or private and public. Bruni also brings up the magnanimity or greatness of souls in Florence,[74] and he closes the third section of his speech by extolling Florence's ability to keep its dignity at all times.[75] Above all, however, he concludes his speech with reference to the cultivation of letters (*littere*) in Florence; not those that are mercenary and sordid but those especially worthy (*digne*) of free men that always flourish "in every princely people" (*in omne principe populo*). For Bruni as for Aristotle, it is the liberal arts that give dignity to a city – precisely humane letters as opposed to civic humanism. The imperialist impulse of the civic spirit is checked by a reminder of the private activities that flourish in peace. Moreover, Bruni takes the occasion to tell or remind the Florentines that there is something nobler than the mercenary spirit, which is the spirit of their ordinary lives, a fact that Florentines recognize when they spend their wealth on objects that adorn their city. And this nobler thing, Bruni happens to say, makes a people "princely," not republican. Here is a morsel for civic humanists to chew on.

Such are limits on Florentine imperialism that appear in Bruni's panegyric, none of them making appeal to international law. They ensure that Florence would not stoop to follow Machiavelli's advice to imitate the fox and the lion. In practice, Machiavelli would reply, Florence cannot conform to Bruni's praise and merely allows the doing of what it should to interfere halfheartedly and inconsistently with doing what it must. He would wonder especially whether Florence actually achieves the independence of the noblest self-absorbed activity, or anything close to it. In the *Laudatio* he might have pointed to the tense, embarrassed treatment of Florence's piety and its relationship to the Church. With this thought we return to the religious question, in which Machiavelli differs most plainly from the humanists, and from which his Renaissance turns toward modernity.

[73] Ibid., 136 49/233 43.   [74] Ibid., 159/251, 165/256, 167/257.   [75] Ibid., 168/258.

Bruni ends the *Laudatio* with the statement that Florence lacks nothing worthy of praise and has nothing more to desire – and yet he offers a prayer seeking defense from every defeat and evil (*ab omni clade maloque*).[76] Bruni prays to God, whose providence, understood as Lady Fortune, Machiavelli wants to beat down and control. That prayer indicates a much greater challenge to Florence's self-sufficiency than Bruni is willing to acknowledge openly. In the fourth section of his speech he describes Florence's government and comes to its outstanding feature, the dominance of the Guelf party that began after the interlude of Ghibelline rule following Florence's defeat at the battle of Montaperti in 1260. But Bruni does not mention either the Guelfs or the Ghibellines, and though he refers to the pope, he does not bring out the parties' connections to Church and empire. Though he speaks of expulsions, he does not mention exiles; his account by contrast with Machiavelli's is straightforward praise of the unnamed Guelfs, who are merely called leaders of the aristocratic party (*optimarum partium duces*).[77] His account of the event certainly qualifies his praise of harmony in Florence, but all ended for the best. Unlike Machiavelli, Bruni does not point to the Church as a source of division; but when listing the excellent kinds of genius in the city, he ignores the clergy. Above all, he says nothing of the differences between the ancient and the modern republic, caused by religion, which might make it difficult for the Florentine republic to live as heir to the Roman republic.[78]

For there were two heirs to Rome, rivals to the Florentine republic, whom Bruni does not mention – the Holy Roman empire and the Roman Church. In each case the relationship to ancient Rome is in doubt, but the strain of establishing it is hardly comparable to the difficulty of making Florence heir to Rome. In the *Laudatio* he makes Florence comprise, and stand for, human perfection. It is the best regime, and "republic" (*res publica*) has the primary sense of best regime that it held in classical political philosophy. The best regime does not depend on anything supernatural for its perfection; it only depends for its continuance on good fortune, for which one must pray. Bruni's republicanism takes responsibility for almost the whole human good; thus it is a way of shunting the Church aside without attacking it directly. It is also a rejection of empire; Ghibelline is not sufficient

---

[76] Ibid., 175/263; cf. the statement on 166/256 that God has favored Florence "many times" (*plurimus*).
[77] Ibid., 171–72/261; cf. Machiavelli, *Florentine Histories*, II 6. Kohl's translation of the *Laudatio* inserts the name of the Guelfs.
[78] On Bruni's "advanced secularism," see James Hankins, *Plato in the Italian Renaissance* (Leiden: Brill, 1991), 61.

answer to Guelf. Bruni retains the Roman use of "republic" as opposed to one-man rule (*unius potestas*), which, he says, prevents genius from flourishing.[79] In principle, Florence's inheritance from Rome gives it the same universality, the same claim to the world, as the empire and the Church. In practice, the genius of Florence keeps it directed upon itself, except for fitful episodes of imperialism. For Bruni, its ambition is to be found in the practice of the liberal arts. Judged by such an end, the Italian principalities and tyrannies could also be found deserving of approval, and so too the emperor and the pope. So Bruni was not a republican ideologue; he did not say with Rousseau that every legitimate government is republican.[80] One might have to say that a republic ordinarily gives a more complete life to a city, but not always or in every circumstance. Bruni's uncivic humanism rules over his civic spirit, limiting his allegiance to a form of government precisely because he demands so much from it. Though he practiced rhetoric, he is not a mere professional rhetorician in the style of Gorgias. Like other humanists, he has absorbed the correction and improvement of rhetoric by Socratic philosophy. His rhetoric is not for sale to any city whatever for any purpose whatever, but it is temporarily on loan to Florence.

Baron was right to say that Bruni was civic-minded, but wrong to think that being civic-minded, in Bruni's opinion and – dare I say? – in truth, always carries one to support republican government. What is civic must be directed by prudence in the situation, as opposed to ideology, which has one solution for all situations. Baron's critics are right to take note of Bruni's adaptability, but wrong if they imply that this means he cannot be civic-minded. It is strange to stress the importance of rhetoric to the humanists and then to dismiss it as unworthy and uninteresting because it is not history. Not every rhetorician is civic, but perhaps it is impossible to be civic without using rhetoric. The adaptability of rhetoric reminds one of the all-around capability of wisdom, which is somehow sovereign over both the civic and rhetoric. It seems to me that on the whole the humanists understood politics better than we do, possibly even better than Machiavelli. We should approach them in a modest spirit.

Neither Bruni nor Machiavelli was a civic humanist, for the very good reason that the combination of civic and humane is impossible without compromising one or the other. What is the civic? Is it what is patriotic or is it what is in accord with moral virtue? Only if one's native country always behaves morally can one make civic and humane coincide. And

---

[79] Bruni, *Laudatio*, 154/247. [80] Rousseau, *Social Contract*, II 6.

such a country would be duty-bound, as we saw in Aristotle's argument, to try to rule the world. What prevents it from doing so would be humane in another sense, the sense of intellectual virtue, that would be precisely uncivic because it would be not a duty or sacrifice but a pleasure, and because it would be not for the common good but for self-perfection. Of course one can speak loosely of civic humanism as humanism which is aware of the claim of the civic, but all humanists, insofar as they listened to Plato, Aristotle, Cicero, or any philosopher in the Socratic tradition, were civic in that way. As humanists, they understood the civic as partly instrumental and subordinate and partly rival to humanism. They never made the error made by today's civic humanists of supposing that the common good never derogates from one's individual good.[81]

Paul Kristeller attempted, unsuccessfully, to stifle civic humanism in its cradle, but his powerful criticism has gained adherents since he first published it in 1955. He warned against a broad use of the term "humanism" in such a way as would connect it with the politics and philosophy of our day – which is just what happened. He argued that humanism was a "peculiarly literary preoccupation" with the *studia humanitatis*; it was the study of a certain set of disciplines and not a certain outlook or philosophy. It was part of, and preoccupied with, the "rhetorical tradition in Western culture." It was a movement of "professional rhetoricians."[82]

"Professional rhetorician" is a useful term of defense against the opinion that the humanist was like an ideologist of our day, who answers all questions from within a simple, universal system, and lacks the suppleness of a rhetorician. But it has perils of its own. It might suggest in the manner of Gorgias that rhetoric is all-powerful or, on the contrary, that rhetoric is a mere instrument without concern for the end for which it is used. In the latter case, one might be tempted to allege that humanism has no connection with what is in a permanent sense humane. But that cannot be so. Kristeller admits, or rather asserts, that humanism has philosophical implications, even that it may contain a "philosophy of man."[83] Somehow humanism in its variety differs from

---

[81] Skinner states the wishful civic humanism succinctly: "if we wish to enjoy as much freedom as we can hope to attain within political society, there is good reason for us to act in the first instance as virtuous citizens, placing the common good above the pursuit of *any* individual or factional ends" (emphasis supplied): "The Republican Ideal of Political Liberty," in *Machiavelli and Republicanism*, 304. For more on this criticism of civic humanism, see Mansfield, *Machiavelli's Virtue*, 31–6, 194–8.

[82] Paul Oskar Kristeller, *Renaissance Thought: The Classic, Scholastic, and Humanist Strains*, rev. ed (New York: Harper and Row, 1961), 10–11, 98.

[83] Ibid., 22, 120; cf. 110. Kristeller's erudition sometimes defeats his formulations.

scholasticism by centering on man rather than God, and in that vague sense it intends to be more humane. The humanists set aside divine revelation, even if they do not proceed in the methodical sense of modern epistemology; they do not regard their main task as that of reconciling human reason with revelation, as did the scholastics. They neither criticize nor devote themselves to Christianity; they accommodate themselves to it. As to the relationship with philosophy, a professional rhetorician in the Renaissance knows from the beginning of Aristotle's *Rhetoric* that rhetoric is the counterpart (*antistrophe*) of dialectic, not altogether distinct from it. And from the same source he would know that the rhetorician must be involved in morality and politics. His reservation against such involvement arises from respect for, if not devotion to, the philosophical life, which is higher – and not from the belief that rhetoric is self-contained and complete in itself like other arts.[84] One cannot repel "civic humanism" with the objection that humanism was neither philosophical nor political. It is rather that the phrase is a dubious combination of two elements in tension.

Bruni indicates that what is humane can never be fully embodied in the civic because it is above civic life; Machiavelli makes it clear that the civic cannot be humane. Bruni's rhetoric allows us to suppose that the civic and the humane might converge, since both are good if not equally good. Machiavelli's rhetoric also exaggerates, but in the contrary direction. He seeks to harden the men of his time and thereafter against two sources of their softness, the ancients and Christianity. So he makes certain that we see that the republican civic spirit is not humane but full of venom and hatred. His republicanism emerges from his deconstruction of the few, the gentlemen or aristocrats who represent morality and civic spirit together. His general advice in politics, found in both *The Prince* and the *Discourses*, is for the prince to ally with the people against the few. Sometimes the result is tyranny modified by the tyrant's desire to make his foundation in the people; sometimes it is a republic led by princes, captains, or tribunes of tyrannical disposition. Neither regime is either civic or humane. Machiavelli is so eager to reject *civic* and *humane* in combination that he denies them in isolation from each other. His contribution to our modern politics is not the combination civic humanism but the alliance of one-man rule and popular consent dating from the sixteenth century or before, which appears in both modern dictatorships and modern republics.

[84] See Aristotle, *Rhetoric*, I 2.1.

CHAPTER 9

*Rhetoric, reason, and republic: republicanisms –
ancient, medieval, and modern*

Cary J. Nederman

The language of classical republicanism has long been recognized as one of the central modes of political discourse in early modern Europe. In returning to the theories as well as practices of the republics of the Greco-Roman world, the early modern republicans sought a model to cope with the tumultuous changes in the politics of their own times.[1] Yet scholars have also come to realize that early modern interest in classical republicanism was hardly exceptional. In many ways, European Renaissance theorists of a "civic humanist" bent were simply carrying forward a republican project which had already commenced during the Latin Middle Ages. Working with largely the same ancient sources as their successors, medieval authors pioneered the republican ideas and language that would be extended and elaborated in the early modern world.[2]

The present study examines some threads of republican theory as it emerged and was restated over more than a millennium and a half. Specifically, the study defends three interrelated claims. First, I argue

Versions of this paper were presented at the Ohio State University and the University of California, Riverside, as well as at the 1997 Annual Meeting of the American Political Science Association in Washington, D.C. Thanks are due to Professors Norma Thompson, Markus Fischer, Ben Fontana, Chris Laursen, and Jim Hankins for their comments on earlier drafts.

[1] See Hans Baron, *The Crisis of the Early Italian Renaissance*, 2 vols. (Princeton: Princeton University Press, 1955) and *In Search of Florentine Civic Humanism*, 2 vols. (Princeton: Princeton University Press, 1988); Zera S. Fink, *The Classical Republicans: An Essay on the Recovery of a Pattern of Thought in Seventeenth-Century England* (Evanston, Ill.: Northwestern University Press, 1962); J. G. A. Pocock, *The Machiavellian Moment* (Princeton: Princeton University Press, 1975).
[2] Quentin Skinner, *The Foundations of Modern Political Thought*, 2 vols. (Cambridge: Cambridge University Press, 1978), I; Skinner, "Ambrogio Lorenzetti: The Artist as Political Philosopher," *Proceedings of the British Academy* 77 (1986): 1–56; Skinner, "The Republican Ideal of Political Liberty," in *Machiavelli and Republicanism*, ed. Gisela Bock, Quentin Skinner, and Maurizio Viroli (Cambridge: Cambridge University Press, 1990); Cary J. Nederman, "The Union of Wisdom and Eloquence before the Renaissance: The Ciceronian Orator in Medieval Thought," *Journal of Medieval History* 18 (1992): 75–95.

247

that the republicanism of antiquity lacked a unitary theoretical starting-point, resting instead on multiple and perhaps incommensurable foundations. Heterogeneous elements may be detected even in the work of a single thinker, such as Marcus Tullius Cicero. A careful examination of Cicero's writings suggests that it may be more appropriate to speak of classical republicanisms. Second, I contend that the gulf between competing versions of classical republicanism was reiterated in differences between late medieval thinkers, such as Marsilius of Padua and Nicholas of Cusa, who were writing within a republican framework. Finally, I demonstrate how the multiplicity of republicanisms also led to fissures in the early modern revival of republican ideals, as revealed in the ambiguous relationship between the works of Niccolò Machiavelli and James Harrington.[3] What unites these three lines of inquiry is the overarching claim that wherever one looks within Western republican discourse – ancient, medieval, or modern – one finds not a single coherent theory, but a diversity of approaches coexisting within an uneasy tension.

This tension is not insignificant. The disparities I detect within classical republican thought generate very different visions of republicanism, both in terms of the duties of governors and the functions of the governed. Regardless of whether such disparities can be reconciled in an ultimate philosophical way (and I remain uncertain about this), we are still confronted with not one but (at least) two paths to classical republicanism, neither of which is more "authentic" or "valid" than the other. Both of these frameworks embrace a conception of the common good as the goal of public affairs, as well as a principle of civic virtue and a doctrine of *vivere civile* – all hallmarks of classical republican thought. To say that one or the other route to republicanism is the "truer" path would simply be absurd, at least as a historical claim (and perhaps as a logical one as well).

In turn, this insight gives us a useful tool for understanding the later dissemination of classical republicanism in the European world. Current scholars have debated widely about the extent of the influence of the classical republican paradigm in more recent times, especially in connection with the development of early modern thought. Some have traced the diffusion of classical republicanism from the Renaissance through to the founding of the American republic, arguing for an essential continuity, a "Machiavellian moment," in the phrase of

---

[3] Permit me to stress that no imputation of historical influence informs this argument. Whether or not succeeding authors read and relied upon their predecessors, I am attempting simply to identify a recurrent intellectual pattern of diversified modes endemic to classical republican theorizing.

J. G. A. Pocock. Others have sternly criticized the view that a uniform revival of classical republicanism may be attributed to the modern world, contending instead that "classical" republicanism must be distinguished from a "modern" variant and that, despite superficial resemblances, different thinkers may be sorted into one or the other category.[4] If I am right, then both interpretations of the later history of classical republicanism are flawed, since each assumes the unified nature of classical republican thought.

RHETORICAL REPUBLICANISM

It is perhaps not too great an exaggeration to say that Marcus Tullius Cicero was the most influential republican thinker of the ancient world. Although many other classical authors contributed significantly to the understanding of the theory and practice of the republic – Polybius, Sallust, and Livy come immediately to mind – Cicero enjoyed the widest audience and most loyal following, both in ancient and in later times. Drawing on Hellenic and Hellenistic philosophies, as well as on his knowledge of Roman history and his personal experiences with the practical requirements of republican rule, Cicero in many ways represented the pinnacle of republican theory as well as statesmanship.[5]

Yet in his political theory, as in his intellectual career more broadly, Cicero underwent a series of changes and developments that lend to his corpus, taken as a whole, a highly unsystematic and perhaps even internally inconsistent quality. (Indeed, this is surely one of the reasons why his reputation as a philosopher and political theorist has been so profoundly tarnished in the twentieth century.) Nowhere is the ambiguous character of Cicero's thought more in evidence than in his republican teachings.[6] In my view, it is possible to isolate two different and competing theoretical defenses of republicanism within the body of his

---

[4] See Paul A. Rahe, *Republics Ancient and Modern: Classical Republicanism and the American Revolution* (Chapel Hill: University of North Carolina Press, 1992).
[5] See Neal Wood, *Cicero's Social and Political Thought* (Berkeley: University of California Press, 1988).
[6] I adopt a neutral stance with regard to the ultimate logical coherence of Cicero's doctrines. It may be that Cicero's thought can be demonstrated to be rigorously cohesive; respected scholars sharply disagree about this. Because of his explicit adherence to the New Academic School of moderate skepticism, Cicero often renders it difficult to gauge his own philosophical principles. On some of these vexed issues, see Julia Annas, "Cicero on Stoic Moral Philosophy and Private Property," in *Philosophia Togata*, ed. Miriam Griffin and Jonathan Barnes (Oxford: Clarendon Press, 1989), 171–3. None of this is directly germane to my present argument, however, since I merely draw attention to important and suggestive differences of emphasis that may be discerned in his various writings – differences that are echoed in later times.

work: one highlighting eloquent speech, the other focusing on the faculty of reason. These divergent positions run parallel to other lingering ambiguities in Cicero's political writings.[7]

The first approach, which is especially prominent in Cicero's writings on rhetoric and oratory, places a premium on public discourse – both among citizens and statesmen – as the basis for the republican regime. In writings such as *De inventione* and *De oratore*, Cicero maintains that the eloquent expression of the common welfare binds the republic together. On the one hand, the leaders of the commonwealth are charged with acquiring the oratorical skills necessary to persuade citizens to accept the laws and policies conducive to the well-being of public affairs. On the other hand, all human beings, regardless of their station, are deemed competent (on the basis of their natural faculties) to discern and judge the pronouncements of orators in public assemblies and proceedings.

Cicero grounds this discursive approach to republican rule on the claim that human nature can only be fully realized through articulate and intelligent speech. While his rhetorical writings do not deny the importance of rationality, they are explicitly critical of the philosophical tradition which glorifies reason to the exclusion or detriment of language. Rather, human beings are both rational and linguistic creatures, simultaneously capable of reasoning and speaking. As Cicero says in the opening paragraph of his youthful *De inventione*, "Wisdom without eloquence leads to very little of value for civic bodies [*civitatibus*], while eloquence without wisdom for the most part performs in an excessive fashion and leads to nothing."[8] Likewise, his mature treatise on rhetoric, *De oratore*, repeatedly subordinates philosophy to oratory, insisting that "eloquence... could never have been attained except by a knowledge of all matters."[9] And even in a nonrhetorical work, such as *De officiis*, he observes that "the fellowship of the entire human race" depends upon a convergence of the rational and linguistic aspects of human nature, "by which the processes of teaching and learning, communicating, discussing and judging associate people together and unite them into a sort of natural fraternity."[10] Speech is, however, accorded primacy in this formulation of human nature:

---

[7] See Walter Nicgorski, "Cicero's Focus: From the Best Regime to the Model Statesman," *Political Theory* 19 (1991): 230–51.
[8] Cicero, *De inventione*, ed. H. M. Hubbell (Cambridge, Mass.: Harvard University Press, 1949), I.1.1. All translations will be my own unless otherwise noted.
[9] Cicero, *De oratore*, ed. E. W. Sutton and H. Rackham, 2 vols. (Cambridge, Mass.: Harvard University Press), II.2.6; cf. II.11.48, II.1.5.
[10] Cicero, *De officiis*, ed. Walter Miller (Cambridge, Mass: Harvard University Press, 1913), I.16.50.

I think that human beings, although lower and weaker than animals in many respects, excel them most by having the power of speech. Therefore, that person appears to me to have won a splendid possession who excels his fellows in that ability by which human beings excel beasts.[11]

It is not enough to possess reason, for rational powers require the faculty of language in order that their discoveries may be disseminated.

In turn, Cicero places eloquent speech at the foundations of human association. In both *De inventione* and *De oratore*, he argues that the very realization of social intercourse requires the activity of an orator acting in concert with his fellow human beings.[12] All human beings possess a potential for sociability implicit in their common rational and linguistic nature. Yet their primordial existence was a scattered and brutish one, devoid of cities, laws, and the fruits of civil community. They would have been destined to remain permanently in this condition, Cicero believes, without the "existence of one from among the infinite multitude of mankind who, either alone or with a few others, could induce what is given to everyone by nature."[13] Such a person was the first orator, who, by the application of reason and eloquence, inspired the establishment of communities, the foundation of cities, and the institution of laws and rights. As Cicero explains:

> At a certain time, a great and wise [*sapiens*] man discovered a natural property contained within the souls of human beings and a great source of opportunity afforded thereby, if one could draw it out and render it better through education ... He transformed them from wild beasts and savages into tame and gentle creatures on account of heeding speech and reason more diligently. It does not seem to me, at least, that a wisdom either silent or lacking speech [*inops dicendi*] could have accomplished the sudden conversion of men from their habits and the conveyance of them into different modes of life ... This seems to be the first birth and lengthy progression of eloquence, and likewise, afterwards, in matters of peace and war it came to be of the greatest utility amongst human beings.[14]

The origins of human association and of oratory are thus identical. Society itself could not have arisen without the primitive orator, who was both a persuasive speaker and a man of special insight and wisdom, capable of recognizing that latent power which existed within all men.

---

[11] Cicero, *De inventione*, I.4.5.   [12] Ibid., I.1 2.2 and Cicero, *De oratore*, I.8.33.
[13] Cicero, *De oratore*, I.8.31.
[14] Cicero, *De inventione*, I.2.2 3. The extent to which this Ciceronian account of the emergence of human social and political relations differs from Aristotle's views has been examined by me in two essays: "Nature, Sin, and the Origins of Society: The Ciceronian Tradition in Medieval Political Thought," *Journal of the History of Ideas* 49 (1988): 3 26; and "The Puzzle of the Political Animal: Nature and Artifice in Aristotle's Political Theory," *Review of Politics* 56 (1994): 283 304.

Cicero urges the latter-day orator to imitate the heroism of his archetype, not only by discovering what is truly good for his fellow creatures, but also by communicating it to them in the most forceful and convincing manner so that they may put it to use. His writings consistently ascribe to the successors of the primeval orator a special duty to maintain and defend the principles of communal life. In *De inventione*, he declares that "eloquence is to be studied . . . all the more vigorously, lest evil men are the most powerful to the detriment of good men and the common disaster of everyone . . . For this [eloquence] attains the greatest advantage for the republic if wisdom, the director [*moderatrix*] of all matters, is present."[15] Likewise, *De oratore* proclaims: "The direction [*moderatione*] and wisdom of the perfect orator preserves not only his own dignity, but also the well-being of most individuals and of the whole republic."[16] It would seem to be precisely the combination of eloquence and wisdom characteristic of the orator which assures that he will speak on behalf of the interests of the entire community. Here a direct contrast between oratory and philosophy is invoked. The philosopher may know the good, but lacks the skill or training to convey it to the multitude. Instead, Cicero states that the realm of so-called "practical philosophy" (philosophy touching on *vita atque mores*) falls more properly within the domain of the orator than of the philosopher.[17] Inherent in the subject-matter of oratory, then, is a regard for fellow citizens which imposes upon the orator an overarching duty to act in the service of public welfare.

The function of oratory, of course, is "to speak in a manner suited to persuade an audience."[18] In the case of deliberative rhetoric – speech which is concerned with "political debate and involves the expression of an opinion"[19] – persuasion must be centered on presentation of one's views in a manner appealing to the whole of the citizen body in order to obtain public assent. Thus, as Cicero remarks in *De optimo genere oratorum*, "The supreme orator is the one whose speech instructs, delights, and moves the minds of his audience . . . To move them [the audience] is indispensible."[20] The orator can only achieve this goal, in turn, by expressing himself in the popular idiom. Oratory

is concerned in some measure with the common usage, custom, and speech of humankind, so that, whereas in all other arts that which is most excellent is

---

[15] Cicero, *De inventione*, I.4.5.   [16] Cicero, *De oratore*, I.8.34.   [17] Ibid., I.15.68–9.
[18] Cicero, *De inventione*, I.5.7.   [19] Ibid.
[20] Cicero, *De optimo genere oratorum*, ed. H. M. Hubbell (Cambridge, Mass.: Harvard University Press, 1949), I.3–4.

farthest removed from the understanding and mental capacity of the untutored, in oratory the very cardinal sin is to depart from the language of everyday life and the usage approved by the sense of the community.[21]

This may even involve the employment of techniques, such as emotional appeals and the manipulation of one's voice, that stand beyond purely rational discourse. Cicero thereby assumes that the orator is beholden to the public whom he seeks to convince. It is one's fellow citizens who, by listening and being moved (or unmoved), are the ultimate arbiters of the republic's honor and advantage, those ends which Cicero regards as the proper subject-matter of deliberative rhetoric.[22] The orator necessarily defers to his audience, rather than commanding them.

In sum, Cicero's account of the discursive foundations of public life ties the role of the statesman to a clear notion of citizenship and civic intercourse. In the discursive view, statesmanship is assimilated to oratory: the man of public affairs is called upon to persuade his fellow citizens to follow the wisest course of action in order to achieve the common good. Eloquent speech must, therefore, be cultivated alongside wisdom as a prized asset for political life; the statesman requires these qualities in order to appeal to and convince an audience. Likewise, even though ordinary citizens may lack the talent and skill of the orator, they are deemed to be competent to judge between competing arguments within the public arena and to choose in accordance with the best and most persuasive (that is, the wisest) case that they hear. Thus, citizenship ought to be construed in an active sense: statesmen seek the approval of citizens, who, by virtue of their inherently rational and linguistic faculties, are all qualified to discern the public good. Public life is a kind of recapitulation of the initial entry of human beings into the social and political order. Hence, this discursive approach has overtly participatory implications; it encourages political actors to conceive of their roles in terms of open rational persuasion and debate leading towards the civic recognition of the public good.

THE RATIONAL REPUBLIC

By contrast, Cicero's alternative account of the foundations of republicanism, which becomes apparent in his philosophical works that are more heavily infused with Stoicism, emphasizes the centrality of reason

---

[21] Cicero, *De oratore*, I.3.12. [22] Cicero, *De inventione*, II.51.157.

alone as the source of public welfare, and concomitantly diminishes the active and discursive dimensions of citizenship.[23] In this version of republicanism, natural reason forms the cornerstone of human social relations. The role of reason is to discover those precepts of natural law that maintain and strengthen the bonds of communal order, and to impose such dictates through law and rulership in a manner consonant with the public good. Of course, Cicero acknowledges that reason is unevenly distributed among human beings. While all people may be minimally rational, some exceed their fellows in the exercise of reason, a fact which qualifies the wise to ascend to positions of authority within the civic body. Indeed, in a well-ordered regime, those lacking fully developed powers of reason ought freely to accede to governance by their betters, on the grounds that wise rule is the strongest safeguard of the common good. The rational powers of statesmen guide the republic for the benefit of citizens, and the people are best governed when they defer to magistrates of superior wisdom.

Cicero's philosophical writings tend to highlight the Stoic-derived view that human beings are inherently rational creatures and that their natural powers of reason constitute the precondition for all social intercourse and political community. In *De finibus*, he declares that

> among the many points of difference between man and the beasts, the greatest difference is that nature has bestowed on man the gift of reason ... It is reason that ... has prompted the individual, starting from friendship and family affection, to expand his interests, forming social ties first with his fellow citizens and later with all mankind.[24]

Similarly, he states in *De legibus* that the human creature "is the only one among so many different kinds and varieties of living beings who has a share in reason and thought, while the rest are deprived of it ... There is nothing better than reason," and hence, it yields the foundation for "that which forms the bond between human beings, that which forms the natural fellowship between them."[25] The centrality of reason is proven, for Cicero, by its divine origin: the rational faculty is what human beings share in common with the gods.[26] Through the medium of nature, the gods instill in all of humankind the "divine element" of

---

[23] On Cicero's relation to the Stoics, see Marcia L. Colish, *The Stoic Tradition from Antiquity to the Early Middle Ages*, second edn, 2 vols. (Leiden: Brill, 1990), I: 61–158.

[24] Cicero, *De finibus*, ed. H. Rackham (Cambridge, Mass.: Harvard University Press, 1931), II.14.45.

[25] Cicero, *De legibus*, ed. C. W. Keyes (Cambridge, Mass.: Harvard University Press, 1928), I.7.22–3, I.5.16.

[26] Ibid., I.7.23 and Cicero, *De finibus*, V.13.28.

reason, which distinguishes people from the remainder of the animal world.

According to Cicero, reason is essential and natural to the human species and its communal life on three counts. First, human beings congregate because reason reveals to them the advantages which stem from cooperation. Cicero explains at great length that when rational creatures work together, discernible benefits abound: protection from the elements and the improvement of productive capacities, no less than the pleasures of social intercourse and the advantages of economic exchange. Reason teaches that persons can live a materially more satisfactory existence in a community than under conditions of solitude.[27] But Cicero also recognizes that rational self-interest is an insufficient basis for a stable and harmonious society. He remarks that "just as we obtain great utility from consent and cooperation among men, so there is no pestilence as detestable as that which men have wrought upon men."[28] If self-interest alone were at the heart of social relations, then no community would endure, since men would only cooperate when it suited them and they would always try to take advantage of or even oppose their fellows whenever personal gain so dictated. Natural reason seeks to resolve this dilemma in two ways: first, through the discovery and dissemination of the virtues, especially justice; and second, by means of the appointment of governors and the formulation of laws whose purpose is to maintain social order by imposing justice upon the community.

Cicero maintains that society, and hence our very capacity to conceive of a public welfare, depends on the cultivation of virtue. He observes that "since, therefore, one may have no doubt how men may be both most helpful and most harmful to men, I state that virtue exists for this reason: to reconcile the minds of men and to bind them to each one's aid."[29] Virtue is directly dependent, in turn, upon the cultivation of the rational faculties: "Virtue is defined as the perfection of reason."[30] Hence, the mark of a harmonious communal setting is the presence of virtue as an ingrained feature of its organization. Cicero singles out and concentrates upon justice, identifying it as the virtue most crucial to the perpetuation of human association. He proclaims that "there is nothing more illustrious nor of wider range than the bond between human beings and the sort of fellowship and useful intercommunication and love among human beings, which . . . is termed justice."[31] In Cicero's view, "the society of humans amongst themselves and the quasi-

---

[27] Cicero, *De officiis*, I.4.12 and Cicero, *De legibus*, I.8.25 6. [28] Cicero, *De officiis*, II.5.16.
[29] Ibid., II.16.17. [30] Cicero, *De finibus*, V.14.38. [31] Ibid., V.23.65.

communal life are maintained" solely on the basis of adherence to just precepts.[32] The absolute prerequisite of social organization is the presence of a commonly recognized and respected principle of justice.

The Ciceronian conception of justice becomes more fully comprehensible when viewed in light of the doctrine of natural law. Cicero holds that nature imposes upon us a certain code or measure of conduct, constituted in particular by the requirement to promote the ends and interests of human society. This idea he expresses by reference to natural law. The commission of an injury (such as theft or fraud) constitutes a violation of natural law precisely because it "is necessarily disruptive of that which is most in accordance with nature, the generation of human society."[33] It is in order to prevent perpetual endangerment to the bonds of society that the law of nature is afforded prescriptive force. Cicero contends that recognition of the dictates of justice emerges "much more effectively from natural reason itself, which is law for human beings and divinity alike."[34] To know what accords with the law of nature, and hence what behavior is required by justice, one reasons about the common good. Our duty on the basis of natural law is always to act in the general welfare when there exists a conflict between private benefit and the general interests of society. Because by "nature there are interests that all have in common," Cicero asserts that "we are all subject to one and the same natural law" and that "we are certainly forbidden to harm another person on the basis of natural law."[35] The Ciceronian doctrine of natural law codifies and authorizes the obligation stemming from justice to value social fellowship above all else.

It is one matter to identify such an obligation, of course, and quite another to enforce it effectively. This is why reason also authorizes the creation of political power to supplement and actualize the sociability natural to human beings. Since the impulse to associate may be diverted by the harm which individuals are capable of causing to one another, Cicero contends that no assurance exists that social relations will continue if left to themselves. In order to remedy the abuses which would have occurred in primitive society, he explains, kings were first appointed and, later, laws were established. In earliest times, Cicero claims, rulers possessed the greatest personal virtue: "Those were formerly selected for rulership who were most just in the opinion of the multitude."[36] Such highly esteemed moral character was necessary because government was conducted without reference to statutory law.

[32] Cicero, *De officiis*, I.7.20.   [33] Ibid., III.5.21 2.   [34] Ibid., III.5.23.   [35] Ibid., III.6.27.
[36] Ibid., II.12.41.

Instead, kings ruled on the basis of their virtuous knowledge of the laws of nature upon which equitable social order was grounded.

But Cicero also recognizes that entrusting unlimited political power to kings was a precarious enterprise. Primitive kingship functioned effectively so long as "a just and good man" occupied the throne. When communities failed to generate such a ruler, however, "laws were invented which would speak to everyone at the same time with the same voice... The reason for constitutional laws is the same as that for kings. For equitable right is always sought."[37] A legal system was substituted for personalized political rule, but the fundamental purpose of both was identical: to guarantee that justice is done and hence that the community is safeguarded. In this sense, the civic law, like the good ruler, must conform to the natural law and the dictates of justice. The special character of civil law, as distinct from natural law, stems from its applicability to persons as citizens rather than as members of the human species. But civil law ought neither to violate the precepts of natural law nor to exempt citizens from their social duties. As Cicero says, "Civil law is not always the same as universal [that is, natural] law; still, universal law should be the same as civil law."[38] The statutes of communities must embrace and cohere with the requirements of what Cicero describes as *verum ius*: civil law is not the product of arbitrary human determination, but reflects a framework engendered by reason.[39] Even when positive law does not prohibit acts which are injurious, no one may engage in such conduct precisely because it is "still forbidden by natural law."[40] In sum, since the purpose of human law is to bring social arrangements into line with the dictates of justice, civil statutes are both subordinate to natural law and lend support to it.

Cicero's privileging of reason consequently yields a basis for civic association different from the one we observed in the case of his rhetorical views. Certainly, he believes that all human beings share in the faculty of reason, and therefore are equal in their capacity to grasp what is just and lawful. In turn, "those for whom these things [reason, justice and law] are held in common are part of the same city (*civitas*)," he remarks in *De legibus*.[41] But it is obvious that all people are not equally rational, and therefore virtuous and law-abiding. This is explained by the fact that reason must be drawn out and improved, until the point when it demonstrates wisdom; and many individuals lack the instruction to realize the potential lying within their faculty. "If bad habits and false

---

[37] Ibid., II.12.41-2. [38] Ibid., III.17.69. [39] Cicero, *De legibus*, I.15.42-16.45.
[40] Cicero, *De officiis*, III.17.69. [41] Cicero, *De legibus*, I.7.23.

beliefs did not twist the weaker minds and turn them in whatever direction they are inclined," Cicero observes, "No one would be so like himself as all men would be like all others."[42] Yet, whatever equality human beings enjoy by birth is in effect eradicated by differences of circumstance, so that wisdom is ultimately achieved by a very few persons, and the multitude remain in a state of ignorance.

The distinction between the wise and the foolish has important implications for the foundations of the republic. Since civil law, properly speaking, has a rational origin in "what is true and just," according to Cicero, only those statutes that are framed and approved by the wise should be counted as valid.[43] Law exists not when it is formally promulgated, but rather when it is established "in the mind of the wise [*in mentes sapientis*]."[44] As *De legibus* explains:

If ignorant and inexperienced people have prescribed deadly poisons in place of true medicines, these cannot be called the prescriptions of physicians; so neither in a people can a statute of any sort be called a law even though the people have accepted it in spite of its being pernicious.[45]

Valid legislation, therefore, must be referred to reason in accordance with nature and justice. No enactment of the multitude, regardless of how overwhelming the popular support, deserves to be accorded respect and obedience unless it is consonant with natural law. And only the wise are qualified to make this determination. As Cicero remarks in *De re publica*, the virtuous ruler "considers the welfare of the people rather than their wishes."[46]

Here one finds the theoretical underpinnings of the *optimates* ("best men") in whose hands Cicero regards the security of government to reside.[47] The well-ordered republic of Cicero's *De re publica* – the constitution most in conformity with nature – was the creation of individuals who "fostered the precepts and discoveries of the wise."[48] Indeed, Cicero reserves the highest praise for the statesman who applies wisdom to the art of politics: "Even though a quiet life devoted to study and the noblest arts will seem happiest to some, the civil life is surely more laudable."[49] In turn, the ideal constitution is balanced and harmonious when the "best men" (embodied by the senate of the republic) enjoy the influence appropriate to their superior learning. *De re publica* commends that stage

[42] Ibid., I.10.29.   [43] Ibid., II.5.11 12.   [44] Ibid., II.5.11.   [45] Ibid., II.5.13.
[46] Cicero, *De re publica*, ed. C. W. Keyes (Cambridge, Mass.: Harvard University Press, 1928), V.6.8.
[47] See Wood, *Cicero's Social and Political Thought*, 194 7.   [48] Cicero, *De re publica*, III.4.7.
[49] Ibid., III.3.6.

in the growth of the republican system when "supreme authority was in the senate with the sufferance and obedience of the people"; and he bemoans the popular grasping after power (in the name of liberty) that leads to the decline in the concord afforded by the republic.[50]

Hence, the rational conception of the republic promotes a passive conception of citizenship as well as an exalted idea of statesmanship. While all human beings are deemed minimally rational, Cicero regards the powers of reason of most of them to be insufficient for sharing directly in the judgment of the common good. Rather, it is up to the statesman, with his wisdom and superior virtue, to serve the public welfare by pioneering and preserving just institutions. There is little requirement that the rational statesman explain himself to, or seek the overt approval of, the citizen body; his responsibility is to a higher wisdom that is valid regardless of public opinion. Indeed, given the distinction between the ignorance of the multitude and the wisdom of the virtuous few, a direct appeal by a statesman to the masses would almost certainly be an act of demagoguery or tyranny, an attempt to destabilize the order of the republic. To employ decidedly modern terminology, the rational statesman governs on behalf, not at the behest, of citizens. The orator, by contrast, can only lead the citizen body by the force of his eloquence, and must accede to the popular will.

REPUBLICANISMS REVISITED: MARSILIUS AND CUSA

The differences in emphasis between the two formulations of Ciceronian republicanism were to be replayed throughout the later history of classical republican thought. This is evident when we turn to two late medieval figures who developed republican themes: Marsilius of Padua and Nicholas of Cusa. Marsilius's republican credentials, and in particular his debt to Cicero, in his *magnum opus*, the *Defensor pacis* (1324), have been well established.[51] Likewise, scholars have noted the extent of Nicholas's dependence upon Marsilian republicanism in his fifteenth-century *De concordantia catholica*.[52] But though superficially borrowing

---

[50] Ibid., II.36.61, III.13.23.
[51] Alan Gewirth, "Republicanism and Absolutism in the Thought of Marsilius of Padua," *Medioevo* 5 (1979): 23–48; Cary J. Nederman, "Nature, Justice and Duty in the *Defensor pacis*: Marsiglio of Padua's Ciceronian Impulse," *Political Theory* 18 (1990): 615–37.
[52] Paul E. Sigmund, "The Influence of Marsilius of Padua on XVth Century Conciliarism," *Journal of the History of Ideas* 23 (1962): 392–402; Jeannine Quillet, "Le *Defensor pacis* de Marsile de Padoue et le *De Concordantia Catholica* de Nicolas de Cues," in *Nicolò Cusano agli inizi del mondo moderno. Atti del Congresso internazionale in occasione del V centenario della morte di Nicolò Cusano. Bressanone, 6–10 September 1964* (Florence: Sansoni, 1970), 485–506.

from the *Defensor pacis* to develop his own arguments, Nicholas's departures from his source indicate a repetition of the tension between the discursive and rational versions of classical republicanism that I have detected in Cicero.

In the *Defensor pacis*, Marsilius stresses the linguistic foundations of the community, following Cicero's account of the formation of the human community as a consensual process in which the multitude is convinced to join into bonds of social and political cooperation by the "persuasion and exhortation" of oratorically gifted individuals, who "guided others successively or simultaneously to the formation of a perfected community, to which human beings are naturally inclined so that they readily complied with this persuasion."[53] In turn, Marsilius ascribes to discourse a continuing role in the conduct of public affairs, as a sort of recapitulation of the original foundation of the community. The framing of legislation, for example, he regards as a function of public speech. He stipulates that draft statutes are to be framed by prudent persons (*prudentes*) who, by virtue of their leisure and superior experience, are best qualified to discover just and useful laws.[54] Yet the wisdom of the few does not entitle them to enact legislation on behalf of the general mass of citizens. Rather,

> Although the multitude cannot by itself discover true and useful matters, still it can discern and judge what is discovered and proposed to it by others, as to whether there should be additions or subtractions or complete changes or rejection. For many things which a man could not initiate or discover by himself can be comprehended and completed after they have been explained to him by someone else.[55]

Thus, the whole body of citizens (which Marsilius terms the *legislator humanus*) must consent to draft statutes in order to give them the status of "coercive commands," that is, laws which the community is obligated to obey.[56]

The *Defensor pacis* ascribes to oratory two pivotal functions in the process of a "bill becoming a law." First, it is assigned to the *prudentes*, when they present their legislative proposals to the citizen body, to "explain" publicly the measures they have recommended; and their fellow citizens are likewise bound to "listen attentively" to the arguments given.[57] The *prudentes* in effect play the role created by the

---

[53] Marsilius of Padua, *Defensor pacis*, ed. C. W. Previté-Orton (Cambridge: Cambridge University Press, 1928), II.22.15. My translations, although often revised, rely upon *Marsilius of Padua: The Defender of Peace*, trans. Alan Gewirth (New York: Columbia University Press, 1956).
[54] Marsilius, *Defensor pacis*, I.12.2, I.13.4.   [55] Ibid., I.13.7.   [56] Ibid., I.10.4 5.   [57] Ibid., I.13.7.

primordial orator: they must attempt to persuade the assembly of citizens that the draft statutes are consistent with justice and contribute to the common good, while it is left to the multitude, whose powers of reason are less well developed, to reflect upon the justifications presented to them and to approve (or withhold approval from) laws. Second, Marsilius views the occurrence of legislative authorization as an occasion for general public discussion and debate amongst the members of the civic body. He contends that:

> if any citizen thinks that something should be added, subtracted, adjusted or completely rejected, he can say [*dicere*] so . . . In the general assembly of citizens, those citizens will have been heard who have wished to make some reasonable statements with regard to them.[58]

Marsilius thereby insists that the whole citizen population must have an opportunity to speak about the matters of communal concern placed before it, and that the words of the populace are ultimately binding. Lest "partiality" creep into the legislative process, the entire citizen body is to enjoy a say in the laws by which it will be governed.[59]

Nicholas of Cusa's adaptation of Marsilius's teachings in *De concordantia catholica* scrupulously excises the discursive dimensions ascribed by the *Defensor pacis* to the process of public deliberation and decision-making. Nicholas instead emphasizes the rational foundations of social and political community. Insisting that reason distinguishes human beings from animals, he asserts that "the exercise of their reason" led men to form associations, adopt laws, and appoint rulers.[60] Human reason, Nicholas maintains, provides access to the precepts of natural law that guides all valid political institutions and powers. But reason is not equally distributed among human beings. Some are "better endowed with reason," and these "wiser and more outstanding men are chosen as rulers by the others to draw up just laws by the clear reason, wisdom and prudence given to them by nature and to rule the others by these laws."[61] Consequently, Nicholas posits a strict distinction between the wise few and the foolish multitude which dictates that the latter can play no direct role in their own rule: "Almighty God has assigned a certain natural servitude to the ignorant and stupid so that they readily trust the wise to help them preserve themselves."[62] Reason dictates the dominance of the few over the many.

[58] Ibid., I.13.8. [59] Ibid., I.12.6, I.13.8.
[60] Nicholas of Cusa, *The Catholic Concordance*, trans. Paul E. Sigmund (Cambridge: Cambridge University Press, 1991), III.Pro.268.
[61] Ibid., II.14.127. [62] Ibid., III.Pro.271.

Nicholas's argument remains within the confines of republicanism to the extent that he embraces a "populist" doctrine of jurisdiction in conjunction with a theory of mixed government.[63] He bases his views, in turn, on the claim that all people – even the most ignorant – are nevertheless held to assent to the terms of their governance, both originally and on a continuing basis. According to Nicholas, the "enslavement" of the ignorant to the wise does not undercut the voluntary character of political arrangements: "Those better endowed with reason are the natural lords and masters of the others but not by any coercive law or judgment imposed on someone against his will."[64] Rather, less rational human beings must in some fashion consent to their own servitude. Since men are equal by nature in power and freedom, Nicholas declares, "the true properly ordered authority of one common ruler . . . cannot be naturally established except by the election and consent of the others, and law is also established by consent."[65] Yet this volitional basis of political community is not deemed by Nicholas to be participatory in character. The consent of the masses in his account has the wholly formal character of silent submission and deference. Insofar as the wise enjoy a privileged access to the reason by which all are governed, there is no cause for public speech or deliberation on the part of the multitude. The wise are instead the natural trustees of the common good: "The rule of the wise and the subjection of the ignorant are harmonized through common laws that have the wise as their special authors, protectors, and executors, and the concurrent agreement of all the others in voluntary subjection."[66] Law and rulership rest upon the rational foundation of natural law that the wise few are particularly qualified to discover and uphold.

REPUBLICANISMS RESTATED: MACHIAVELLI AND HARRINGTON

The late medieval dichotomy within republicanism – that between discursive and rationalistic conceptions of governance – prefigures a similar division among early modern adherents to the classical republican tradition, perhaps illustrated most strikingly by the works of Niccolò Machiavelli and James Harrington. According to Pocock, Harrington

---

[63] See Brian Tierney, *Religion, Law, and the Growth of Constitutional Thought, 1150–1650* (Cambridge: Cambridge University Press, 1982), pp. 66–71; James M. Blythe, *Ideal Government and the Mixed Constitution in the Middle Ages* (Princeton: Princeton University Press, 1992), pp. 253–8; and Antony Black, "Christianity and Republicanism: From St. Cyprian to Rousseau," *American Political Science Review* 91 (1997): 652.

[64] Nicholas of Cusa, *The Catholic Concordance*, II.14.127.   [65] Ibid.   [66] Ibid., III.Pro.275.

walks directly in Machiavelli's footsteps, circulating classical republicanism beyond the confines of Italian (especially, Florentine) writers, into the English tradition, and eventually across the Atlantic.[67] Harrington is a key player in the early modern revival of classical republicanism, distinctive for the way in which he Anglicizes Machiavelli, rendering the latter palatable to his audience.

Pocock's reading of Harrington has lately been challenged by a number of scholars on a range of grounds. Jonathan Scott has argued that in substance Harrington is really more indebted to that antirepublican, Hobbes, than to Machiavelli, in spite of the words of praise reserved for the latter and the scorn heaped on the former.[68] Although Paul Rahe and Gary Remer find different grounds for this disjunction between Machiavelli and Harrington, they share Scott's basic conclusion that Harrington was *not* a classical republican, but instead pioneered a distinctively modern republican framework whose similarities to its classical predecessor are mainly superficial.[69]

I argue that both approaches to Harrington (and by extension, Machiavelli) are flawed in precisely the same way, that is, to the extent that they adopt a unitary and prescriptive view of the nature of classical republicanism. In my view, Machiavelli and Harrington each may be counted as classical republicans, albeit in very different senses: Machiavelli draws upon the discursive dimensions of classical republican thought, whereas Harrington's republicanism relies more heavily upon the rationalist strain. In this sense, both authors deserve a place in an account of the early modern retrieval of classical republican doctrines (*pace* Scott, Rahe, and Remer), even as their republicanisms take on distinct complexions that cannot be equated or assimilated (*pace* Pocock).

It is well known that one of the central themes of Machiavelli's *Discourses* is the defense of the view that the popular elements within the community form the best safeguard of civic liberty as well as the most reliable source of decision-making about the public good.[70] In particu-

---

[67] Pocock, *The Machiavellian Moment*, 383–400; James Harrington, *The Political Works of James Harrington*, ed. J. G. A. Pocock (Cambridge: Cambridge University Press, 1977), pp. 6–42.

[68] Jonathan Scott, "The Rapture of Motion: James Harrington's Republicanism," in *Political Discourse in Early Modern Britain*, ed. Nicholas Phillipson and Quentin Skinner (Cambridge: Cambridge University Press, 1993).

[69] Rahe, *Republics Ancient and Modern*, 409–29; Gary Remer, "James Harrington's New Deliberative Rhetoric: Reflection of an Anticlassical Republican," *History of Political Thought* 14 (1995): 532–57.

[70] For a convenient summary, see Mark Hulliung, *Citizen Machiavelli* (Princeton: Princeton University Press, 1983), 32–5.

lar, Machiavelli contrasts the constancy and trustworthiness of the people, who are often accused of fickleness and ineptitude, with the improbity of the nobility, who are commonly regarded to be the "natural" leaders of a republic. What permitted Rome to avoid public corruption and to extend its empire for so many centuries, Machiavelli believes, was precisely the fact that ordinary citizens demanded and were accorded such a large hand in public determinations. The people thus thwarted the use by patricians of public power to pursue private interests. The apparent "tumults" between the popular and elite segments of the Roman population were in fact the key to Rome's success.[71]

Machiavelli's praise for the role of the people in securing the republic is supported by his confidence in the generally illuminating effects of public speech upon the citizen body.[72] Near the beginning of the first *Discourse*, he notes that some may object to the extensive freedom enjoyed by the Roman people to assemble, to protest, and to veto laws and policies. But he responds that the Romans were able to maintain liberty and order because of the people's ability to discern the common good when it was shown to them. At times when ordinary Roman citizens wrongly supposed that a law or institution was designed to oppress them, they could be persuaded that:

> their beliefs are mistaken . . . [through] the remedy of assemblies, in which some man of influence gets up and makes a speech showing them how they are deceiving themselves. And as Tully says, the people, although they may be ignorant, can grasp the truth, and yield easily when told what is true by a trustworthy man.[73]

The reference to Cicero (one of the few in the *Discourses*) confirms that Machiavelli has in mind here a key feature of classical republicanism: the competence of the people to respond to and support the words of the gifted orator when he speaks truly about the public welfare.

Machiavelli returns to this theme and treats it more extensively at the end of the first *Discourse*. In a chapter intended to demonstrate the superiority of popular over princely government, he argues that the people are well-ordered, and hence "prudent, stable and grateful," so long as room is made for public speech and deliberation within the

---

[71] Niccolò Machiavelli, *The Chief Works and Others*, ed. Allan Gilbert (Durham, N.C.: Duke University Press, 1965), 200 3.

[72] In a volume that came to hand too late for me to make proper use of it, Maurizio Viroli argues at length for the importance of the background of classical rhetoric to the understanding of all of Machiavelli's political writings. See *Machiavelli* (Oxford: Oxford University Press, 1998), 73 113.

[73] Machiavelli, *The Chief Works and Others*, 203.

community. Citing the formula *vox populi, vox dei*, Machiavelli insists that:

> public opinion is remarkably accurate in its prognostications . . . With regard to its judgment, when two speakers of equal skill are heard advocating different alternatives, very rarely does one find the people failing to adopt the better view or incapable of appreciating the truth of what it hears.[74]

Not only are the people competent to discern the best course of action when orators lay out competing plans, but they are in fact better qualified to make decisions, in Machiavelli's view, than are princes. For example, "the people can never be persuaded that it is good to appoint to an office a man of infamous or corrupt habits, whereas a prince may easily and in a vast variety of ways be persuaded to do this."[75] Likewise, should the people depart from the law-abiding path, they may readily be convinced to restore order: "For an uncontrolled and tumultuous people can be spoken to by a good man and easily led back into a good way. But no one can speak to a wicked prince, and the only remedy is steel . . . To cure the malady of the people words are enough."[76] The contrast Machiavelli draws is stark. The republic governed by words and persuasion – in sum, ruled by public speech – is almost sure to realize the common good of its citizens; and even should it err, recourse is always open to further discourse. Nonrepublican regimes, because they exclude or limit discursive practices, ultimately rest upon coercive domination and can only be corrected by violent means.

Just as Nicholas of Cusa carefully excised the linguistic dimension of Marsilius's republican theory, so James Harrington's *The Commonwealth of Oceana* (1656) seems to have detoured around the discursive elements of Machiavelli's classical republicanism, even as the work lauds the Florentine for having "retrieved" the prudence of the ancients.[77] But Harrington's elision, unlike Nicholas's, is conscious and explicit; in preferring the government of Venice to that of Rome, and to a lesser extent, Sparta to Athens, he manifests overt hostility to public speech. Rome and Athens, he asserts, were both ruined by the "storms" arising from the "debate of the people."[78] Far preferable is Venice which, like its alleged Lacedaemonian exemplar, never sanctions public debate: "Nor shall any commonwealth where the people in their political capacity is talkative ever see half the days" of Sparta and Venice, "but

[74] Ibid., 316. [75] Ibid. [76] Ibid., 317. [77] Harrington, *Political Works*, 161.
[78] Ibid., 263.

being carried away by vain-glorious men ... swim down the sink."[79] Indeed, in his own ideal commonwealth of Oceana, popular discussion of political affairs is punishable by no less a penalty than death.[80]

Harrington's abhorrence of public speech is tied to a set of premises that we have already identified within the rationalistic side of classical republicanism: namely, that public decision-making must be conducted in accordance with a strict principle of right reason, accessible only to the wise few, who therefore take it upon themselves to serve as guardian of the people for the sake of the common benefit. Harrington expressly distinguishes three concepts of reason – as self-interest, as group interest, and as the interest of the whole – and contends that only the latter should be taken into consideration in the formation of laws and public policies. Following a long quotation from Hooker, Harrington concludes, "There is a common right, law of nature, or interest of the whole, which is more excellent, and so acknowledged to be by the agents themselves, than the right or interest of the parts only."[81] But the problem is how the "common right" may safely be discovered and converted into the law of the land. In Harrington's view, this cannot be achieved by the people as a whole, since he observes that nature itself generates clear differences between human beings and, in particular, produces a "natural aristocracy" of the wise who are clearly more adept in their faculties of understanding. This group of individuals,

> though it be small, will be discovered and ... lead the herd ... Wherefore this can be no other than a natural aristocracy diffused by God throughout the whole body of mankind to this end and purpose, and therefore such as the people have not only a natural but a positive obligation to make use of as their guides.[82]

As with Nicholas, Harrington thinks that the foolish or ignorant will – especially in times of "common concernment, difficulty or danger" – recognize that it is desirable to be led by the "excellent parts" in whom special "virtue or authority" resides.[83]

Harrington institutionalizes this distinction between the wise few and the foolish multitude in his construction of the constitution of Oceana. The natural leaders form the body of the senate, whereas the foolish are represented in a popular assembly (or "prerogative tribe") composed of 1,050 delegates. The functions of these two groups differ markedly. The senate is charged with debating public affairs and with decreeing laws

[79] Ibid., 264.   [80] Ibid., 251.   [81] Ibid., 171 2.   [82] Ibid., 173.   [83] Ibid., 172 3.

and policies; within its halls, discussion of proposals is to be open and unrestricted, and its members are deemed free to express disparate and conflicting opinions, until some conclusion is achieved.[84] That this will not lead to disorder, Harrington believes, stems from the fact that the procedures of debate will occur strictly in accordance with the precepts of reason, and thus will shun emotional and inflammatory oratory.[85] Senators are also assigned to give to the popular assembly a weekly public lecture which has a purely instructional or pastoral aim, rather than a deliberative goal.[86]

The prerogative tribe, by contrast, performs a completely passive role: strictly enjoined from debating the senate's decrees, its members instead either affirm or reject the proposals presented to them. This has the effect of ensuring that the senators do not attempt to employ their authority to pass measures that reflect either private or group interest.[87] The popular assembly thus has the primary purpose of checking potential abuses of power. But it can do no more than this. Harrington ascribes to the prerogative tribe no positive or active functions; it cannot air grievances, suggest issues or topics for legislation, make any sorts of changes in proposals, nor even question the wisdom of the senatorial decrees. In short, the popular assembly is participatory only in the weakest imaginable sense of expressing a dull "yea" and "nay" to those measures with which it is presented. It cannot even debate amongst its membership the reasons for giving or withholding its consent.[88] Although Harrington, unlike Nicholas of Cusa, lends institutional weight to the process by which the ignorant populace is permitted involvement in government, the prerogative tribe is a far cry from Machiavelli's free people, who must be convinced of the goodness of a course of public action and who are deemed competent to discern between competing points of view. Starting with the principle that reason is a special competence of the few, Harrington's republicanism must exclude public speech from the well-ordered constitution.

---

[84] Ibid., 155 7. [85] Ibid., 266.
[86] Ibid., 283. In this connection, Harrington does mention Machiavelli's reference to Cicero (discussed above) "that the people, albeit not so prone to find out the truth of themselves, as to follow custom or run into error, yet, if they be shown truth, not only acknowledge and embrace it very suddenly, but are the most constant and faithful guardians of it" (284). But Harrington places an emphasis on this passage of the *Discourses* different from that of its original intent: whereas Machiavelli cited Cicero in support of the active and relatively incorruptible role of the people in their own governance, Harrington (true to form) concentrates on the passive mentality of the people who are thereby in need of instruction (regular lectures) by their superiors.
[87] Ibid., 172, 416 17. [88] Ibid., 281 3.

CONCLUSION

In surveying some key moments in the history of classical republicanism, then, it seems unwarranted to adopt a unitary and prescriptive view of classical republican doctrines. As the case of Cicero illustrates, defenses of classical republicanism might issue from competing (and potentially conflicting) theoretical foundations. Thus, disparate later expressions of republicanism – such as one finds in Marsilius, Nicholas, and Harrington as well as Machiavelli – may still be counted equally as classical: some draw upon the discursive dimensions of classical republican thought, whereas others rely more heavily upon the rationalist strain. In this sense, the retrieval of classical republican doctrines involved the dissemination of republicanisms of distinct complexions that resist equivalence or assimilation to a single teaching.

There are perhaps some worthwhile lessons in this historical analysis for contemporary theorists who seek to revive the republican paradigm. Pocock's claim of a direct lineage from classical republicanism to the foundations of the American republic, for instance, becomes more complicated in view of the diversity of such republicanisms available. Should the American appropriation be seen as a debt to the Machiavellian version, with its emphasis on an active populace engaged in public discourse, or to the Harringtonian variant, according to which the citizen body is to bow passively and silently before a natural aristocracy of wise elites? Or ought American republicanism to be regarded as an attempt to effect a compromise (or to chart an entirely different route) in relation to these alternatives?[89] Once we dispense with the assumption that classical republicanism subscribed to a single set of doctrines or premises, we raise new and important issues about the cross-cutting and ambiguous impact of republican thought on more recent political institutions and values.

At the same time, the acknowledgment of multiple, and incongruent, theoretical strands within the classical republican tradition may help to assuage some of the concerns that liberals have expressed about the contemporary revival of republicanism. As Don Herzog has observed, republicans "have advanced a remarkably hazy doctrine," with regard to the mechanisms of public deliberation and participation as well as the content of the common good to be sought.[90] In some ways, this may be

---

[89] Some of these issues are taken up in the articles by C. Bradley Thompson, Karl Walling, and Paul Rahe contained in a symposium on "American Faces of Machiavelli" published in *Review of Politics* 57 (1995): 389–481.

[90] Don Herzog, "Some Questions for Republicans," *Political Theory* 14 (1986): 473, 486–8.

traced to the tendency among current republicans (in one or another communitarian guise) to cling to a unitary model of classical republicanism that obscures the divergent strains within the tradition. To the extent that tensions within republicanism are openly admitted and the relative merits of disparate accounts appraised, it becomes possible to refine the doctrine in a manner more apt to facilitate a convincing response to liberal critics.

In this sense, then – and *pace* Herzog[91] – the history of republican thought *does* matter for contemporary debates. This is not merely because modern republicans, just like liberals, seek the foundations of their own framework in the past. Rather, reflection on the internal tensions that have repeatedly manifested themselves within classical republicanism stimulates recognition of the variety of theoretical options which the tradition affords. What contemporary republicans ought perhaps to seek is not *the* true account of republicanism, but instead the version of republican doctrine that proves to be the most theoretically as well as practically satisfactory, given the political dilemmas and challenges that confront us at the dawn of the twenty-first century.

[91] Ibid., 474–8.

CHAPTER 10

Situating Machiavelli

Paul A. Rahe

Of all the figures in the long, complex, and convoluted history of political thought, none is quite as difficult to situate properly as Niccolò Machiavelli. The problem is by now an old one: it bedeviled interpreters from the outset. It arises in large part because Machiavelli penned not one but two political classics and because they appear to be at odds with one another as to whether virtuous republics are decidedly and in all respects preferable to principalities governed ruthlessly in accord with the ruler's self-interest.

Machiavelli composed his *Prince* and his *Discourses on Livy* in the second decade of the sixteenth century after the collapse of the Florentine republic and the reestablishment of Medici rule. The two works circulated widely in manuscript for some time thereafter, both in Florence and abroad; and, within five years of their author's death in 1527, they were published in Rome under the imprimatur of Machiavelli's patron Clement VII, the second of the two Medici popes.[1] Almost immediately after the appearance of these two works in printed form, an inquisitive English visitor to Florence named Reginald Pole

In citations I have used the standard abbreviations for classical texts provided in *The Oxford Classical Dictionary*, third edition, ed. Simon Hornblower and Antony Spawforth (Oxford: Oxford University Press, 1996). Where appropriate, the ancient texts and more recent works are cited by the divisions and subdivisions employed by the author or introduced by subsequent editors (that is, by book, part, chapter, section number, paragraph, act, scene, line, Stephanus page, or by page and line number). In particular, to make it easier for those who cannot read Italian, I have, where pertinent, included in my citation of Machiavelli's *Discourses on Livy* the paragraph numbers added in the one generally reliable English translation: Niccolò Machiavelli, *Discourses on Livy*, ed. Harvey C. Mansfield and Nathan Tarcov (Chicago: University of Chicago Press, 1996). My own rendering of Machiavelli's Italian will often vary from that of Mansfield and Tarcov but is much indebted to it nonetheless. Unless otherwise indicated, all of the translations are my own. In writing this chapter, I have profited from suggestions made by James Hankins, Vickie B. Sullivan, Robert Eden, William Connell, and James W. Muller.

[1] For the pre-publication and publication history of Machiavelli's works, see Adolph Gerber, *Niccolò Machiavelli: Die Handschriften, Ausgaben und Übersetzungen seiner Werke im 16. und 17. Jahrhundert* (Turin: Bottega d'Erasmo, 1962). It was under the commission of Clement VII that Machiavelli composed the *Florentine Histories*.

was told by one or more of Machiavelli's compatriots that the author of the *Discourses on Livy* had written *The Prince* solely in order to trip up the Medici and bring about their demise. Machiavelli had purportedly acknowledged as much himself. Although Pole was not inclined to entertain this claim,[2] others who learned of the report were perfectly prepared to do so,[3] and the tendency for students of the subject to discount *The Prince* on one ground or another and to treat the *Discourses on Livy* as representative of Machiavelli's real thinking has had adherents ever since – especially in the English-speaking world, where in some quarters Machiavelli's apparent espousal of republicanism has long inspired admiration.

Alberico Gentili is a case in point, and Henry Neville is another. In a scholarly volume on the conduct of embassies, which he dedicated to Sir Philip Sidney and published in 1585, not long before he was created Regius Professor of Civil Law at Oxford University, Gentili singled out as "precious" the *Discourses on Livy*, described their author as "*Democratiae laudator et assertor*," termed him "a very great enemy to tyranny," and claimed that he had written *The Prince* not "to instruct the tyrant but to expose openly his secret deeds and exhibit him naked and clearly recognizable to the wretched peoples." "It was," he explained, "the strategy of this most prudent of all men to educate the people on the pretext of educating the prince."[4] Ninety years thereafter, when Neville

---

[2] See the report in his *Apologia ad Carolum Quintum* (1539), in *Epistolarum Reginaldi Poli*, ed. Angelo M. Quirini, 5 vols. (Brescia: J. M. Rizzardi, 1744 57), I: 137 52 (at 151 2), as cited in L. Arthur Burd, "Introduction," in Niccolò Machiavelli, *Il Principe*, ed. L. Arthur Burd (Oxford: Clarendon Press, 1891), 36 8. The full Latin text of Pole's discussion of Machiavelli has been reprinted as an appendix to Heinrich Lutz, *Ragione di stato und christliche Staatsethik im 16. Jahrhundert* (Münster: Aschendorffsche Verlagsbuchhandlung, 1961), 48 62. In this connection, see Peter S. Donaldson, *Machiavelli and Mystery of State* (Cambridge: Cambridge University Press, 1988), 1 35, 87 8. It is by no means inconceivable that Machiavelli engaged in such special pleading when, towards the end of his life, the Medici were overthrown, the republic was for a brief time restored, and he sought to regain the office he had lost in 1512.

[3] See, for example, Giovanni Matteo Toscano, *Peplus Italiae* (Paris: Morelli, 1578), 52, and André Rossant, *Les meurs, humeurs et comportemens de Henry de Valois* (Paris: P. Mercier, 1589), 11. Although Pole's *Apologia ad Carolum Quintum* was not published in printed form until the eighteenth century, what he said therein almost immediately found its way into diplomatic reports: see *Letters and Papers (Foreign and Domestic) of the Reign of Henry VIII*, ed. J. W. Brewer, James Gairdner, and R. H. Brodie (London: Longmans, 1862 1910), XIV:1, no. 200.

[4] Alberico Gentili, *De legationibus libri tres* (London: Thomas Vautrollerius, 1585), 3.9 (Sig. oiii). The pertinent passage is quoted at length in L. Arthur Burd, "Introduction," in Machiavelli, *Il Principe*, 63 4. For an English translation, see Alberico Gentili, *De legationibus libri tres*, trans. Gordon J. Laing, 2 vols. (New York: Oxford University Press, 1924), II 156. Cf. Diego Panizza, "Machiavelli e Alberico Gentili," *Il pensiero politico* 2 (1969): 476 83, with Donaldson, *Machiavelli and Mystery of State*, 86 110, and then consider, in this connection, Patrick Collinson's account of the manner in which Gentili's English contemporaries were inclined to think of the English polity in republican terms: see "The Monarchical Republic of Queen Elizabeth I," *Bulletin of the John*

published his English translation of Machiavelli's works, he thought it appropriate to invent and add to his edition a letter from the author of *The Prince* describing that work as "both a Satyr against" tyrants, "and a true Character of them."[5] This way of reading Machiavelli was not just a passing phenomenon. In our own day, Garrett Mattingly revived the argument,[6] and he was by no means the last to suggest something of the sort.[7]

In more recent years, however, Anglo-American admirers of Machiavelli's writings in praise of republicanism have tended in another direction, following the lead of Hans Baron and justifying a preference for the *Discourses* over *The Prince* on the less outlandish presumption that the former is the later and the more mature work: the enigma disappears, they contend, if one simply supposes that Machiavelli initially pursued one line of reasoning and then, either upon reflection or in response to altered circumstances, changed his tune.[8] As Professor Connell points out in his contribution to this volume, this approach has not attracted support on the continent.[9] There are dissenters as well in the United States,[10] and it is not difficult to see why. To begin with, it is by no means

---

Rylands University Library of Manchester 69 (1987): 394 424. Traiano Boccalini's satirical account of his contemporaries' response to Machiavelli points in the direction of Gentili's conclusions: see *De'ragguagli di Parnaso* (Venice: P. Farri, 1612 15), 1.89. This work was translated into English in 1626 by William Vaughan and again in 1656 by Henry, earl of Monmouth.

[5] See *The Works of the Famous Nicholas Machiavel, Citizen and Secretary of Florence* (London, 1675), as cited in Felix Raab, *The English Face of Machiavelli: A Changing Interpretation, 1500–1700* (London: Routledge and Kegan Paul, 1964), 218 21 (at 220). For a discussion of the letter's authorship, see ibid., 267 72.

[6] See Garrett Mattingly, "Machiavelli's *Prince*: Political Science or Political Satire?" *The American Scholar* 27 (1958): 482 91.

[7] For variations on these themes with antecedents of their own, see Mary Dietz, "Trapping the Prince: Machiavelli and the Politics of Deception," *American Political Science Review* 80 (1986): 777 99, and Stephen M. Fallon, "Hunting the Fox: Equivocation and Authorial Duplicity in *The Prince*," *Proceedings of the Modern Language Association* 107 (1992): 1181 95.

[8] Consider, for example, Quentin Skinner, *The Foundations of Modern Political Thought*, 2 vols. (Cambridge: Cambridge University Press, 1978), I: *The Renaissance*, 152 86 (esp. 154, n. 1); *Machiavelli* (New York: Hill and Wang, 1981), 21 77, 96 (esp. 96); and "Political Philosophy," in *The Cambridge History of Renaissance Philosophy*, ed. Charles B. Schmitt, Quentin Skinner, Eckhard Kessler, and Jill Kraye (Cambridge: Cambridge University Press, 1988), 389 452 (esp. 430 41), in light of Hans Baron, "Machiavelli the Republican Citizen and Author of *The Prince*," revised and reprinted in Baron, *In Search of Florentine Civic Humanism: Essays on the Transition from Medieval to Modern Thought*, 2 vols. (Princeton: Princeton University Press, 1988), II: 101 51. Baron's essay on Machiavelli, which first appeared in 1961, was intended as a sequel to his two-volume *magnum opus*: *The Crisis of the Early Italian Renaissance: Civic Humanism and Republican Liberty in an Age of Classicism and Tyranny*, 2 vols. (Princeton: Princeton University Press, 1955). See Baron, "The Course of My Studies in Florentine Humanism (1965)," in *In Search of Florentine Civic Humanism*, II, 182 93 (esp. 191 3).

[9] See above, chapter 1.

[10] See, for example, Harvey C. Mansfield, Jr., *Machiavelli's New Modes and Orders: A Study of the Discourses on Livy* (Ithaca: Cornell University Press, 1979), esp. 79, n. 1; Mark Hulliung, *Citizen Machiavelli* (Princeton: Princeton University Press, 1983); Paul A. Rahe, *Republics Ancient and Modern: Classical Republicanism and the American Revolution* (Chapel Hill: University of North

clear that *The Prince* was completed before Machiavelli began the *Discourses*: the evidence regarding composition can most easily be interpreted to suggest that Machiavelli was working on them both at the same time and that each was composed with an eye to the other.[11] Furthermore, even if it could be shown that *The Prince* was in finished form before Machiavelli began to pen the *Discourses*, there would be no doubt that they were written in the same decade in quick succession; there is nowhere even a hint on Machiavelli's part that the *Discourses* constitute a repudiation of *The Prince*; and we have no indication in his letters or elsewhere that he sought to prevent the latter from being circulated and posthumously published. In this matter, the republican wish would appear to be father to the dismissive thought. One cannot so easily escape the quandary that arises from the fact that Machiavelli wrote two seemingly opposed and apparently comprehensive works on the nature of politics.

Even if one could do so, however, the fundamental difficulty would persist, for the author of the *Discourses on Livy* appears to be no less willing than the author of *The Prince* to dispense his advice indiscriminately – not just to republics and their citizens, but to princes, to aspirants to one-man rule, and even to those whom he singles out as tyrants.[12] In any case, as Machiavelli's popular reputation over the centuries would lead

Carolina Press, 1992), 260 7; Victoria Kahn, *Machiavellian Rhetoric: From the Counter-Reformation to Milton* (Princeton: Princeton University Press, 1994), esp. 3 84, 243 8; and Vickie B. Sullivan, *Machiavelli's Three Romes: Religion, Human Liberty, and Politics Reformed* (Dekalb, Ill.: Northern Illinois University Press, 1996).

[11] Note the apparent cross-referencing: Niccolò Machiavelli, *Discorsi sopra la prima deca di Tito Livio*, 2.1.3, 20, 3.19, 42 and *Il principe* 2, 8, in Niccolò Machiavelli, *Tutte le opere*, ed. Mario Martelli (Florence: Sansoni, 1971), 147, 176, 225 6, 250, 258, 269. Then, see Felix Gilbert, "The Composition and Structure of Machiavelli's *Discorsi*," reprinted in Gilbert, *History: Choice and Commitment* (Cambridge, Mass.: Harvard University Press, 1977), 115 33. Although there is much of value to be found in David Wootton, "Introduction," in Niccolò Machiavelli, *The Prince*, ed. and trans. David Wootton (Indianapolis: Hackett Publishing Company, Inc., 1995), xi xliv, I remain unpersuaded by his attempt to explain away the apparent references within *The Prince* to the *Discourses on Livy*.

[12] In considering what to make of Machiavelli's largesse in this particular (*Discorsi* 1.16.3 5, 19, 21, 25 7, 30, 32, 33.5, 40 3, 45.3, 51, 55.5, 2.12 14, 18.5, 20, 23.3, 24, 27 8, 31, 3.3 6, 8, 11, 15, 22 3, 26.2, 27, 29 30, 34.3, 38, 42 4, in *Tutte le opere*, 99 101, 104 6, 108 10, 112 16, 123 8, 133, 138, 161 4, 173, 176, 180 4, 186 88, 191 2, 198 213, 216 17, 221 2, 228 31, 233 7, 242, 246 7, 249 52), one should keep in mind the fact that the *Discourses* are addressed neither to the citizens of republics as such nor to "those who are princes," but rather to "those who, for their infinite good parts, deserve to be" princes for these may, in the end, become princes, as happened in the case of Hiero of Syracuse: see *Discorsi*, Ep. Ded., in *Tutte le opere*, 75. The manner in which the ethos of *The Prince* periodically reappears in the pages of the *Discourses* is all too often ignored by students of the latter: see, for example, Skinner, *The Foundations of Modern Political Thought*, I: 180 6, and *Machiavelli*, 48 77; and the work dedicated to him by his student Maurizio Viroli, *From Politics to Reason of State: The Acquisition and Transformation of the Language of Politics, 1250–1600* (Cambridge: Cambridge University Press, 1992), 154 77.

one to expect, the author of the *Discourses* turns out to be an exceedingly slippery figure even when he appears in classical republican guise.[13] This is already abundantly evident in the preface to the first book of that work. In the opening sentence, Machiavelli presents himself as a revolutionary innovator: he compares himself with Columbus, arguing that it is "no less perilous to discover new modes and orders than to search unknown waters and lands," and contending that the "new modes and orders" which he discovered constitute "a road as yet untrodden by anyone." Then, a few sentences thereafter, he suddenly and unexpectedly reverses course and presents himself as an advocate for a return to patterns of behavior long ago abandoned.

In the latter passage, Machiavelli at first draws attention to the honor accorded in his day to classical antiquity – to the manner in which ancient art was then sought after and imitated, to the degree to which "the civil laws" and the "medicine" of his day, were "nothing other than judgments [*sentenze*] handed down by ancient jurisconsults" and "the experiments carried out by ancient physicians." Then he laments the fact that "in ordering republics, in maintaining states, in governing kingdoms, in ordering the military and administering war, in judging subjects, and in increasing empire, neither prince nor republic is to be found that has recourse to the examples of the ancients." This failure he traces "not so much" to "the weakness [*debolezza*] into which the present religion has conducted the world" or to "the evil done many Christian provinces and cities" by the "ambitious idleness [*ambizioso ozio*]" of the clergy as to his contemporaries not possessing "a true knowledge of histories, through not drawing from reading them that sense nor from savoring them that taste that they have in themselves." In composing an extended commentary on the histories of the Roman writer Livy, Machiavelli would appear to be attempting to make available to his readers the crucial "knowledge" that they lack.[14]

It is no wonder, then, that those inclined to envisage Machiavelli as a partisan of republicanism and to treat the *Discourses on Livy* as his greatest and most revealing work are tempted also to see it as "a wholehearted defence of traditional republican values" presented "in a wholeheartedly traditional way."[15] To conceive of the book in this fashion, however,

---

[13] This was appreciated from the start: see Kahn, *Machiavellian Rhetoric*, 60–165.
[14] Machiavelli, *Discorsi*, 1 Proemio, in *Tutte le opere*, 76.
[15] See Quentin Skinner, "Machiavelli's *Discorsi* and the Pre-Humanist Origins of Republican Ideas," in *Machiavelli and Republicanism*, ed. Gisela Bock, Quentin Skinner, and Maurizio Viroli (Cambridge: Cambridge University Press, 1990), 121–41 (at 141), which is reprinted in slightly revised form as Skinner, "The Vocabulary of Renaissance Republicanism: A Cultural *longue-durée?*" in *Language and Images of Renaissance Italy*, ed. Alison Brown (Oxford: Clarendon Press,

they must ignore or dismiss as a mere rhetorical flourish Machiavelli's claim to have discovered genuinely "new modes and orders" and to have entered upon "a road as yet untrodden by anyone." Whether Machiavelli's thinking with regard to republics is traditional or radically novel deserves extended consideration.

THE REVIVAL OF CLASSICAL REPUBLICANISM

The two most distinguished proponents of the view that Machiavelli was a restorer of classical political norms are J. G. A. Pocock and Quentin Skinner. Since the former's claim that Machiavelli is best understood as an Aristotelian has come under sustained and quite effective assault,[16] and since elsewhere I have myself argued in detail (against Pocock and others) that there is a chasm dividing the species of republicanism that Aristotle observed in classical Greece and the sort that first emerged in Machiavelli's thinking and then was appropriated, further developed, and articulated by his successors in early modern Britain and elsewhere,[17] I will focus my attention here more narrowly on the argument presented by Skinner. In part, I suspect, because Skinner's hypothesis has never been fully presented in a comprehensive work, it has received much less attention than it deserves.[18]

It would be easy to suppose that Skinner accepts Pocock's argument, and they are often lumped together in the secondary scholarship on the history of republicanism by those who have not read closely. This is understandable. Nowhere does Skinner directly challenge Pocock's foundational hypothesis; he consistently refers to *The Machiavellian Moment* as a book to which he owes a considerable debt;[19] and, of

---

1995), 87 110. For a summary statement along the same lines, see Skinner, "Political Philosophy," 434 41. For a more detailed argument to similar effect, see Viroli, *From Politics to Reason of State*, 11 177 (esp. 154 77).

[16] Cf., for example, J. G. A. Pocock, *The Machiavellian Moment: Florentine Political Thought and the Atlantic Republican Tradition* (Princeton: Princeton University Press, 1975), esp. 183 218, with Vickie B. Sullivan, "Machiavelli's Momentary 'Machiavellian Moment': A Reconsideration of Pocock's Treatment of the *Discourses*," *Political Theory* 20 (1992): 309 18.

[17] See Rahe, *Republics Ancient and Modern*, 15 541.

[18] Note, however, John Charvet, "Quentin Skinner on the Idea of Freedom," *Studies in Political Thought* 2 (1993): 5 16, and Alan Patten, "The Republican Critique of Liberalism," *British Journal of Political Science* 26 (1996): 25 44 (esp. 25 36).

[19] See, for example, Quentin Skinner, "The Idea of Negative Liberty: Philosophical and Historical Perspectives," in *Philosophy in History: Essays on the Historiography of Philosophy*, ed. Richard Rorty, J. B. Schneewind, and Quentin Skinner (Cambridge: Cambridge University Press, 1984), 193 221 (at 203, n. 21); "The Paradoxes of Political Liberty," in *The Tanner Lectures on Human Values*, vol. VII, ed. Sterling M. McMurrin (Salt Lake City: University of Utah Press, 1986), 227 50 (at 237, n. 31); and "The Republican Ideal of Political Liberty," in *Machiavelli and Republicanism*, 293 309 (at 300, n. 32).

course, he repeatedly insists that Machiavelli was a "classical republican." It is nonetheless clear from the details of his argument that he is persuaded that Aristotle and Machiavelli must be relegated to two opposed camps. In fact, Skinner's chief aim is to refute as inadequate the widespread presumption summed up in Alasdair MacIntyre's claim that "the crucial moral opposition" to be found in the history of political thought is that "between liberal individualism in some version or other and the Aristotelian tradition in some version or other."[20] This task he pursues by trying to show that such a taxonomy cannot accommodate Machiavelli – who represents a third and highly attractive alternative.

Skinner takes as his starting-point the now familiar distinction, drawn by Jeremy Bentham and elaborated by Isaiah Berlin, between positive and negative liberty: in time-honored fashion, he treats Aristotle and Thomas Aquinas as proponents of positive liberty and Thomas Hobbes and John Locke as proponents of negative liberty.[21] The Aristotelian tradition, he tells us, operates on two premises: "that we are moral beings with certain characteristically human purposes" and that "the human animal is *naturale sociale et politicum*, and thus that our purposes must be essentially social in character." From these premises, it concludes that "we can only be said to be fully or genuinely at liberty . . . if we actually engage in just those activities which are most conducive to *eudaimonia* or 'human flourishing,' and may therefore be said to embody our deepest human purposes."[22] For their part, Hobbes and Locke deny these premises, reject this conclusion, and assert that the only form of liberty worth worrying about is freedom from external constraint. "Much of the debate between those who think of social freedom as a negative opportunity concept and those who think of it as a positive exercise concept may thus be said to stem from a deeper dispute about human nature. The argument is *au fond* about whether we

---

[20] Cf. Alasdair MacIntyre, *After Virtue* (Notre Dame: Notre Dame University Press, 1981), 241, with Skinner, "The Republican Ideal of Political Liberty," 293. Note also Skinner, "The Paradoxes of Political Liberty," 249 (esp. n. 52).

[21] See Skinner, "The Idea of Negative Liberty," 193–221; "The Paradoxes of Political Liberty," 227–50; and "The Republican Ideal of Political Liberty," 293–309. Skinner puts particular emphasis on the example of Hobbes: see Skinner, "Thomas Hobbes on the Proper Signification of Liberty," *Transactions of the Royal Historical Society* 40 (1990): 121–51. His aim is to refute the Hobbesian analysis of negative liberty as it is revived and presented in Isaiah Berlin, *Two Concepts of Liberty: An Inaugural Lecture Delivered Before the University of Oxford on 31 October 1958* (Oxford: Oxford University Press, 1958). See Skinner's own inaugural lecture: *Liberty Before Liberalism* (Cambridge: Cambridge University Press, 1998), 1–11, 59–68, 77–86, 101–20 (esp. 113–16).

[22] Skinner, "The Republican Ideal of Political Liberty," 295–98 (esp. 296).

can hope to distinguish an objective notion of *eudaimonia* or human flourishing."²³

This radical bifurcation of political thought between Aristotelianism and liberalism Skinner finds politically confining and taxonomically misleading. To escape its limits, he challenges a presumption which is shared, so he believes, by liberal individualists as well as by the admirers of Aristotelianism: "that it is only if we can give a content to the idea of objective human flourishing that we can hope to make sense of any theory purporting to connect the concept of individual liberty with virtuous acts of public service." To prove his case, he sets out to examine in detail what he takes to be a third "tradition of thought about social freedom," Roman in origin, in which "the negative idea of liberty as the mere non-obstruction of individual agents in the pursuit of their chosen ends was combined with the idea of virtue and public service in just the manner nowadays assumed on all sides to be impossible without incoherence."²⁴ His intention is to demonstrate that "our inherited traditions of political theory . . . embody two quite distinct though equally coherent views about the way in which it is most rational for us to act in order to maximise our negative liberty."²⁵

This is not the place for a thorough examination as to whether Skinner's account of liberalism in this regard is a caricature or not.²⁶ What matters for our purposes here is twofold: that Skinner conceives of

---

[23] Skinner, "The Idea of Negative Liberty," 193–8 (esp. 197). See also Skinner, "The Republican Ideal of Political Liberty," 293–301. In distinguishing negative liberty as opportunity from positive liberty as exercise, Skinner is adopting the terminology of Charles Taylor, "What's Wrong with Negative Liberty?" in *The Idea of Freedom*, ed. Alan Ryan (Oxford: Oxford University Press, 1979), 175–93.
[24] Skinner, "The Idea of Negative Liberty," 197.
[25] Skinner, "The Republican Ideal of Political Liberty," 307.
[26] See, however, Charvet, "Quentin Skinner on the Idea of Freedom," 12–14; Patten, "The Republican Critique of Liberalism," 25–36; and my review of Skinner's *Liberty Before Liberalism*, forthcoming in *The Review of Politics* 62 (2000). Here, I can only suggest that readers note Thomas Hobbes, *Leviathan*, ed. Edwin Curley (Indianapolis: Hackett Publishing Company, Inc., 1994) I.xv, where Hobbes does precisely what Machiavelli is said by Skinner to have done: he derives an elaborate theory of social and political virtue and obligation from an understanding of self-interest that is presented as being free from any notion of "objective human flourishing" and that is linked with a fierce rejection of the very idea of positive liberty. In Locke, this teaching concerning what we might call "the liberal virtues" is connected with an instrumental defense of political freedom and with the contention that public vigilance and even a measure of public participation are required for liberty's preservation: see Nathan Tarcov, "Locke's *Second Treatise* and 'The Best Fence Against Rebellion,'" *The Review of Politics* 43 (1981): 198–217 (esp. 211–17), and *Locke's Education for Liberty* (Chicago: University of Chicago Press, 1984), and Thomas L. Pangle, "Executive Energy and Popular Spirit in Lockean Constitutionalism," *Presidential Studies Quarterly* 17 (1987): 253–65 (esp. 259–64). Note also Rahe, *Republics Ancient and Modern*, 249–520 (esp. 291–315, 364–98, 445–520). See below, notes 84–5.

the intellectual historian as "a kind of archaeologist" whose "excavation" can bring "buried intellectual treasure back to the surface," and that he hopes – by digging up the illiberal alternative represented by Machiavelli, by dusting it off, and presenting its rediscovery as an occasion for rumination – to make it possible for us to "recapture a vision of politics based not merely on fair procedures but on common meanings and purposes" without our being thereby forced to adopt a natural teleology of the sort championed by Aristotle and Thomas Aquinas.[27] To this project, Skinner has returned repeatedly in the course of the last fifteen years – most recently in his inaugural lecture as Regius Professor of Modern History at Cambridge University.[28] The classical republican Machiavelli that emerges from his quest to transcend the limits of liberal individualism and find a link between an "individual liberty" emptied of all positive content and "virtuous acts of public service" is a tough-minded communitarian: the very model of a modern social democrat.

THE ROMAN LEGACY

For his argument concerning Machiavelli's adherence to a school of thought that he once called "classical republican" and now prefers to speak of as "neo-Roman,"[29] Skinner prepares the way with a detailed and controversial account of the nature of the political thinking that prevailed within the public sphere in the late medieval and Renaissance Italian city-states. The development of civic ideology within these communities, he contends, transpired well before the moral and political theory of Aristotle became widely available in the latter part of the

---

[27] See Skinner, "The Republican Ideal of Political Liberty," 308, and *Liberty Before Liberalism*, 101 20 (esp. 112, 116 18). Note also Skinner, "The Idea of Negative Liberty," 198–202.

[28] In addition to the article, the book, and the five book chapters already cited, see Quentin Skinner, "Machiavelli on the Maintenance of Liberty," *Politics* 18 (1983): 3–15; "Ambrogio Lorenzetti: The Artist as Political Philosopher," *Proceedings of the British Academy* 72 (1986): 1–56; and "On Justice, the Common Good, and the Priority of Liberty," in *Dimensions of Radical Democracy*, ed. Chantal Mouffe (London: Verso, 1992), 211 24. Skinner's restatement in his inaugural lecture *Liberty Before Liberalism* owes much to the work of Philip Pettit: "Negative Liberty, Liberal and Republican," *European Journal of Philosophy* 1 (1993): 15 38; "Liberalism and Republicanism," *Australasian Journal of Political Science* 28 (1993): 162 89; and *Republicanism: A Theory of Freedom and Government* (Oxford: Clarendon Press, 1997).

[29] For our purposes here, the distinction is insignificant. The shift in terminology came about when Skinner turned his attention to Machiavelli's admirers in Britain. He wanted to include Algernon Sidney and Henry Neville in his discussion of the school of thought represented by Machiavelli, and he was understandably reluctant to describe as republicans figures who, after the Restoration, gave lip-service to the cause of constitutional monarchy. See Skinner, *Liberty Before Liberalism*, 1 57 (esp. 11, n. 31; 54 5, nn. 174, 176 7).

thirteenth century and even longer before the Florentine political crisis of 1402, which was singled out as the catalyst for humanism's civic turn by Hans Baron;[30] and it took place under the influence of arguments advanced not by Aristotle, but by Cicero, Seneca, and Sallust. To this end, Skinner provides extensive evidence that, from the early twelfth century on, these arguments were echoed in the treatises on the *Ars dictaminis* penned by the *dictatores* who taught rhetoric in the law schools of late medieval Italy and that the same arguments reappear in the treatises on city government written from the 1220s on for the guidance of the *podestà* and the other magistrates who served the Italian cities.[31] By the time that Leonardo Bruni articulated these notions in the civic orations on which Hans Baron placed so much weight,[32] they had long been the common currency of civic discourse in the *Regnum Italicum*.[33] "It was," Skinner insists, "from these humble origins, far more than from the impact of Aristotelianism, that the classical republicanism of Machiavelli, Guicciardini, and their contemporaries originally stemmed. The political theory of the Renaissance, at all phases of its history, owes a far deeper debt to Rome than to Greece."[34]

Skinner's ultimate purpose in pointing to this early humanist revival of Roman republican thinking is unstated, perhaps because of his reluctance to take issue directly with the argument advanced by Po-

[30] See Baron, *The Crisis of the Early Italian Renaissance*, I: 3–63.
[31] See Skinner, "Ambrogio Lorenzetti," 1–31 and "Machiavelli's *Discorsi* and the Pre-Humanist Origins of Republican Ideas," 121–34. For the view that Skinner is seeking to correct, see Hans Baron, "The Memory of Cicero's Roman Civic Spirit in the Medieval Centuries and in the Florentine Renaissance," in *In Search of Civic Humanism*, I: 94–133. I prefer to speak of Skinner's *dictatores* as "early humanists" for the reasons evident from a comparison of Paul Oskar Kristeller, "Humanism and Scholasticism in the Italian Renaissance," in *Renaissance Thought and its Sources*, ed. Michael Mooney (New York: Columbia University Press, 1979), 85–105, with Ronald Witt, "Medieval 'Ars dictaminis' and the Beginnings of Humanism: A New Construction of the Problem," *Renaissance Quarterly* 33 (1982): 1–35. For Skinner's earlier discussion of this literature, see *The Foundations of Modern Political Thought*, I: 28–48, 71–84. See also Viroli, *From Politics to Reason of State*, 11–30, and Patricia J. Osmond, "Sallust and Machiavelli: From Civic Humanism to Political Prudence," *Journal of Medieval and Renaissance Studies* 23 (1993): 407–38 (esp. 407–20).
[32] See Baron, *The Crisis of the Early Italian Renaissance*, I: 38–60, 163–245, 351–78, II: 395–400, 422–39. See also Baron, "The Florentine Revival of the Philosophy of the Active Political Life" and "A Defense of the View of the Quattrocento First Offered in *The Crisis of the Early Italian Renaissance* (1970)," revised and reprinted in *In Search of Florentine Civic Humanism*, I: 134–57, II: 194–211.
[33] Skinner's most recent discussion of Leonardo Bruni's *Laudatio Florentinae urbis* appears to have been written before he came to appreciate the importance of the *dictatores*, but it is well worth noting that his comparison of Machiavelli's *Discorsi* with Bruni's civic rhetoric in this context tracks closely the case that he subsequently makes in comparing the former work with the treatises of the *dictatores*: note "Political Philosophy," 408–21 (esp. 418–21); then, cf. ibid., 434–41, with "Machiavelli's *Discorsi* and the Pre-Humanist Origins of Republican Ideas," 123–41.
[34] Skinner, "Ambrogio Lorenzetti," 56.

cock. His intention is nonetheless clear. He is persuaded, by Machiavelli's own claims, that the Florentine's purpose in writing the *Discourses on Livy* is to revive classical republicanism; he recognizes that Machiavelli and Aristotle represent different and radically opposed schools of thought; and, for methodological reasons, he is eager to situate Machiavelli within a recognizable and established linguistic context. That Machiavelli should be *sui generis*, that he should be a radical innovator, promoting genuinely "new modes and orders" and opening up "a road untrodden by anyone," is to a linguistic contextualist such as Skinner virtually unthinkable.[35] This is why he depicts the *Discourses on Livy* as "a wholehearted defence of traditional republican values" presented "in a wholeheartedly traditional way."[36] Skinner has a great deal at stake in defending such an account. Given his recognition that Machiavelli rejects the Aristotelian tradition, if he is to vindicate his approach to intellectual history, he must show that the dominant civic ideology of the Italian city-state was Roman and not Greek. In consequence, Skinner's Machiavelli appears as Cicero, Seneca, Sallust, and Livy *redivivus*.

CICERO AND ARISTOTLE

Proof of the Renaissance debt to Rome is not, however, all that is required if Skinner is to make good his claims. He must demonstrate also that, on the crucial question of positive and negative liberty, Cicero, Seneca, Sallust, and Livy are at odds with Aristotle, and this he manifestly fails to do. Skinner touches on this question only once and then only in passing. After briefly alluding to "the doctrine that Aquinas and his disciples derive from the Aristotelian thesis of natural sociability," he turns to what he calls "another and strongly contrasting tradition of thought" according to which "we are not innately social or political animals at all." The tradition that he has in mind is a "doctrine, stoic and anti-Aristotelian in origin," that "stems in its most

---

[35] Skinner's principal essays on historical method are conveniently collected in *Meaning and Context: Quentin Skinner and his Critics*, ed. James Tully (Princeton: Princeton University Press, 1988), 29–134. For criticism directed at these and Skinner's response: see ibid., 135–228 and 231–88. In this connection, see also Skinner, *The Foundations of Modern Political Thought*, I: x–xiii. Note as well J. G. A. Pocock, "Languages and Their Implications: The Transformation of the Study of Political Thought," *Politics, Language and Time: Essays on Political Thought and History* (New York: Athenaeum, 1973), 3–41. Cf. Michael P. Zuckert, "Appropriation and Understanding in the History of Political Philosophy: On Quentin Skinner's Method," *Interpretation* 13 (1985): 403–24.

[36] Skinner, "Machiavelli's *Discorsi* and the Pre-Humanist Origins of Republican Ideas," 141. See also Viroli, *From Politics to Reason of State*, 154, 176–7.

influential version from the moral and rhetorical writings of Cicero and Seneca."

Cicero's *De inventione* opens with a classical statement of the case. "There was once a time when men wandered about in the fields in the manner of wild beasts." "They conducted their affairs without the least guidance of reason," and "no one recognized the value inherent in an equitable code of law." Nor should we think of them as willingly abandoning this way of life; rather "they cried out at first against any innovations." From this Cicero infers that, since we now live under the rule of law, "a great and wise man" must at some point have succeeded in persuading us to abandon our natural and brutish ways. The shift to our present social and political life is seen, in short, not as the fruit of our own decision, rationally and voluntarily made; it is seen as the achievement of an heroic figure who is held up for our admiration throughout this tradition of thought: the wise lawgiver. It must have been due to such a *vir sapiens*, Cicero insists, that men were first persuaded "to keep faith, follow the rules of justice and work for the common good." And it must have been due to his combination of eloquence with *sapientia* that he managed to impose these rules upon reluctant and brutish men, "inducing them to submit without violence to the dictates of justice."

Skinner then concludes that "Seneca later adopts essentially the same viewpoint, adding that *sapientia* ought above all to act 'as our mistress and ruler,' since 'it is wisdom which disposes us to peace and calls mankind to concord.'" This understanding of the origins of the political community was the one eventually taken up by the *dictatores* of late medieval Italy.[37]

This discussion of Cicero, Seneca, and the *dictatores* would settle the question were it not for the fact that Cicero's account of the origins of the political community is perfectly compatible in all crucial respects with Aristotle's claim that man is a political animal. Aristotle nowhere asserts that man is naturally social; and though he does compare human beings with the ants, the cranes, the bees, and the wasps, he nowhere claims that they are gregarious in precisely the same way. That which distinguishes man from the other animals and makes him political is not the brutish, herdlike behavior of the naturally sociable but his possession of *logos*: his capacity for reason and speech concerning the advantageous, the just, and the good; a capacity which, among other things, makes it possible for him to laugh. This deliberative, judgmental capacity is rarely developed fully except within a self-governing political community such as the Greek *polis*, but it is not the case that men enter this or

---

[37] Skinner, "Ambrogio Lorenzetti," 17–20, citing Cicero, *Inv. Rhet.* 1.2.2, *Leg.* 1.22.58, *Off.* 1.43.153, and Seneca, *Ep.* 85.32, 90.26–7.

any other less satisfactory political community in search of the development of this capacity. Rather, they leave their brutish ways, abandon their solitary or herdlike existence as wild beasts, and enter the political community in search of security and material well-being. They enter it seeking mere life. Only thereafter do they stumble on the good life. Their deliberations characteristically begin with advantage, but they cannot stop there: precisely because men are political by nature, these deliberations inevitably come to be concerned with the just and the good. The desire for mere life may bring the *polis* into being, but it is the desire to live nobly and well that sustains it. In describing the genesis of the *polis*, Aristotle nowhere suggests that it is spontaneous. His self-governing community has an inventor – a wise lawgiver, a *vir sapiens* of just the sort that Cicero has in mind – who calls it into being and shapes its character. This inventor of the *polis* Aristotle singles out as the greatest benefactor of human kind.[38] Cicero's account of the origins of the political community is merely an elaboration of what Aristotle has to say.[39]

It is important to stress that, when Skinner denies that Cicero conceives of "the shift to our present social and political life ... as the fruit of our own decision, rationally and voluntarily made," he misrepresents the thinking of the Roman. As Professor Nederman points out in his contribution to this volume, Cicero's *vir sapiens* is able to persuade human beings to join the political community precisely because, even in their brutish state, they already "possess a potential for sociability implicit in their common rational and linguistic nature."[40] Indeed, in the very works drawn upon by Skinner's *dictatores*, in *De inventione* and in *De officiis*, Cicero insists in good Aristotelian fashion that it is "the capacity for speech" above all else that enables man to "excel" the other animals and that "by means of teaching, learning, communicating, discussing, judging, it conciliates human beings with one another and

---

[38] Aristotle, *Pol.* 1252b27 1253a39. See 1278b15 30, 1280a25 1281a10, 1283b42 1284a3; *Eth. Nic.* 1097a15 1098b8, 1169b16 18. Cf. *Hist. An.* 487b33 488a13 with *Part. An.* 673a8. In making this argument, I contend elsewhere, Aristotle was articulating the common sense of the matter in classical Greece: see Paul A. Rahe, "The Primacy of Politics in Classical Greece," *American Historical Review* 89 (1984): 265 93, and *Republics Ancient and Modern*, 27 54.

[39] Cf. Cary J. Nederman, "Nature, Sin, and the Origins of Society: The Ciceronian Tradition in Medieval Political Thought," *Journal of the History of Ideas* 49 (1988): 3 26, who neglects Aristotle's brief allusion to the genesis of the political community and draws a sharp contrast between Cicero's account and that of the peripatetic.

[40] See chapter 9, above. See also Cary J. Nederman, "The Union of Wisdom and Eloquence Before the Renaissance: The Ciceronian Orator in Medieval Thought," *Journal of Medieval History* 18 (1992): 75 95.

joins them in a sort of natural alliance [*societas*]" conducive to their advancement in "justice, equity, and goodness." The task of Cicero's *vir sapiens* was not manipulation. It was rational persuasion, and its accomplishment presupposed "that there is, within the souls of human beings, matter and opportunity for the greatest things, if there is anyone able to draw that matter out and render it better through instruction." To transform men "from wild beasts and savages into tame and gentle creatures," he had only to encourage them to heed "speech and reason with greater eagerness."[41] In so far as the early humanists of late medieval Italy drew on Cicero who was, as Skinner puts it, "their veritable Bible in matters of moral and political philosophy,"[42] they imbibed a political doctrine indistinguishable from that of Aristotle in all respects pertinent to this discussion – a political doctrine at the center of which stood a notion of positive liberty. It would not be difficult to demonstrate the same regarding Seneca and his influence. There can be no doubt that the Stoics, to the extent that they were civic-minded, understood what Skinner calls "social freedom" in a manner informed by "an objective notion of *eudaimonia* or human flourishing."

By now, Skinner may be aware that Cicero and Seneca do not serve his argument at all well – for, in one of his more recent formulations, he is silent concerning the influence of Seneca on the *dictatores*, and he has quietly dropped his claim that Cicero was "their veritable Bible." Instead, he contends that these early humanists "owed an even deeper debt to Sallust's histories" than to Cicero, "and in particular to the opening of the *Bellum Catilinae* with its explanation of the rise and fall of republican Rome."[43] And in another yet more recent statement, in which he ignores the early humanists and focuses his attention more narrowly on Machiavelli and his admirers in seventeenth-century England, Skinner stresses the influence of Livy and his restatement of the prevalent Roman conviction that the loss of political liberty on the part of a people is tantamount to their enslavement.[44] Unless, however, it can be shown that Sallust and Livy adopted a doctrine of negative liberty and rejected out of hand the very notion of positive liberty, the fact that these two Roman historians were so influential does nothing to shore up Skinner's argument. There is, in any case, ample reason to suppose that the predominant Roman understanding of citizenship, especially in their day, was Aristotelian in substance, if not also in

---

[41] Cicero, *Off.* 1.16.50, *Inv. Rhet.* 1.1.1 2.3, 4.5.   [42] Skinner, "Ambrogio Lorenzetti," 6.
[43] Skinner, "Machiavelli's *Discorsi* and the Pre-Humanist Origins of Republican Ideas," 122–3.
[44] Skinner, *Liberty Before Liberalism*, 36–57.

origin.⁴⁵ In contrasting classical Roman thought with Aristotelianism, Skinner would appear to be making a distinction where there is for the purpose of his analysis little, if any difference. He splits where he should lump.

SELF-GOVERNMENT AND LIBERTY

It is unclear why Skinner erred in this fashion. He is an exceedingly careful and industrious scholar, and he has a well-earned reputation for philosophical rigor. In this case, however, the source of his confusion may be conceptual. The notions of negative and positive liberty are not mutually exclusive. As Skinner's principal examples – Thomas Hobbes and Isaiah Berlin – indicate, one can embrace the former while rejecting the latter notion of liberty as meaningless. But an Aristotelian cannot do the reverse. For someone persuaded that man is a political animal and that, in general, he can best fulfill his nature within a self-governing community, the notion of exercise central to the very idea of positive liberty presupposes the opportunity inherent in negative liberty. To use Skinner's language, only in a community in which the citizen body is unobstructed in "the pursuit of" its "chosen ends" can we be free to make the appropriate choices and to "engage in just those activities which are most conducive to *eudaimonia* or 'human flourishing' and may be said to embody our deepest purposes." Thus, the Aristotelian proponents of popular political participation would have at least as great a stake in securing the conditions for negative liberty as their Machiavellian opponents.⁴⁶

We should not, then, be shocked to discover that the Roman notion propagated by Livy – that the loss of liberty on the part of a people is tantamount to their enslavement – was, like most Roman notions, in its origin Greek.⁴⁷ Nor should we be surprised to learn that this notion is linked closely in the pertinent texts with an Aristotelian understanding

---

⁴⁵ See Claude Nicolet, *The World of the Citizen in Republican Rome* (Berkeley: University of California Press, 1980).
⁴⁶ The same point has been made from an Hegelian perspective: see Charvet, "Quentin Skinner on the Idea of Freedom," 5 16.
⁴⁷ In the very passage of *Leviathan* (II.xxi.8 9) to which Skinner repeatedly returns, Hobbes singles out Aristotle as this notion's proponent: see *Pol.* 1317a40 b16. It was, in any case, commonplace: cf. Aeschylus, *Pers.* 50, 74 5, 234, 241 2, 402 4, 584 97; Herodotus, 7.101 4, 135 6; and Euripides, *Hel.* 276, *Iph. Aul.* 1400 1 with Isocrates, 4.131 2, 150 2, 181 2, 5.107, 120 4, *Ep.* 3.5, 9.19; Plato, *Resp.* 4.435e-436a; Aristotle, *Pol.* 1285a15 29, 1313a34 b10, 1327b23 36. See also Hippocrates, *Airs, Waters, and Places* 12, 16.

of liberty as a positive exercise concept.[48] When Skinner singles out the conviction "that personal liberty can only be fully assured within a self-governing form of republican community" and identifies it as "the heart and nerve of all" of the "theories of citizenship" that he considers to be "classical republican" in character, he has not seized upon a feature that distinguishes the thinking of Machiavelli from that of Aristotle.[49]

Thomas Hobbes understood this perfectly well: in a fierce assault on those who assert personal liberty's dependence on republican self-government, presented in a passage of *Leviathan* to which Skinner himself quite often recurs, Hobbes lumped Cicero and Aristotle together. Then, almost as an afterthought, he alluded in an unmistakable fashion to Machiavelli – who was preeminent, as he well knew, among those who "by reading of these Greek and Latin authors . . . from their childhood have gotten a habit . . . of favouring tumults."[50] The fact that Cicero, Seneca, Sallust, Livy, and the early humanists all shared in the conviction so emphasized by Skinner in no way demonstrates that in their understanding of liberty they were opposed to Aristotle and in Machiavelli's camp. In the event, as Professor Blythe's contribution to this volume might be taken to suggest,[51] the appropriation of Roman republican thinking by the early humanists seems, if anything, to have helped pave the way for their successors' adoption of Aristotle's *Politics*.[52] One may justly doubt whether the humanists of the Quattrocento were any less enthusiastic in their embrace of the author of the *Nicomachean Ethics* than their rivals the scholastics, but if they were, as

---

[48] See Rahe, "The Primacy of Politics in Classical Greece," 265–93 and *Republics Ancient and Modern*, 27–54.
[49] Skinner, "The Idea of Negative Liberty," 207–8.
[50] Hobbes, *Leviathan* II.xxi.9. See Skinner, "The Idea of Negative Liberty," 194–6, 212–13; "The Paradoxes of Political Liberty," 227–31, 245; "The Republican Ideal of Political Liberty," 294–6; and *Liberty Before Liberalism*, 4–11, 59–60, 68, 77, 85, 97 n. 2. Although, in one of his articles, Skinner even quotes extensively from the pertinent passage, he seems not to have appreciated its significance for the argument that, at the time in which he published it, he was presenting elsewhere: "Thomas Hobbes on the Proper Signification of Liberty," 140–1. For Machiavelli as the premier champion of "tumults," see below.
[51] See above, chapter 2.
[52] Well before the recovery of Aristotle's ethical and political works in the Latin world, argues Cary J. Nederman in an important series of articles now collected in a single volume, their influence had by this and other quite similar routes become pervasive: see Nederman, *Medieval Aristotelianism and its Limits: Classical Traditions in Moral and Political Philosophy, 12th–15th Centuries* (Aldershot: Variorum, 1997). On this question, Viroli's valuable survey of the evidence would appear to put him at odds with his mentor: see *From Politics to Reason of State*, 11–125, 201–80.

some insist,[53] it was presumably because these civil servants, teachers, diplomats, courtiers, and political propagandists recognized that those of their contemporaries who embraced the *vita activa* owed a debt of gratitude to Cicero for his one significant departure from Aristotle – his elevation of statesmanship over the contemplative life.[54]

CLASSICAL REPUBLICANISMS?

It might be tempting to suppose that one could salvage a part of Quentin Skinner's argument and make sense of his attempt to make a classical republican of Machiavelli by adopting the argument advanced by Professor Nederman in his contribution to this volume. Professor Nederman contends that "the republicanism of antiquity lacked a unitary theoretical starting-point," that it rested "instead on multiple and perhaps incommensurable foundations," and that the resulting contradictions come to light when one compares the arguments that Cicero advanced regarding statesmanship in his rhetorical works with those advanced concerning the same subject in his political and philosophical works. To be more precise, he distinguishes "the discursive" or "rhetorical republicanism" of Cicero's rhetorical writings from the "rational . . . republicanism" evident in his political and philosophical dialogues. He, then, suggests that Marsilius of Padua and Niccolò Machiavelli were advocates of the former and Nicholas of Cusa and James Harrington of the latter.[55]

Professor Nederman's treatment of Cicero's thinking has one great virtue and one grave vice. The virtue is that he has drawn attention to one of the crucial tensions that characterizes classical republican thought; the vice is that he has failed to ask whether the rhetorical and philosophical perspectives can be reconciled. This is of particular importance because this tension would appear to be typical of classical republicanism as a whole. It is certainly present in Aristotle's *Politics*. In the first book, we are told that man is a political animal, that his capacity for speech distinguishes him from the animals and gives him his political

---

[53] Cf., for example, Richard Tuck, "Humanism and Political Thought," in *The Impact of Humanism on Western Europe*, ed. Anthony Goodman and Angus McKay (New York: Longman, 1990), 43–65 (esp. 47–56), who asserts that the humanists tended to repudiate the scholastic subordination of the Roman moralists to Aristotle and to interpret the latter in light of the former. But on the centrality of Aristotle for both humanist and scholastic moral philosophy see David Lines, "The Importance of Being Good: Moral Philosophy in the Italian Universities, 1300–1600," *Rinascimento* n.s. 36 (1996): 139–93.

[54] Cicero, *Off.* 1.43.152–5. Note, in this connection, *Rep.* 6.13.13, 24.26–26.29.

[55] See above, chapter 9.

character, and that the *polis* enables him to develop that distinctive capacity, and we are led to conclude that a man excluded from such a self-governing community is likely to lead a bestial life. In the third book, where Aristotle elaborates further on this point, we are nonetheless given to understand that the best regime is a monarchy in which the one best man rules by virtue of his character and wisdom.[56] If Cicero is at odds with himself, then so is Aristotle.

Professor Nederman seems to have been misled by the categories that he deploys – for the juxtaposition that he sets up would only make sense if the discursive, rhetorical republicanism advocated by Cicero was not also a rational republicanism – if the public square, as envisaged by Cicero, was merely a locus for idle chatter and rhetorical manipulation, for discourse as opposed to rational discourse; if Cicero's discursive republic was a community in the grips of a false dream fostered by an oratorical illusionist. In fact, of course, as is illustrated in the very passages from *De officiis, De inventione, De oratore,* and *De optimo genere oratorum* that Professor Nederman cites, Cicero's mantra is the unity of "reason and speech [*ratio et oratio*]." In defending rhetoric against its detractors, he may insist that "wisdom without eloquence is of little profit to cities," but he then goes on to add that "most of the time eloquence without wisdom does them great harm, and it never brings them profit." In consequence, Cicero sides emphatically with Aristotle against Gorgias, insisting that oratory is not autonomous, making it "a part of political science," and contending that the orator must be "learned" in the branch of philosophy that deals with "life and its ways [*mores*]" and that he must be capable of assessing and reconciling "the honorable [*honestum*] and the advantageous [*utile*]." Cicero's orator achieves his end as a wise lawgiver in deploying his eloquence in support of practical wisdom – above all, by appealing to the reason of his listeners in ordinary language that they can understand.[57]

In much the same fashion, the speech that distinguishes Aristotelian

---

[56] Cf. Aristotle, *Pol.* 1252b27 1253a39, 1278b15 30, and 1280a25 1281a10 with 1283b20 84b33, and see P. A. Vander Waerdt, "Kingship and Philosophy in Aristotle's Best Regime," *Phronesis* 30 (1985): 249 73, and W. R. Newell, "Superlative Virtue: The Problem of Monarchy in Aristotle's 'Politics,'" *Western Political Quarterly* 40 (1987): 159 78.

[57] Cicero, *Off.* 1.16.50, *Inv. Rhet.* 1.1.1 5.7, 2.51.156 59.178, *De Or.* 1.3.12, 6.20, 8.31 34, 15.68 9, 2.2.5 6, *De optimo genere oratorum* 1.3 4. There is nothing in any of these passages to justify Professor Nederman's claims that for Cicero "the realm of so-called 'practical philosophy' . . . falls more properly within the domain of the orator than of the philosopher" and that "the orator necessarily defers to his audience, rather than commanding them." See above, chapter 9. Cicero's point is, rather, that the orator must make practical philosophy his province and that, by means of persuasion, he stoops to conquer.

man from the animals is *logos* or rational speech. This means that man possesses more than mere voice (*phone*) – that he can do more than communicate his feelings and appeal to the passions of his listeners. For Cicero, as for Aristotle, *logos* is something more refined than the capacity to introduce private feelings and passions into the public arena: it enables the human being to perform as no other animal can; it makes it possible for him to perceive and make clear to others through reasoned discourse the difference between what is advantageous and what is harmful, between what is just and what is unjust, and between what is good and what is evil. It is the sharing of these things, they insist, which constitutes the household and the political community, each as a moral community, (*koinonia*).[58]

Aristotle's discussion of man's political character is rendered compatible with his preference for monarchy by the same logic that renders Cicero's rhetorical writings compatible with his philosophic and political dialogues. Both authors are persuaded that the quality that distinguishes man from the animals distinguishes men from one another: both embrace a doctrine of differential moral and political rationality. In many of the passages that Professor Nederman quotes, Cicero emphasizes the unequal distribution of reason among men. The *vir sapiens* singled out in the rhetorical works as the political community's founder is nature's nobleman. Indeed, in both *De inventione* and in *De oratore*, Cicero stresses that, in developing his potential in *ratio et oratio*, a man can come to "surpass" other human beings in the very sphere in which they are most superior to the other animals.[59]

On this matter, Aristotle is notoriously blunt. We exclude slaves from the political community, he explains, because some men are by nature lacking in the capacity for prudential deliberation (*to bouleutikon*) regarding the advantageous, the just, and the good; we exclude women, though they possess this capacity, because it is without authority (*akuros*) over them; and we exclude children because they possess it in incom-

---

[58] Cf. Cicero, *Off.* 1.16.50 17.58, *Inv. Rhet.* 1.1.1 2.3, 4.5, 5.6 7, 2.51.156 9.178, *De Or.* 1.3.12, 6.20, 8.31 34, 15.68 9, 2.2.5 6, with Aristotle, *Pol.* 1252b27 1253a39, 1278b15 30, 1280a25 1281a10, 1283b42 1284a3; *Eth. Nic.* 1097a15 1098b8, 1169b16 18, and then see Cicero, *Off.* 1.4.11 7.24, 2.5.16 17, 12.41 42, 3.5.21 6.27, 17.69; *Fin.* 2.14.45 47, 5.13 14.38, 23.65 66; *Rep.* 2.36.61, 3.2.3 4.7, 22.33, 25.37, 31.43 35.48, 5.4.6 6.8; *Leg.* 1.6.18 16.45, 22.58 24.63, 2.5.11 13.

[59] The pertinent passages (Cicero, *Inv. Rhet.* 1.4.5, *De or.* 1.8.32 3) need to be read in light of Cicero's insistence on subordinating *oratio* to *ratio* (*Off.* 1.16.50 17.58, *Inv. Rhet.* 1.1.1 5.7, 2.51.156 9.178, *De Or.* 1.3.12, 6.20, 8.31, 34, 15.68 9, 2.2.5 6) and in light of his commitment to a notion of differential moral and political rationality: *Off.* 1.4.11 7.24, 2.5.16 17, 12.41 42, 3.5.21 6.27, 17.69; *Fin.* 2.14.45 7, 5.13 14.38, 23.65 6; *Rep.* 2.36.61, 3.2.3 4.7, 22.33, 25.37, 31.43 35.48, 5.4.6 6.8; *Leg.* 1.6.18 16.45, 22.58 24.63, 2.5.11 13.

plete form. There can be no doubt that Cicero agrees.[60] An aristocratic presumption underlay classical practice both Greek and Roman. When, with an eye to classical authors such as Aristotle and Cicero, Alexis de Tocqueville spoke of the ancient republic as "an aristocracy of masters," he spoke the truth.[61]

The aristocratic and even monarchical bent evident in Aristotle's discussion of regimes and in Cicero's more narrowly political and philosophical works is merely the extreme expression of a principle inherent in all genuine classical republicanism. Whether public deliberation is desirable depends on the character of the citizens – on their natural gifts; on the *paideia* to which they have been subjected; on whether, by inclination and an education to virtue, they have been sufficiently liberated from the dominion of the passions to be able to reason together in public concerning the transcendent common good. Otherwise, where reason remains enslaved to the passions and genuine virtue is unattainable, the most that one can hope for from the citizen is a shrewd calculation of individual self-interest and its fierce, resolute pursuit. In the absence of a citizenry educated in moral virtue for freedom, or in those circumstances in which a community is endowed with an individual or with a handful of men who are decisively superior to their compatriots in virtue and wisdom, it is entirely appropriate that a monarchy or aristocracy be established. The classical republicanism of Aristotle and Cicero was not an ideology blindly dictating partisan regime preferences; it was a way of thinking about human association that left ample room for the exercise of political prudence.

That Cicero should have emphasized public deliberation in his rhetorical works and the rule of reason in his philosophical works is, to say the least, rhetorically appropriate. He also had good political grounds for giving emphasis in *De re publica* and *De legibus* to the aristocratic and even monarchical implications of the classical republicanism that he espoused. After all, the Roman republic was a mixed regime, not a simple democracy: as Cicero quite rightly insists, it had always depended for leadership and guidance on the Roman senate and on the aristocracy serving in its ranks. Moreover, long before Cicero's time, the republic had expanded to such an extent as to render full public deliberation virtually impossible. In principle, the ordinary citizens of the republic were welcome to attend a *contio* to listen to their betters

[60] Cf. Aristotle, *Pol.* 1260a4 13 with Cicero, *Rep.* 3.25.37 8.
[61] Alexis de Tocqueville, *De la démocratie en Amérique*, 2.1.3, in *Oeuvres, papiers et correspondances*, ed. J.-P. Mayer, 14 vols. to date (Paris: Gallimard, 1951 89), I: 2 22.

contend in speech, but in Cicero's day only a small proportion of the voting population could actually do so – and, even in times of crisis, a much, much smaller proportion actually did.[62] By that time, as Claude Nicolet has demonstrated, citizenship had become virtually meaningless for most Romans.[63] The understanding projected in Cicero's rhetorical works was a nostalgic vision of a discursive regime no longer viable. That developed in his more broadly political works was designed to inform political reflection in an age when the vast extent of Rome's empire; the rise of great military magnates such as Marius, Sulla, Pompey, and Caesar; and the recurrence of civil war had demonstrated that, if Rome was to survive, it required a *rector*.

If, in a later age, Marsilius of Padua was at odds with Nicholas of Cusa regarding political matters, it was not because they had imbibed from the ancients different versions of republicanism. Marsilius thought it appropriate that legislative authority within the community be exercised by its "weightier part [*valentior pars*],"[64] and he did so for the same reasons that Nicholas championed the wise few against the foolish multitude. They were both committed to the principle of differential moral and political rationality. If they were at odds with regards to its implications, it was because they faced substantively different situations requiring different emphases or because the exercise of prudence had led them to different conclusions as to what was appropriate in similar circumstances. Those who think along the same lines need not always reach the same conclusions.

It is worth adding here that the principle of differential moral and political rationality helps explain the apparent inconsistencies in the behavior of a humanist such as Leonardo Bruni. As Professor Hankins has observed in his contribution to this volume, Bruni was not a republican ideologue. In his capacity as a public orator and magistrate, in his service to the papacy, and in his accomplishments as a scholar, he pursued a single humanist program, Isocratean, Aristotelian, and Ciceronian in its foundations. Whether, at any given moment, it had an overtly political dimension depended on circumstances and on the

---

[62] For a series of studies exploring the prominent role played by public deliberation and popular participation at various stages in the evolution of the republic, see Fergus Millar, "Political Power in Mid-Republican Rome: Curia or Comitium," *Journal of Roman Studies* 79 (1989): 138–50; "The Political Character of the Classical Roman Republic, 100–151 B.C.," *Journal of Roman Studies* 74 (1984): 1–19; "Politics, Persuasion, and the People before the Social War (150–90 B.C.)," *Journal of Roman Studies* 76 (1986): 1–11; and *The Crowd in the Late Republic* (Ann Arbor: University of Michigan Press, 1998).

[63] Nicolet, *The World of the Citizen in Republican Rome*, 129–398.

[64] See Marsilius of Padua, *The Defensor Pacis of Marsilius of Padua*, ed. C. W. Previté-Orton (Cambridge: Cambridge University Press, 1928) 1.12.3.

dictates of prudence in those circumstances with regard to the promotion of virtue and learning.⁶⁵ Flexibility of the sort displayed by Bruni was expected of humanists. Their project was the instruction of rulers and their moral and political improvement, not the encouragement of any particular political regime.⁶⁶

The centrality of the principle of differential rationality to the species of republicanism embraced by the ancient Greeks and Romans helps also to explain a phenomenon uncovered by Dr. Hörnqvist in his contribution to this volume.⁶⁷ It was perfectly natural that imperialism should be almost as much a focus of the civic humanist project as liberty itself. Conquest and dominion were so fundamental to the classical republican endeavor that the ancients found it difficult to think of freedom without thinking at the same time of empire over others.⁶⁸ As is amply evident in Pericles' Funeral Oration and in Vergil's famous encomium on Rome,⁶⁹ the principle of differential rationality justifies not only the enslavement of men incapable of managing their own affairs but the subordination of peoples lacking in sufficient measure the virtues requisite for self-rule.⁷⁰

The same point can be made with regard to Professor Najemy's contribution to this volume: it is in no way surprising that, in the wake of their bitter experience under the Ciompi, wealthy and even moderately prosperous Florentines should be attracted by a way of thinking about politics that is aristocratic at its heart.⁷¹ For perfectly understandable

---

⁶⁵ See above, chapter 5. For another example illustrating the range of practical positions open to the humanist, see Cary J. Nederman, "Humanism and Empire: Aeneas Sylvius Piccolomini, Cicero, and the Imperial Ideal," *Historical Journal* 36 (1993): 499–515.
⁶⁶ See James Hankins, "Humanism and the Origins of Modern Political Thought," in *The Cambridge Companion to Renaissance Humanism*, ed. Jill Kraye (Cambridge: Cambridge University Press, 1996), 118–41. Note also Delio Cantimori, "Rhetoric and Politics in Italian Humanism," *Journal of the Warburg and Courtauld Institutes* 1 (1937): 83–102.
⁶⁷ See above, chapter 4.
⁶⁸ See, for example, J. A. O. Larsen, "Freedom and its Obstacles in Ancient Greece." *Classical Philology* 57 (1962): 230–4.
⁶⁹ Cf. Thucydides 2.34–46 with Vergil, *Aen.* 6.847–53.
⁷⁰ This helps explain why the great minds of the classical age were inclined to dispute as to whether the subjects of the Great King were servile by nature, by education, or because of the climate: cf. Aeschylus, *Pers.* 50, 74–5, 234, 241–2, 402–4, 584–97; Herodotus, 7.101–4, 135–6; and Euripides, *Hel.* 276, *Iph. Aul.* 1400–1 with Isocrates, 4.131–2, 150–2, 181–2, 5.107, 120–4, *Ep.* 3.5, 9.19; Plato, *Resp.* 4.435e–436a; Aristotle, *Pol.* 1285a15–29, 1313a34–b10, 1327b23–36. See also Hippocrates, *Airs, Waters, and Places* 12, 16. Note Cicero, *Rep.* 1.33.50.
⁷¹ See above, chapter 3. Note, in this connection, Lauro Martines, *Power and Imagination: City-States in Renaissance Italy* (Baltimore: Johns Hopkins University Press, 1979), 7–217 (esp. 191–217), and John M. Najemy, *Corporatism and Consensus in Florentine Electoral Politics, 1280–1400* (Chapel Hill: University of North Carolina Press, 1982). See also Najemy, "The Dialogue of Power in Florentine Politics," in *City States in Classical Antiquity and Medieval Italy*, ed. Anthony Molho, Kurt Raaflaub, and Julia Emlen (Ann Arbor: University of Michigan Press, 1991), 269–88.

reasons, those threatened by that revolutionary movement had turned against the old principle, derived from the Roman law governing the management of waterways by private corporations, which had provided the undergirding for guild-republicanism and the other species of self-government that developed in the late Middle Ages. The notion that all legitimately concerned in a matter should have a say – *Quod omnes tangit ab omnibus tractari debeat* – was simply too democratic in its implications.[72] Instead of sharply distinguishing a discursive from a rational republicanism, Professor Nederman should have spoken of rational republicanism's discursive and more aristocratic or even monarchical moments.

SPEECH AND REASON IN MACHIAVELLI

Professor Nederman's treatment of Machiavelli deserves a separate discussion as a matter of particular interest. In effect, by pointing to the handful of passages in which Machiavelli attributes to the *popolo* a capacity for profiting from public debate and by suggesting that he be classed as a discursive republican, Professor Nederman is asking that we reconsider whether Machiavelli meets the requirements that he would have to meet if J. G. A. Pocock were to be justified in claiming that he was a classical republican on the Aristotelian model.

Here, we must pause to remind ourselves what this would entail. The classical republican argument, articulated by Aristotle and Cicero on the basis of their observation of Greek and Roman practice, was grounded in the conviction that the distinctive human feature is man's capacity for moral and political rationality. It eventuated in an understanding of politics and the common good that transcended the simple pursuit of material interest: politics, as Aristotle insists, may begin with

[72] Cf. *Codex Iustinianus*, 5.59.5.2 with *Digesta*, 39.3.8, and see Gaines Post, "Corporate Community, Representation, and Consent," in *Studies in Medieval Legal Thought* (Princeton: Princeton University Press, 1964), 27–238, and consider Riccardo Fubini, "From Social to Political Representation in Renaissance Florence," in *City States in Classical Antiquity and Medieval Italy*, 223–39. See also Yves M.-J. Congar, "Quod omnes tangit ab omnibus tractari et approbari debet," *Revue Historique de droit français et étranger*, fourth ser., 36 (1958): 210–59; Peter N. Riesenberg, "Civism and Roman Law in Fourteenth-Century Italian Society," *Explorations in Economic History* 7 (1969): 237–54; and Riesenberg, "Citizenship at Law in Late Medieval Italy," *Viator* 5 (1974): 333–46. Note also Pierre Michaud-Quantin, *Universitas: Expressions du mouvement communautaire dans le Moyen-Age Latin* (Paris: J. Vrin, 1970), and Arthur P. Monahan, *Consent, Coercion, and Limit: The Medieval Origins of Parliamentary Democracy* (Leiden: Brill, 1987). Though Skinner eventually notices the frequent citation of this principle by his *dictatores*, in his earlier discussions of the juridical foundations of medieval communalism, he makes no mention of it: cf. Skinner, *The Foundations of Modern Political Thought*, I: 3–12 and "Political Philosophy," 390–5 with "Ambrogio Lorenzetti," 21. Viroli's recent discussion of the political ethos of the medieval and Renaissance city-state is defective in the same way: *From Politics to Reason of State*, 11–125.

the concern for mere life but it is sustained by the desire to live nobly and well. Public deliberation begins with the question of advantage but somehow can never escape the question of justice and the good. For politics to achieve what it can, however, the citizens must receive a moral and intellectual education: they must become virtuous. Their *paideia* in virtue, the development of their natural potential in this regard, is the first concern of the Aristotelian and Ciceronian lawgiver.

For this conception to make sense, however, there must be a foundation in nature for right and wrong: it must be meaningful to speak of the genuinely advantageous, the just, and the good. It matters little whether one refers to natural right, as Aristotle does, or to natural law in the manner of Cicero, the Stoics, and Thomas Aquinas: if moral reason is to be the foundation for republicanism, there must be something in the way of the noble and good to reason about. In short, if discursive republicanism is not to descend into idle chatter and mere rhetorical manipulation, if there is to be a genuine link between *ratio* and *oratio*, if eloquence and wisdom are to be united, it must in principle be feasible "to distinguish" what Skinner calls "an objective notion of *eudaimonia* or human flourishing."

This, as Skinner repeatedly emphasizes, Machiavelli manifestly refuses to do: his "point of departure is not a vision of *eudaimonia* or real human interests, but simply an account of the 'humours' that prompt us to choose and pursue our various ends."[73] His republicanism is, in fact, grounded on the conviction that all talk of natural human ends is nonsense: he mentions neither natural right nor natural law, and his account of virtue is strictly instrumental. Politically, Machiavelli can perhaps best be described as a disciple of Heraclitus. The foundation of his teaching concerning politics is his claim that "all the things of men are in motion and cannot remain fixed." By this he meant to convey something closely akin to what Thomas Hobbes and David Hume had in mind when they asserted that reason is the slave of the passions. As

---

[73] Skinner, "The Idea of Negative Liberty," 217. See also Skinner, "The Republican Ideal of Political Liberty," 302, 306 7. This dimension of Skinner's argument is absent from the work of his student Maurizio Viroli who, in discussing Italy's civic tradition, draws no sharp distinction between Cicero and Aristotle and who presents us, in his brief and exceedingly circumscribed account of the *Discourses*, with a Machiavelli more reminiscent of Pocock's disciple of Aristotle than of Skinner's advocate of negative liberty: consider *From Politics to Reason of State*, 154 77, in light of ibid., 11 125. Cf., however, ibid., 201 9, and then note ibid., 281 95. Viroli's failure to discuss the *Discourses* in detail and his reliance in the pertinent passage (ibid., 154 77) on quotations from other works is indicative of the difficulties inherent in the attempt to fit Machiavelli's republican teaching within the framework of traditional Greek, Roman, Italian, and Florentine reflection on this subject.

Machiavelli put it by way of explanation, "the human appetites" are "insatiable"; "by nature" human beings "desire everything" while "by fortune they are allowed to secure little"; and since "nature has created men in such a fashion" that they are "able to desire everything" but not "to secure everything," their "desire is always greater than the power of acquisition [*la potenza dello acquistare*]." As a consequence of accepting this doctrine, the Florentine dismissed as utopian the moral and political teachings advanced by his classical and Christian predecessors; and under its guidance, he rejected the Aristotelian doctrine of the mean, arguing that the pursuit of moderation is a species of folly and contending that in a world in constant flux there simply is not and cannot be "a middle road [*via del mezzo*]."[74] One must take one's political bearings, he asserted, from a fact putatively admitted by "all who reason concerning civic life [*vivere civile*]": that anyone intent on setting up a republic and ordaining its laws must "presuppose that all men are wicked [*rei*] and that they will make use of the malignity of their spirit whenever they are free and have occasion to do so."[75]

To be sure, Machiavelli does attribute an importance to "good examples," and he contends that they "arise from good education."[76] But though he affects to admire the ancients, the education that he has in mind is neither Greek nor Roman, neither Aristotelian nor Ciceronian: it is not a product of moral training and habituation; it is in no way aimed at liberating men from the dominion of their passions; and intellectual virtue is not its completion. Its goal is, rather, to shape, direct, and fortify the spirited passions, and the prevalence of Christianity is the greatest obstacle to this accomplishment in his day.

As we have already seen, in the preface to the first book of his *Discorsi*, Machiavelli alludes to "the weakness into which the present religion has conducted the world" and to "the evil done many Christian provinces and cities" by the "ambitious idleness" of the clergy. There, however, he places his greatest emphasis on the absence of "a true knowledge of histories," contending that his contemporaries do not get "from reading them that sense nor from savoring them that taste that they have in themselves." This happens, we are told, because Machiavelli's contemporaries take pleasure in "hearing of the variety of incidents they

---

[74] Cf. Machiavelli, *Discorsi* 1.6.4, 37.1, 2 Proemio 2 3, in *Tutte le opere*, 86 7, 119, 145, with Thomas Hobbes, *Leviathan*, I.iii.3 5, viii.14 16, and with David Hume, *A Treatise of Human Nature*, ed. L. A. Selby-Bigge (Oxford: Clarendon Press, 1888), II.iii. In this connection, see Markus Fischer, "Machiavelli's Political Psychology," *Review of Politics* 59 (1997): 789 829.
[75] Machiavelli, *Discorsi* 1.3.1, in *Tutte le opere*, 81.
[76] Machiavelli, *Discorsi* 1.4.1, in *Tutte le opere*, 82.

contained without otherwise thinking of imitating them, judging imitation not only difficult but impossible – as if heaven, the sun, the elements, men had varied in motion, in order, and in power from what they were in antiquity." Machiavelli's task in the *Discorsi* is "to draw men from this error." What this means, however, only becomes evident later when Machiavelli traces "the weakness of present-day men" to "their weak education and their slight information concerning things" and then hints that what causes them to "judge ancient judgments in part inhuman, in part impossible" are "certain . . . opinions" peculiar to modernity. These "modern opinions" may not have to do with a variation in the motion, order, and power of heaven, the sun, and the elements, but they do pertain to such a transformation – one, worked by divine grace, in the situation of men. For his part, Machiavelli insists that "men . . . have and have had always the same passions" and that, if "their works are more virtuous in this province at present than in that, and in that more than in this," it is "in accord with the form of education from which those people have derived their mode of living."[77]

Because the Christian religion "makes us esteem less the honor of the world," Machiavelli expresses a preference for that of the ancient Romans, which esteemed this honor "very much" and "lodged in it the greatest good." Thereby, this religion rendered its adherents "in their actions more ferocious" than their modern counterparts.

> This can be assessed from a consideration of many of their institutions, starting with the magnificence of their sacrifices in contrast with the humility of ours, where there is a certain pomp more delicate than magnificent but no ferocious or spirited action. Here there was no lack of pomp or magnificence of ceremony, but there was added the action of the sacrifice, full of blood and ferocity, with a multitude of animals suffering butchery. This sight, being terrible, rendered men similar to itself. Besides, the ancient religion did not beatify men if they were not full of worldly glory, as were captains of armies and princes of republics. Our religion has conferred more glory on men who are humble and contemplative than on those who are active. It has then lodged the greatest good in humility, abjectness, and contempt for human things; the other lodged it in greatness of spirit, strength of body, and all other things suited to making men very strong. And if our religion requests that you have in yourself strength, it wishes you to be apt more to suffer than to do something strong. This mode of living, then, seems to have rendered the world weak and to have given it in prey to wicked men, who can manage it securely, seeing that the collectivity [*università*] of men, in order to go to paradise, think more of enduring their thrashings than of avenging them.

---

[77] Cf. Machiavelli, *Discorsi* 1 Proemio with 3.27.2, 43, in *Tutte le opere*, 76, 233 4, 250.

In concluding this diatribe against what his admirer James Harrington would later dub "priestcraft," Machiavelli raises the possibility that Christianity only "appears" to have rendered "the world . . . effeminate and heaven disarmed," and he invites future theologians to recast it as a more worldly doctrine, suggesting, with malice aforethought, that the troubles which he identifies arise less from Christianity itself than "from the cowardice of those who have interpreted our religion according to idleness [*ozio*] and not according to *virtù*."[78]

Machiavelli did not think that Christianity's replacement by paganism or its reform in light of the dictates of *virtù* would suffice as a guarantee of the "good education" that he sought.[79] Thus, when he suggested that "good examples arise from good education," he immediately added that "good education [arises] from good laws, and good laws from the tumults [*tumulti*] which many so inconsiderately condemn." From his premise that the founder of a republic must operate on the presumption that all men are wicked, he drew a series of conclusions which astonished his contemporaries and which would have surprised the ancients at least as much: that classical Rome was as a republic Lacedaemon's superior, that in a republic the people are safer and better guardians of liberty than the nobles, and that Roman liberty was rooted in a salutary political turbulence.[80]

In Machiavelli's judgment, those who are inclined to denounce political turmoil and to argue for social and political harmony "have not considered how it is that in every republic there are two diverse humors – that of the people, and that of the great ones [*grandi*] – and that all the laws that are made in favor of liberty are born from this disunion." To those who thought this last claim preposterous, he replied that "every city ought to have modes by which the people can vent their ambition," arguing that "the demands of a free people are seldom pernicious and rarely endanger their liberty: they arise from oppression or from the suspicions that they entertain that they are about to be oppressed." It is in the context of denouncing the well-known hostility

---

[78] See Machiavelli, *Discorsi* 2.2.2, in *Tutte le opere*, 149 50, and note Mark Goldie, "The Civil Religion of James Harrington," in *The Languages of Political Theory in Early-Modern Europe*, ed. Anthony Pagden (Cambridge: Cambridge University Press, 1987), 197 222. For what Machiavelli really thinks regarding the true nature of Christianity, see *Discorsi* 3.1.4, in *Tutte le opere*, 196 7. In this connection, see also Sullivan, *Machiavelli's Three Romes* passim (esp. 15 59, 119 90).

[79] Had he thought such an expedient sufficient, there would be warrant for Isaiah Berlin's vision of him as a restorer of pagan antiquity against Christianity: cf. Berlin, "The Originality of Machiavelli," in *Studies on Machiavelli*, ed. Myron P. Gilmore (Florence: Sansoni, 1972), 147 206.

[80] Machiavelli, *Discorsi* 1.4 5, in *Tutte le opere*, 82 4.

to political discord of authorities such as Cicero, Sallust, and Skinner's early humanists that Machiavelli advances the claim that Professor Nederman so emphasizes, citing Cicero in defense of popular participation in public deliberation – and adding a crucial qualifier: that, when the "opinions" of the people *as to the existence or likelihood of such oppression* "are false, there is a remedy in the public assemblies where a good man can stand up and, in speaking, demonstrate to the people that they are in error."[81] It is his rejection of the classical notion of moral and political rationality and his reduction of public reason to multitudinous private calculations of material self-interest that underpin Machiavelli's populist turn.

The crucial fact, Machiavelli insists, that one has to keep always in mind is that the people "have less of an appetite for usurpation" than the *grandi*; if one ponders the ends which "the nobles" pursue and those pursued by "the ignoble," one will recognize that the former's purposes arise from "a grand desire for domination" and the latter's "solely from a desire not to be dominated" – that the former "desire to acquire" while the latter "fear to lose what they have acquired."[82] If, then, the people are better guardians of liberty than the nobility, it is not because they possess any natural inclination for justice but because a defect in "appetite" renders them more timid and less likely to exploit the opportunities presented to them. Machiavelli makes much of "the popular desire . . . to be free," but he insists that only "a very small part" of the people "desire to be free in order to command; all the others, who are infinite in number, desire liberty in order to live securely." Thus, "the common utility" that ordinary men draw "from a free way of life [*vivere libero*]" is extremely prosaic, even bourgeois: "being able to possess one's things freely without any suspicion, not having grounds for doubting the honor of women and of children, not fearing for oneself."[83] It was not for nothing that Peter Laslett, some years ago, suggested that John Locke be considered "Machiavelli's

---

[81] Cf. Machiavelli, *Discorsi* 1.4.1, in *Tutte le opere*, 82–3, with Cicero, *Amic.* 25.95.

[82] Machiavelli, *Discorsi* 1.5.2, in *Tutte le opere*, 83–4. At the end of the chapter, Machiavelli opens up the possibility that the majority of the well-to-do are, in this crucial regard, a part of the *popolo* in that they are driven to further acquisition by the fear of losing what they have: *Discorsi* 1.5.4, in *Tutte le opere*, 84. This leaves one to wonder whether, when he speaks of "the nobles" and "the ignoble," Machiavelli has in mind a distinction grounded in convention or in nature. Consider what he has to say about the behavior of the *plebs* once it has secured what it has acquired: *Discorsi* 1.37, in *Tutte le opere*, 119–20. The uncharacteristic ambition that the plebeians then display would appear to stem from that of the natural aristocrats in their number: *Discorsi* 1.16.5, in *Tutte le opere*, 100–1.

[83] Machiavelli, *Discorsi* 1.16.3–5, in *Tutte le opere*, 100–1.

philosopher."[84] One takes a giant step from Machiavelli's position towards that of Skinner's liberal individualists and one severs the last tenuous link connecting the Florentine's understanding of the purpose of liberty with that of the ancients when one follows through on the logic of Machiavelli's populism, adopts the amendment suggested by Skinner's English "neo-Romans," and grounds the polity exclusively on the desire of the *popolo* for security while subordinating to that desire quite systematically the vain aspirations of the *grandi* for honor, glory, conquest, and command.[85]

Later, when Machiavelli once again sounds his populist theme, he underlines even more emphatically the elements within his argument that mark his break with the ancients, and he signals this theme's novelty, its radicalism, and its significance for his teaching as a whole by directly attacking his authority, Livy. This time, he explicitly debunks the classical presumption that the wise and virtuous few are superior to the foolish and vicious many. In doing so, he points to the fact that, if a legislator really must presuppose that "all men are wicked and that they will make use of the malignity of their spirit whenever they are free and have occasion to do so," there is no place for the classical republican principle of differential moral and political rationality. Not just Livy, he contends, but "all the other historians" and, indeed, "all the writers" are profoundly mistaken. In fact, all are in error who have preceded Machiavelli and who have therefore been unable to profit from his discovery of the "new modes and orders" that constitute "a road as yet untrodden by anyone" – for they all denounce "the multitude" as "vain and

---

[84] Note Peter Laslett, "Introduction," in John Locke, *Two Treatises of Government*, ed. Peter Laslett, second edn. (Cambridge: Cambridge University Press, 1967), 86 7, and see Tarcov, "Locke's *Second Treatise* and 'The Best Fence Against Rebellion,'" 198 217 (esp. 211 17); Pangle, "Executive Energy and Popular Spirit in Lockean Constitutionalism," 253 65 (esp. 259–64); and Harvey C. Mansfield, Jr., *Taming the Prince: The Ambivalence of Modern Executive Power* (New York: The Free Press, 1989), 121 211. The confusion that besets Skinner's attempt to distinguish liberalism from the sort of republicanism that he champions is especially visible in the concluding remarks of his student Maurizio Viroli: see *From Politics to Reason of State*, 281 95. Cf. Charvet, "Quentin Skinner on the Idea of Freedom," 12 14, and Patten, "The Republican Critique of Liberalism," 25 36.

[85] It is no accident that Skinner's "neo-Romans" are wedded to the language of individual rights: consider Skinner, *Liberty Before Liberalism*, 18 21, in light of ibid., 59 67, and see Rahe, *Republics Ancient and Modern*, 399 541. When Machiavelli rejects the classical notion that the quest for honor and glory points beyond itself to the pursuit of virtue and human excellence or, indeed, to anything higher than fame itself, he not only eliminates the ground for distinguishing the wise and virtuous few from the foolish and vicious many; as he knows all too well, he prepares the way for the collapse of his own distinction between the *grandi* and the *popolo*: consider Pindar, F215 (Bowra) and Theognis, 1104a 1106 (West) in light of Aristotle, *Eth. Nic.* 1123b35 1124a2; then, see *Il Principe* 18 (at the end), in *Tutte le opere*, 284.

inconstant." Livy in particular is wrong when he claims that "the nature of the multitude" is such that "it either serves humbly or dominates proudly." The truth is that "all men in particular and princes especially can be accused of the defect" which these writers attribute to the people, "for everyone who is not regulated by the laws would make the same errors as the multitude unshackled [*sciolta*]." Indeed, "all" are "equally" apt to "go astray when all can go astray without looking back [*sanza rispetto*]." In any case, it makes no sense to compare such a multitude with kings who are subject to the law: to them one should compare "a multitude in the same fashion regulated by laws" – such as "the Roman people who, while the republic remained uncorrupt, never served humbly or dominated proudly."

In practice, Machiavelli informs us, "a prince unshackled from the laws will be more ungrateful, various, and imprudent than the people." This is not due to the "diverse nature" of the prince and the people but to the relative timidity of the latter – to "their having more or less respect [*rispetto*] for the laws under which the one and the other live." If, when "the one and the other are unshackled, one sees fewer errors in the people than in the prince," and their errors are less severe and more easily remedied, it is evidently because the people are defective in appetite and, when lacking genuine leaders as "heads," hopelessly irresolute: "to a licentious and tumultuous people a good man can speak, and they can easily be returned to the good way." Thus, if one wishes to "cure the malady of the people, words are sufficient," but "to cure that of the prince requires iron." The real danger that arises when "a people is completely unshackled" stems not from what the people might do but from the opportunity that this offers to those of their "heads" who possess an appetite for command: "in so much confusion a tyrant can be born."[86]

Machiavelli insists that Livy, "all the other historians," and "all the writers" in general are united in embracing the classical republican principle of differential moral and political rationality, and he puts considerable effort into defending the *popolo* against the charge that arises from what he takes to be a false presumption. He does, however, concede the superiority of princes in one particular – "in ordaining laws, forming civil life, ordaining new statutes and orders." The people are superior, he tells us, only in "maintaining things" already "ordained." Because of its defect in appetite, the populace seems unable to initiate.

---

[86] Note Livy 6.7, 14, 24.25, and consider Machiavelli, *Discorsi* 1.58 in light of 1.2.3, 44, 54, and 57, in *Tutte le opere*, 79–80, 126–7, 136, 139–42.

In fact, it needs guidance from "someone" of sufficient appetite "in whom it has faith" – for, often, "deceived by a false image of the good, the people desire their own ruin." Fortunately, in judging between orators of "equal *virtù*," the populace tends to "the better opinion." Rarely, says Machiavelli, are the people "incapable" of discerning "the truth that they hear." It is as if they are in possession of "an occult virtue" enabling them to "foresee their own ill and their good." To exercise that virtue, however, they must be turned away from false images of the good and liberated from all abstract notions and from every glittering moral and political "generality." "By finding a mode in which they have to descend to particulars," he tells us, "one can make the people open their eyes."[87] It was with this argument in mind that Machiavelli's great admirer James Harrington banned public deliberation in the manner described by Professor Nederman, for he knew that the orators on opposing sides are only rarely "equal in *virtù*," and he had learned from observing the religious conflicts that broke out soon after Machiavelli's death just how common it is for the people to be distracted and "deceived by a false image of the good" and to "desire their own ruin" when not somehow forced by well-designed institutions "to descend" to the "particulars" of their own material self-interest.[88]

Of course, in defending populism, Machiavelli is inclined to speak not just of "virtue" and "corruption," but of "the common good" – and to do so in a manner that many critics of liberal individualism find morally appealing. For example, when considering the "unshackled," he observes that "the cruelty of the multitude" is deployed only "against those who, they fear, will lay hold of the common good" while that of the prince is deployed "against those who, he fears, will lay hold of his own good."[89] The contrast might be taken as an indication that peoples and princes somehow differ in character, but, as we have seen, this is not Machiavelli's view: he never budges from his position that a legislator must presume all men wicked. In any case, his common good is not really held in common: it cannot ground a politics of "common meanings and purposes." In Machiavelli's republic, the individual citizen is no more interested in a good not privately his own than is the prince: it

---

[87] Machiavelli, *Discorsi* 1.47, 53.1, 54, 58.3, in *Tutte le opere*, 129 30, 134, 136, 141 42.
[88] See Rahe, *Republics Ancient and Modern*, 408 26. See also Jonathan Scott, "The Rapture of Motion: James Harrington's Republicanism," in *Political Discourse in Early Modern Britain*, ed. Nicholas Phillipson and Quentin Skinner (Cambridge: Cambridge University Press, 1993), 139 63, and Gary Remer, "James Harrington's New Deliberative Rhetoric: Reflections of an Anticlassical Republican," *History of Political Thought* 4 (1995): 532 57.
[89] Machiavelli, *Discorsi* 1.58.4, in *Tutte le opere*, 142.

simply happens to be the case that the material interests of the common people in the aggregate coincide more or less with the material interests of the community as a whole; and if a minority loses out, this is a matter of no concern. Machiavelli traces the popular "affection for living in liberty [*vivere libero*]" not to any high-minded notion of honor, glory, nobility, or virtue nor to any appreciation on the part of the people of the intrinsic dignity of political liberty itself, but to their recognition of the simple fact that "cities have not grown either in dominion or riches when not in a condition of liberty." Machiavelli has conquest and tribute, profit and acquisitions, and nothing nobler in mind when he writes, "It is not the particular good but the common good which makes cities great, and without a doubt this common good is not observed if not in republics."[90]

What this means is that Machiavelli's populism is modern. It rests not on any conviction that man is by nature a political animal endowed with moral and political rationality, nor on any judgment as to the human capacity to transcend private interest in pursuit of a transcendent common good, nor on any belief that the human potential for *ratio et oratio* points towards justice, equity, and even the good. In fact, as Professor Mansfield points out in his contribution to this volume, Machiavelli's populism presupposes that *ratio et oratio* are always secondary: that deeds, especially deeds of violence, are prior to and determinative of words.[91] There is for this reason nothing in Machiavelli's own account of the origins of civil society comparable to the references in Cicero to nature's provision to man of the capacity for reason and speech.[92] Machiavelli's populism rests, then, solely on his commonsense recognition that, while ordinary human beings may not be as skilled as some among them in searching out the consequences of various courses of action, they are perfectly capable, when presented with the arguments by two orators of equal ability, of judging what they have to say – at least when induced to descend to the particulars of their own lives and made to weigh these arguments as they pertain to their own material interests. No one, Machiavelli implies, is as good a judge in calculating his own self-interest thus narrowly understood as is the individual concerned.

[90] Machiavelli, *Discorsi* 2.2.1, in *Tutte le opere*, 148. The qualification added at the end deserves particular attention.
[91] See chapter 8.
[92] Consider *Discorsi* 1.1–2 (esp. 2.3), in *Tutte le opere*, 77–81, in light of Mansfield, *Machiavelli's New Modes and Orders*, 28–41, and see Harvey C. Mansfield, Jr., "Necessity in the Beginning of Cities," reprinted in Mansfield, *Machiavelli's Virtue* (Chicago: University of Chicago Press, 1996), 57–78.

When viewed from this vantage point, Machiavelli's understanding of republican politics would appear to have a certain Augustinian flavor: it presupposes as ineluctable the human depravity that the ancient Greeks and Romans thought it possible by way of *paideia* to transcend. His understanding certainly has more in common with the guild republicanism of the later Middle Ages than with the classical republicanism championed by some from among the scholastics and the Renaissance humanists.[93] Like that guild republicanism, it promotes a politics of material interest.[94] Its focus is mere advantage rather than "the middle ground" where private and public advantage are reconsidered and reinterpreted within a horizon defined by justice and the transcendent good.[95] It operates in accord with the dictum of Roman law devised for the government of corporations in the private, economic sphere: *Quod omnes tangit ab omnibus tractari debeat.* It reduces the political in a manner sanctioned by Augustine and the Church Fathers to what the ancients had considered subpolitical.[96] The one difference separating Machiavelli from the bishop of Hippo and from the guildsmen of the medieval communes is that there is no room within the Florentine's conception of republican politics for original sin and divine grace. Of course, this defect is as a difference decisive, for it liberates his politics from all moral limits as well as from ecclesiastical tutelage. It is certainly hard to imagine Machiavelli seriously posing to himself Augustine's question: "In so far as concerns this life of mortal men, which is conducted and brought to conclusion within a few days, what does it matter under whose rule lives a man who is destined to die

[93] See John M. Najemy, "*Arti* and *Ordini* in Machiavelli's *Istorie Fiorentine*," in *Essays Presented to Myron P. Gilmore*, vol. I: *History*, ed. Sergio Bertelli and Gloria Ramakus (Florence: La Nuova Italia, 1978), 161–91; *Corporatism and Consensus in Florentine Electoral Politics*, 301–17 (esp., 315–17); and "Machiavelli and the Medici: The Lessons of Florentine History," *Renaissance Quarterly* 35 (1982): 551–76. For a corrective to the propensity, evident in Skinner and others, to draw a sharp distinction between the political thought of the scholastics and that of the humanists, see James M. Blythe, *Ideal Government and the Mixed Constitution in the Middle Ages* (Princeton: Princeton University Press, 1992).

[94] In this connection, see Antony Black, *Guilds and Civil Society in European Political Thought from the Twelfth Century to the Present* (London: Methuen, 1984). For the Florentine experience, see John M. Najemy, "Guild Republicanism in Trecento Florence: The Successes and Ultimate Failure of Corporate Politics," *American Historical Review* 84 (1979): 53–71, and *Corporatism and Consensus in Florentine Electoral Politics*, 3–317.

[95] I have elsewhere collected and discussed the evidence for what the Greeks had in mind when they spoke of *to meson*: see "The Primacy of Politics in Classical Greece," 265–93 (esp. n. 52), and *Republics Ancient and Modern*, 34–48, 53–57, 124, 207, 209, 371–92, 414–18, 467–8, 472–9, 562–72, 581–614, 672–3, 777 (with 812–13, nn. 81, 83–4, 89–91). For the dependence of advantage on justice and the good, see Paul A. Rahe, "Thucydides' Critique of *Realpolitik*," *Security Studies* 5:2 (Winter, 1995): 105–41.

[96] See Paul A. Rahe, "The Constitution of Liberty Within Christendom," *The Intercollegiate Review* 33:1 (Fall, 1997): 30–36.

– as long as those who rule do not force him to commit impious and iniquitous deeds?"[97]

SITUATING MACHIAVELLI

As should be evident by now, Quentin Skinner has never shown any inclination to attribute to Machiavelli any commitment to natural teleology. He has, in fact, paid especially careful attention to the elements in Machiavelli's analysis that set him apart from those with whom he nonetheless wishes to see him aligned. Some time ago, Skinner drew attention to the shocking novelty of Machiavelli's claims with regard to political strife, and he has emphasized as well the manner in which the Florentine's endorsement of tumults not only sets him against Cicero's call for a *consensus omnium* and *concordia ordinum* and Sallust's preference for civic solidarity but also puts him at odds with the hostility to factionalism that permeated the civic rhetoric of the *dictatores* in late medieval Italy, that of their Renaissance humanist successors, and even the thinking of Machiavelli's younger friend Francesco Guicciardini,[98] whose tough-mindedness is the subject of Professor Moulakis' and Professor Brown's contributions to this volume.[99]

Moreover, Skinner has closely examined the way in which Machiavelli "silently" made "one alteration . . . to the classical analysis of the virtues needed to serve the *communes utilitates*." As he notes, Machiavelli finds place in his discussion for prudence, courage, and temperance, but then "erases the quality of justice, the quality that Cicero in *De officiis* had described as the crowning splendour of virtue." Skinner finds this "immensely important" it is, he says, "small in appearance but overwhelming in significance." Machiavelli's repudiation of "the crucial" Ciceronian "contention that the observance" of justice "is invariably

---

[97] Augustine, *De civ. D.* 5.17.
[98] Consider Skinner, "Machiavelli's *Discorsi* and the Pre-Humanist Origins of Republican Ideas," 135 6, in light of ibid., 128 34, and see Skinner, *The Foundations of Modern Political Thought*, I: 180 6, and *Machiavelli*, 65 7. In this connection, see Francesco Guicciardini, *Ricordi*, ed. Ettore Barelli (Milan: Biblioteca Universale Rizzoli, 1977), C 123, B 14, 95, 124; then, consider Guicciardini, "Considerazioni sui Discorsi del Machiavelli," in Francesco Guicciardini, *Opere inedite*, 10 vols. (Florence: Barbèra, Bianchi, e comp., 1857 67), I: 12 14. It was by means of his fascination with intestine conflict that Machiavelli distinguished himself as a historian from classical republicans such as Leonardo Bruni: *Istorie fiorentine* Proemio, in *Tutte le opere*, 632 3. For a further examination of this last theme, see Harvey C. Mansfield, Jr., "Party and Sect in Machiavelli's *Florentine Histories*," reprinted in Mansfield, *Machiavelli's Virtue*, 137 75; and Gisela Bock, "Civil Discord in Machiavelli's *Istorie Fiorentine*," in *Machiavelli and Republicanism*, 181 201.
[99] See above, chapters 6 and 7. See also Viroli, *From Politics to Reason of State*, 178 200, and Athanasios Moulakis, *Republican Realism in Renaissance Florence: Francesco Guicciardini's Discorso di Logrogno* (Lanham: Rowman and Littlefield, 1998).

conducive to serving the common good . . . takes us to the heart of his originality and his subversive quality as a theorist of statecraft." It "represents an epoch-making break with the classical republican analysis of the cardinal virtues; its suddenness and completeness can hardly be overemphasized."

But then, after saying all of this, Skinner with a suddenness and completeness all his own reverses course, writing that "it is scarcely less important to emphasize that this represents Machiavelli's sole quarrel with his classical authorities. The result of his analysis of *virtù* and its connections with *libertà* is impeccably Ciceronian in character." Machiavelli, he explains,

> not only centres his entire account around the qualities of courage, temperance and prudence; he regularly refers to these attributes as elements of virtue as well as preconditions of liberty . . . At the heart of Machiavelli's political theory there is thus a purely classical message, framed in the same play on words that the classical republican theorists had all exploited. If we ask in virtue of what qualities, what talents or abilities, we can hope to assure our own liberty and contribute to the common good, the answer is: in virtue of the virtues.[100]

Nowhere does Skinner ponder whether Cicero's contention that the virtues are politically useful exhausts his understanding of virtue. Nowhere in his various discussions of Machiavelli and the ancients does he pause to consider whether the Florentine's critique of civic solidarity and of the Ciceronian teaching regarding justice might not have a larger significance.[101]

---

[100] Skinner, "The Idea of Negative Liberty," 208–17 (esp. 214–17). See also Skinner, "Political Philosophy," 438–9, and "Machiavelli's *Discorsi* and the Pre-Humanist Origins of Republican Ideas," 136–7. In earlier formulations, Skinner gave equal weight to Machiavelli's other quarrel with his classical authorities his endorsement of tumults: see *The Foundations of Modern Political Thought*, I: 180–6, and *Machiavelli*, 53–77. Viroli diverges from Skinner in contending that the endorsement of tumults is Machiavelli's sole innovation: *From Politics to Reason of State*, 154–77 (esp. 154).

[101] Skinner's attentiveness to Machiavelli's alteration of Cicero's teaching on the virtues nonetheless marks a considerable advance on Marcia Colish's thoroughgoing attempt to reconcile the two: cf. Colish, "Cicero's *De officiis* and Machiavelli's *Prince*," *Sixteenth Century Journal* 9 (1978): 81–93, and Tuck, "Humanism and Political Thought," 43–65 (esp. 56–8), with Skinner, *Machiavelli*, 34–47, and see Hulliung, *Citizen Machiavelli*, 189–218. Note also Skinner, *The Foundations of Modern Political Thought*, I: 128–38. Colish is, of course, right to emphasize that, in *De officiis*, where Cicero makes a systematic attempt to reconcile the *honestum* with the *utile*, he does so by blunting the sharpness of the distinction drawn by the Stoics, but she errs in supposing that this brings him close to Machiavelli. Aristotle is the presiding genius here: Cicero's reformulation of the Stoic teaching arises from his conviction that man is by nature a political animal. While he interprets the *honestum* as it pertains to individual citizens in light of the *utilitas rei publicae*, he is careful to limit that same *utilitas rei publicae* in light of the *honestum*: his Rome is attentive to the demands of justice and the transcendent good in a fashion inconceivable for Machiavelli's predatory republic.

I would submit that the two changes made by Machiavelli are, indeed, "immensely important," "overwhelming in significance," "subversive," and "epoch-making" – that, in fact, they change everything, and that they have a common root. When Machiavelli jettisons natural teleology, he abandons the central tenet of classical republicanism. To be precise, he rejects the common Greek and Roman conviction that man is a political animal and that his political character stems from his capacity to discern and make clear to others in rational speech the linkage between the advantageous, the just, and the good. When he rejects this conviction, he reduces reason to mere calculation, and he transforms the virtues from ends in themselves into mere means for personal defense and material gain. Then, when he "erases the quality of justice" on the grounds that it sometimes fails to serve personal defense and material gain, he alters forever the character of the virtues that remain, eliminating thereby the distinction between courage and ferocity, temperance and resolution, prudence and cunning – and rendering the civic ideal of social solidarity utterly implausible.[102] When he does all of this in its "suddenness and completeness," he points the way to genuinely "new modes and orders" and opens up "a road untrodden by anyone" which leads on to the substitution of institutions with teeth in them for the *paideia* in moral and political virtue that was the true "heart and nerve of all classical republican theories of citizenship."[103] Skinner is aware of the novel character of Machiavelli's institutional focus: he has written on the subject with considerable insight.[104] But he fails fully to appreciate its significance, and he therefore neglects to draw between Machiavelli and the Romans the distinction required in cases where there is a substantive difference. Here, he lumps where he should split.

BEYOND LINGUISTIC CONTEXTUALISM

It is perhaps time that we abandon the attempt to square the circle; cease speaking of Machiavelli as a civic humanist, classical republican, or

---

[102] For a far more radical investigation of Machiavelli's teaching on this question than Skinner seems willing to contemplate, see Harvey C. Mansfield, Jr., "Machiavelli's Virtue," in Mansfield, *Machiavelli's Virtue*, 6–52.
[103] Cf. Skinner, "The Idea of Negative Liberty," 207–8.
[104] See Skinner, "Machiavelli on the Maintenance of Liberty," 3–15 (esp. 8–13) and "Political Philosophy," 439–41. I would qualify Skinner's account, however, in one particular: although Machiavelli's defense of political strife can be said to be the inspiration for James Harrington's championing of bicameralism, in Machiavelli himself it eventuates in a defense of tumults. See Rahe, *Republics Ancient and Modern*, 420–4.

neo-Roman; and turn back to the question whether and how *The Prince* and the *Discourses on Livy* can be reconciled. After all, Lord Macaulay suggested a plausible point of departure long ago, when he wrote, "Il principe traces the progress of an ambitious man, the Discourses the progress of an ambitious people. The same principles on which, in the former work, the elevation of an individual is explained, are applied in the latter to the longer duration and more complex interest of a society." Even Quentin Skinner admits that "for all the many differences between *The Prince* and the *Discourses*, the underlying political morality of the two books is . . . the same."[105] The real obstacle to understanding would appear to be our timidity, our reluctance to contemplate the linkage between the species of republicanism pioneered by Machiavelli and his teaching in *The Prince*,[106] and our unwillingness to acknowledge the debt owed Machiavel by the liberal republicanism that we have inherited from his seventeenth- and eighteenth-century admirers.[107]

That our contemporaries should be skeptical as to whether liberal individualism can equip us with "a vision of politics based not merely on fair procedures but on common meanings and purposes" is entirely understandable, and it is perfectly in keeping with a prudent appreciation for the advantages afforded by the modern secular state that they should be wary of what Skinner calls "the Aristotelian and Thomist assumption that a healthy public life must be founded on a conception of *eudaimonia*." But that a predatory imperialism of the sort practiced by Machiavelli's Rome can do more than to provide a basis for reconciling private with public greed we may justly doubt, and there are good grounds as well for wondering whether one can articulate a politics of "common meanings and purposes" linking "individual liberty with virtuous acts of public service" solely on the basis of the calculation "that, if we wish to maximise our own individual liberty, we must cease to put our trust in princes, and instead take charge of the public arena ourselves."[108] If a politics of virtue, informed by "common meanings

---

[105] Cf. Thomas Babington Macaulay, "Machiavelli," in *Critical, Historical, and Miscellaneous Essays*, 6 vols. (New York: Hurd and Houghton, 1860), I: 309, with Skinner, *The Foundations of Modern Political Thought*, I: 182–4. Note also Skinner, *Machiavelli*, 34–47, 53–77. Cf., however, Viroli, *From Politics to Reason of State*, 126–77.

[106] For a resolute attempt to come to grips with the unity of Machiavelli's two books without forcing either into a superficial conformity with the other, see Leo Strauss, *Thoughts on Machiavelli* (Glencoe, Ill.: The Free Press, 1958).

[107] For correctives, see Mansfield, *Taming the Prince*, passim (esp. 121–278); Paul A. Rahe, "Thomas Jefferson's Machiavellian Political Science," *Review of Politics* 57 (1995): 449–81; and the other essays collected in *Machiavelli's Republican Legacy*, ed. Paul A. Rahe, forthcoming.

[108] Skinner, "The Idea of Negative Liberty," 197 and "The Republican Ideal of Political Liberty," 308.

and purposes," is what Quentin Skinner and those who wish to draw a sharp distinction between liberalism and republicanism really seek, they are looking in the wrong place – for not even an alchemist can extract gold from dross.

If we are ever fully to appreciate Machiavelli's originality, we will have to abandon the quest to situate him within an intellectual matrix by reducing him to it. He wrote within an intellectual context, to be sure. In making his arguments, he deployed an inherited normative vocabulary. He was flesh and blood: he lived in a particular time and place; he spoke Italian and was educated in a particular tradition; he had access to some books and not to others. If he wanted to communicate with contemporary readers and to persuade them, he had to accommodate himself to certain conventions. If we ignore all of this, we are likely to misapprehend what he wrote. All of this is true, all too true – but none of it proves that, in any substantive way, the particularities of Machiavelli's situation restricted what he could think or even say.

Machiavelli was a master of rhetoric who delighted in seizing upon traditional forms and arguments and reversing all the polarities.[109] It is now widely acknowledged that, in taking up the genre of the mirrors of princes, he turned it to a set of purposes quite foreign to that tradition.[110] In the *Discourses on Livy*, as we have seen, he appropriates the moral vocabulary of Cicero's *De officiis*; and then, by restricting himself to a consideration of virtue's utility, he strikes justice from the canonical list and transforms the very character of courage, temperance, and wisdom or prudence. Ordinary human beings may think within a framework determined by inherited assumptions and the available vocabulary. But there was nothing ordinary about Niccolò Machiavelli. To do justice to the trickster who gave to the devil his moniker "Old Nick," we must restore to the study of intellectual history a notion of agency – for when

---

[109] As John Najemy ("Machiavelli and the Medici," 555, n. 10) observes, "Machiavelli's tendency to appropriate and yet consciously to subvert his sources . . . makes any search for *their* influence on *him* a one-sided approach to the problem. Because he did not depend uncritically on these sources, the identification of their traces . . . can never serve to 'explain' why Machiavelli wrote as he did on any particular theme. In other words, the text is not a function of its sources; rather, it emerges from the confrontation of Machiavelli's language with them." Patricia Osmond ("Sallust and Machiavelli," 437) is quite right to emphasize, with regard to Machiavelli, that many Renaissance readers were less interested in understanding figures such as Sallust and Livy than in "selectively borrowing, imitating, adapting whatever seemed to suit their aims."

[110] Cf. Allan H. Gilbert, *Machiavelli's Prince and Its Forerunners* (Durham, N.C.: Duke University Press, 1938), with Felix Gilbert, "The Humanist Concept of the Prince and *The Prince* of Machiavelli," in *History: Choice and Commitment*, 91–114, and see Robert Hariman, "Composing Modernity in Machiavelli's *Prince*," *Journal of the History of Ideas* 50 (1989): 3–29; then, note Skinner, *The Foundations of Modern Political Thought*, I: 118–38, *Machiavelli*, 21–47, and "Political Philosophy," 409–16, 423–34, and Viroli, *From Politics to Reason of State*, 96–106, 126–54, 238–80.

Machiavelli comes to the defense of classical republicanism, he is doing to it just what he did to the mirrors of princes and to Cicero's teaching concerning the virtues: with a wink and a nod and an occasional propitiatory word to console the pious humanist partisans of the ancients and beguile their modern heirs, he is turning that tradition on its head.[111] If a genuine admiration for classical antiquity was the distinguishing feature of the Renaissance, Machiavelli was the man who killed it once and for all.

[111] In this connection, see Mansfield, *Machiavelli's New Modes and Orders* passim; Sullivan, *Machiavelli's Three Romes*, 57 117; and Hankins, "Humanism and the Origins of Modern Political Thought," 134 7.

Index of manuscripts and archival documents

Florence, Archivio di Stato
  Balìe 17, 95, 208
  Capitoli, Protocolli 7, 82
  Carte Bagni (scaff. 43/III), filza 65 (ins. 15), 197
  Consulte e pratiche 52, 189, 190
  Consulte e pratiche 57, 184
  Miscellanea repubblicana 109, 192
  Notarile antecosmiano 9636, 191
  Notarile antecosmiano 14183, 191
  Provvisioni 185, 194
  Signori e collegi, Deliberazioni (ord. aut.) 96, 194

Florence, Biblioteca Mediceo-Laurenziana
  Ashburnham 1918, 163
  Martelli 8, 156
  Plut. XIII, 5, 193
  Plut. XIII, 8, 193

Florence, Biblioteca Nazionale Centrale
  Banco rari 341, 193
  Naz. II V 10, 156

Florence, Biblioteca Riccardiana
  Ed. rari 341, 192
  Ricc. 784, 148

Florence, Opera del Duomo, Archivio
  Antifonario C 11, 193

London, British Library
  Harl. 2268, 148, 149

Paris, Bibliothèque Nationale
  lat. 16089, 55

Turin, Archivio di Stato
  MS J a VI 35, 149

Vatican City, Biblioteca Apostolica Vaticana
  Vat. lat. 3477, 148
  Vat. lat. 5223, 148

General index

active and contemplative lives, 8, 31, 60, 71–3, 88, 100, 203, 286
Albizzi, Maso degli, 207, 219
Albizzi, Rinaldo degli, 84, 157, 158, 176, 207
Alessandri, Alessandro degli, 101
American constitutional thought, 221
American Revolution, ideology of, 2, 3, 21–2, 26, 80, 268
Aquinas, Thomas, 34, 37–40, 55, 59, 61–2, 63, 276, 278, 293, 306
Arendt, Hannah, 226
Aristides, Aelius, 144, 186
aristocracy, 39, 243
Aristotle, 4, 8, 16, 34–5, 55, 66–7, 73, 110, 170, 172–3, 177, 203, 205, 217, 218–19, 228, 236, 237, 275, 284, 306
 Ethics, 56, 204, 285
 Politics, 35, 64, 66, 240, 285, 286
 Rhetoric, 230, 246
Arnold of Brescia, 36
ars dictaminis, 53, 72, 279, 282, 283, 303
Augustine, St., 45, 49, 51, 57, 58, 193, 235, 302
Augustus, Roman emperor, 41, 42, 47
Azo, the glossator, 54–5

Bacon, Francis, 228
Bailyn, Bernard, 21–2, 227
Baron, Hans, 7, 8, 11, 12, 15–18, 20, 24–6, 30–1, 35–7, 43–4, 70–1, 73–4, 75–7, 105–7, 120, 141–2, 143, 151, 159–60, 181, 202, 223–6, 229–30, 244, 272, 279
Bartolus of Sassoferrato, 68
Beard, Charles, 21
Beccadelli, Antonio, "il Panormita", 158
Bentham, Jeremy, 276
Benzo d'Alessandria, 54
Berlin, Isaiah, 276, 284
Biglia, Andrea, 159n, 166
Black, Antony, 35
Blair, Tony, 2
Blythe, James M., 8, 285

Bodin, Jean, 198
Bouwsma, William J., 18
Brown, Alison, 10, 303
Brucker, Gene, 157
Bruni, Leonardo, 8, 9, 11, 12, 16, 27, 71, 73–4, 78, 85–6, 98–9, 100–2, 105, 108, 125, 143–78, 200, 202, 215, 228–32, 234–5, 236–46, 279, 290
 Commentarius rerum suo tempore gestarum (*Commentary on the Events of His Own Time*), 171
 De militia (*On Knighthood*), 143, 154
 De primo bello punico (*On the First Punic War*), 147
 De studiis et literis (*On Literary Study*), 176
 Epistula ad magnum principem imperatorem (*Letter to the Great Prince-Emperor*), 173
 Epistulae familiares (*Letters to his Friends*), 160–1, 173
 Historiae Florentini populi (*History of the Florentine People*), 79, 85–6, 106, 132, 133, 145,162, 163, 164, 170–71, 173, 205
 Isagogicon moralis disciplinae (*Introduction to Moral Philosophy*), 147, 176
 Laudatio Florentinae urbis (*Panegyric of the City of Florence*), 9, 35–6, 79, 98–9, 100, 101–3, 117, 123–4, 125, 126–9, 143, 144–51, 157, 160–4, 169–71, 187, 202, 204–5, 229–38, 240–4
 Oratio in funere Ioannis Stroze (*Funeral Oration for Nanni Strozzi*), 95, 143, 151–9, 164–7, 171–2, 187
 Περὶ τῆς τῶν Φλωρεντίνων πολιτείας (*On the Polity of the Florentines*), 174–5, 203–4
 Preamble to the Statutes of the Guelf Party, 105
 Translation of Aristotle's *Ethics*, 147, 204
 Translation of Aristotle's *Politics*, 173, 202, 203
 Translation of St. Basil, *Ad adolescentes*, 147
 Vita di Dante (*Life of Dante*), 90–2, 100–1
Burckhardt, Jacob, 16, 202, 224, 225, 226

310

General index

Caesar, Gaius Julius, 41, 42, 47, 121, 216, 231
Capponi, Gino, 83, 133, 136, 138
Capponi, Neri, 133
  Commentari della guerra o dell'acquisto di Pisa
  (*Commentaries on the War or Conquest of Pisa*),
  133
"Cambridge School", 2, 19
capitalism, 20, 21
Capra, Bartolomeo, 158–9
Castellani, Michele, 156
Cavalcanti, Giovanni, 84, 157, 165–6
Charlemagne, king of the Franks, 36, 45
Chartier, Roger, 183, 196
Christianity, 235, 246, 294, 295–6
Chrysoloras, Manuel, 156
Church, Roman, 45–8, 52, 114, 243–4
Cicero, Marcus Tullius, 6, 9, 16, 31, 35, 36, 53, 59, 60, 70–3, 97, 110, 167–8, 170, 216, 220, 248–59, 280–90, 292, 303, 304, 307, 308
  De finibus bonorum et malorum (*On the Standards of Good and Evil*), 254–5
  De inventione (*On Invention*), 250–2, 282, 287, 288
  De legibus (*On Laws*), 254, 257, 258, 282, 288
  De officiis (*On Duties*), 97, 250, 255, 256, 287, 288
  De optimo genere oratorum (*On the Best Kind of Orator*), 252, 287
  De oratore (*On the Orator*), 167, 250–2, 287, 288
  De re publica (*On the Commonwealth*), 258, 289
  Epistulae familiares, 167–8
  Partitiones oratoriae, 168
Ciompi rebellion, 83–5, 175, 206, 208, 291
citizenship, 111, 112, 127, 219, 283, 285, 290
civil society, 60
Clinton, William Jefferson, 2
Columbus, Christopher, 274
common good, 11, 14, 20, 33, 37, 39, 61, 62, 63, 73, 138, 178, 239, 245, 256, 264, 268
communitarianism, 2, 5, 12, 13, 22, 24
Connell, William J., 7, 8, 272
consent, popular, 211, 213–14, 219, 246, 262
constitutions, history of, 38–41, 43
constitutions, theory of, 37, 40–1, 66–70, 153, 200–22, 238–9
contemplative life: *see* active and contemplative lives
Cornazzano, Antonio, 149
corruption, 222

Dante Alighieri, 36, 68, 90–2, 178, 238
Dati, Gregorio, 79, 87–9, 107, 117–20, 123, 133
  Istoria di Firenze (*History of Florence*), 113, 117–19, 123, 141
Daub, Susanne, 151

David, king of Israel, 185, 186, 190, 194, 195
Davis, Charles Till, 25, 36–7, 47, 58
Decembrio, Pier Candido, 149–51
deliberation, 211, 220–1, 262, 265–7, 282, 288–9
Delors, Jacques, 2
democracy, 21, 25, 39, 62, 68, 271
Demosthenes, 187
despotism, 56–7, 62
Donatello, 185–6, 190

education, 100–1
Engelbert of Admont, 34, 42–3, 46, 62–3, 66–8
Epaminondas, 167
equality, 76, 107
equality, legal, 107, 111, 116, 213, 221
Este, Niccolò III d', 157, 165, 166
Etruscans, 153

family, as metaphor for republic, 100–3
Fanfani, Amintore, 20
Field, Arthur M., 175n
Florence, festivals in, 180–1, 192–3
Florence, imperial myth of, 11, 127, 130–2
Florus, Lucius Annaeus, 36
Frederick I Barbarossa, Holy Roman emperor, 45
Fubini, Riccardo, 24

Gentili, Alberico, 271
Gilbert, Felix, 17–21
Girolami, Remigio de', 36, 70
Gottolengo (or Ottolengo), battle of, 154–5
Greenblatt, Stephen, 182
Guicciardini, Francesco, 10, 19, 179, 180, 181, 193, 189, 192, 196, 198, 200–2, 207, 211–17, 218–19, 221, 303
  Dialogo del reggimento di Firenze (*Dialogue on the Government of Florence*), 10, 184, 195,197, 200, 215
  Discorso di Logrogno (*On Bringing Order to Popular Government*), 197, 200, 212–17
  Ricordi (*Maxims*), 181–2, 195, 214, 221
  Storie fiorentine (*Florentine Histories*), 200, 207
guild republicanism, 12, 81–4, 292

Hankins, James, 12, 30, 53, 73, 78–80, 290
Harrington, James, 5, 262–3, 265–8, 286, 296, 300
Hartz, Louis, 21
Hebrews, ancient polity of, 38, 39, 43
Hegel, Georg Wilhelm Friedrich, 225, 227
Hegelianism, 225
Heidegger, Martin, 227

Henry of Rimini, 54
Heraclitus, 293
Hercules, 185, 186, 189, 190, 193, 194
Herzog, Don, 268–69
Hobbes, Thomas, 184, 198, 263, 276, 284, 285, 293
Hörnqvist, Mikael, 12, 291
human society, origins of, 57, 59–60
Hume, David, 293

ideology, 80–1, 125, 130, 176–7, 245
  Guelf, 114, 117, 120, 124, 125, 128, 208
imperialism, 11, 13, 25, 106–42, 146, 147, 240–2, 244; *see also*: signory

Jerome, St., 45
John of Paris, 34, 64, 69–70, 72
John of Salisbury, 36
just war, 205, 240
Juvenal (Decimus Junius Juvenalis), 36

Kent, Dale, 158
knighthood, 154–5
Kristeller, Paul Oskar, 72, 245

Landino, Cristoforo, 193
Laslett, Peter, 297
Latini, Brunetto, 56, 72
Lazaro da Padova, 147
legitimacy, 10, 51, 52, 95, 126, 154, 172–3, 174n, 204, 208, 209, 211, 217
Lewis, Ewart D., 66
liberalism, 3, 6, 13, 277–8
liberty, 6, 11, 105–112, 114, 124–5, 179–9
  "negative", 6, 8, 11, 116–17, 283
  "positive", 6, 8, 11, 116–17, 283
Livy (Titus Livius), 110, 150, 274, 280, 283, 284, 285, 298–9
Locke, John, 2, 4, 22, 23, 26, 276, 297
Loschi, Antonio, 113, 115–16, 120, 142
Lucan (Marcus Annaeus Lucanus), 36
Lupold of Bebenberg, 52

Macaulay, Thomas Babington, 306
Machiavelli, Niccolò, 5, 6, 8, 9, 10, 12, 14, 16–19, 26, 27–9, 183, 197, 198, 224–46, 262–5, 270–6, 278, 280, 286, 292–308
  Discorsi sopra la prima deca di Tito Livio (*Discourses on Livy*), 17–18, 28, 232, 233, 234, 236, 246, 263–5, 270–4, 280, 294–301, 306, 307
  Discursus florentinarum rerum (*Discourse on Florentine Affairs*), 198
  Il principe (*The Prince*), 17–18, 28, 232, 233,
234, 246, 270–3, 306
  Storie fiorentine (*Florentine Histories*), 236
MacIntyre, Alasdair, 27, 276
Manent, Pierre, 5
Mansfield, Harvey C., Jr., 9, 13, 198, 214–15, 217, 220, 301
Marcus de Canetulo, 148
Marsilius of Padua, 34, 49–50, 53, 54, 64–5, 71, 72, 259–62, 286, 290
Martines, Lauro, 73
Marxism, 2, 3
marzocco, heraldic lion of Florence, 141, 185–6, 193
Mattingly, Garrett, 272
Medici, Alessandro de', duke of Florence, 196
Medici, Cosimo de', 149, 175, 184, 189–91, 193
Medici, family, 189–94, 206
Medici, Lorenzo de', 188, 191–3, 206, 212
Medici, Piero de', 190, 206
Medici, regime, 12, 91–2, 156, 175, 196–7, 206–7, 212
meritocracy, 153–4, 216
Michelangelo Buonarroti, 194
millenarianism, 23
mixed regime, 62, 68
modernity, 9–10, 26, 201
Moerbeke: *see* William of Moerbeke
monarchy, 33, 4, 46–7, 49, 52, 56, 57, 61, 67, 68, 69, 151
Montesquieu, Charles de Secondat, baron de, 198, 217, 226
Morelli, Giovanni di Pagolo, 87, 88, 89–90, 96–7
Moses, 39
Moulakis, Athanasios, 10, 197, 198, 303

Najemy, John M., 11, 74, 142, 178n., 197, 212, 214, 216, 291
Nederman, Cary J., 9, 32n., 63, 72, 282, 286–8, 292, 297, 300
Neville, Henry, 271–2
Niccoli, Niccolò, 106, 126
Nicholas of Cusa, 259–62, 265, 266, 267, 286, 290
Nicolet, Claude, 290
Niccolò da Tolentino, 166
nominalism, 66–9

Ockham, William (of), 50–2, 66, 69
oligarchy, 10, 25, 63, 68, 77, 150, 176, 206, 207, 209–10, 213, 239
Ordinances of Justice, 153
Oresme, Nicole, 34, 43, 48–9, 54, 66
Otto of Freising, 45

Palmieri, Matteo, 79, 88, 93–5, 97–8, 101, 108, 128, 131–41, 218
  Città di vita (*City of Life*), 132
  De captivitate Pisarum (*The Capture of the Pisans*), 131–41
  Vita civile (*Civic Life*), 93, 94, 97–8, 101, 128, 134, 136, 137
Pandolfini, Agnolo, 93, 101, 134
papacy, 47, 48, 51, 69, 70, 114, 209
Parenti, Marco, 88, 103
Parte Guelfa, 84
participation, civic, 8, 11, 30, 40, 54–60, 65, 66, 70, 76, 87–92, 116, 211–12, 226, 267
Pascal, Blaise, 183
Paul the Deacon, 36
Pazzi conspiracy, 188, 191, 194
Pazzi, Guglielmo de', 185
Peter of Auvergne, 34, 55–6, 57
Petrarca, Francesco, 31, 36, 71, 72, 223
Piccinino, Niccolò, 166
Piccolomini, Aeneas Silvius, 52, 53n
Pisa, Florentine conquest of, 118–19, 131–41, 145
Pizolpasso, Francesco, 160
Plato, 97, 150, 217, 235, 236
Platonism, 132
Plutarch, 167
Pocock, J. G. A., 1–2, 5, 6, 8, 12, 22–3, 24, 32, 143, 203, 226, 227, 248–9, 268, 275, 279, 292
Pole, Reginald, 270–1
Pollaiuolo, Antonio, 190, 194
Porcari, Stefano, 149
private property, 21, 23–4
Prodi, Romano, 2
Ptolemy of Lucca, 8, 32, 34, 36, 37, 40–2, 46–8, 53, 57–61, 63, 67, 68, 69, 70, 172

Quintilian (Marcus Fabius Quintilianus), 146n, 168

Rahe, Paul A., 5, 9, 177, 263
realist constitutionalism, 10, 197, 201–2, 218–22
reason of state, 222
Remer, Gary, 263
rhetoric, 25, 31, 72, 74, 79, 126, 143, 160, 161, 167–9, 220, 229–30, 232, 234, 235, 244, 245, 246, 249–53
Rinuccini, Alamanno, 79, 103, 179–80, 184, 194
  De libertate (*On Liberty*), 184, 187, 188–9, 194
Rinuccini, Cino, 113–16, 122
  Risponsiva alla Invettiva di messer Antonio Lusco (*Response to the Invective of Antonio Loschi*), 113, 115–16, 122

Roman empire, 8, 31–53
  theology of, 43–53
Roman law, 52, 55, 68, 219, 257–8, 292
Roman republic, 31–3, 35–43, 44, 47, 57, 61, 62, 68, 109, 120–4, 146, 204–5
Rousseau, Jean-Jacques, 5, 244
Rubinstein, Nicolai, 14, 25, 36, 44, 107–8, 129
Rucellai, Bernardo, 19

Salerno, Giannicola, of Verona, 149
Sallust (Gaius Sallustius Crispus), 6, 36, 53, 54, 110, 280, 283, 285, 297, 303
Salutati, Coluccio, 31, 37, 71, 79, 108, 114–17, 120–3, 126, 127–8, 144, 182, 206
  Invectiva in Antonium Luschum Vicentinum (*Invective against Antonio Loschi of Vicenza*), 113, 116, 122
  Missive (*Public Letters*), 114–15, 121, 182
Santosuosso, Antonio, 144
Savonarola, Girolamo, 58, 197, 215
Scala, Bartolomeo, 188, 194–5
  Excusatio Florentinorum (*A Justification of the Florentines*), 188
Scott, Jonathan, 263
Seigel, Jerrold E., 78, 144
Seneca (Lucius Annaeus Seneca), 6, 280, 281, 283, 285
Servius, 36
Shalhope, Robert E., 22
Sidney, Sir Philip, 271
signory, 112
Skinner, Quentin, 2, 5, 6, 8, 13, 19, 25–6, 53, 54–5, 65, 129–30n, 179, 197, 226, 227, 275–286, 293, 297, 298, 303–7
Smalley, Beryl, 36, 53
socialism, 2, 6, 13, 24
Soderini, Niccolò, 184
Solon, 152
Sombart, Werner, 20
sovereignty, 11, 201, 204–5, 208, 213, 222
Stefani, Marchionne di Coppo, 84–5, 87, 99–100
Stoics, 252, 254, 283, 293
Strozzi, Carlo, 154, 156, 165
Strozzi, Nanni, 152–5, 164–7
Strozzi, Palla, 91–2, 156, 167

Tacitus (Marcus Claudius Tacitus), 231, 238
Thucydides, 152–3, 186, 291
Tocqueville, Alexis de, 289
Trexler, Richard C., 131
Tuck, Richard, 73
tyranny, 33, 37, 41, 46, 49, 61–2, 194, 216, 239, 246

Valerius Maximus, 36
Valla, Lorenzo, 150
Verres, Gaius, 195
Vettori, Francesco, 181, 192, 196
Villani, Filippo, 223
Villani, Giovanni, 36
Villani, Matteo, 117, 125, 128
Virgil (Publius Vergilius Maro), 36, 291
Viroli, Maurizio, 129
virtue(s), 8, 9, 23, 30, 33, 36, 39, 42, 51, 56–61, 63, 65, 90, 92–5, 98, 1136–7, 146, 204, 218, 240, 257
vita civile (*vivere civile, vivere libero, vivere politico*), 14, 88, 111, 203, 248, 297, 301
Viti, Paolo, 151

Weber, Max, 227
William of Moerbeke, 34
Witt, Ronald G., 41–2
Wood, Gordan S., 21–2

Ideas in context

Edited by QUENTIN SKINNER (*General Editor*),
LORRAINE DASTON, DOROTHY ROSS and JAMES TULLY

1 RICHARD RORTY, J. B. SCHNEEWIND and QUENTIN SKINNER (eds.)
   Philosophy in History
   Essays in the historiography of philosophy
   pb: 0 521 27330 7

2 J. G. A. POCOCK
   Virtue, Commerce and History
   Essays on political thought and history, chiefly in the eighteenth century
   pb: 0 521 27660 8

3 M. M. GOLDSMITH
   Private Vices, Public Benefits
   Bernard Mandeville's social and political thought
   hb: 0 521 30036 3

4 ANTHONY PAGDEN (ed.)
   The Languages of Political Theory in Early Modern Europe
   pb: 0 521 38666 7

5 DAVID SUMMERS
   The Judgement of Sense
   Renaissance nationalism and the rise of aesthetics
   pb: 0 521 38631 4

6 LAURENCE DICKEY
   Hegel: Religion, Economics and the Politics of Spirit, 1770–1807
   pb: 0 521 38912 7

7 MARGO TODD
   Christian Humanism and the Puritan Social Order
   hb: 0 521 33129 3

8 LYNN SUMIDA JOY
   Gassendi the Atomist
   Advocate of history in the age of science
   hb: 0 521 30142 4

9   EDMUND LEITES (ed.)
    Conscience and Casuistry in Early Modern Europe
    hb: 0 521 30113 0

10 WOLF LEPENIES
    Between Literature and Science
    The Rise of Sociology
    pb: 0 521 33810 7

11 TERENCE BALL, JAMES FARR and RUSSELL L. HANSON (eds.)
    Political Innovation and Conceptual Change
    pb: 0 521 35978 3

12 GERD GIGERENZER *et al.*
    The Empire of Chance
    How probability changed science and everyday life
    pb: 0 521 39838 X

13 PETER NOVICK
    That Noble Dream
    The 'objectivity question' and the American historical profession
    pb: 0 521 35745 4

14 DAVID LIEBERMAN
    The Province of Legislation Determined
    Legal theory in eighteenth-century Britain
    hb: 0 521 24592 3

15 DANIEL PICK
    Faces of Degeneration
    A European disorder, c. 1848–c.1918
    pb: 0 521 45753 X

16 KEITH BAKER
    Inventing the French Revolution
    Essays in French political culture in the eighteenth century
    pb: 0 521 38578 4

17 IAN HACKING
    The Taming of Chance
    pb: 0 521 38884 8

18 GISELA BOCK, QUENTIN SKINNER and MAURIZIO VIROLI (eds.)
    Machiavelli and Republicanism
    pb: 0 521 43589 7

19 DOROTHY ROSS
    The Origins of American Social Science
    pb: 0 521 42836 X

20 KLAUS CHRISTIAN KOHNKE
    The Rise of Neo-Kantianism
    German Academic Philosophy between Idealism and Positivism
    hb: 0 521 37336 0

21 IAN MACLEAN
Interpretation and Meaning in the Renaissance
The Case of Law
hb: 0 521 41546 2

22 MAURIZIO VIROLI
From Politics to Reason of State
The Acquisition and Transformation of the Language of Politics 1250–1600
hb: 0 521 41493 8

23 MARTIN VAN GELDEREN
The Political Thought of the Dutch Revolt 1555–1590
hb: 0 521 39204 7

24 NICHOLAS PHILLIPSON and QUENTIN SKINNER (eds.)
Political Discourse in Early Modern Britain
hb: 0 521 39242 X

25 JAMES TULLY
An Approach to Political Philosophy: Locke in Context
pb: 0 521 43638 9

26 RICHARD TUCK
Philosophy and Government 1572–1651
pb: 0 521 43885 3

27 RICHARD R. YEO
Defining Science
William Whewell, Natural Knowledge and Public Debate in Early Victorian Britain
hb: 0 521 43182 4

28 MARTIN WARNKE
The Court Artist
The Ancestry of the Modern Artist
hb: 0 521 36375 6

29 PETER N. MILLER
Defining the Common Good
Empire, Religion and Philosophy in Eighteenth-Century Britain
hb: 0 521 44259 1

30 CHRISTOPHER J. BERRY
The Idea of Luxury
A Conceptual and Historical Investigation
pb: 0 521 46691 1

31 E. J. HUNDERT
The Enlightenment's 'Fable'
Bernard Mandeville and the Discovery of Society
hb: 0 521 46082 4

32 JULIA STAPLETON
Englishness and the Study of Politics
The Social and Political Thought of Ernest Barker
hb: 0 521 46125 1

33 KEITH TRIBE
Strategies of Economic Order
German Economic Discourse, 1750–1950
hb: 0521 46291 6

34 SACHIKIO KUSUKAWA
The Transformation of Natural Philosophy
The Case of Philip Melancthon
hb: 0 521 47347 0

35 DAVID ARMITAGE, ARMAND HIMY and QUENTIN SKINNNER (eds.)
Milton and Republicanism
pb: 0 521 64648 0

36 MARKKU PELTONEN
Classical Humanism and Republicanism in English Political Thought 1570–1640
hb: 0 521 49695 0

37 PHILIP IRONSIDE
The Social and Political Thought of Bertrand Russell
The Devolopment of an Aristocratic Liberalism
hb: 0 521 47383 7

38 NANCY CARTWRIGHT, JORDI CAT, LOLA FLECK and THOMAS E. UEBEL
Otto Neurath: Philosophy between Science and Politics
hb: 0 521 45174 4

39 DONALD WINCH
Riches and Poverty
An Intellectual History of Political Economy in Britain, 1750–1834
pb: 0 521 55920 0

40 JENNIFER PLATT
A History of Sociological Research Methods in America
pb: 521 64649 9

41 KNUD HAAKONSSEN (ed.)
Enlightenment and Religion
Rational Dissent in Eighteenth-Century Britain
hb: 0 521 56060 8

42 G. E. R. LLOYD
Adversaries and Authorities
Investigations into Ancient Greek and Chinese Science
pb: 0 521 55695 3

43 ROLF LINDNER
The Reportage of Urban Culture
Robert Park and the Chicago School
hb: 0 521 44052 1

44 ANNABEL BRETT
Liberty, Right and Nature
Individual Rights in Later Scholastic Thought
hb: 0 521 56239 2

45 STEWART J. BROWN (ed.)
William Robertson and the Expansion of Empire
hb: 0 521 57083 2

46 HELENA ROSENBLATT
Rousseau and Geneva
From the First Discourse to the Social Contract, 1749–1762
hb: 0 521 57004 2

47 DAVID RUNCIMAN
Pluralism and the Personality of the State
hb: 0 521 55191 9

48 ANNABEL PATTERSON
Early Modern Liberalism
hb: 0 521 59260 7

49 DAVID WEINSTEIN
Equal Freedom and Utility
Herbert Spencer's Liberal Utilitarianism
hb: 0 521 62264 6

50 UYN LEE TOO and NIALL LIVINGSTONE (eds.)
Pedagogy and Power
Rhetorics of Classical Learning
hb: 0 521 59435 9

51 REVIEL NETZ
The Shaping of Deduction in Greek Mathematics
A Study in Cognitive History
hb: 0 521 62279 4

52 MARY MORGAN and MARGARET MORRISON (eds.)
Models as Mediators
pb: 0 521 65571 4

53 JOEL MICHELL
Measurement in Psychology
A Critical History of a Methodological Concept
hb: 0 521 62120 8

54 RICHARD A. PRIMUS
The American Language of Rights
hb: 0 521 65250 2

55 ROBERT ALUN JONES
   The Development of Durkheim's Social Realism
   hb: 0 521 65045 3
56 ANNE McLAREN
   Political Culture in the Reign of Elizabeth I
   Queen and Commonwealth 1558–1585
   hb: 0 521 65144 1
57 JAMES HANKINS (ed.)
   Renaissance Civic Humanism
   Reappraisals and Reflections
   hb: 0 521 78090 X

Made in the USA
Columbia, SC
24 August 2017